Women and Sex Roles

A Social Psychological Perspective

Women and Sex Roles
A Social Psychological Perspective

Irene H. Frieze
University of Pittsburgh

Jacquelynne E. Parsons
University of Michigan, Ann Arbor

Paula B. Johnson
University of California, Los Angeles

Diane N. Ruble
Princeton University

Gail L. Zellman
Rand Corporation

In collaboration with

Esther Sales
University of Pittsburgh

Jeanne Marecek
Swarthmore College

Gwendolyn Lewis
University of Pittsburgh

Joan Hertzberg

Deborah Lee

W • W • Norton and Company • *New York* • *London*

Dedicated to all women everywhere

FIRST EDITION

Library of Congress Cataloging in Publication Data
Main entry under title:
Women and sex roles.

  Bibliography: p.
  Includes index.
  1. Women—Psychology.   2. Sex role.
3. Women—Social conditions.   I. Frieze, Irene H.
HQ1206.W873   1978   301.41'2   78–15651
ISBN 0 393 01163 1   cloth edition
ISBN 0 393 09063 9   paper edition

1 2 3 4 5 6 7 8 9 0

Acknowledgments

Grateful acknowledgment is made for permission to print the following:

Chapter 4

Box 3: Reprinted with permission of author and publisher from Sherman, Julia A, "Field Articulation, Sex, Spatial Visualization, Dependency, Practice, Laterality of the Brain and Birth Order." *Perceptual and Motor Skills,* 1974, 38, 1223–35.

Box 5: Kagan, J., and Kagan, N., "Individuality and Cognitive Performance," from P. H. Mussen (ed.), *Carmichael's Manual of Child Psychology* (Vol. I, 3rd edition). New York: John Wiley & Sons, Inc., 1970.

Box 6: Inge K. Broverman, et al., "Sex-Roles Stereotypes: A Current Appraisal." *Journal of Social Issues,* Vol. 28, No. 2 (1972), pp. 59–78, an excerpt.

Chapter 8

Box 1: Glick, P. C. and Norton, A. J., "Perspectives on the Recent Upturn in Divorce and Remarriage." *Demography,* 1973, 10 (3), 301–14.

Box 8: Figure 9.2, from *Indicators of Trends in the Status of American Women,* by Abbott L. Ferriss, © 1971 Russell Sage Foundation, New York.

Chapter 9

Box 2: From *Childhood and Society,* by Erik H. Erikson, with the permission of W. W. Norton & Company, Inc. Copyright 1950, © 1963 by W. W. Norton & Company, Inc.

Box 3: From *Psychology Today* Magazine. Copyright © 1975, Ziff-Davis Publishing Company.

Box 4: Figure from Birnbaum, J. A., "Life Patterns and Self-Esteem in Gifted, Family Oriented and Career Committed Women," in Mednick, et al., *Women and Achievement: Social and Motivational Analyses.* Washington, D.C.: Hemisphere, 1975.

Chapter 10

Box 1: Illustration of ovulation during the menstrual cycle, from R. C. Benson, *Handbook of Obstetrics and Gynecology* (6th edition). Los Altos, Calif.: Lange Medical Publications, 1977.

Box 3: Neugarten, B. L., and Kraines, R. J., "Menopausal Symptoms in Women of Various Ages." *Psychosomatic Medicine,* 1965, *27* (3), 266–73.

Chapter 11

Box 3: A. C. Kinsey, W. B. Pomeroy, C. E. Martin, and P. H. Gebhard, *Sexual Behavior in the Human Female.* W. B. Saunders Company, 1948, 1953.

Box 4: A. C. Kinsey, W. B. Pomeroy, and C. E. Martin, *Sexual Behavior in the Human Male.* W. B. Saunders Company, 1948.

Box 5: Masters, W. H., and Johnson, V. E., *Human Sexual Response.* Boston: Little, Brown, 1965.

Box 6: Masters, W. H. and Johnson, V. E., *Human Sexual Response.* Boston: Little, Brown, 1965.

Box 7: Masters, W. H. and Johnson, V. E., *Human Sexual Response.* Boston: Little, Brown, 1965.

Chapter 12

Box 5: V. A. Valle and I. H. Frieze, "Stability of Causal Attributions as a Mediator in Changing Expectations for Success." *Journal of Personality and Social Psychology,* 1976, *33* (5), 579–87. Copyright © 1976 by the American Psychological Association.

Chapter 14

Box 1: Rosenkrantz, S. Vogel, H. Bee, I. Broverman, and D. Broverman, "Sex Role Stereotypes and Self-Concepts in College Students." *Journal of Consulting and Clinical Psychology,* 1968, *32,* 287–95. Copyright © 1928 by the American Psychological Association.

Chapter 15

Box 5: Paula Johnson, "Women and Power: Toward a Theory of Effectiveness." *Journal of Social Issues,* Vol. 32, No. 3 (1976), pp. 99–110.

Contents

Preface

The psychological study of women and of sex roles has become an increasingly important subfield within psychology since we first began thinking of writing this book in the late sixties. At that time, there was little empirical research on women, and there were no comprehensive books on empirical psychological research relating to women. It was then that we decided to survey what literature we could find in various psychological writings so that we could better understand ourselves as women and psychologists and so that we could begin to integrate this material into a coherent statement. We formed a teaching team which planned and taught a course called "The Psychology of Women" at the University of California at Los Angeles. As we taught what we had learned, our ideas began to further evolve and coalesce. We finally felt ready to begin writing this book.

We have all been teaching courses in the psychology of women or the psychology of sex roles since that time. This book represents our current thinking about the empirical research and theory in these areas. It is intended to be a basic text for courses in the psychology of women, sociology of women, women's studies, and sex roles. With our backgrounds in various areas of psychology, we have been able to write a book which provides a wide and basic coverage of the major subfields within psychology. However, our common focus has been to review the research and theory in all areas of psychology relevant to women from a social psychological perspective.

We all share a feminist perspective. We hope that the material in this book will not only add to the scholarly understanding of women and sex roles, but that it will also help women and men to achieve greater freedom of choice for themselves through presenting material relevant to their daily lives and helping them to understand the psychological processes which reinforce sex roles. Although we do not believe that truly value-free science exists, we have attempted to present material in an unbiased way so that the reader may draw her or his own conclusions. Allowing for individual freedom of choice is the strongest expression of feminism we know.

In planning this book, we asked several people to help us write chapters for which they had the special expertise necessary. We were pleased to have Esther Sales contribute a chapter on adult development and collaborate on the final chapter. Jeanne Marecek wrote a chapter on women and therapy. Gwendolyn Lewis took major responsibility for the chapter analyzing the changes in women's roles, and Deborah Lee and Joan Hertzberg contributed the initial drafts of the clinical theories chapter. In addition, several others helped us with planning chapters and gathering information. Julie Croke was very helpful in the initial work on the classical theories of sex-role socialization chapter. Karen Trocki contributed much material for the chapter on changes in women's roles. Rosalyn Katz worked on the women's adult development chapter. Initial planning and background work on the sexuality chapter was done by Theresa Christerson Mason. Anstiss McIver Markowitz provided material in the areas of sex roles. We found all of these contributors to be very helpful.

We have received the help and support of so many other people over the years that it is impossible to acknowledge everyone individually. We are grateful, though, to all of our colleagues, students, and friends who have commented upon or provided additional references for various chapters. The feedback from the hundreds of students who have read earlier versions of these chapters has been especially helpful in clarifying presentations and making discussions relevant for college students. Specifically, we would like to thank Shirley Angrist, Jeanne Brookes-Gunn, Inge K. Broverman, Anne Clarke, Patrick Dorien, Nina Feldman, Jacqueline D. Goodchilds, Kathy Grady, the late Marcia Guttentag, Carolyn Hanson, Jerre Levy, Maureen McHugh, Denise Nelesen, Mary Brown Parlee, Bertram H. Raven, Aletha Huston Stein, Susan R. Vogel, and Richard Willis for their valuable comments on earlier versions of one or more chapters.

Beverly Stewart has worked many hours to compile our bibliography. Our spouses, lovers, and friends have also helped us, each in a particular way, and we are especially grateful to them. Finally, our Norton editor, Don Fusting, has continued to give us friendly encouragement and help throughout the long process of writing this book.

IRENE H. FRIEZE
JACQUELYNNE E. PARSONS
PAULA B. JOHNSON
DIANE N. RUBLE
1978   GAIL L. ZELLMAN

Women and Sex Roles
A Social Psychological Perspective

1 The Psychology of Women and Sex Roles

There are a number of questions which are of major concern to those studying the psychology of women and sex roles, which will be raised in various contexts throughout this book. These include:

1. What are the effects of sexism or prejudicial attitudes upon women and men today? How do these limit options for both sexes?
2. What is the reason for differences between women and men? Do these differences have a biological basis or are they based solely upon the values and teachings of our culture?
3. What are the psychological effects of traditional sex roles upon women and men? How are these sex roles changing? What will be the effects of these changes on the lives of women and men?
4. What factors serve to maintain traditional sex roles? Will these factors show changes?

Unfortunately, each of these questions can be answered in many ways, depending upon which data one looks at and how the data are interpreted. As we discuss in Chapter 2, there are many examples of sexism or biased thinking in social psychological research. Thus, it is difficult to know which studies should be accepted and which should be questioned or completely rejected. This book is an attempt to carefully review the existing research and draw conclusions about what this research can tell us about the basic theoret-

---

Irene Frieze was the primary author of this chapter.

ical questions listed above. It is essential for the readers to develop critical attitudes of their own in evaluating the data presented in this book and in reading any other reports of research in the future. There is no such thing as value-free science. Any supposedly "objective" research is based on numerous subjective decisions which affect both the results and the interpretations drawn.

THE EFFECTS OF SEXISM

Sexist attitudes can affect both the study of psychology and the practice of psychotherapy. The widespread belief that women's personalities are different in fundamental ways from those of men might also be considered sexist since there are few valid research studies which in any way support this assumption (Pleck, 1976). In fact, there is more difference between two individuals regardless of sex than there is between women and men on the average. People also vary in their behaviors from day to day and from situation to situation, so that it is difficult to say about any group of people that they are always behaving in a particular way (Bem and Allen, 1974). However, most people do believe that women and men are different and that they should be different (Broverman, et al., 1972). Such beliefs affect the way people treat one another in many ways. For example, they influence the ways in which we raise children. They also determine what we expect of men and women we do not know well, in terms of what we talk to them about or ask them to do. The effects are widespread, operating on a face-to-face level with acquaintances, and also on more abstract levels of employment, government, and other institutions.

The indirect effects of sexism are not as obvious, but they may have even more pervasive and long-term effects. Some of our scientific understanding of people and their behavior comes from the social sciences, and the findings of these sciences are dependent upon the attitudes of the people conducting this research. Biases in research are especially dysfunctional if the researcher is unaware of her or his own biases and does nothing to counteract them. Chapter 2 discusses some of the ways in which biases enter research design and practice in more detail.

Sexist attitudes can also be seen in the various theories of the female personality (see Chapter 3). These personality theories are a major basis of much of the clinical work which attempts to use psychological insights to help people cope more effectively with their lives. Just like other people, therapists can sometimes have sexist attitudes. Unfortunately, this can affect the ways in which they analyze their patients. This can perhaps be best seen in a concrete example.

Imagine the case of a young woman who has been living with her lover for the past year. Sally and John are both premed students doing well in school and they both work part time. John wants to get married and have children since he feels that their part-time jobs would provide them enough income for a reasonably comfortable life even if they did have children. He feels that it would be better to have children now rather than waiting until they are in medical school or until after they finish. If they wait, they will be too old to enjoy them, he feels. All this is very upsetting to Sally. She dislikes disagreeing with John but she is afraid that children will interfere too much with school and she is also not completely convinced that she wants to marry John.

Sally finally decides to seek therapy after an incident in which she became especially irritated at John for not helping around the house, and he responded by hitting her several times. She tells the therapist about the incident and her general state of upset and depression. She blames herself for not being more supportive to John since he was trying to finish a term paper. She also worries that she is not being fair to him by refusing to get married.

After hearing her story, the therapist may feel that Sally is working against her own true desires to marry John. Her lack of emotional support of him at a particular stressful time indicates her underlying feelings of hostility towards John. He speculates that she may unconsciously want John to be more dominant and to insist that she marry him and that by allowing her to be so independent, he is really frustrating her desires to be taken care of by a strong man. Although the therapist would never tell her his suspicions, they will influence his therapeutic approach. For example, he may attempt to get Sally to talk about her relations with her father to see if she is projecting her attitudes about him onto John and expecting John to take over the role of her father. The therapist may also reinforce any positive statements she makes about marriage and children since he feels that this is what Sally really wants.

There are a number of sexist assumptions being made by this hypothetical therapist. First, he does not take Sally's desires for a medical career seriously. His whole concern is with her relationship with John. Although he assumes that Sally should support John's efforts in school, there is no similar assumption that John should be supportive of Sally's efforts. Sally mentions being concerned with John not helping with housework. Again, the therapist ignores this, rather than helping to work out an equitable arrangement. Certainly, if John had come to therapy and said he was doing all or most of the housework, this would have been questioned and seen as somewhat unusual by the therapist. Additionally, the therapist disregarded the violence of John towards Sally. This could have been seen as a major violation of Sally's freedom to speak openly to John and that she should make sure this never happens again. Finally, it has been assumed that Sally really wanted marriage and children. A therapist with different assumptions might have seen Sally's hesitation to marry and have children as realistic if she desired to have a medical career. All these sexist assumptions become more obvious if the reader substitutes a man's name for Sally and a woman's name for John in this example.

These are just some of the ways in which sexist attitudes may operate in our society. Box 1 suggests some other exercises for the reader which can help in further identifying sexism.

ORIGINS OF SEX DIFFERENCES

We all know that men dress and act differently than women do. Girls seem to prefer different activities than boys. Thus, many believe that the basic differences between the sexes start at a young age and continue throughout our lives, and that these differences have a biological origin. Others see differences resulting from socialization or from variations in the ways we raise girls and boys. These people believe that each society has its own values for how the sexes should behave and trains its youngsters according to these values. Part II outlines some of these arguments in more detail and discusses the supporting evidence for each of them. Although we conclude that the culture is a major influence in socializing children for their later adult roles, we also find on careful review of the data that there are relatively few basic personality differences between boys and girls. Thus, it appears that many apparent differences between men and women are not fundamental personality differences, but are the result of the roles we assign to the sexes and our reinforcement of varying behaviors for each sex.

Box 1   Identifying Sexism

1. Ask a friend if she or he would like to work for a woman. After your friend answers "yes" or "no," ask her or him to tell you why. What assumptions is your friend making about women?

2. Make a list of ten major personality characteristics which you feel are important in understanding people. Rate three of your female friends and three of your male friends on each of these traits, as being high, average, or low. Do you find that all the women are alike and that all the men are alike? Are the men and women always different on these traits? What does this tell you about the basic differences between women and men?

3. What is the image of women portrayed on television? Do you feel that you (if you are a woman) are like these women? What is the image of men which is portrayed on television? Do the men you know fit this image?

4. Find examples of sexist thinking in psychology textbooks.

Even though culture is a major factor in shaping behavior, there is no question that biological differences have an impact. This can be seen in our reactions to two infants. One is active and irritable; it cries a lot and dislikes being held. Another is relaxed and enjoys being touched or held. It smiles and likes attention. People are much more likely to hold the second and will probably spend more time smiling and talking to it. Such a child may then learn to talk earlier and may develop a more positive feeling about other people. If this child is also a girl, she will be reinforced for "feminine" behavior, both because of her unique behaviors and people's reactions to them, and because people want her to act in "girl-like" ways. There is some evidence that girls are slightly more likely to be like the second child than like the first. Thus, this biological difference may indirectly lead to what we think of as a basic sex difference (girls are more social).

Biology may also be important in that people react to one's apparent biological sex. Girls are expected to be weaker and cry more. If they do these things, no one pays much attention to them. However, if a boy does these "girl" things, he may be severely reprimanded.

The biological events in our own lives also affect us. Girls have reactions to their first menstruation. The little girl may feel she is growing up and may begin to act more grown up after menstruation. Another girl may react to the same event with frustration and anger. Her behavior may then be very childish or she may adopt a tomboy role as a reaction against being female. Another girl may accept menstruation as part of life and may continue as before enjoying sports and strenuous physical activities. Similar variations in reactions occur with other biological events such as pregnancy or menopause. They can also be seen with reactions to sickness or aging. We all experience our bodies in unique ways. Women may share some physical experiences, but most of the evidence could suggest that individual variations are of even more importance.

All this leads us to conclude that understanding the origins of sex differences is a very complex task. Box 2 gives some exercises for the reader to personally explore these issues.

PSYCHOLOGICAL IMPLICATIONS
OF TRADITIONAL SEX ROLES

Sex roles affect all of us in major ways. Part III of this book discusses roles and their impact upon sexuality and achievement. It also discusses some of the conflicts implicit in traditional roles which can lead to psychological difficulties for women. Chapter 9 focuses on how traditional roles operate at various points in the life cycle for women. The traditional female role for a woman in her twenties is very different than the role requirements for a woman in her forties. Children are a very central focus for the young married

Box 2   Socialization of Sex Differences

1. Observe children of various ages playing. How sex-typed are their activities? At what ages are children most and least sex-typed?
2. Notice the clothes children are wearing. Do girls wearing dresses act differently from those wearing pants?
3. Go to a maternity ward and observe the reactions to male and female children. How do people know what sex the infants are? Do people talk or act differently towards girls and boys? Are the infants dressed differently?
4. When you were growing up, were you treated differently than your brothers or sisters? Did you learn that there were certain things that girls did and certain things that boys did? Who told you this?

woman, but as the children become older and more independent, the mother has more and more free time. She frequently begins to develop more interests outside the home as this happens. For the traditional married woman with young children, her role means almost total dedication to the needs of her children and husband. She has little "free" time. If she attempts to work out-side the home, she may well be emotionally and physically exhausted much of the time. Thus, for her, there are high costs associated with the traditional female role. However, as she and the children get older, the costs often diminish. Assuming that the somewhat older woman can develop interests to fill her time, she will become more and more self-confident and satisfied with her life. However, if she attempts to cling to her mother role, she may again suffer high costs as the children mature and finally leave the home to begin their own adult lives.

Data presented in Chapter 8 suggest that the traditional roles of women may be changing somewhat. More and more women are working outside the home before they have children and even after the children are born. This change may suggest that the costs of this new approach to the woman's role will be even higher for the woman with young children. However, these women may have an easier time building their lives as the children get older, since they will already have major activities in addition to the children. These role changes for women will also affect men. For the married man, if his wife also works outside the home, this will mean that he does not have the entire financial responsibility for the family. However, it may also mean that he will be asked to take a more active role in child care and housework. This in turn may affect the socialization of children in the next generation. There is evidence now that children of mothers who chose to work outside the home are more independent and less traditional in their sex-role values.

These are just some examples of the ways in which sex roles currently influence behavior and how our lives may change as sex-role definitions change. Box 3 lists a few exercises relating to sex roles. Chapter 18 more fully explores the implications of various role options for women's lives.

FACTORS MAINTAINING TRADITIONAL ROLES

Many factors serve to maintain traditional roles. Such factors, which relate directly and indirectly to the expression of power, are the focus of Part IV. As mentioned earlier, people have prejudices about women which cause them to limit the options available to women in terms of jobs and political power, among other things. Chapter 14 discusses these prejudices in more detail and shows some of the reasons these are so hard to change. For example, we learn some of our prejudices from our parents and from our culture. Thus, there is a tendency to perpetuate the same beliefs from generation to generation. Our friends and acquaintances also influence us. If we change our beliefs and they do not, it becomes difficult for us to talk to them and they will attempt to change us so that we will be consistent with their views.

Forces towards the maintenance of traditional roles also operate in more subtle ways. Chapter 15 discusses how women are taught to sit and stand in ways which communicate low status. Some nonverbal behaviors, such as keeping one's legs together or not spreading one's arms too much, are considered as proper feminine behaviors by many people. Thus, if a woman wants to appear to be high-status nonverbally, she will at the same time be forced to be "unfeminine" in her nonverbal behavior. Nonverbal forces also operate

Box 3 Looking at Adult Sex Roles

1. Talk to your parents about their lives. How is your own life different from that of your parents thus far? How might it be the same or different as you get older? What influences did your parents feel were important in shaping their lives? How did sex-role expectations influence your mother? Your father?

2. Do a survey of your friends to find out how important they feel a woman's menstrual cycle is in determining her moods. Keep a daily chart of your moods (and of your friends' moods, if possible). What factors seem to be most important in determining your moods and those of your friends? Do women's moods fluctuate more than men's?

3. Interview a young married woman with children, a married woman without children, and a single woman, who are all about the same age. How do each of these women spend their time? What are their major concerns? What do each of them see as the advantages and the disadvantages of their life-style?

in other ways to maintain traditional roles. Women are taught not to take up too much space or to ask for privacy. Rather, they should always be available to their children or others who might need them. This results in it being harder for women to do projects requiring high degrees of concentration, which again perpetuates the myth that women are not as competent as men.

On a broader scale, if women are to gain true equality in our society, they will need better representation in local and national government. Chapter 17 deals with some of the reasons that women have not gained more political power and suggests some issues which might serve to unite women more. This chapter also discusses some of the personal difficulties encountered by women politicians. Such women face all the sexism and prejudice that women in general must contend with, but because they seek a demanding occupation which requires the support of many people, they must be able to overcome this. At the same time, such a woman must free herself of guilt over not giving enough time to her children or not having children at all. For this reason, many women enter politics when they have already raised a family. The woman politician must also contend with the attitudes of other legislators, many of whom may be quite old and traditional in their views. Finally, she must overcome personal feelings of lack of confidence that she will not be able to do the job. She must often do this in an environment which provides her little if any emotional support. Obviously, this is much to ask of anyone; it is no wonder we have so few women entering politics. Although we need more women in politics to help in changing laws and overcoming institutionalized sexism, for many women the demands are too great.

We hope that this book will allow women and men to see more clearly what their role choices and the consequences of these are, so that they can make better decisions about their own lives. The final chapter of the book outlines some of these choices in more detail. As people gain more information about these issues, this will be another force operating to change traditional roles.

Part I

Psychology and Women

2   Doing Psychological Research

"We are like the fish who is unaware that his environment is wet. After all, what else could it be? Such is the nature of all man-conscious ideologies. Such is the nature of America's ideology about women" (Bem and Bem, 1970).

Research psychologists share the nonconscious ideologies our society holds about women, and these ideologies are incorporated into the research they perform. A nonconscious ideology is a set of beliefs and stereotypes of which one is unaware because of a failure to imagine any alternatives. Generally, these beliefs are held by most members of any given culture. Scientists and scholars are often no exception. They, too, can share their culture's nonconscious ideologies. However, when academic disciplines incorporate stereotypes into their theories and methodologies, the implications are far-reaching in terms of the effects on each discipline.

It is the purpose of this chapter to examine how and why these nonconscious ideologies about women have affected psychology, and what the implications of this have been. The errors and oversights outlined here apply to the methods traditionally employed in the study of biological aspects of sex differences, as well as to much of social, clinical, personality, and developmental psychological research. The incorporation of nonconscious assumptions about women into psychology is antithetical to empirical psychology's basic job—the study of how and why people act as they do. What psycholo-

---

Paula Johnson was the primary author of this chapter.

gists have neglected in the study of people is the fact that there are female people, as well as male people, and the fact that our behavior expectations for the two sexes are quite different. What psychologists did do was to consider male behavior as normative. That is, they considered what males are as what all humans are or should be, and largely ignored females. In addition, whether studies included females or not, they were done with a lack of awareness of the dynamics of sex roles. This bias has meant that the study of both males and females has suffered from an unquestioning acceptance of male roles.

The study of sex differences has also suffered. Often sex differences were either assumed to be so obvious or so mysterious that they did not warrant study. For example, when a behavior pattern characteristic of women but not men could not be explained, a "women's mysteries" explanation was invoked, and the behavior was not further studied. Even though certain sex differences have been examined, this research has incorporated stereotypic views of the sexes. Each of these biases has had consequences for the validity of psychology as a science, and has served to reinforce and perpetuate inaccurate assumptions about women.

In assessing the impact of sexism in empirical psychology, certain basic questions will be explored:

1. Has empirical psychology neglected the study of women?
2. Has psychology made biased assumptions about women? If so, how and why has this happened?
3. What implications do such biases have for the science of psychology and our society?

SEXISM

Although sexism, like racism, has been associated and described with much rhetoric, it is possible to use the term to define objectively observable phenomena. Sexism is prejudice against one sex (Allport, 1954). Thus, to the extent that prejudice can be measured and its consequences observed, sexism can be documented. Sexism, like racism, can take many forms—from social behavior, to verbal abuse, to discrimination and physical injury. It need not necessarily imply any conscious maliciousness on the part of the person or the institution which exhibits it. Instead it may reflect that the differences between men and women are nonconsciously assumed to mean that women are less able human beings. The results of this assumption can be, and usually are, very insidious.

Sexism can also be viewed in terms of its even more subtle institutionalized ramifications. Institutional sexism is harder to identify since it is a result of rules, regulations, and traditions that may not result directly from the decisions of one or more sexists. But the rules, regulations, and traditions end up supporting a sexist ideology. Tied into these broader nonconscious traditions and into institutionalized sexism are the individual decisions of researchers. For example, psychologists have not studied women because women generally have not been considered important. This is analogous to newspapers not covering women because women's activities are not considered newsworthy. Both psychologists and newspaper people have had, at best, an accurate perception of the social reality of the world. Women simply have not occupied earth-shaking positions—the decision-making, negotiating, administrating, influencing positions. At worst, there has been overt prejudice against women—a belief that they are too inconsequential to be studied. These beliefs were most likely rooted in the nonconscious ideologies about women, rather than reflective of a conscious hostile attack of womenkind. Along with the sexism against women goes an equally nonconscious and sexist set of assumptions regarding the positive, normal, and natural character of the male world. As a result, the impact of sex roles on the male world was also not examined. Box 1 presents some examples of sexism in the social sciences. From these examples it is clear that sexism can appear in many areas of a research psychologist's thinking and methods.

Box 1   Examples of Sexism

It is sexism when a woman psychologist writes a monograph about creativity in college women and the reviewer tells her that perhaps creativity in college women is worth a journal article but surely not a monograph.

It is sexism when a student in political science wants to write a paper on the role of women in the Chinese revolution, an important topic, and is told that she should write a paper on the role of the military in the Chinese revolution.

It is sexism when Kinsey's demolition of the vaginal orgasm myth was overlooked when it was published in 1953. It is true that Masters and Johnson (1966) had the anatomy more accurately presented because of their research techniques, but the essential facts were in *Sexual Behavior in the Human Female*. Yet these vital facts were not publicized. Thousands of women still thought there was something wrong with them. For information to spread, two things are necessary—first the information itself and second some person of the group in whose interest it is to have the new facts known. It was only when there was a women's movement that these conditions were met. Thus it was not until *Human Sexual Response* (1966) was published that these facts were made generally public.

SOURCE: Bart, 1971.

HISTORICAL BACKGROUND
OF SEXISM IN PSYCHOLOGY

Since the inception of the scientific study of psychology in the late 1800s, numerous traditions have grown up among research psychologists, traditions which are still carried out by institutions and individuals. Since these traditions have, in part, led to subtle biases in research related to women, and sex roles, they will be examined briefly in order to better understand how sexism in research has developed.

Psychology grew out of the fields of philosophy and experimental biology. As psychology developed, several areas and methodologies of studying animal and human behavior evolved. For example, methods of introspection (the detailed reporting of subjective experience of a stimuli by trained subjects) were developed to study perception; free association developed out of the psychoanalytic tradition as a means of studying the unconscious, and several years later, methods of objective and quantifiable observation grew out of the behaviorist school. These traditions became the research and therapy systems that exist today in psychology.

A controversy that is particularly relevant to the ways women are viewed by psychologists has sometimes raged and has at other times flowed unobtrusively through all of psychology, from the early days right up to the present. This controversy concerns the relative contribution of herdity and environment to human activities—the nature-nurture controversy. This basic controversy has led some psychologists to tend to interpret all their research findings in terms of the innate nature of persons, while others see their data in terms of environmental effects. As related to the psychology of women, the former school is associated with the "anatomy is destiny" views of Freud, Jung, and some of their followers (see Chapter 3). The other viewpoint, in its extreme form, holds that *all* differences between the sexes (other than differences in sex organs) are learned.

By 1924 social psychology acknowledged the roles of both innate predispositions and learned social responses (Allport, 1924). This belief that behavior is determined jointly by innate factors and learning is predominate today. However, in spite of this common recognition of the importance of both these factors, the polarity between these two points of view has continued to exist in social psychology and other fields (e.g., developmental, clinical, personality, learning, perception, physiological). Even today, despite attempts at objective methodology, a researcher can explain the behavior of women or the presence of sex differences in terms of whatever biases or orientation he or she has. One person may find female passivity in a given experiment and conclude that women are innately more passive. Another may point to the effect of situational variables in the experiment, or explain the difference in terms of a general sexist oppression in a society which reinforces passivity for women.

One of the latent functions of most research on women and sex differences has always been to support the researcher's political position on the status of women in society by seeking to find innate sex differences compatible with existing roles, or by attacking the status quo either in an attempt to show that sex differences do not exist to any meaningful extent, or that their cause is not innate, and therefore is subject to change. More often, the latter, so-called feminist, position is overtly referred to as the biased point of view. If a position is taken that is consistent with the current (nonfeminist) noncon-scious ideologies, it is rarely questioned. But if a position questions the prevailing ideologies, it is subject to attack and continually forced to justify its findings. There is no evidence that feminists are or ever were more biased than antifeminists. For example, findings of female superiority in many early studies of verbal skills did not lead to the conclusion that women were superior in these areas (Wooley, 1910). Conclusions were much more tentative. One may consider whether such restraint would have marked the interpretations if the results had been reversed to favor males.

During the early study of psychology, a number of practices originated which still affect the nature of the research done and the kind of information collected. Many of these traditions influence the way psychological study is conceived, carried out, and interpreted. One such tradition is that of male resarchers studying male subjects. This tradition came about because psychological research was, and still is, conducted at universities, primarily by male professors. It was not until the 1920s that women were educated at major universities. Prior to that time, they were educated at elite women's colleges, such as Vassar and Wellesley. Later, land-grant colleges admitted women. However, these schools were primarily staffed by men. The few women who were on the faculty tended to be primarily teaching and service oriented, rather than research oriented (Bernard, 1971). Thus, the research institutions were staffed by males with the bulk of the research being conducted on the readily available male students. In the early days, "experiments" often were done using the professor or a graduate student as the only "subject." There are still a great many similarities between the way experiments were done at the turn of the century and today. Some of these practices have had sexist results. For example, because white male students have been traditionally used to test and develop theories, there is a larger amount of psychological knowledge about white males, and theories which apply only to white males (Schultz, 1969).

METHODS OF PSYCHOLOGICAL RESEARCH

Psychology now employs several methodologies to answer questions on human behavior (Campbell and Stanley, 1966). The four main types are experiments, nonexperimental observations, surveys and correlational research, and case studies. In experiments which are the most rigorous and scientific of these methods, the investigator controls both the situations that occur (the independent variables) and the measurements of the subjects' feelings, attitudes, or behavior. While nonexperimental observation is more typical of anthropology, psychologists occasionally use this technique by informally observing or systematically rating natural ongoing behavior. In this way the antecedents of the behavior are not controlled, but the measurements can be. Survey methods are often used in social and political psychology to measure people's current attitudes about various issues. Other correlation techniques include the investigation of the relationship of various personality tests to each other or to other variables. Case studies are most often used in the field of clinical psychology. These studies of one person may lead to more depth of understanding even though they lack control and generality. In fact, some of the most influential psychological theories have grown out of the case-study approach, for example, psychoanalytic theory and Piaget's cognitive developmental theory.

Each of these methodologies can suffer from the effects of nonconscious sexist ideologies. Both surveys and observations tend to have the same type of biases as measurements in experiments. Case studies can have biases that follow the same principles as those present in designing experiments. Thus, for purposes of brevity, all biases will be discussed in terms of an experimental methodology.

BIASES IN PSYCHOLOGY: WHAT ARE THE FACTS?

When a psychologist puts an experiment together, there are many ways in which the methodology can work against the accumulation of accurate knowledge of what women are like. A survey of the evidence suggests that psychologists do not know much about women (Weisstein, 1971). As things now stand, much research has indeed been extremely biased. However, there is a growing body of literature that has not made the mistakes to be outlined here. Some examples of nonbiased research can be found in the growing field known as the psychology of women. In studying the psychological literature, one needs to keep in mind the errors that researchers can make that distort what women are like, and how to judge research on the basis of its accuracy in the treatment of sex roles.

The following errors in methodology are common to psychology, and reflect and result in biases in the study of women:

1. Use of only male subjects in the experiment.
2. Not testing for sex differences.
3. Building theories by eliminating data from females that do not correspond to data from males.

4. Lack of knowledge of sex roles and how they influence behavior.
5. Exclusive use of male experimenters and investigators.
6. Ignoring important experimental and situational influences, including the use of male-biased tasks.
7. Viewing behaviors as dichotomous rather than integrated, especially conceptualizing masculinity and femininity as mutually exclusive.
8. Incorporating the value system prevalent in this culture.

Each of these problems can introduce bias at the various stages of an experiment. In the experimental process psychologists form a hypothesis about how and why people act the way they do, and then test it out. Though such testing attempts to be as objective as possible, there are openings for bias every step of the way. Box 2 outlines the stages of a psychological experiment and presents an example from the laboratory. These stages will be examined one by one, along with the biases that can enter into each one.

Box 2   Stages of an Experiment

Stage I: Formulation of the Problem
The researcher chooses an area of research (e.g., conformity) and forms a hypothesis (e.g., people will conform to group pressure against their better judgment unless they receive minimal social support).

Stage II: Operationalization of the Hypothesis
The researcher finds a way to test the hypothesis (e.g., show subjects a list of lines and ask which is shortest. Have a group of people disagree with the subject. In one condition, all disagree with the subject; in the other, all but one disagree. The independent variable is the amount of agreement about the lines; the dependent variable is whether the subject is swayed).

Stage III: Choice of Subjects; Choice of Experimenters
The researcher may choose someone else to carry out the experiment. The researcher also chooses the subject population to be used in the experiment.

Stage IV: Data Collection
The experimenter collects the data based on standardized measures of reactions to the independent variables (the group setting, the degree of disagreement from the group norm, the actual sizes of the lines).

Stage V: Analysis and Inference from the Data
The researcher or others analyze the data by statistical tests. The researcher looks at results and draws conclusions. If the hypothesis is supported, results are published.

Stage I. Formulation of the Problem

The kinds of theories and hypotheses that psychologists test wax and wane with the current interests of the discipline. Certain kinds of behavioral phenomena may be considered to be important areas of study at one time but not another, or by one area of psychology but not others. For example, in social psychology, if one looks at the major journals, interest trends are clearly evident and shifts in these trends occur over time. In the past these areas defined as important have generally excluded women. Research has usually been carried out on white, middle-class males, concerning issues of importance to them. For example, studies on decision making are conceptualized in terms of decision making in the male world, like clinical judgments or international relations. There are relatively few studies of family decision making. Even in fields in which there are more women, such as developmental or clinical psychology, there is still a relative lack of study of issues relevant and important to females. Women, their traditional roles, and the issues about which they are concerned have not been considered important until the last few years. Examples of these areas are love, marriage, empathy, female sexuality, nurturance, helping, birth control, pregnancy, and menopause. Similarly, researchers who study "women's issues" have typically been considered second-rate as a result of these biases (Bart, 1971).

The predominance of male researchers may also affect these interest trends. There are many fewer female than male psychologists, as is true in most professional pursuits (Epstein, 1970). While some women are active in research publication, the smaller number of women in the profession results in most studies being conceived and carried out by males (Centra, 1974). Consequently, most research done at any one time concerns topics of interest to men. In addition to problems in choice of topics, male bias may also mean that potential group differences are never considered. For example, those experiments authored by females are tested for sex differences significantly more often than those authored by males (Harris, 1971). Also, women may be likely to have different styles of investigation that contribute to new perspectives on behavior (Carlson, 1972).

After choosing the general area of research, the direction of the hypothesis can be affected by sex-role stereotyping as well. Clearest examples might be in areas in which an experimenter *is* testing for sex differences, such as "females conform more than males." Or, if the researcher (R) is using only one sex or the other for the experiment, he or she may nonconsciously form hypotheses in terms of stereotypes. Thus, sex-role assumptions come into play regardless of the subjects used.

Stage II. Operationalizing of the Hypotheses

Once R has formed the hypotheses, he or she has to find a way to test them out. R has to operationalize them—to translate the general concept into the specifics of the experiment. Situational factors (i.e., the context in which the experiment takes place) play a role in this translation, and can unintentionally bias the experimental results and the conclusions reached. The contexts and the tasks can be biased so that each sex may respond differently. For example, one study found that men do better on problems when they are described as masculine tasks; whereas women do better if the same test is labeled feminine (Milton, 1959). The competitiveness of the situation is also an important factor which influences the performance of men and women differently (Condry and Dyer, 1976; Frieze, et al., 1975). Other relevant situational factors include the sex of the experimenter (E), the sex composition of the group in which the tests are given, and the differential familiarity of materials to males and females.

When R chooses the materials and procedures for the experiment, he or she is often unaware of or may not consider the differential saliency or meaningfulness of these to the two sexes. There is some evidence suggesting that some of the reported differences between women and men are not due to inherent or stable personality characteristics of the person, but to the differential sensitivity to the tasks presented to them. For example, a host of studies show that women are more conforming, yield more to group pressure, and are more suggestible than men. This has been interpreted in psychoanalytic terms (as discussed in the next chapter), as a result of the weaker superego of females because they have not thoroughly resolved the Oedipal conflict, and thus are more dependent on the evaluations of others in guiding their behavior. It has also been interpreted as a reflection of the cultural prescriptions that women be docile, compliant, and submissive. However, there are studies that have *not* found that women yield to pressure and conform more than men. Typically such exceptions are regarded as just that, exceptions to the rule, but it is also possible that there is something more systematic involved.

A review of the literature on conformity reveals that in most of the experimental situations, subjects were asked to make judgments about activities or stimuli which were clearly male related, such as political or economic affairs and geometric designs suggestive of mechanical or mathematical relevance (Sistrunk and McDavid, 1971). Relatively few studies asked the subjects to evaluate or make judgments about female-related topics, such as domestic management, design, fashion, or family affairs. Perhaps conforming behavior is related to saliency, meaningfulness, or relevance. It might be that researchers were finding that women conformed more because they were asking them to make judgments about things that were not as relevant to them, and about which they had less information than men.

In one study a list of sixty-five statements were compiled that had been previously categorized by students as fact or opinion, and as of masculine, feminine, or nonsex-stereotyped interest. Subjects (S) were asked to agree or disagree with the items. Pressures toward conformity were applied by giving the subjects information about the majority opinion of a group of two hundred students on each item. S's were told that these opinions were included only for the subjects' interest. The "majority" answers were actually wrong for the fact statements and randomly varied for the opinion statements. Conformity was measured by seeing how many males and females agreed with these false "majority" opinions. No sex differences in conformity were found. Men and women conformed equally often to the majority. However, females conformed more on items previously rated as of masculine interest, and males conformed more on items previously judged to be of feminine interest. There was no sex difference on the neutral items. These results suggest that the situational factor of saliency or familiarity can affect how men and women respond (Sistrunk and McDavid, 1971). Thus, researchers need to take sex-role considerations seriously when planning an experiment, or they are apt to bias the results in favor of more or less conformity, dependence, aggression, or other factors.

Stage III. Choice of Subject (S) and Experimenter (E)

Once the hypotheses have been operationalized, the experimenter must decide who will be studied and who will actually conduct the study. Each of these decisions can introduce further bias into the investigation.

Sex of Subject (S). Most students of psychology are aware of psychology's propensity to overuse students and middle-class samples because they are conveniently available for study. Somewhat less well known is psychology's tendency to study males rather than females and to overlook the importance of gender as an independent variable. When psychologists carry out a study, they recruit subjects in various ways. For a survey study, researchers now draw random samples of the community, or focus on groups they are particularly interested in, such as medical doctors, political candidates, black school children, et al. However, most laboratory studies are carried out at universities, which have a convenient group to serve as subjects—students. Many psychology departments have set up subject pools or groups of students available to participate in experiments. They typically are students enrolled in large introductory psychology courses who are given course credit for participation.

Although it is no longer the case that available subjects are primarily male, several factors have contributed to the continued overuse of male subjects. First, psychologists occasionally try to replicate previous studies. In order to exactly replicate earlier results, the same, all-male samples must be used. Second, it is often inconvenient to have to use twice as many subjects;

this increase is required if one is to use both males and females and test for sex differences. Also, theories which are developed to explain male behavior may be explicitly limited to male subjects. If one wants to extend or test such a theory, all-male samples are a necessity. Finally, the male-as-norm ideology may make it seem unnecessary to include females as subjects.

A survey of the issues of the *Journal of Abnormal and Social Psychology* for 1958 documented the neglect of the study of women and sex differences in the 298 studies surveyed (Carlson and Carlson, 1960). Thirty-eight percent used males only, 21 percent did not report the sex of subject, 36 percent used both males and females, and 5 percent used females only. Of the 108 studies that had used both male and female subjects, only 32 reported tests for sex differences; 22 of these (or 69 percent) found statistically significant sex differences. It is unclear if this 69 percent represents an actual frequency of sex differences or if other studies simply did not report on their tests for these differences since they found no such differences or any sexual variations were statistically nonsignificant. Journals are biased toward the publication of "significant" findings, that is, statistically unlikely to occur by chance. Therefore, many of the results which show no differences are never reported. If all the 108 studies reviewed earlier which used both sexes actually tested for sex differences but only 22 found them, then the actual frequency of male-female differences would have been 20 percent rather than 69 percent. It is important to know which of these figures more accurately represents reality, but unfortunately without all the data we cannot. It is possible that our current conceptualizations of sex differences may reflect inaccurate generalizations based on those few studies which do report differences.

The construction of theories from work on primarily one sex is another source of bias resulting from the scarcity of studies using female subjects. For example, achievement motivation (the desire to be successful, see Chapter 12) has often been studied only in men. Of the fifteen studies on achievement in one collection, only one—a field study on children—examined sex of subject as a factor, and that one did indeed find differences (Atkinson and Feather, 1966). The other studies used only male subjects. It is ironic to note that several of these studies looked at demographic characteristics such as race, class, and education to justify the use of the subject population they had chosen, but did not mention sex. Because of this male bias in the subjects, social psychology texts caution readers to consider the discussion of theories of achievement motivation as applicable to males only (e.g., Brown, 1965).

There are at least two possible reasons for the relative absence of female subjects from the work on achievement motivation. First, there may be a nonconscious assumption that it is not important to study women because they "obviously" are not interested in achievement. Second, early data collected on achievement in women was dropped when it did not fit consistently with the male data (see McClelland, et al.; 1953). Study of female achievement was largely ignored until the last few years (Chapter 12).

Earlier, it was suggested that males were often studied because they were conveniently available. When investigating families, however, it is the female who is more available for study. For example, studies of schizophrenia and other mental disturbances in children have often focused on females. Theories of schizophrenogenic mothers abound. Fathers were not systematically studied until 1972, probably because fathers are usually at work during the day, while the mothers are at home with the children; this made the mothers easier to study. In addition to convenience, there are theoretical reasons for not studying fathers. Many of the clinical theories (see Chapter 3), as well as our cultural myths, stress the importance of the mother in the normal development of the child. This is not to question whether or not maternal behavior is important in schizophrenia, but to point to the less than scientific way in which the theory came about—when the father was ignored. Our society has highly negative as well as highly positive stereotypes of mothers, and psychology has often accepted these stereotypes, rather than looking at the facts directly.

Clinical theories, such as those about mothers, suffer from particular methodological problems. Clinicians derive their theories from case studies of individuals. One of the problems with this approach is that the clinician is basing his theory on a highly unusual sample of people—those who seek psychological help. Clearly these people have some difficulties and are probably not representative of all men or all women. Thus for clinicians' case studies, the subject sample is as biased as the white, middle-class, male college student sample used for most psychological experiments. The result is that studies of general issues such as female sexuality have been done with clinical populations and then are unjustifiably generalized to all women.

The study of cyclical mood changes by physiological psychologists provides another example of the effects of a nonconscious ideology on research. Our society believes that women are overly emotional and unstable while men are the opposite. Research until quite recently has reflected these beliefs. The study of cyclical mood and behavior changes has focused on women's menstrual cycles, largely ignoring other cycles that might be unique to men or common to both sexes (see Chapter 10). The point here is that this research has studied biological effects only to the extent that they paralleled our stereotypes, with the result of constricting knowledge in the area. Women's emotional nature has been often assumed to be innately related to their cycles. Even the study of animal physiology and behavior has incorporated our stereotypes of women. For example, female monkey behavior has been interpreted in terms of human female stereotypes. Typically, researchers have focused upon aggressive male behavior and have assumed that females are always submissive to males. However, females may actually be more aggressive in controlling certain decisions (Lancaster, 1973).

Regardless of whether it is males or females that are ignored, studying one sex alone can distort our theories of human behavior, especially when common stereotypes are left unquestioned.

Sex of Experimenter (E). The sex of the experimenter (E), the person who actually carries out the experiment, can also influence the results of the study. Although most published studies do not state the sex of the experimenter, when they do test for the effects of the sex of E, the reported results are often significant (Harris, 1971). The sex of E has been found to be an important variable in studies of schizophrenia (e.g., Klein, Cicchetti, and Spohn, 1967); conformity (e.g., Beloff, 1958); need for affiliation (e.g., Exline, 1962); empathy (e.g., Tomlinson, 1967); classroom learning (e.g., Page, 1958); verbal conditioning (e.g., Sarason and Minard, 1963); and E bias (e.g., Rosenthal, 1966). In each of these studies, the subjects responded differently when the experiment was run by different sex E's. In addition, the sex of the experimenter has also been found to interact with the sex of the subject. Male and female subjects react differently toward male and female E's. However, it must be kept in mind that journals tend to publish only significant results. Consequently, studies which tested and failed to find significant effects for the sex of E may be underrepresented in the journals.

Stage IV: Data Collection

After all the procedures have been established and the decisions have been made as to who will be studied and who will actually run the experiment, then the study can begin. Once again, in the data collection stage, several opportunities exist for potential bias.

Expectations of E. Regardless of their sex, E's bring into the experiment assumptions about behavior of males and females and often react to the two sexes differently, thereby effecting the results of the "controlled" experiments they perform. This effect is the *self-fulfilling prophecy:* we expect that men and women will behave in certain ways, and when they do, our stereotypes are confirmed. All too often, however, we are unaware of the probability that our expectations affect the person's responses.

Studies of both animals and humans show that the expectations of the experimenter can influence results, even in controlled experiments. In one experiment people were shown photographs of faces, and asked to rate whether the person was a successful person or a failure. Twenty experienced E's were given identical instructions to read to their subjects, and told not to deviate from these. However, ten E's were told that the previous findings indicated the photograph had been rated as successful, and the other ten were told the photograph had been rated a failure. Each experimenter obtained results that fulfilled his or her expectations (Rosenthal and Jacobson, 1968). Evidently, they communicated these expectations to their subjects, probably nonverbally.

These experiments showed that rigorous experimental psychology is not immune to the self-fulfilling prophecy. To avoid this, many experiments are run "blind"—i.e., the experimenter does not know the hypothesis. But in sex-role research, many of the expectations about women and men are nonconscious, and may affect data gathering in subtle ways even in "blind" experiments. The self-fulfilling prophecy remains a serious problem in clinical psychology. Because the situation is less controlled, therapists can more readily create the behavior they expect in a patient. If, then, theories of behavior are developed from such expectations, their validity is doubtful.

One particular area in which the formulization and operationalization of the problem has lead to biases in data collection is in the study of masculinity and femininity. As early as 1904, psychologists have attempted to develop measures of masculinity and femininity (Ellis, 1904). There have been several basic problems with this research, stemming first from the way the measurement devices were constructed. Masculinity and femininity were conceived to be mutually exclusive; the two ends of a simple, bipolar dimension (Constantinople, 1973). That is, people were seen as necessarily either all masculine or all feminine. Also, it was often considered abnormal (by people who used these scales) if males scored feminine or females scored masculine.

These masculinity-femininity scales generally consisted of interest items that had yielded sex differences in pilot subject populations, for example, "I'd rather be a dress designer than a forest ranger." While it seems clear that these scales were measuring the degree of alignment of an individual with sex-role expectations of this society, the M-F scales purported to measure a more basic underlying psychological dimension. This goal was not achieved (Constantinople, 1973).

Recently, traditional concepts of masculinity and femininity have been questioned (e.g., Mead and Kaplan, 1965). Some suggest that we should not look at the concept of masculinity and femininity as polar ends of a single continuum (Bem, 1974; Bem and Bem, 1970; Carlson, 1972). Some have proposed a new conceptualization of masculinity and femininity as two independent trait constellations (Bem, 1974; Spence, et al., 1975).

Individuals of either sex can be highly "masculine," highly "feminine," or androgynous. An androgynous person is one who may act according to sex-role stereotypes or not, depending on the circumstances of the situation. Such a person is both instrumental and expressive, both assertive and yielding, both "masculine" and "feminine." Furthermore, because androgynous people fail to fit the traditional model of masculinity or femininity, psychology has not studied androgynous people, despite the possibility that they might be the most interesting and psychologically the more healthy individuals.

Stage V: Analysis and Inference from the Data

Once the experimenter has gathered data, more biases can enter into the statistical analyses and into the researcher's interpretation of the results. For example, if statistically significant sex differences are found, these may be interpreted to mean that all women are different from all men. Instead, nearly all research shows overlapping distributions for men and women. Thus, although the average score may be different for the two sexes, there are many women on the "masculine" side of the average and many men on the "feminine" side. In fact, most research, even that showing "significant" differences, points to great similarities between men and women rather than differences.

A second problem in the interpretation of sex differences is the tendency to assume that these differences are due either to innate differences or entirely to socialization. These interpretations are implicitly made in spite of the fact that the data may offer no insight into the origin of differences found. Although either assumption is equally biased when unsupported by data, the non—status quo viewpoint that socialization is responsible for sex differences is most often perceived as being biased for the reasons discussed earlier.

Another problem is that women have been accused of being biased when they study women. However, if one assumes that someone is too emotionally involved to write about their own group, then men should not be allowed to write about men. Instead, only women should write about men because men would not be objective in writing about themselves. These arguments grow out of the idea that only an outsider can be objective enough to interpret social reality. However, recent ethnic movements have held just the opposite—that only an insider can understand a minority group's value system and accurately interpret what are the causes and effects of behaviors. It is fairly well accepted by psychologists that in the case of blacks and other minorities it is difficult for a dominant group to study a minority group with which they do not share many values and experiences. The same logic leads one to conclude that it may not be as reasonable for men to study women as for *women* to study women. Biases due to self-interest may indeed enter in, but the perceptions, values, and living experiences of women can also bring in valuable insights in each of the stages of carrying out an experiment. This does not necessarily mean that all females can study women better than all males. What is needed is a well-informed outlook in sex roles in order to interpret the data correctly, and it is hoped that either a man or a woman would be able to develop this outlook.

There are many areas open to biases in an experiment. The possible biases are summarized in Box 3. By being aware of the kinds of mistakes that can be made, psychologists can perform better experiments, and we can know what to watch out for in evaluating these experiments. Some questions that might be asked of any study are: How were hypotheses formed? Was the status quo

Box 3   Errors in Experimental Psychology: What to Watch Out For

Stage I: Formulation of the Problem

1. Study only areas of life with which males are familiar.
2. Formulize hypotheses without considering sex-role stereotypes.

Stage II: Operationalization

1. Use of male-oriented tests and situations.
2. Looking at all behavior as a result of internal processes.

Stage III: Sex of Subject and Experimenter

1. Using all male subjects.
2. Not testing for effects of sex of the experimenter.
3. Theory building while ignoring one sex.

Stage IV: Data Collection

1. Ignoring the effects of the experimenter's expectations on the subjects' behavior.
2. Construction of instruments that bias direction of findings (e.g., M-F scales).

Stage V: Analysis and Interpretation

1. Viewing behavior in terms of stereotypes.
2. Interpreting sex differences as absolute rather than overlapping.
3. Publication of significant results only.
4. Ignoring personal experience.
5. Considering the feminist interpretation as being the biased interpretation.

---

assumed or opposed without examination? Did the operationalization and data collection allow for interpretation of results from an informed outlook on sex roles?

Methodological issues in the psychology of women are important for several reasons. First, to be a science, psychology should strive to become aware of its biases and assumptions so that it can move toward truth, or at least toward a valid perspective on social reality. Second, psychological findings about women and sex differences affect people's lives. One example of how findings and the influence of stereotypes affect lives is in governmental policy. Politicians seem to be more interested in using empirical data for making social policies, as evidenced by the various presidential commission reports on violence, pornography, and other social issues. Chapter 17 discusses the use of data and assumptions about women in the United States Senate discussions of the Equal Rights Amendment. The point is that unbiased data are needed for these decisions.

In order to be a better science, and to be able to present accurate material from a more balanced value system, psychology needs to rethink its methods. The goal is to have a science which is unpolluted by the misuse and manipulation of sex-role concepts, and to have valid knowledge in the psychology of women and the psychology of sex differences, as well as an informed psychology of men.

3 Theories of Feminine Personality

Deborah Lee and Joan Hertzberg

During the early part of the twentieth century a dramatic change took place in psychology, which revolutionized the way in which psychologists look at the human mind. The person responsible for this was Sigmund Freud; his ideas formed the basis of psychoanalytic theory.

Today, much of the field of personality is derived from the psychoanalytic tradition. Psychoanalytic theories and constructs are directly applied in clinical settings and set the tone for the psychiatric treatment of women and men. This has had a great impact upon clinical practice. Psychoanalytic theory has also had wide acceptance by the general public, and it has been a major influence in the formation of our basic conceptions of femininity. Thus, whether filtered through the therapist's office, the university classroom, or the mass media, women have accepted these concepts and have tried to mold themselves to fit them.

As with most theories, personality theories have been subject to much criticism from time to time. More recently, there has been much concern with the way in which these theories have described the behavior and personality of women. This chapter will critically review the psychoanalytic literature on feminine personality, with a special emphasis on some of the assumptions of this literature. Since they deal specifically with defining feminine personality and the special problems of women, we will look at Freud,

This chapter was done with the assistance of Irene Frieze, Jacquelynne Parsons, and Diane Ruble.

Deutsch, Horney, Thompson, Jung, and Erikson. Freud will serve as the starting point for this review since he was the precursor for the other theorists and his work has had such a major influence upon these later thinkers as well as upon society in general.

SIGMUND FREUD: PSYCHOANALYTIC THEORY

Sigmund Freud (1856–1939) was the most influential of the clinical theorists. Although considered quite radical by many of his contemporaries, Freud's ideas met with increasing enthusiasm in both the psychological and medical communities and, then, in many fields of academic study. His ideas have had a tremendous impact not only on psychology and psychiatry, but also upon broader American and European culture. Few people in our society are not at least somewhat familiar with psychoanalytic theory and such basic Freudian ideas as unconscious motivation, the Oedipus complex, ego defenses, and the importance of early mother-child interactions.

Although much of Freud's personality theory is oriented toward men, he did develop a theory of feminine personality, which he derived in part from his earlier theories of the male. However, he cautioned against conceptualizing male and female development as being completely analogous. Specifically, he suggested that a child's personality development depends on whether the child is a boy or girl, especially after the first two to three years of life. Freud considered his theories to be rudimentary and tentative, and stated that he would modify them as he obtained new data and his theories did, in fact, evolve over his lifetime. Nonetheless, many of Freud's speculations about women remain basic to psychoanalytic theory today, despite the lack of corroborating research data.

In order to understand Freud's theory of feminine personality, it is important to examine several basic ideas which underlie much of Freudian thinking. These include:

1. The existence of an unconscious reservoir of repressed thoughts and desires which is the source of all motivation. Psychoanalysts consider their field to be the scientific study of this unconscious aspect of personality.
2. An emphasis on sexuality as a primary motive for human functioning. Freud postulated that a strong sexual instinct exists both in childhood and throughout later life.
3. The idea that human males and females are basically bisexual, that depending on their particular pattern of development and their extent of inborn "masculinity" or "femininity," people can become heterosexual, homosexual, or bisexual.
4. The essential indivisibility of normal and abnormal. Freud believed that the same psychodynamic principles underlie both normal and abnormal behavior.

5. The belief in the biological, sexual, and social inferiority of women. This assumption strongly affects Freud's theory of male and female development.
6. A focus on early childhood as a period of critical importance for personality development. All people are seen as passing through a set sequence of developmental stages. The three most important stages occur in the first five years of life.

Male and Female Development

Freud felt that many of our basic feelings were unconscious and that unconscious sexual thoughts were of primary importance for understanding people's behavior. However, these sexual thoughts or fantasies were believed to be dependent upon one's stage of development.

Freud felt that everyone passed through a series of developmental stages, each of which was characterized by a focus upon a different area of the body. This focus had sexual connotations; psychic energy during each stage was oriented toward gratification associated with the specific body area.

According to Freudian theory, until approximately age four (allowing leeway for individual variation), boys and girls pass through first the oral and then the anal stages of development. Since there are no sex differences in these areas, boys and girls are alike sexually in these stages. Freud described both sexes as "little men" (Freud, 1933/1965). In the oral stage, children are focused primarily on the mouth and lips and the bottle or the mother's breast. In the anal stage, the central concern is the anus and the elimination and retention of feces. During these two stages both sexes regard their mother as the primary love object, since she is associated with both oral and anal activities.

Girls and boys diverge in their development, according to Freud, in the phallic stage, which occurs at approximately age four. At this point, the focus of sexual fantasies for boys is the penis and for girls the clitoris. The boy's feelings of love for his mother become more sexual during the phallic stage, and he becomes jealous of his father. However, he also fears the jealousy of his father toward him and worries about his father punishing him by castration. Since the boy's external genitals are his central focus, castration would be the worst punishment he could imagine. His castration anxiety is greatly increased when he first observes that girls lack external genitals. He assumes they have already lost their penises and that he too could lose his valued organ. Since girls lack a penis, the boy also assumes they are inferior to him, a normal feeling, according to Freudian logic, which will persist through later stages of male development (Freud, 1925/1974).

Mainly as a result of his castration anxiety, the boy represses his desire for his mother and his fear and hostility toward his father. This process is facilitated by the mother's rebuff of her son's overtures toward her. The boy replaces his feelings of rivalry toward his father with identification with him.

During this process he assumes the values of his father; they form what Freud labeled as the superego, a reservoir of moral values. This identification is the normal resolution of the Oedipal complex. However, if the feminine components of his personality are too strong or other problems have arisen in his development, he may identify instead with his mother and take on a "feminine," homosexual sex-role orientation.

Resolution of the phallic stage begins for the girl when, in comparing herself to boys, she discovers that she lacks a penis. Freud believed that girls, upon discovering this difference, feel

> seriously wronged, often declare that they have "something like it too," and fall victims to "envy for the penis," which will leave ineradicable traces on their development and the formation of their character and which will not be surmounted in even the most favorable cases without a severe expenditure of psychical energy. (*Freud, 1933/1965, p. 589.*)

The girl's first reaction to this "traumatic discovery," according to Freud, is to deny that she does not have a penis. Eventually, however, she must face the fact that not only does she lack a penis, but that she shares this fate with her mother and all other females. She may believe that once she had a penis, but that somehow she lost it. In any case, she blames her mother for her lack of a penis. Because she holds her mother responsible for her "loss" and because the mother also lacks the "highly valued" penis, Freud believed that the mother, and all females, become greatly devalued in the eyes of the girl (as well as boys). Thus, the girl begins to regard men with profound envy, and joins all males in disdaining women.

The girl's "penis envy" motivates her to renounce her love for her mother and turn to her father, while at the same time she renounces her clitoris and shifts her erotic focus to the vagina, the mature female sex organ according to Freud (1938). Her shift of love to her father derives from her desire to possess his penis. She believes that she can take in the father's penis, thereby unconsciously perceiving her vagina in a new positive light. She also comes to equate penis and child: She takes her father as a love object in order to have a child by him, which symbolically represents attaining a penis. This process places the girl in a position of unconscious competition with her mother. Thus, according to Freudian theory, the girl playing with dolls is really expressing her wish for a penis. The original penis-wish is transformed into a wish for a baby, which leads to love and desire for the man as bearer of the penis and provider of the baby.

The shift from clitoral to vaginal sexuality is basic to Freud's developmental theory, since to him the clitoris is "masculine" and clitoral sexuality must be eliminated if mature femininity is to develop. One of the immediate consequences of penis envy to Freud is that the girl struggles to renounce her clitoral masturbation, which may remain a conflict for her throughout childhood. It is, after all, difficult for the girl to give up this activity which has provided her with such pleasure. She does so, according to Freud, because of the terrible narcissistic wound of not possessing a penis.

For a girl, the "discovery of castration" initiates her Oedipus complex. However, Freud believed that girls remain in the grips of Oedipal conflicts for an indeterminate length of time, and never fully escape them. However, partial resolution does occur through the girl's identification with her mother as a symbolic means of possessing her father. She then acquires her superego—a set of moral values from her mother—and her feminine identity. However, Freud concluded from this developmental difference between boys and girls, that women cannot have as strong a superego as men, since the motive for its formation (in men, fear of castration by their fathers) is lacking. Thus, in Freud's view, women remain forever morally and ethically undeveloped compared with men.

Although never completely resigned to their "femininity", Freud believed that women gain some relief from the birth of their first child. Finally, with birth, there issues forth from the woman's own body a mass of protoplasm which symbolically represents the penis, and she is at last fulfilled. The birth of a son is all the more gratifying, for it provides the woman with a real penis, beyond the symbolic one.

A woman, according to Freud, usually responds to the Oedipal stage according to one of the following patterns: 1) She may renounce sexuality in general; 2) She may develop the "normal" feminine attitude, with all eroticism concentrated in the vagina. This occurs at the later genital stage; or 3) She may cling to her clitoral "masculine" sexuality in obstinate self-assertion. Abnormal resolution of these phallic stage conflicts can lead to masculine identification and homosexuality, or to overly strong "penis envy" and masculine behavior.

Although only one of these three paths involves the renunciation of sexuality, Freud did believe that the libido, or human sexual force, functions less effectively in women than men. He stated that the libido is essentially active or "masculine" but that it also covers passive or "feminine" aims. According to Freud, the libido is more constrained "when pressed into the service of the feminine function" (1933/1965, p. 595). In short, he believed that the normal process of female development demands more sexual repression than male development.

After passing through the phallic stage and Oedipal conflict, both sexes enter the latency stage which lasts until the time of puberty. During this time, about which Freud wrote comparatively little, the child has no central erogenous focus and sexuality is largely repressed. Finally, with the final stage, the genital stage, both girls and boys are oriented toward heterosexual intercourse. This means that the girl's erotic focus is the vagina while for the boy it remains the penis. For both sexes, though, the concern is with intercourse rather than masturbation.

Freudian Theory: A Critique

Source of Data. Although Freud believed that the childhood years were crucial in terms of personality development, he actually did very little work with children. His theories are largely based on clinical data from his patients, most of whom were adults. Freud's method of treatment was called psychoanalysis. This involves retelling dreams and other important memories with an attempt to look behind them through association to unconscious memories of childhood. Freud believed that the adult problems of his patients had their origins in their early childhood conflicts. He also felt that this free recall material derived from people in therapy illuminated psychic processes shared by "healthy" people. Of his method, Freud wrote:

> . . . We are only within our rights if we study the residues and consequences of the emotional world in retrospect, in people in whom these processes of development had attained a specially clear and excessive degree of expansion. Pathology has always done us the service of making discernable by isolation and exaggeration conditions which would remain concealed in a normal state. (*1933/1965, p. 585.*)

The unconscious material, *as interpreted by Freud,* forms the basic data for his theory.

Freud recognized the limited, tentative nature of his formulations about women and, in fact, wrote very little about them. Addressing the women in his audience, he remarked in 1933: "If you want to know more about femininity you must interrogate your own experience or turn to the poets, or else wait until science can give you more coherent information" (1933/1965,p. 599). Science has come up with more coherent information since 1933, and much of it refutes Freuds's tentative theories of feminine personality (e.g., Sherman, 1971).

Masculine Bias. One of the main points of Freud's theory, namely the biological inferiority of women, based on their lack of a penis, is not really a formulation which is easily tested. It is rather a matter of value, a subjective viewpoint. It is Freud's *belief* in biological inferiority of women rather than any observation of women's actual opportunities in society which principally influenced his ideas on the nature and destiny of women. This assigning of values to biology has provoked widespread criticism of Freud's theory of women, although it was consistent with the Victorian values of his time.

An example of this masculine bias is that Freud takes the male as the norm for his theories. Freud is, of course, not alone in this; his approach is validated by most of (at least) Western civilization and most of its psychology. However, Freud's theories provide us with an instructive example of masculine bias. The essence of this bias is that the female is seen as an inadequate male. There are a number of problems with this approach, the main one being that a woman is not a man. Males and females exist with certain inherent and socially conditioned differences. Assigning one sex a higher value than the other seems a useless exercise.

Freud's references to women as inadequate men pervade his writings about women. A woman must accept the "reality" of her castration, the "fact" of her organic inferiority. The clitoris is "actually" a masculine organ, a rudimentary penis. As later writers have pointed out, the penis, in contrast, is never referred to as a "bloated clitoris" (Rotkin, 1973). The pre-Oedipal little girl is described as a "little man." Many basic human activities, such as reading and social action, are considered "masculine" and a girl or woman who engages in them is demonstrating her "penis envy by masculine protest." As stated above, even childbearing is actually an expression of penis envy, according to Freud.

Anatomy Is Destiny. Another basic criticism of Freud's work is that he largely ignored the social context of people and their behavior. "Anatomy is destiny" has become a slogan to characterize his position. In analyzing his patients and in formulating his theories, Freud took as given the social reality in which their symptoms unfolded. Thus, the extent to which his observations hold true in other social contexts with other values remains unknown. Biology never exists in a vacuum, and from birth every biological creature lives in a social and cultural world, with conditioned expectations, assumptions, categorizations, and values. Freud's ignoring of these factors does not in itself disprove his theories. It is conceivable that biophysical features might have deterministic consequences in people's lives. But this assumption is treated as fact by Freud and by many of his followers.

The anatomy-is-destiny viewpoint in Freudian thinking has been strongly criticized. Empirical evidence, to date, does not convincingly document such basic Freudian notions as penis envy, the Oedipal complex, the vaginal orgasm, and so on. While there is considerable evidence that girls and women envy the male role for its greater social power and privilege, there is little evidence for female envy of male anatomy (Sherman, 1971). Experimental evidence also does not support the Oedipal shift from mother to father. Both sexes, at ages four and six, remain primarily attached to their mother, given child-rearing practices in which the mother is primary caretaker.

Some clinical evidence also fails to support Freud (Money, 1965; Stoller, 1968). In certain cases, normal gender identity can be established in contradiction to anatomy. It has been found that individuals, whether biological males or females, who lacked female hormones or female genitalia but whose parents raised them as females, attained a core gender identification of female, and developed "normal" patterns of feminine personality. The main contribution of this work is to emphasize the particular importance of learning in human sexual identification, even in the absence of the sex-appropriate physiology central to psychoanalytic theory (see Chapters 5, 6, and 7).

A Masculine View of Female Sexuality. With regard to Freud's ideas about female sexuality, the evidence is contradictory. While it is true that many women are repressed and conflicted with regard to sex, there is no evidence that this repression is based on female physiology apart from social factors (Chapter 11; Sherman, 1971). Freud's notion of the vaginal orgasm, a separate "mature" orgasm which is centered exclusively in the vagina, is one aspect of his theory which has quite convincingly been disproved by later experimental evidence which demonstrates that both the clitoris *and* the vagina are involved in any female orgasm.

By defining women's sexuality in terms of the vagina, Freud defined women in terms of what pleases heterosexual men, namely vaginal penetration. Women who cannot attain their "mature" vaginal sexuality are defined as frigid. They may suffer silently in self-blame, seek expensive treatment in psychoanalysis to "cure" their "repression" which is denying them (and their mates) a "mature" sex life, or they can lie to attract a man and convince him that his potency is intact by providing "his woman" with full vaginal satisfaction. This equation of "mature" sexuality with intercourse is an extremely masculine orientation, as well as defining sexuality in exclusively heterosexual terms.

Penis Envy. Freud's concept of penis envy is essential to his theory of feminine personality. The evidence for penis envy is clinical, based on childhood memories of adult patients. According to Freud, the phenomenon of penis envy is quite common. However, the bulk of empirical research does not support the theory of penis envy (Sherman, 1971). Most well-documented studies of Oedipal-aged children find little evidence of castration anxiety in boys, and even less evidence of penis envy in girls. Almost all studies which report evidence of penis envy as an important factor in the psychic life of adult women can be shown to be seriously methodologically flawed. Other than the clinical reports, there is no strong evidence that penis envy exists as a trait of normal adult women, let alone as the crucial influential phenomenon described by Freud. However, it is important to distinguish between envy of the actual penis, and envy of the male role. There is much evidence that many females envy the male role and its privileges. It is possible that under certain circumstances, a girl may react to a penis with any number of feelings, including envy, admiration, as well as bewilderment, curiosity, laughter, and disgust. Envy is only one of these reactions and is probably not the most common.

Freud's Contributions

Freud was basically concerned with the functioning of the adult personality—particularly male personalities. His ideas about unconscious motivation are still widely accepted. Other major contributions include his recognition of childhood sexuality and the overall importance of sexual motives; his focus on early development, specifically recognizing the intensity and sexuality involved in a child's attachment to parents; and his recognition of the influence of biological factors on behavior. However, later thinkers have modified some of these Freudian concepts.

Although sexual motives may well be highly important for all ages of people, it is not proven that they are *the* primary motivators of human behavior, as Freud felt they were. Similarly, early childhood development has important implications for the adult personality, but Freud's extreme emphasis on the early childhood years has not been supported by empirical data. For example, some of the childhood events Freud felt were so important have not been found in later research. Thus, there is no evidence that penis envy is a universal phenomenon, nor that its presence in normal girls leaves permanent scars. Also Freud's theory of penis envy gives a one-sided and essentially distorted impression, since he does not deal correspondingly with the phenomenon of "womb envy," or woman envy in men and boys, an issue some theorists such as Erikson have discussed in some detail. Also, the adult personality is not fully developed by the early teens as Freud implied. Social conditions can lead to personality changes at any age and much personality development occurs after puberty (see Chapter 9). Finally, although the authors disagree on the overall importance of biology in determining differences between the sexes, we would concur that biological factors, including sex differences in hormones, have some impact upon understanding variations in human behavior.

DEVELOPMENT OF PSYCHOANALYTIC THEORY

Freud's work, although initially criticized, came to be widely accepted by other psychologists. Those following his ideas most closely include Helene Deutsch. Others, such as Karen Horney, Erik Erikson, Clara Thompson, and Carl Jung, made more radical deviations in their own interpretations of Freud and are therefore known as neo-Freudians. All of their theories, however, can be criticized to a greater or lesser degree for some of the issues raised in the critique of Freudian theory. They all tend to rely heavily upon clinical observations as a basis of their ideas. Many of them use the white male experience as the norm for all of humanity (as do many modern experimental psychologists). The following section reviews some of the specific ideas of these later theorists.

Helene Deutsch: Variations on the Freudian Theme

Helene Deutsch was born in 1884 and worked closely with Freud, doing clinical psychoanalysis and writing about psychoanalytic theory. Her clinical and theoretical work on feminine psychology was highly praised by Freud.

He particularly valued her work on frigidity and masochism; her contributions to the theory of pre-Oedipal development in which the girl is primarily attached to her mother; and her ability as a woman analyst to serve as a mother-substitute for women patients in therapy.

Helene Deutsch, unlike Horney, Thompson, and other women psychoanalysts, stayed very close to Freud's basic theories. She extended Freud's ideas in equating femininity with passivity, a correspondence which she felt was a universal tendency in all cultures, although she believed there were variations in degree and form. To Deutsch, woman's activity is directed inward, and enriches her inner life with intuition, subjectivity, and general affectivity, which Deutsch considered characteristic of femininity. However, her passivity contributes to the masochism also associated with femininity. Deutsch considered the girl's pre-Oedipal relationship to her mother to be extremely complex and important. She pointed out that it is not uncommon for a girl to fantasize a partnership with her mother which excludes the father, often assigning him to a passive role (Deutsch, 1945, pp. 61–63). Deutsch also discussed the psychology of reproduction in detail, formulating a complex theory of the relationship of mother to child during pregnancy.

To Deutsch, pleasure in intercourse is due to the expectation of parturition, an "orgy of masochistic pleasure" (Deutsch, 1924/1970). The clitoris was considered to play an inhibitory role and to be totally superfluous to the healthy adult woman's sexuality. Deutsch believed that orgasm is essentially a male phenomenon, and that the vagina is properly limited to a passive-receptive sucking function (1945). Intercourse for the truly feminine woman should exclude orgasm, and should rather consist of slow relaxation, without vaginal contractions (1960/1970).

Many aspects of Deutsch's theory are not in keeping with more current data. For example, women have orgasms which do involve pulsations in the vaginal walls and changes in the clitoris (Masters and Johnson, 1966). Other research shows that women are not essentially passive (Chapter 4). Nonetheless, Deutsch had some interesting insights, particularly her emphasis on the importance of the early mother-daughter relationship and her idea that a woman's sexuality may extend to include her experiences of birth, pregnancy, and lactation. In any event, her own life stands out in contrast to her theory of woman doomed to passivity.

Karen Horney: Criticism of Freudian Thinking about Women

Karen Horney (1885–1952), another of the original psychoanalysts who worked closely with Freud, wished to correct what she considered to be fallacies in his work. She differed from Freud principally in two areas: 1) She emphasized the importance of social and cultural values as the context for biophysical phenomena. 2) She proposed the radical idea that women might have a psychology of their own, not derived from analogies to men.

Horney believed that there was a remarkable similarity between Freud's theory of feminine personality, and ideas little boys have about girls, rather than actually reflecting the thinking of the girls themselves. For example, Horney pointed out that it was much more probable that boys, rather than girls, would believe that members of both sexes should normally have penises. From this Freudian assumption came all the other assumptions about the girl feeling sad and then fearing that she has been mutilated because she has lost her penis. She also believed that boys, not girls, fear castration as punishment and feel that the lack of a penis implies inferiority. The boy, being unable to imagine how a girl can ever get over her great loss, then imagines that she will always long to be a man and may even wish vengeance against men because they have what she lacks.

Horney shared Freud's belief that penis envy was a regular feature of a little girl's development, but she differed from Freud in several important aspects of his theory. She viewed penis envy as an aspect of mutual envy between sexes. However, she believed that the source of penis envy was the greater ease with which a boy could view and handle his genital in urination and masturbation. She also saw this envy as resulting from the girl's recognition of the superior status awarded to males. She argued that the clitoris "legitimately belongs to and forms an integral part of the female genital apparatus" and was not simply a small penis (Horney, 1926). One problem for girls, according to Horney, was anxiety related to the relative inaccessibility of their genitals and fear of being penetrated. The latter worry she traced to a little girl's fantasy of being penetrated by the comparatively huge penis of her father.

A similar form of anxiety existed for boys; their desire was for the sexual possession of their mother. However, this wish had negative consequences for the boy, who was then made aware of the smallness and insignificance of his penis in relation to his mother's vagina. These perceptions were seen as the basis for the development of male feelings of sexual inadequacy, loss of self-respect, and fear of rejection (Horney, 1935).

Although emphasizing the anxiety in female development as well as male development, Horney specifically and effectively refuted psychoanalytic ideas about female masochism. She demonstrated that cultural factors such as lack of effective outlets for sexual expression for women, the belief in the inferiority of women, the economic dependence of women on men, and the restriction of women to emotionally centered spheres of life could adequately account for the female tendency toward masochism. In view of these factors, she felt that the pervasiveness of female masochism had been greatly overestimated by Freud.

Karen Horney also wrote on a number of other topics of importance to women: the economic, social, and psychological aspects of the relationship between the sexes, marriage, motherhood, monogamy, menstruation, men's problems with women, and the masculine bias in society.

Clara Thompson: Interpersonal Psychoanalysis

Clara Thompson (1893–1958) also emphasized the interaction of social factors with women's biology in personality development. She was originally trained in classical psychoanalytic methods, and went on to work with Harry Stack Sullivan, sharing with him a clinical approach which emphasized interpersonal relations. In general, Thompson's orientation to clinical theory was that neurotic traits were more a product of culture than one's sex. She stated that while biological factors could not be ignored, psychological difficulties were a result of a sociohistorical situation which could not adequately provide for the fulfillment of biological needs.

She criticized Freud for his view of penis envy as manifesting biological inferiority. She placed "penis envy" in a social context by pointing out its use as a symbol for both men and women. For women, she believed, the penis gave concrete manifestations for feelings of inferiority, while for men it came to symbolize aggressive impulses. Like Horney, Thompson argued that many of the behaviors of women which a Freudian analyst probably would interpret as penis envy, were actually the result of envy of male status. In a competitive and patriarchal culture, women could be expected to feel envy apart from biological sex differences. Typical reactions to envy by both sexes, in her view, included attempts to excel in competitiveness, withdrawal from competition, or efforts to gain revenge over one who had excelled and thereby precipitated envy.

Thompson, in rejecting Freud's view of the inferiority of the clitoris, assumed that girls and boys in their "phallic" stage of development get equal autoerotic satisfaction from their genitals. She believed, though, that the male urinary function might appear superior to both sexes (Thompson, 1950). Beyond this difference, Thompson believed children's genital comparison might well be part of their general experimenting with life, a mutual, nonproblematic activity. These impressions derived from Thompson's own clinical practice.

Thompson also challenged Freud's assertion of the biological base for such "feminine traits" as narcissism, weak superego, and psychic rigidity. For all of these, she offered convincing social explanations.

Thompson did not merely criticize Freud, but proposed an extensive, though unfinished, theory of her own about woman's psychology. Her entire theory was grounded in her observations of sociohistorical phenomena. For example, she believed that the decline of the family as a vital social and economic unit created a transitional situation with particular problems for women. These included a loss in the value given for work in the home and conflicting demands and expectations for women between modern and traditional values. Conflicts relating to these social situations could translate themselves into neurotic symptoms.

Thompson believed one of modern woman's most serious conflicts concerned childbearing. She wrote that women were trained to believe that adequate sexual fulfillment (including childbearing) was not compatible with self-development and creative self-expression. This was at least partly a result of lack of social supports for creative activity for the woman with children. Thompson also challenged Freud's concept of the equivalence of a penis with a baby. She stated that "childbearing is a sufficiently biologic function to have value for its own sake. Surely only a man could have thought of it in terms of compensation or consolation" (1964, p. 232).

Thompson also held that problems continued for women after their children were grown. At this time, she stated, a woman might suffer from the absence of clear role models for her self-definition, and had to find new ways to integrate her life. Yet, to the extent that the woman moved toward independence, she experienced the disapproval of her parents, of the man she loved, as well as society at large. Her other problems at this time might include the onset of menopause and diminished self-esteem due to the cultural ideal of youthful beauty. Here again, Thompson integrated biological and social factors in her analysis.

According to Thompson, another problem for women in this society was the absence of any well-developed sense of their own sexuality. A woman's training in sexual insecurity and insincerity contributed to her diminished sense of self. The cultural undervaluation of female sexual organs led to the woman's lack of pride in her own genitals and lack of acceptance of her entire body. Thompson also felt that the cultural inhibition of woman's sexuality discouraged her intellectual development and sense of personal initiative. Unlike Freud, however, she did not attribute women's sexual inhibitions to any biological inferiority.

Another original contribution in Thompson's theory was that woman's difficulty with sex was further compounded by the prevalent puritan phobia about cleanliness. The male in intercourse rid himself of the "dirty" products of sex. The woman was left to carry around the semen; worse yet, she lacked sphincter control in her vagina, and the semen dripped out. In a "sphincter morality" woman's sense of dirtiness and unacceptability was an integral part of her sense of sexuality.

Significant to Thompson is the fact that a woman could, and frequently did, have intercourse without desire, for reasons ranging from rape to feeling that the man's pleasure and needs were more important than her own. This situation was prevalent due to the combined effect of two deeply ingrained cultural beliefs: that the female was sexually and biologically inferior to the male; and that female sexual satisfaction was considered less important than male satisfaction.

Finally, Thompson was not overly optimistic about the prospect of any immediate change:

> Any attempt to change a cultural pattern produces conflict in the people involved. Those who have had the advantage previously and have little or

nothing to gain from the change, i.e., in this case men, furnish a strong resistance to the change. The result may be increasing the woman's inferiority feelings or her sense of guilt in wanting to be different. (Thompson, 1964, p. 259.)

While Thompson did not present any comprehensive developmental theory, she did provide valuable information to relate the woman's inner life to her experience of her body. She also provided suggestions for some of the biological differences between men and women which may underlie and interact with the cultural situation.

Carl Jung: Analytic Psychology

Carl Jung (1875–1961) was a disciple of Freud's until 1913, when the two parted over a number of fundamental disagreements (Jung, 1961). Jung disagreed with Freud's insistence that all motives could ultimately be reduced to the sexual. Another difference was Jung's greater emphasis on the individual's aims, sense of purpose, and creative development as a whole person. Finally, Freud emphasized the importance of early childhood development, while Jung was also concerned with the development of the individual during the adult years. Jung was particularly concerned with old age in some of his writings. Jung was also interested in the history of humanity and its influence on the individual psychology, and built this idea into his theory.

Jung felt that racial memories were present in the personality in the form of unconscious archetypes. Archetypes include images of types of people about whom one has emotional responses. For example, one common archetype is the mother. This archetype represents not only a person's actual experiences with her or his own mother and observations of other mothers, but also the collective history of every person's experiences with mothers as well as prehuman memories of mothering (Jung, 1943/1953).

Two archetypes are of particular importance to the understanding of the female personality: the *animus* and the *anima*. The animus is the woman's masculine archetype and her unconscious male personality. The anima is the man's feminine archetype and his unconscious female personality. The animus was said to be formed, like any archetype, by images of all the men a woman had known, as well as her inherited images based upon the collective unconscious. To the extent that the animus is completely unconscious, Jung believed that a woman would project her animus onto actual men she knew. Similarly, men were believed to project their female anima onto women. Jung believed that these archetypes had a strong survival value for both sexes since they helped them to understand one another. However, by projecting part of their own personality onto the other sex, people might also deceive themselves about the true personalities of others, since their projections could interfere with an accurate perception. Thus, archetypes serve both functional and dysfunctional roles. Jung felt that by bringing them into one's conscious experience, the negative aspects could be minimized; by integrating both female and male aspects of oneself into one's conscious personality, one could be a more complete person. It was only by the "union of opposites" that women or men would reach their full human potential.

Jung's use of masculine and feminine archetypes can be seen as giving a biological and spiritual basis to the traditional male and female stereotypes. His theories could be used to give a scientific rationale for the traditional roles of men and women. However, his stress on the integration of the male and female aspects of one's personality can also be seen as one means of achieving androgyny.

Erik H. Erikson: The Inner Space

Erik Erikson (1902–   ) is a leading contemporary psychoanalyst working within the neo-Freudian tradition. He has specifically addressed himself to the issue of feminine personality and has done some experimental work in studying the psychology of women, although his major interest is in children and their development. Erikson accepts most basic principles of Freudian personality theory, but his emphasis is more on social and cultural factors in continual *interaction* with the biological factors, which he maintains are basic to all sex differences, including differences in personality.

With regard to female personality, Erikson's departures from Freud are primarily in emphasis. He believes that Freud erred in his emphasis on "what is not there" in woman, namely the absence of the penis. While this lack might be the central preoccupation of some disturbed girls, Erikson has stated that the normal pattern for females is to focus on what does exist, namely, "an inner bodily space—with productive as well as dangerous potentials" (Erikson, 1968, p. 296). By "inner space" Erikson is referring to the vagina and the uterus, which he regards as the fundamental female sexual and reproductive organs. He makes no reference to the clitoris.

Erikson has explicitly criticized Freud for projecting onto women an essentially masculine view of femininity. He has rejected Freud's view of the feminine experience as essentially negative and traumatic, and writes about femininity as a positive, moral force in society which could counteract what he feels is an overemphasis on masculine values and viewpoints. He emphasizes women's role as mothers as central to the feminine personality. He believes that a woman's potential for motherhood is the central focus in her identity, and that her other personality characteristics derive largely from her childbearing and child-rearing potential. Erikson has acknowledged that a woman may function in the world as an individual aside from her role as mother, but he regards her participation in nonmothering roles as secondary to her primary function.

Erikson's emphasis on the positive healthy aspects of femininity is part of his overall tendency to emphasize health rather than pathology. Erikson has disagreed with Freud that normal functioning can be completely understood from the study of pathological functioning. He believes that many of Freud's ideas about females do not apply to normal girls and women.

Erikson has also made some interesting observations about men and their responses to women. He has acknowledged the general male response of awe and disquiet with regard to the female reproductive function, a phenomenon he has labeled "womb envy." He has stated that this aspect of the male psychology is more important than "penis envy" in females.

While Erikson's version of psychoanalytic personality theory has been largely derived from his clinical observations, he is also well known for a study which utilized children's play as a projective device. In this study, he provided children between the ages of ten and twelve with a variety of blocks and toys, and instructed them to set up on a table "an exciting scene from an imaginary motion picture" (Erikson, 1951). According to Erikson, the structures made by girls emphasized "inner space," while those of the boys emphasized "outer space." More specifically, male structures were dominated by strong movement and the arresting of movement, high towers, and exterior scenes. In contrast, girls produced structures which Erikson describes as static, peaceful, and intruded upon from the outside. Walls around the structures were not high, and sometimes included an elaborate doorway. Erikson characterizes the mood of the girl's structures as "goodness indoors," while the boys emphasized "caution outdoors" (Erikson, 1968, p. 301). Erikson related these sex differences in the play constructions to the anatomical difference between the sexes. He believed that social factors influence the choice of themes, but that these factors are not sufficient to provide an adequate explanation for the structural differences. This study has been widely criticized, however, on methodological grounds (Marmor, 1973; Sherman, 1971), and for an inadequate accounting of social factors (Millett, 1970).

In summary, Erikson is valuable for his effort to reinterpret the psychoanalytic view of femininity in a more positive and primary light; his recognition of the importance to feminine personality of a woman's maternal functions; and, especially, his understanding of male psychology with regard to women. But he still sees the woman's maternal function as *the* determinant of her personality, and he appears to underestimate the weight of social factors in determining a woman's personality. His switch from Freud's negative view of women to a romantic, idealized, maternal view of women is equally male-identified.

Although several of the clinical theories of female personality reviewed in this chapter share a negative perception of women, either in terms of viewing women as inadequate men or restricting their female-role behaviors to biologically defined female functions, they all offer many positive contributions. These theories stress the importance of emotion and personal experience, and believe in studying the whole person rather than one specific aspect of the person's behavior. These values are shared by many feminists today. However, modern, empirical, experimental psychology is not yet able to analyze the whole person as a unit and has great difficulty studying emotions. The intent of the following chapters in this book is to allow us to begin to put some of the pieces together so that new theories of female personality can be developed which more accurately reflect the findings of empirical psychology.

4 Sex Differences in Personality and Abilities

Interest in and beliefs concerning the nature of sex differences date back to ancient times. Throughout much of history, apparent differences between men and women have been considered natural and innate. Even today, most people believe there are differences between men and women and boys and girls in many areas of personality or intelligence. According to the beliefs or stereotypes held by most people in our society, the average woman is passive, dependent, quiet, gentle, unintelligent, and generally inferior to the average man. The average adult male, on the other hand, is believed to be active, aggressive, independent, neither quiet nor gentle, intelligent, and superior to women. How valid are such stereotypes? Are these commonly held beliefs verified by data on how women and men actually behave? Although in many instances the data are incomplete and/or inconsistent, it appears as though the actual differences between the sexes are not as great as many believe. Many studies have either failed to find the expected differences or found them to be relatively small.

DEFINING PERSONALITY

Traits

Sex differences are just one of the many differences between groups of people. Others include age differences, social-class differences, race differences, and

Diane Ruble was the primary author of this chapter.

general personality differences. Psychologists' interest in these differences derives from a common-sense observation that people vary in their characteristics in fairly obvious, consistent, and predictable ways. People respond in different ways to the same situation. For example, before an exam, some people are very talkative while others are very quiet; some are self-confident, others are not. How do we explain these behavioral differences? One common way is to infer that a person's behavior is an external manifestation of a stable underlying disposition, a *trait* (Mischel, 1971). Thus, we say that Joe is talkative because he's an extrovert, or that Sally lacks confidence before the exam because she has low self-esteem.

The use of trait concepts has advantages in addition to providing *explanations* for behavior. They also allow us to *predict* behavior and create a sense of stability in the world. Because we think Joe is an extrovert, we assume he will be talkative and outgoing not only before the exam but in most situations. Consequently, we might make an extra effort to invite him to a party, whereas we might overlook someone we had labeled an introvert.

Another advantage of trait concepts is that they allow the reduction of a complicated set of observations, thus preventing a kind of information overload. Suppose you are asked to describe your closest female friend. One way to do this is to begin listing some of the things that you have observed about her: "She listened intently while I talked about my troubles for two hours last week. She spoke in a loud and angry voice to a male classmate who called her a 'dumb blonde.' She got A's in all her classes last semester." However, it is unlikely that this is the kind of description you would give. It is cumbersome and inefficient, both for you to remember and to communicate to others. Instead, you would probably infer from your friend's various behaviors some underlying traits and use these in your description: "She is warm, sympathetic, somewhat verbally aggressive, and smart." This trait description may be less accurate in many cases than the detailed behavioral description, but it conveys quickly and simply information about global characteristics you feel your friend possesses.

Thus, for at least the two reasons described above—predictability and information reduction—people seem to be motivated to see behaviors in terms of traits. Recently, however, psychologists have suggested that these stable differences among people are more apparent than real. Global personality dispositions are much less global than most theories and most common-sense beliefs have assumed them to be (Mischel, 1968; 1969):

> . . . on virtually all of our dispositional measures of personality substantial changes occur in the characteristics of the individual longitudinally over time and, even more dramatically, across seemingly similar settings cross-sectionally. (*Mischel, 1969, p. 1012.*)

Research on delay of gratification provides a good example of how human behavior varies according to situation. This research involves peoples' ten-

dencies to wait an indefinite period of time for a large reward rather than settling for a small reward, which they can have immediately. There is some
degree of consistency for a given individual over time. But much more
impressive is the variability which different situations will evoke in an individual. A three-year-old, who in one situation is only able to wait for thirty
seconds, may be able to delay gratification up to an hour if cognitive and at-
tentional conditions are properly arranged (Mischel, 1969).

These data would suggest two major conclusions. First, behavior is a function of situations as well as traits. Second, situational factors are usually
deemphasized relative to trait explanations. That is, the mind perceives continuity and stability in spite of actual discontinuity and instability. It is important to keep those points in mind when examining any set of indivdiual-
difference traits. Sex differences are no exception.

Situational Factors

What kinds of situational factors must be considered in looking at sex differences? The most obvious is that males and females are differentially distributed across possible situations. As a hypothetical example, assume that
children are typically most active and aggressive when they are outdoors. Assume further that parents keep girls indoors more than boys. This combination of factors would probably lead us to conclude that boys are dispositionally more aggressive and assertive than girls, thereby ignoring the
impact of the different situations in which boys and girls are most often seen.

There is another way in which situational factors are related to sex differences. Most studies attempt to "control" for situational factors by making
the external situation the same for males and females. (See also Chapter 2.)
However, this approach ignores the problem that what is overtly the same
may be psychologically very different for diffrent groups of individuals. Consider as a non–sex-difference example a study of age differences in help-seeking behavior. The experimenter gives children at two age levels a difficult
task to perform and measures the number of times they look at the experimenter or ask for help. The experimenter is careful to control the situation by
using exactly the same task for the two age groups. Results indicate that
younger children look at the experimenter and ask for help more frequently
than the older children. Can one conclude that the younger children are
dispositionally more help-seeking? No. It is possible, and in fact likely, that
the situations were not psychologically equivalent for the two age groups.
The task was probably much more difficult for the younger children than for
the older children. Thus, it is not surprising that the younger children were
in more need of assistance.

Males and females may also perceive the same external situation in very
different ways. For example, it is not the same psychological situation for a
woman to enter a room with five men sitting in it as it is for a man to enter

the same room. The woman is likely to become much more aware of her gender than the man, which in turn may differentially affect self-perceptions and behaviors. For example, one study found that the mere presence of certain proportions of males and females affected responses of the members of a group. Females described themselves as more competitive and males described themselves as more introverted when they were the only member of their sex in a group than did members of other group compositions. These differential sex-related perceptions or reactions can be due to different expectations of what is appropriate behavior for a male versus a female in a given situation (Ruble and Higgins, 1976). People usually try to behave according to the expectations of others. Inappropriate sex-typed behavior violates role expectations and is likely to meet disapproval of some kind (Darley, 1976). Thus, aggressive/assertive behaviors which are considered to be "masculine" may not appear to be traits of women because women are not expected to behave in this way. Women's roles also do not typically support such characteristics.

This social psychological view of sex differences will underlie the review of trait differences to follow. One mut constantly ask to what extent apparent sex differences in behavior may reflect implicit demands for how males and females should act in the immediate situation rather than stable and general differences in traits of males and females.

MEASURING SEX DIFFERENCES

If you were asked to provide concrete evidence that males are more aggressive than females or that females are more dependent than males, how would you go about it? One possible approach is to ask a group of males and a group of females to describe how aggressive they are. If the males describe themselves as more aggressive and the females describe themselves as more dependent, you would have some supportive evidence. But there are problems with this approach. Your data only tell you how males and females think about their aggressive and dependent tendencies, not how they actually behave. Perhaps the two sexes have different definitions of what "aggressive" and "dependent" mean. Perhaps they are only conforming to the stereotypes of how males and females are supposed to behave, so they may report having behavior consistent with the stereotypes even if they do not feel they actually behave that way. Thus, the data may not be measuring aggression and dependency at all, at least not as usually defined.

For these reasons, it is important to know how to define and measure traits. For every possible trait for which sex differences are believed to exist, the trait can be defined and measured in numerous ways. Two types of data are most common: observations of behavior and paper-and-pencil measures or verbal report.

For the first, an observer records certain selected aspects of the subject's behaviors, which are believed to represent underlying personality traits. For example, nursery-school children may be observed during play. Observers might record frequency of hitting to indicate aggression, or the frequency of assistance to a younger child to indicate nurturance. For the second, either the subject or people who know the subject are asked to describe selected attributes of the subject. For example, they may fill out rating scales like the following:

How aggressive is X?

/___/___/___/___/___/___/___/___/___/

not at all   moderately   very

aggressive   aggressive   aggressive

Specific types of observational and paper-and-pencil measures are summarized in Boxes 1 and 2.

There are some major differences between observational and paper-and-

Box 1   Observational Measures of Sex Differences

Type

1. Direct observation: trained observers rate the quantity and quality of particular behaviors of subjects in a natural or semi-natural setting.

2. Projective: an attempt to measure unconscious aspects of behavior. The subject is given an ambiguous stimuli and asked to describe it, tell a story about it, or manipulate it in some way. The purpose of the task is disguised, and the subject is free to respond as he or she likes.

3. Experimental: the subject responds to particular stimuli in the controlled setting of a laboratory.

Examples

a. Count the number of times a child hits another in a playground.

b. Rate the extent to which a child clings to the mother in the home.

a. A child is asked to play-act a story with dolls and a doll house. An observer counts the number of hostile or aggressive acts in playing with dolls in a doll-house.

b. A college student is asked to tell a story in response to a picture of two men standing at a window. The experimenter rates the extent to which themes of affiliation appear in the story.

a. Count the number of aggressive responses (physical or verbal) children will imitate after observing an aggressive model.

b. Rate the extent to which a subject's answers or judgments are influenced by group pressure.

Box 2   Paper-and-Pencil and Verbal Report Measures of Sex Differences

Type

1. Self-report and personality inventories: subject fills out a questionnaire or a scale rating personal traits, interests, preferences, or behaviors according to her/his own opinion. Typically such scales record a subject's general reaction to hypothetical situations or to general items or questions rather than specific situations.

2. Interviews and rating scales by teachers or parents of subject: teachers, parents, or others rate the subject on various traits, interests, preferences, or behaviors, based on past experience and knowledge of the person being rated, and not on specific situations.

3. Sociometric devices: subjects list one or a few peers who are best described by a particular word or phrase.

Examples

a. Children answer yes or no, or true or false to a list of questions or statements such as "Does it make you uneasy to cross a bridge over a river? or "I am happy most of the time."

b. College students rate themselves on bipolar items such as high vs. low self-confidence, submissive vs. dominant.

a. Parents rate their children on a continuum from high to low on terms such as quarrelsome, negativistic, etc.

b. Teachers rate their students on a continuum from high to low on attributes such as approval seeking, overdependence, friendliness, etc.

Children nominate peers on the basis of items such as
Who pushes or shoves children?
Who says mean things?

---

pencil measures. Observational studies are usually more concerned with discrete, overt behaviors, such as hitting. In addition, the subjects are usually not completely aware of what is being studied and are thus not as likely to bias their actions. In direct observation in a natural setting (e.g., a playground), the subject may not even be aware that she or he is being studied at all. Similarly, projective tests, a second type of observational measure, are concerned with unconscious motives and behaviors and attempt to disguise the true purpose of the study. The subject is merely asked to respond in some way (e.g., tell a story) to ambiguous stimuli. These responses are coded for their implicit motivational concerns. Finally, experimental studies in a laboratory also attempt to hide the specific nature of the behaviors under observation. The subjects may be told the study involves punishment effects (i.e., administering shock) on learning, when, in fact, the focus is retaliatory aggression.

In contrast, paper-and-pencil studies make it fairly clear to the subject what is being investigated. Thus, this kind of measure is most liable to expectation-induced bias. Since, subjective impressions rather than specific, discrete behaviors are being rated, sex-role stereotypes are able to exert a fairly powerful influence over the ratings. For example, when ratings of dependency in young children are made, girls are perceived as much more dependent than boys; but these sex differences do not appear when direct observations of behavior are made (Maccoby and Jacklin, 1974). It is as though parents and teachers assume that girls are dependent and ignore behavioral evidence to the contrary.

Self-ratings are likely to be similarly affected. Since people are influenced by their own sex-role expectations and what they feel is expected of them, it is difficult to report objectively on the existence of a particular trait within themselves. Instead, they may respond to questions about their feelings or behavior in terms of what they perceive is expected of a "normal" person of their sex.

There are also potential biases in observational data, though they are typically not as strong as for paper-and-pencil measures. Observers may interpret behavior in terms of expectations about sex differences which they have been socialized to hold. These expectations could bias the ratings in at least two ways. First, observers may rate people as having the traits they would expect them to have. That is, they would "see" relatively more nurturant behaviors by females and relatively more aggressive behaviors by males. Second, sex-role expectations may cause observers to magnify any deviations from the expected role. That is, a rather low intensity strike at an object may be labeled aggressive if performed by a girl but playful or nonaggressive if performed by a boy (Meyer and Sobieszek, 1972). In part, this definitional problem arises because the kinds of cues that result in a behavior being labeled, for example, aggressive or dependent, are not usually well defined and may not be consistent for all males and females.

In addition to problems with measures, there are sometimes problems selecting a comparable sample of males and females. Most studies draw a random sample of males and females from the same elementary or high school or college, which in general should produce comparable samples. However, for cultural reasons, low-ability boys are more likely than girls to drop out of elementary and high school. Thus with older school children, there is an increasingly select sample of boys as compared to girls. This differential dropout rate may result in an "artificial" compression of differences in which girls excel and an "exaggeration" of differences in which boys excel (Maccoby and Jacklin, 1974). For example, sex differences in verbal abilities may "disappear" in upper grades because there are fewer low-ability boys to lower the boys' average scores.

Finally, there are biases in the reporting and interpretation of data. In psychology, as well as other social sciences, there is a strong trend for publication of "significant differences." Typically, if the odds are less than five out of a hundred that a particular difference between two groups could have been obtained by chance, then the difference is considered statistically significant. For example, suppose one observes that women seem to like spinach more than men. If this occurs more often than would be expected by chance then it would be concluded that there is a significant sex difference in spinach liking. If no significant differences are found, results are often not published (see Chapter 2). This means that the psychological literature probably over-represents differences between the sexes (Maccoby and Jacklin, 1974).

Assuming that the differences in a study are statistically significant, this does *not* mean that all males are different from all females. It only means that the average male in the sample differs from the average female. For any trait, there is a large amount of variation *within* a sex, and the distributions of scores for the two sexes overlap considerably. Box 3 shows the range of scores for boys and girls taken from a study on spatial skills. As the figure shows, boys have a higher mean score than girls. However, many of the girls scored better than many of the boys. Thus, on the basis of a significant sex difference, one cannot assume that all girls are poor in spatial ability.

Box 3   **Hypothetical Distribution of Scores from a Study of Sex Differences in Spatial Skills***

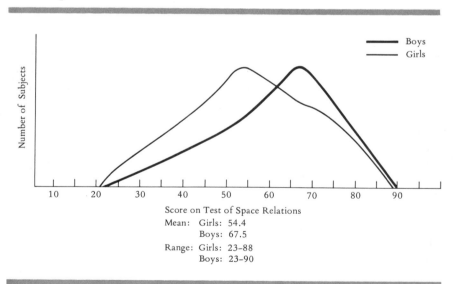

Score on Test of Space Relations
Mean: Girls: 54.4
        Boys: 67.5
Range: Girls: 23–88
        Boys: 23–90

SOURCE: Sherman, 1974. The distribution curves are only assumed, but the means and ranges are taken directly from Sherman's study.

SEX DIFFERENCES IN PERSONALITY

The term "personality" can have many meanings. One common usage refers to a person's charm—"Susan really has a good personality." In another sense, personality refers to the uniqueness of every individual—their special pattern of traits or the organization of their various traits and behaviors. The psychological study of *sex differences* in personality is concerned with how the average female differs from the average male for a particular trait. This chapter will consider five such aspects of personality: aggression, dependency, nurturance and affiliation, emotionality, and self-concept.[1]

Aggression

What comes to mind in response to the word "aggressive?" One may see a child hitting or shoving another, quarreling, or breaking things. These images and many others are implicit in measures of aggression. These measures include directly observing behavior; ratings of aggressiveness in children by teachers, parents, or peers; rating oneself for aggression (as on a personality inventory); aggressive themes in fantasy stories; and various miscellaneous measures such as giving electric shocks to another person.

The studies of aggression have yielded some of the most consistent findings for any personality or ability area. The stereotype that males are more aggressive than females has been strongly supported. Most of forty-eight studies reviewed (Oetzel, 1966), as well as more recent research (e.g., Maccoby and Jacklin, 1974), found males to be more aggressive than females. This consistency is especially noteworthy given the range of measures that have been used. Such a generalization across measures supports the belief that males are more aggressive on the average than females. Furthermore, the fact that these differences emerge quite early in life and are found cross-culturally suggests that biological factors may be involved (Maccoby and Jacklin, 1974; Rohner, 1976; Whiting and Edwards, 1973).

What does this sex difference mean? Aggression is usually conceptualized in terms of overt, physical behavior, such as hitting. But there is more than overt behavior involved in aggression. A good definition must include an underlying motive, the intent to injure another person or object. Is a person aggressive who shoves another out of the way of an oncoming car? Probably not. On the other hand, is it aggressive when a person passively avoids or ignores another person who is trying to be friendly? Probably yes.

There are several indications that females may not differ much from males in aggressive motivation or drive. In nonphysical measures of aggression, the differences are less clear and in some instances more aggressive behavior is

---

[1] Conclusions in the following sections are based on the total number of *consistent* findings and on the direction of findings.

found for females than for males. For example, out of the six studies that dealt with verbal aggression, five found no differences and one showed girls to be more aggressive (Oetzel, 1966). Similarly, studies of female- and male-group reactions to a newcomer found that girls exhibited more "indirect" forms of aggression than boys (Feshbach, 1969; Feshbach and Sones, 1971). That is, the girls rejected and excluded the newcomer more, an action which in its hostile intent may be equivalent to direct physical or verbal assault.

Situational variables based on sex-role expectations may be important determinants of aggressive behavior. Several studies show that differences may disappear when the situation is modified to remove the normal constraints placed on females displaying aggression. For example, girls initiated as many aggressive responses as boys when they were offered a reward for doing so, but were less aggressive in a free-choice situation (Bandura, Ross, and Ross, 1961). Similarly, females were found to be as aggressive as males when the privacy of their aggressive act was assured (Mallick and McCandless, 1966) and when told by the experimenter that their aggressive responses (giving an electrical shock to another person when she or he made an error) should produce faster learning (Leventhal, Shemberg, and Van Schoelandt, 1968). These results are consistent with findings that females may be more anxious and guilty about aggression than males (e.g., Sears, 1961) and may therefore avoid being aggressive except where aggression is explicitly sanctioned.

In sum, there is strong support for the hypothesis that males *behave* more aggressively than females at all ages. However, other research suggests that these sex differences in overt aggression may be partly due to the masculine sex-typing of aggressive responses. That is, females recognize that aggressive behavior is culturally defined as unfeminine, and thus they will be anxious about responding aggressively and will tend to exhibit such responses only in a private, permissive situation or in an indirect way. This would be especially true for overt physical aggression, the type of aggression where sex differences are maximized.

Dependency-Related Traits

What does it mean to be dependent? A typical definition of dependency— "reliance on others for help, approval, and attention" (Nevill, 1974)—seems to involve a number of different but related behaviors. Psychologists who observe people interacting usually consider dependency in a child to mean behaviors such as clinging to the mother or help-seeking. Psychologists using an experimental approach usually focus on two dependency-related behaviors—suggestibility and conformity. Suggestibility in an experimental situation typically refers to the extent to which opinions or attitudes are changed by means of some persuasive communication or direct-influence attempt, such as propaganda. A similar construct, conformity, is typically defined in experimental settings as the extent to which subjects will modify their own judgment of an event to agree with responses of other members of a group.

Females are believed to be more passive and dependent, and more easily influenced than males. However, empirical verification of these stereotypes is much less clear than the support for the aggressive stereotype. Differences are particularly small for children. Of thirteen *observational* studies of sex differences in dependency, six found no difference and the rest were evenly divided as to which sex was more dependent (Oetzel, 1966). Similarly, of forty-eight observations of children's touching and proximity to parents, and resistance to separation from a parent, eight found girls more dependent, seven found boys more dependent, and the rest showed no differences (Maccoby and Jacklin, 1974).

It should be noted, though, that most *rating* studies found that more girls are rated—by teachers, peers, or parents—as being dependent. The inconsistency in results across the two methodologies may reflect the impact of stereotypic expectations. The same sex-typed expectations that lead individuals to rate "the average females" on the high end of a scale labeled "dependency" would probably operate in making them rate any particular girl or woman as being more dependent. These expectations might even bias their perceptions of specific behaviors so that they were consistent with these expectations.

There also seems to be a developmental pattern in sex differences in dependency. Findings with young children have been very inconsistent and have predominantly failed to find sex differences. Studies with older children and adults, however, have consistently found more women to be (or to rate themselves as) higher on dependency-related traits than men. This developmental pattern may indicate that as they get older, girls learn to conform to certain sex-typed expectations. It is also possible, though, that the developmental pattern is simply due to the different ways of measuring dependency at different ages. Studies with young children are primarily observational in nature, while rating scales or experimental studies are more frequently used for older children and adults. These data seem to suggest that with some kinds of measures and especially at older ages, females are more dependent than males.

Recently, the legitimacy of assuming that females are generally more dependent at any age has been questioned. Current research fails to show consistent sex effects in dependency-related behaviors (Maccoby and Jacklin, 1974). It is not clear if these newer findings are due to actual changes in men and women or if they are due to changes in experimental procedures. For example, situational variables, such as the content of the stimulus materials, have a marked effect on conformity behavior. In particular, women conformed more than men on male-related issues (e.g., economics or political affairs), while men were more easily influenced than women on female-related issues (such as fashion or design). On neutral issues, there was equal conformity. Thus, previous generalizations concerning sex differences may have been partly due to a greater use of male-related tasks in experiments (Sistrunk and McDavid, 1971).

Therefore, contrary to stereotypic conceptions, females are not consistently more dependent than males. Even with measures or subject samples where this dependency was found more in females, many of the difference findings may be due to observers generalizing from stereotypes or to factors in the experimental situation that bias the results.

Social Orientation

As with most personality characteristics, the term "social orientation" can refer to many different sorts of behaviors or dispositions: interest in and desire to be near other persons; cooperation; helping; social sensitivity; mothering; empathy. The majority of studies reported that females as compared to males were rated or observed to be relatively more nurturant and higher on need for affiliation and as showing greater interest in or positive feelings for others (Oetzel, 1966). These findings were again consistent with stereotypes that females are more tactful, gentle, aware of feelings of others, and easily able to express tender feelings (Broverman, et al., 1972). Most of these studies were done with older children or adults; in cases where young children were included, sex differences were less clear, though they still tended to favor the girls (Oetzel, 1966).

Recent studies have cast doubt on the generality of this sex difference. First, women's supposedly greater interest in other people does not seem to result in their having more ability to judge emotions (Tagiuri, 1969) or being more sensitive to social cues (Maccoby and Jacklin, 1974), though there is some indication of sex differences in empathy (Hoffman, 1977). Second, studies measuring a social orientation in task situations usually find no sex differences (Ruble, 1975; Ruble and Nakamura, 1972) and when differences have been found they are contradictory, sometimes favoring girls (e.g., Pepitone, 1972) and sometimes favoring boys (e.g., Ruble, Feldman, and Boggiano, 1976). Third, there have been several findings that contradict the stereotype that females are more cooperative than males (Cook and Stingle, 1974; Bedell and Sistrunk, 1973).

The inconsistencies between these findings and previous studies may be attributed, in part, to differential responsiveness of the sexes to certain situational factors, such as competitive set or characteristics of the other player. Males may tend to be more attentive to the situational context and to be competitive or cooperative depending on how they perceive the situation. Females may, on the other hand, respond more to the characteristics of the other player. Thus, they may be more cooperative towards women than towards men (Bedell and Sistrunk, 1973). Fourth, females have not always been found to be more affiliative or socially interactive than males (e.g., Becker, 1967; Loo, 1972). In fact, boys have been more frequently higher in positive social interaction with peers (Maccoby and Jacklin, 1974).

Therefore, findings from early research suggest the conclusion that females are moderately more socially oriented and nurturant than males. However, many of these studies consisted of paper-and-pencil measures and were thereby heavily subject to bias from stereotyping. In contrast, many recent studies have found no differences in these behaviors or found that the differences are related to complex situational factors. Thus, at present, the extent of sex differences in social orientation remains inconclusive.

Emotionality

Novels, movies, advertisements—all abound with the stereotype that women are more emotional than men. The emotional women is believed to become flustered in the most minor crisis. She is seen as sensitive, often fearful and anxious, and cries easily. She is moody—sometimes bubbling over with joy; sometimes irritable, lethargic, and depressed. However, there has been a sex bias in what behaviors are labeled emotional (Sherman 1971). Emotionality usually refers to fearfulness, anxiety, moodiness, neuroticism, as opposed to acting-out behaviors and maladjustments. Acting-out behaviors such as aggression, antisocial behavior, and psychopathy are more characteristic of males but these are not labeled as indicating emotionality.

What evidence is there that females are in fact more emotional in these stereotypic ways—anxious, fearful, moody? Slightly over half of twenty-six pencil-and-paper studies of sex differences in anxiety found girls and women to be more anxious than males, while the rest found no difference (Oetzel, 1966). With regard to fearfulness, females appeared to be somewhat higher when rating-scale measures were used (e.g., Spiegler and Liebert, 1970; Wilson, 1966; 1967), but observational studies of sex differences in fearfulness or responses to a fearful stimulus in young children have not produced consistent results (Bronson, 1970; Maccoby and Jacklin, 1973; Stern and Bender, 1974). Finally, findings concerning reactions to frustration have been somewhat inconsistent, though emotional reactions decline at an earlier age for girls than for boys (Maccoby and Jacklin, 1974).

These studies appear to support the stereotype that females are more emotional than males, at least after early childhood. However, investigations of anxiety and fearfulness have mostly used paper-and-pencil measures. Since cultural expectations are that "a real man is afraid of nothing" or that "boys don't cry," a reasonable alternative explanation of rated differences is that females are simply more willing to report anxieties and fears than males are. In fact, a few studies have found direct support for this hypothesis (Spiegler and Liebert, 1970; Wilson, 1967). In these studies people who reported few fears or anxieties were also likely to score high on a measure of social desirability (the tendency to respond in a culturally approved way).

A possible additional problem with paper-and-pencil emotionality scales is that the content of the items may be sex-biased. For example, there are relatively few items dealing with anxieties typically associated with men (e.g., anxiety over money and business) on the Manifest Anxiety Scale, one of the standard self-report anxiety scales. Therefore it is not possible to determine whether total score differences reflect true sex differences in underlying anxiety, or in overt expression of anxiety, or are simply an artifact of the sex-typed item content (Jahnke, Crannell, and Morrissette, 1964).

Some studies have tried to avoid the problems of rating scales by using physiological measures of emotionality. Increases in heartbeat, pulse, respiration, and skin conductance are assumed to indicate an increase in emotional arousal. In contrast to overt behavioral or self-report studies, which usually reported females to be more emotionally responsive, physiological measures yielded inconsistent results (Kopacz and Smith, 1971). These findings suggest that overt measures may be more affected by social expectations concerning emotionality in women than the more covert, physiological measures.

These studies taken together would suggest that consistent sex differences in fearfulness and anxiety are found only with paper-and-pencil measures, which are subject to bias from stereotyping. Thus, whether or not females are more emotional than males remains to be determined.

Self-concept

Self-concept—the way one thinks about or evaluates oneself—is affected by factors such as physical attributes (height, weight, attractiveness), athletic abilities, intellectual capacity, personality traits, and perceptions of how others view oneself. What does it mean, then, to say one person has a more positive self-concept than another? Psychologists have generally tried to develop scales which measure a global feeling of satisfaction or dissatisfaction with oneself, incorporating items that cover a broad range of relevant characteristics. Differences in self-concept on these measures then refer to level of positive or negative self-evaluation. A positive self-concept indicates feelings of satisfaction with one's abilities and conduct. Self-concept also refers to feelings of being a good person or being worthy (Sears, 1970).

Males are stereotyped as being more self-confident than females, but empirical verification of this belief has been weak except in achievement-related areas. There have been few studies that have directly compared the level of positive self-concept of males and females on standardized scales. Studies using one of the standard personality scales typically have not examined sex differences or have not found any (Coopersmith, 1967; Primavera, Simon, and Primavera, 1974). Of thirty-nine comparisons of males and females on various measures of self-esteem, females were high on nine, males on six, and there were no differences on the remaining twenty-four (Maccoby and Jacklin, 1974).

It thus appears that the sexes do not differ on generalized measures of self-esteem. However, for studies of achievement-related competence or expectations for success, it has been reasonably well established that females perceive themselves to be less competent than men. Compared to males, females have relatively negative evaluations of their own abilities, performance, and likelihood of future success (Crandall, 1969; Frieze, 1975; Maccoby and Jacklin, 1974; Parsons, et al., 1976).

A more indirect approach to self-concept is the study of stereotypic traits and values. There have been numerous indications that men and masculine attributes are more highly valued than women and feminine attributes. There is evidence that the masculine poles of various attributes are more often considered to be socially desirable than the feminine poles, and that both sexes rate males as more worthwhile. Also, masculine activities are generally preferred over feminine activities, and many more women than men recall a desire to be the opposite sex (Broverman, et. al., 1972). Consistent with this general trend, occupational prestige decreases when increased proportions of women in a given profession are anticipated (Touhey, 1974). Specifically, people rated professions such as physician and college professor lower when they were led to expect an increase in women than when they thought the percentage would remain the same.

These stereotypes appear to be incorporated into self-descriptions (Rosenkrantz, et al., 1968). Even a negatively valued feminine-typed trait like passivity is incorporated into a woman's self-image, simply because it is seen as an integral part of femininity. Logically, this incorporation of a negative trait should lead women to have more negative self-concepts than men. However, females do not evaluate themselves as less worthwhile on standard self-concept scales.

Indirect inferences concerning sex differences in self-concept can also be drawn from projective measures. A series of studies have examined drawings of the human figure by children of various ages. The sex of the first figure they draw has often been used as a projective indicator of strength of sex-role identification, but it also could be considered an index of the child's valuing of a particular sex. Thus a girl might draw a picture of a girl either because she identified with girls or because she felt that girls were better than boys. The tendency for girls and boys to draw a figure of the same sex as themselves first appears to be strongly age related. That is, for young children, a higher percentage of girls than boys draw same-sex figures first, but after the age of eleven or twelve, the pattern reverses (Oetzel, 1966). Boys then show an increase in the percentage of same-sex figures drawn, while girls show a decrease (e.g., Laosa, Swartz and Holtzman, 1973). Thus, with increasing age, both sexes may learn to value the male role more and prefer to draw more male figures. A more recent study, however, indicated that this pattern may be changing (Tolor and Tolor, 1974). A greater percentage of girls drew their own sex in this study than previously. This shift may indicate that more positive values are being assigned to the contemporary female role.

In sum, it is clear that stereotypic feminine attributes are devalued relative to male attributes. Nevertheless, females do not have consistently less positive self-concepts than males, except in areas related to achievement.

SEX DIFFERENCES IN INTELLECTUAL ABILITIES

Do the sexes differ on any of the components of intelligence such as mathematical skills or verbal skills? This section will review sex differences in five areas of intellectual functioning—verbal skills, memory, mathematical and spatial skills, and cognitive styles.

Verbal Skills

The common stereotype is that females are superior to males in all types of verbal skills. However, differences favoring females are not as strong and persistent as is usually thought, especially after early childhood. There is a wide range of verbal skills. Articulating well as a young child, having the ability to communicate ideas well, possessing reading skills and breadth of vocabulary—all are types of verbal skills.

Early reviews of sex differences in intellectual ability suggested that girls had a head start over boys in speaking ability, reading, spelling, grammar, and vocabulary, and that girls' superiority persisted through the early school years and then declined (Maccoby, 1966; Oetzel, 1966; Sherman, 1971). However, a recent summary arrived at a somewhat different set of conclusions. There are few consistent differences during the early years, but by age ten or eleven, girls begin to surpass boys in verbal performance. From this age through high-school and college years, girls outscore boys in a variety of verbal skills (Maccoby and Jacklin, 1974). Finally, in a few types of verbal skills, there has been no evidence of difference at any age, particularly in the areas of verbal reasoning (Oetzel, 1966; Kellaghan and MacNamara, 1972) and communication skills (Higgins, 1976).

Memory

The ability to store and reproduce information is obviously a basic and important part of learning. Do males and females differ in this basic process? Psychologists have generally studied memory capacities with two types of measures—free recall and recognition—both of which are often utilized in a single study. Free recall is essentially the ability to write or recite from memory a list of items (e.g., words or sentences) previously read or heard. Recognition refers to the ability to identify items that were previously presented from among a larger set of items.

Past reviews of sex differences in cognitive abilities have often reported that females average better scores on memory tests than males (Anastasi, 1958; Garai and Scheinfeld, 1968). However, these studies are inconsistent. Females were superior on four of eleven studies, males superior on two. There were no differences on the remaining five (Oetzel, 1966). More recent research suggests a slight tendency for females to excel on some memory tasks (Maccoby and Jacklin, 1974; May and Hutt, 1974). In general, however, research findings are too inconsistent to support the conclusion that females perform better on the average than males on tests of memory. It is likely that inconsistencies are due to aspects of experimental procedures that differentially favor one sex or the other. Some sex-difference findings may be traced to differences in verbal skills, instructional conditions, or content of the items.

Mathematical Skills

The predominance of men over women in science and mathematics is often attributed to sex differences in mathematical abilities. It is generally believed that males are more interested in and adept at mathematics, but it is only in reasoning and problem solving that differences favoring males are found (Oetzel, 1966; Maccoby and Jacklin, 1974).

Why do men often perform better than women on tests of reasoning and problem solving? One possibility is that the two sexes may be differentially responsive to or interested in the content of the problems. Typical problems may be oriented to masculine-typed interests and values. Some studies have varied the masculine/feminine content of the word problems, but have kept the underlying logic the same to see if women do better on problems with feminine content. For example, Box 4 shows two word problems. Both involve measurement, but one involves mixing cement (masculine content); the other involves mixing a cake (feminine content). In such problems women do significantly better on feminine- than on masculine-typed items (Milton, 1950). Recent studies have generally supported the conclusion that varying masculine/feminine item content affects sex differences in problem-solving performance (Graf and Riddel, 1972; Leder, 1974).

An additional problem in interpreting sex-difference findings is that male superiority in mathematical problem solving may reflect differences in skills other than reasoning ability *per se*. In particular, males average better performance on tasks involving spatial perception (see the next section). Many

Box 4   Sample Masculine/Feminine Mathematical Reasoning Problem

Masculine/Feminine Sex Typing of Problem

M   A certain quantity of cement to be mixed in a wheelbarrow needs exactly 6 pints of water added to it. The only suitable containers available are a 4-pint and a 9-pint one. How can you manage? (An outside tap is nearby.)

F   You are baking a cake. You have already mixed the sugar, butter, eggs, and flour, and now you are ready to add exactly 6 ounces of water as written in the recipe. However, the only suitable containers available are a 4-ounce and a 9-ounce measuring cup. How can you manage?

SOURCE: Leder, 1974.

mathematical word problems involve spatial orientations. Thus, it is not clear if sex differences in mathematics would remain if the visual-spatial aspect of problems were removed (Sherman, 1971).

Finally, situational factors may influence problem solving. Research has demonstrated that the sex of the experimenter and the sex composition of the group with which they are working affects the problem-solving performance of females. Girls and women do better on math tests when examined by a female rather than a male (Pedersen, Shinedling, and Johnson, 1968). Also, women are more effective in solving a particular problem when they are in mixed-sex groups rather than all-female groups (Hoffman and Maier, 1961).

Why should the sex of the experimenter or group composition affect mathematics performance? It is possible that sex-role awareness or expectations may vary with the situation. Perhaps a male experimenter makes females more anxious or aware of stereotypes that females are poor in mathematics. Whatever the explanation, the implications of the findings are quite important. The large percentage of male mathematics teachers may create a situation that produces or at least perpetuates superior quantitative ability in males (Pedersen, et al., 1968). Thus, the educational structure may serve to maintain sex differences in mathematics, to the detriment of girls.

Spatial Skills

Another common explanation for why women do not abound in the scientific and mathematical professions is the supposed inferiority of women on tasks involving spatial skills. In general spatial skills refer to the ability to visually manipulate, locate, or make judgments about the spatial relationships of items located in two- or three-dimensional space. For example, measures include puzzles in which the subjects must orient pieces properly to form a design or locate smaller figures in a larger design; judgment tasks in which subjects must adjust a bar or rod to be perfectly horizontal or vertical against a tilted background; and body-orientation tests.

On the average, males do better than females on tasks involving visual spatial skills (Maccoby, 1966; Tyler, 1965). In two major reviews, one listed eighteen studies of spatial orientation, and males averaged better performances than females in twelve (Oetzel, 1966); in the other, male superiority on visual-spatial tasks was found quite consistently in adolescents and adults (Maccoby and Jacklin, 1974).

As with many traits and abilities, there seems to be a developmental trend for these sex differences. Differences typically do not appear in young children, but grow during the high-school years (Maccoby and Jacklin, 1974). This trend is consistent with the reasoning of investigators, who have attributed sex differences in spatial skills to sex-role—related interests and practice. That is, boys more than girls may be allowed to explore and manipulate their environment and/or encouraged to play with materials, such as mechanical toys, that develop spatial skills. Some studies have suggested that role-related factors are involved in sex differences in spatial abilities. For example, there were no sex differences in spatial skills in several samples of non-Western or nonindustrialized peoples (Berry, 1971). Also, the sex differences that emerged at age fourteen were only for subjects who indicated same-sex preferences. Girls who said they would prefer to be boys did as well as boys on the spatial task (Nash, 1975). Finally, males were generally more likely to engage in activities in their daily lives that were similar to the formal tests of spatial perception and thus received more practice at this type of task (Sherman, 1967). In fact, some studies have shown that with extended practice on certain spatial tasks, the sex differences are reduced to insignificance (Goldstein and Chance, 1965).

Thus, the area of spatial skills provides one of the most consistent sex-difference findings among older children and adults. This difference is less easy to attribute to situational factors involving sex-typed expectations or interests than many other traits and abilities, since distinct stereotypes do not exist in this area. However, the different life experiences of boys and girls may be an underlying causal factor for the difference.

Cognitive Styles

Many students mention that they are interested in learning how men and women "think" differently. Although it is hard to know what thinking differently really means, let us look at the area known as *cognitive styles*. Cognitive styles refer generally to individual differences in information processing or information seeking during the course of problem solving (Coop and Sigel, 1971).

Differences in cognitive styles can occur at several phases of the problem-solving process. People can differ in the way they attend to information, the kinds of information they store, or in the way they analyze the information. Box 5 presents four stages that are part of a problem-solving experience, describes a cognitive style that is relevant to each stage, and presents the typical findings for each style.

A general construct underlying many cognitive-style variables, including those in Box 5, is the presence or absence of an analytic approach. The term "analytic" refers to the ability to overcome the influence of the general context in perceptual or judgmental processes (Sherman, 1967). The analytic individual is able to perceive an item as separate from its background and to break, set, or restructure the situation (Maccoby and Jacklin, 1974). The most frequently studied analytic style is called *field independence* (see Box 5), usually measured by the Rod-and-Frame Test (RFT) or the Embedded Figure Test (EFT). For the RFT, subjects are placed in a completely darkened room; all they can see are a luminous square frame and a luminous rod in its center. The rod and the frame may be tilted to the left or right independently of each other. The subject's task is to indicate when the rod is truly upright and perpendicular to the ground, regardless of the position of the frame. People who are able to accurately identify "true vertical" are termed field independent. People who are heavily influenced by the position of the frame, and are thus inaccurate, are termed field dependent.

The EFT is a much simpler test to administer than the RFT. Subjects are asked to identify a figure hidden in a camouflaging background. Field-independent persons are not affected by context and can identify the figure quite easily while field-dependent people have more difficulty in doing this.

Are there sex differences in field dependence/independence? Males were more field independent than females in eleven out of thirteen studies (Oetzel, 1966). More recent studies have been basically consistent with this trend (e.g., Harley, Kalish, and Silverman, 1974), though reports of no difference have not been uncommon (Maccoby and Jacklin, 1974). However, consistent sex differences do not emerge until after early elementary school. In studies of preschool children, either no differences were found, or girls were found to be more field independent than boys (Coates, 1974).

In spite of the sex differences in field dependence/independence, the conclusion is not necessarily that males are more analytic than females (Sherman, 1967). Since the measures typically used to measure field dependence/ independence are really tests of visual spatial perception, they may not be applicable to more general analytic ability (Sherman, 1967, 1971, 1974). Similarly, tests of analytic style which do not involve spatial skills, such as verbal abstraction or selective listening, typically have not found consistent sex differences (Sherman, 1967; Maccoby and Jacklin, 1974). Thus, findings of sex differences in field independence tell us nothing about analytic thinking; they only support the conclusion made earlier that males often do better than females on visual spatial tasks.

Therefore, in answer to the question of whether men and women think

Box 5 Four Stages of Problem Solving and Relevant Cognitive Styles

Problem-Solving Stage	Example Cognitive Style	Sex-Difference Findings
1. Encoding—perceptual and attentional processes	Field dependence/independence (Witkin, et al., 1962)—individual differences in perceiving the environment. Field-independent persons are more likely to differentiate the parts of a given stimulus, while field-dependent persons are more likely to perceive it globally, as a whole.	Differences when they exist usually show males to be more field independent and females to be more field dependent after early school years.
2. Memory—the ways in which information is stored	Leveling-sharpening (Holzman and Gardner, 1960)—individual differences in processing sequentially presented information. Levellers merge new stimuli with old ones, while sharpeners maintain a separation among current and previous stimuli.	Males more likely than females to be sharpeners on some tasks.
3. Generation of hypotheses—production of possible alternative routes to solving the problem	Analytic conceptual style (Kagan, et al., 1964)—the tendency to analyze visual stimuli in terms of component parts. For example, when asked to sort or categorize items in some way, an analytic person would sort on the basis of similarities among some components of the stimuli (e.g., all have feathers).	Few sex differences, though when they occur, males tend to be classified as more analytic than females.
4. Evaluation—the extent to which the individual pauses to reflect on the quality of his/her hypothesis	Reflection-impulsivity (Kagan, 1966)—individual differences in the tendency to reflect on the validity of alternative solutions. The reflective child takes his/her time in selecting an answer and makes few errors. The impulsive child chooses a response immediately and makes many errors.	Consistent sex differences are not reported.

SOURCE: Kagan and Kagan, 1970.

differently, we have to answer that we do not know. Box 5 describes moderate differences in some cognitive styles, but it is not clear what these mean in terms of problem-solving efficiency. For example, is it "better" to be a leveler or a sharpener? In addition, as long as major cognitive style tasks also involve spatial skills, we do not know to what extent thought processes are involved in the differences. Certainly, there are many individual differences in cognitive styles, but sex is probably not a major dividing line along which these differences fall.

RECONSIDERING SEX DIFFERENCES

What kinds of generalizations can we draw concerning sex differences in personality and abilities? First, there is little support for the belief that there are many strong and consistent differences between males and females. Nevertheless, it appears that when studies in a given area are taken as a whole, any resultant differences do lie in the direction of the predominant stereotype in that area (see Box 6). The table shows the apparent strength of observed differences based on conclusions drawn earlier in the chapter. Differences mentioned are always *in the direction of the stereotype.*

As Box 6 shows, the findings are moderately consistent for only some measures and subject populations. Of all the traits listed, the strongest difference is in physical aggression. Strong differences also exist for spatial skills, which are not associated with a specific stereotype and therefore are not listed in the table.

A second generalization is that often when sex differences are observed, they may result from the methodology employed or may represent differences along a dimension other than what is supposedly being studied. Many elements of an experimental situation may include sex-role biases that are irrelevant to the question the investigator is asking and yet affect the results in systematic ways. For example, we described a study which found that girls did better than boys on mathematical problems when the examiner was female instead of male, while the opposite was true for boys. Thus, if in most studies the examiner is male, one would be led to conclude erroneously that males average better performance on mathematical tasks than females. A female examiner would have found different results. Similar biases may be introduced when the content of a problem on issue is oriented toward the stereotypic sex-typed interests of one sex or the other. Often when these kinds of situational factors are controlled, sex differences can be reversed, eliminated, or greatly reduced.

With reference again to Box 6, all the methodological problems may mean that one reason there is empirical support for many stereotypes is that a sufficient number of studies simply elicit stereotypic responding. Certainly it would not be unreasonable to conclude that weaker findings of differences

Box 6   Comparison of Stereotypes with Actual Findings

Stereotype	*Strength of Finding*
Aggression	
Males aggressive; females not at all aggressive.	1. Strong consistent differences in physical aggression. 2. Inconsistent findings with indirect aggression.
Dependency	
Females submissive and dependent; males dominant and not at all dependent.	Weak differences, which are more consistent for adults than for children.
Nurturance	
Females tactful, gentle, and aware of feelings of others; males blunt, rough, and not at all aware of feelings of others.	Moderate differences on some measures. Overall, findings are inconclusive.
Emotionality	
Females emotional and very excitable in a minor crisis; males not at all emotional nor excitable in a minor crisis.	Moderate differences on paper-and-pencil measures. Overall, findings are inconclusive.
Self-concept	
Males very self-confident; females not at all self-confident.	Moderate differences on some measures.
Verbal Skills	
Females very talkative; males not at all talkative.	Moderate differences on some measures, especially for young children.
Math Skills	
Males like math and science very much; females dislike math and science very much.	Moderate differences on problem-solving tests, especially after adolescence.

SOURCE FOR STEREOTYPES: Broverman, et al., 1972.

(e.g., dependency) may be little more than a reflection of sex-biased situational factors. The fact that in many areas the magnitude of differences increases developmentally (along with sex-role awareness) is consistent with this conclusion. If differences are based on learning, they would be expected to increase with age.

IMPLICATIONS OF SEX-DIFFERENCE RESEARCH

Results of sex-difference research can have implications for public policy. The policy may be at a formal level (e.g., whether or not laws justify sex discrimination), but the policy implications at an informal level are just as important. Findings of sex differences reach the general public in a greatly oversimplified form (Holter, 1970). Although most authors are careful to explain that most differences *between* the sexes are much smaller than differences *within* sexes, such a fact is not always known by decision-making people (managers, teachers, counselors, parents) or properly acknowledged in policy recommendations.

Many people are interested in sex differences for practical reasons, for example, whether to hire a man or a woman for a particular position, or how to counsel male and female students about which courses to take or what occupations they might consider. According to the reasoning of many such people, if women are more nurturant, they should pursue careers such as teaching or nursing, where their true skills can be maximized. If men are more aggressive or assertive, it is they who should handle tough professional jobs such as courtroom lawyers or management personnel. If women lack mathematical and spatial skills, they should be counseled away from scientific courses and applications.

One difficulty with this is that the research has revealed few sex differences that are consistent. Secondly, even when differences do arise, there is much overlap in the distributions of all males and of all females on the particular trait. Thus, the small average differences tell one little about any particular boy or girl. There is a difference in the *average* level of spatial skills between men and women. This does not mean, though, that there are not some women who would make excellent engineers or astronauts. We should not exclude them from these careers because of average differences which do not apply to them as individuals. Nor should we exclude girls from shop courses because more boys are mechanically adept than girls. This is like denying all men driver's licenses because men are more likely to be color-blind than women (Bernard, 1974b). Rather we need to be aware of each individual's unique skills and deficits.

Part II

The Origins of Sex Differences

5 Is Anatomy Destiny?
Biology and Sex Differences

That men and women differ from one another is indisputable. They dress differently, have different hair styles, do different things with their time and, for the most part, play different social roles. Some explanations for these differences center around the issue of the relative contributions of biological and socialization factors. At one extreme, it has been argued that men and women are destined by biology to play different social roles and to have their own distinct personalities. Freud, as evidenced by his statement, "anatomy is destiny," was one of the early proponents of this view. He felt that the general anatomical differences between girls and boys produced inevitable sex differences in adult temperament and personality. Other more recent biological theories stress hormones, genes, and developmental rates as key factors, but still see biological factors as primary determinants of sex differences. At the other extreme, men and women are seen as very similar in all but their reproductive functions; in this view, differences in sex roles are assumed to be the results of socialization and not biology. Today, many feminists argue this latter point of view.

However, most scientific investigators today do not take a simple either/or position concerning the determinants of sex differences. Instead, they see human development as the result of the interaction between an individual's biological make-up and experience with the environment. While there is agreement that human behavior is influenced by both innate and environ-

Jacquelynne Parsons and Diane Ruble were the primary authors of this chapter.

mental factors, there is considerable debate over the relative importance of each and the mechanism of interactions between these two factors. The crux of the debate lies in the relative role biology plays in creating sex-role differences.

For political reasons, the public debate often reverts to the more simplistic issue of whether sex roles are primarily the result of biology or socialization. Advocates of the socialization view argue quite strongly that biology ought not be considered important unless the evidence overwhelmingly indicates that biology creates a universal difference making virtually every woman different from every man on key variables other than reproduction. It is feared by some advocates of social change that the political pressure for new social roles will decrease if people believe that men are destined by their biology to have the qualities necessary for leadership and power, while women are not. Based on this fear, many feminists are biased against biological evidence, preferring to accept a socialization explanation of sex differences if the biological data leaves any room for doubt. Furthermore, since most behavior is multiply determined and since it is extremely difficult to separate the effects of biology and socialization on any given human behavior, it is fairly easy to let this bias lead to an underplaying of the importance of biology.

While sympathetic with these political concerns, it is our view that both the socialization and biological evidence ought to be carefully evaluated and that real progress in sex-role change depends on an accurate understanding of the factors underlying current sex-role behaviors. In this chapter, we will attempt to evaluate the evidence relevant to biological explanations of sex differences. Research on this subject is still in the preliminary stages. Therefore much of what is said in the chapter will be, by definition, tentative.

EXPLORING BIOLOGICAL FACTORS

There are a number of ways to explore the issue of biological factors in sex differences. Initially, it is useful to try to determine which kinds of differences are most likely to have biological origins. Two approaches to examining this initial question will be discussed in the first half of this chapter. First, the literature on very early sex differences in behavior will be reviewed. Studies of very young infants provide one useful source of data for evaluating the influence of biology. If sex differences in behavior are present at or near birth, it is possible that these differences are innate. That is, since socializing agents have not had much time to affect the behavior of a very young infant, it is unlikely that differences found in this age group have been created by socialization practices.

The search for anthropological universals provides a second source of relevant data. If it can be shown that males and females differ cross-culturally on some behaviors, roles, or other related variables, despite wide variations in cultural patterns, then there is reason to speculate about possible biological pecursors. Conversely, if it can be shown that males and females do not differ consistently cross-culturally, then a biological argument is weakened. However, since many cultures emphasize similar sex-role socialization goals, and since biological processes can be modified to some degree by experience, the interpretation of anthropological findings within either a socialization or a biological framework is very speculative.

The second half of the chapter will focus on specific biological mechanisms that might underlie the behaviors that yield the most consistent cross-cultural and developmental sex differences. A wide variety of biological theories have been proposed, including genetic inheritance of specific traits, differential specialization of the hemispheres of the brain, and effects of different levels of hormones early in development. In addition to discussing these specific mechanisms, we will describe the methods of testing the theories and the difficulties of each for generalizing to normal human development.

INFANT SEX DIFFERENCES

One way of investigating the role of nature in the creation of sex differences is to look for sex differences in the behaviors of infants. Since it can be assumed that the effects of culture accumulate with age, any effects of culture should be at a minimum in infants. If sex differences in behavior are found at or near birth, there is reason to suspect that biology contributed to this difference. In contrast, if the sex differences do not appear until later in life it is difficult to determine whether biology is responsible for the behavioral differences or not. However, no matter how close to birth sex differences appear, cultural training and experience may already have had an effect:

> In the delivery rooms of many hospitals it is the custom to wrap the newborn baby in either a pink or blue blanket, depending on its sex as determined by the appearance of the genitalia. From this moment on, the child's maleness or femaleness is constantly reinforced. It is difficult, then, to determine the extent to which the child's learning of his [or her] sex role may be influenced by underlying biological predispositions. (Hamburg and Lunde, 1966, p. 15).

Methodological Issues

The task of examining sex differences in very young infants and attempting to relate them to later behaviors is not an easy one. First, the methodological problems of testing young infants are enormous. For example, one must control for the state of the infant; a crying or hungry infant is likely to respond quite differently from a sleeping or peaceful one. It is also important to select characteristics that are stable over time in each individual. A recent study of newborns found only twelve out of thirty-one possible behaviors that showed enough stability to be used for longitudinal anlysis (Bell, Weller, and Waldrop, 1971). Some of the more stable behaviors included tactile sensitivity of the heel during sleep, sucking rate, formula consumption relative to body weight, and crying following removal of a pacifier. More general patterns of crying and body movements showed great day-to-day fluctuation.

A second difficulty arises when one attempts to relate the kinds of things that infants do to characteristics of older children and adults. For example, in the study mentioned above only one of the twelve behavior patterns examined in the newborn revealed a sex difference. Males were able to lift their chins higher than females when placed on their stomachs. It is difficult to intuit what kinds of later characteristics such a difference would produce. Nevertheless, some infant responses have been related to later behavior patterns (Bell, et al., 1971; Kagan, 1971). For example, tactile sensitivity in infancy was related to vigor, assertiveness, and persistence in the later preschool years. Thus, it clearly would be of interest to know whether infant sex differences are found in tactile sensitivity.

A third methodological problem is that observers of infant behavior nearly always know the sex of the children they are rating. Thus, as discussed in Chapter 4, their stereotypic biases could affect their ratings. For example, in one study, observers rated the same infant as displaying different emotions and different levels of emotional arousal when it was described as a girl than when it was described as a boy (Condry and Condry, 1976).

There are some indications that the sexes do differ in rate of maturation. Based on evidence such as rate of bone ossification (Roche, 1968) and pattern of electroencephalographic recordings (Engel and Benson, 1968), one study concluded that females are one to six weeks more mature than males at birth (Garai and Scheinfeld, 1968).[1] However, this skeletal advantage of girls does not appear to last beyond the first year (Maccoby and Jacklin, 1974), and it does not tell much about the rates of development in other systems. In fact, evidence from one study suggests that the functions of the orbital cortex may develop earlier in males than in females (Goldman, et al., 1974).

While there may be maturational differences in some areas, the evidence to date does not indicate unequivocally that one sex is consistently ahead of the other. Nevertheless, when there are significant sex effects it is generally the female who is the more mature. Thus one should be cautious in interpreting sex differences found in young children which may be as much a reflection of a temporary maturational difference as of a permanent sex difference.

Early maturational differences could produce effects that are still evident

[1] Studies investigating other indices of early development have not found that girls are consistently ahead of boys. See Hindley, 1967; Hindley, et al., 1966; Scott, et al., 1955; Bayley, 1933; 1965; Frankenburg and Dodds, 1967; Gardner and Swiger, 1958.

long after the maturational differences have disappeared. It is possible that these early differences set into motion a chain of interaction patterns between children and their parents or between children and their environment that reinforce and maintain certain behavior patterns, coping strategies, or cognitive styles. For example, a less colicky baby is perhaps more easily soothed by a mother's words of comfort. In turn, the baby's responsiveness reinforces the mother's talking and verbal interaction between the pair increases. Consequently because the baby is exposed to more verbal stimulation, she may learn to speak earlier. She should then elicit even more verbal stimulation from her parents and her language development will be further accelerated.

Although there are difficulties assessing stable characteristics in infants and interpreting what sex differences mean at this age, there are some findings relevant to the concerns of this chapter. The following sections focus on characteristics of infants that may act as precursors to the major stereotypic sex differences.

Aggression

Activity Level. Two lines of reasoning suggest that activity level in infancy may be a precursor of later aggressive/assertive behaviors. First, exposure before birth to testosterone, a male hormone, has been related to both the general activity levels and the aggressive behaviors of animals and possibly humans. Since male fetuses are exposed to more testosterone than female fetuses, it could be predicted that males will be both more active throughout their lives and more aggressive in a variety of situations.

A second argument linking infant activity level to later aggression suggests that aggression may be the result of parent-child interactions which are directly influenced by the infant's activity level (Bell, 1968). An infant who is very active and awake much of the time may get into more trouble and cause extra work for the parents. In turn, the parents may become more impatient and more willing to punish the child. Thus, differences in activity levels in children may directly affect interactions with parents which, in turn, will affect development. If boys are more active, this might then indirectly lead to socialization patterns which would make them more aggressive.

Some research has provided initial support for the hypothesis that male infants are more active than female infants. For example, one study found that at three weeks of age, males on the average slept one hour less than did females (Moss, 1967). However, in more recent studies, the results indicate that there are no consistent sex differences in the general level of infant activity, at least prior to one year of age.[2] These data cast doubt on the importance of prenatal testosterone for understanding later aggressiveness in boys.

[2] See Bell, et al., 1971; Clarke-Stewart, 1973; Kagan, 1971; Maccoby and Jacklin, 1974.

Although boys are the more active sex if any sex differences are found, these biological effects alone do not appear to account for the consistently higher aggressiveness of boys.

Irritability. There is some evidence that male infants are more irritable than female infants. For example, one study found that males from one to three months of age cried and fussed more than females (Moss, 1967). However, such findings depend on a variety of other factors, such as birth order, specific age at testing, and prenatal and delivery complications. But, again, when differences are found, it is usually the male infants who are the more irritable. These early sex differences may be a function both of the greater immaturity of male infants at birth and of the higher incidence of pregnancy and birth complication for male infants (Bell, et al., 1971). Infants who experience birth complications are generally more irritable, and there is a much higher rate of such complications among male babies (Parmalee and Stern, 1972). The likelihood of finding sex differences in irritability decreases when the experimental sample consists of only boys and girls who have undergone normal deliveries. But, it is also possible that greater irritability in males is due to genetic or prenatal hormonal factors.

Whatever the cause of this early difference in irritability, it could begin a social interaction pattern that would lead to boys being more negative, resistive, and aggressive than girls. In a manner similar to that described above for activity level, the circular interactive processes operating in parent-child relationships could turn the irritable baby into the aggressive child. Irritability might elicit harsher behaviors from parents. In turn, since children imitate their parents, irritable children might display harsher, or more aggressive, behaviors which in turn would elicit more punitive behaviors from the parents.

Nurturance and Social Orientation

Smiling and Response to Faces. The popular stereotype is that females are more nurturant and oriented toward the social environment than males are. Two areas of infant behaviors that may be precursors of such difference are smiling and responsiveness to human faces. If female infants smile more or earlier and respond more positively to human faces than males, a possible conclusion is that females are *naturally* more social. Alternatively, parents may act more positively toward a smiling, responsive infant. A few studies have reported that infant girls respond and interact more positively with their mothers (Beckwith, 1972; Clarke-Stewart, 1973). Similarly, infant girls but not infant boys vocalize (coo and gurgle) more to faces than to geometric forms (Kagan, 1971). In contrast, at least two studies have failed to find sex differences in infant vocalization patterns (Clarke-Stewart, 1973; Lewis, 1969).

Furthermore, while infant girls vocalize more to faces than infant boys, there was no evidence of sex differences in the smiling responses to the faces in these same infants (Lewis, 1969).

Nurturance. Thus, the data supporting infant differences in "sociability" are equivocal at best. Furthermore, studies of early nurturing behaviors in preschoolers also fail to find consistent sex differences. For exmple, while girls have been observed to draw and talk more about people (Goodenough, 1957), in other research no sex differences in friendliness with peers, positive interactions with adults, or smiling were found among children who were twenty-seven to thirty-three months old (Bell, et al., 1971). Similarly, in a more recent study, preschool boys were equally as likely to reinforce the behaviors of their peers as girls (Eisenberg, 1974). Thus the question of whether females are naturally more nurturant or socially oriented must remain open.

Independent and Dependent Behavior

Attachment Behaviors. One infant behavior that is commonly associated with dependence is separation anxiety, that is, distress or crying when the child's parent is leaving or out of the room, unwillingness to play when the parent is gone, or clinging to the parent in a novel environment. Another related behavior is fear of strangers, indicated by crying or clinging to the parent when a stranger is present. In general the results from studies investigating both of these behavior patterns suggest that there are no consistent sex differences in the incidence of either separation anxiety or the fear of either strangers or novel situations. One commonly cited study did report sex differences in separation anxiety. In this study, eleven-month-old females stood and cried when separated from their mothers by a barrier. In contrast, boys of the same age spent more time trying to remove the barrier. It was also found that girls sat and played quietly with their toys and spent more time closer to their mothers while boys played more actively with their toys and spent more time exploring their environment (Goldberg and Lewis, 1969).

However, other studies have not replicated these sex differences. For example, one study found that boys cried as much as girls in one situation, while girls cried more than boys in a second situation (Jacklin, et al., 1973). Similarly, in a study of attachment behaviors of ten-, fourteen-, and eighteen-month-old children, no significant sex differences were reported in children's dependency on their mothers (Coates, Anderson, and Hartup, 1973). On the basis of these findings and many others, Maccoby and Jacklin (1974) concluded that attachment-related behaviors in early childhood apparently are not differentiated by sex.

What We Know about Sex Differences in Infants

All these studies taken together suggest that there are few, if any, distinct differences between male and female infants.[3] Boys may be more active and irritable on the average, but the differences are small. It does not appear that biological factors alone operating prenatally and in early infancy can explain the much more obvious differences between the activities and interests of older children. However, parents may respond differentially to smiling, nonirritable infants than to infants who cry a great deal. These parental responses interact with sex-role expectations and may serve to reinforce or counteract them (see Box 1).

Thus, the current state of knowledge on infant characteristics leave unanswered the question of biological determinants of sex differences. However, a given sex difference need not show up as a difference in infancy for it to have

---

Box 1   Possible Interactions between Baby's Characteristics and Parental Responsiveness

Baby A	*Baby B*
[More likely to be a girl]	[More likely to be a boy]

Baby's Characteristics

Physically mature	Physically immature
Sleeps a lot	Cries a lot
Vocalizes to faces	Active and therefore gets into trouble
Smiles at faces	

Parent Response

Affectionate	Irritable
Responsive when child does cry	Not necessarily responsive to child's frequent cries
Talks to child	Uses physical restraints and punishments

Child Response

Affiliative—likes people, expects people to satisfy needs	Aggressive
Early vocalization	Expects to get needs satisfied through own efforts

---

[3] With regard to sex differences in exploratory behavior and in intellectual and perceptual capabilities, there is little evidence of male or female advantage. See Maccoby and Jacklin, 1974.

a biological basis. It is common for biologically based systems to emerge and develop at points in the life cycle other than infancy. For example, the hormonal system does not reach maturity until puberty. Consequently, we would not necessarily expect sex differences—such as aggression, nurturance, or sexuality—that might be influenced by the male and female gonadal hormones to emerge prior to the onset of puberty. However, separating the influence of socialization from the influence of biology at this point in a person's development is extremely difficult. Along with the biological changes, cultural expectations of sex-appropriate behavior patterns also undergo a marked shift at puberty, making changes at this time even more difficult to assess.

ANTHROPOLOGICAL RESEARCH

Anthropologists have developed another approach to the question of the underlying bases of sex differences: the search for cultural universals. If one or more behavioral differences is consistently found across most cultures, despite varying cultural patterns, then it is argued that there is reason to believe that these differences may reflect basic human biological realities (Goldberg, 1973). To give an extreme example, if in every culture only women bear children, then it is reasonable to suspect that men are biologically incapable of this function. Such an argument can be extended to other more subtle behavioral patterns which are also virtually cultural universals. Even though scientists may not yet understand the biological mechanisms that might be involved, cross-cultural consistencies would nevertheless imply that such mechanisms may indeed exist and that continuing research could lead to a more complete understanding at some future time.

However, deciding what constitutes a cultural universal is not always clear cut. Advocates of the socialization view cite cultural exceptions as evidence against a biological argument (McClelland, 1976; Mead, 1935). Protagonists of the biological view have countered this argument quite appropriately with this rebuttal: varying environmental factors could easily have resulted in diverging evolutionary paths that could have altered the relevant biological mechanisms in some cultural groups. Thus they argue that a few notable exceptions do not rule out the possibility of biological precursors. And at present, what constitutes a *few* exceptions is a value judgment rather than a scientific decision.

Division of Labor

All cultures use sex as one criteria for assigning roles. In addition, they all expect there to be certain inevitable temperamental differences between the sexes that suit men and women for their assigned roles. While the differentiation appears to be universal, the magnitude of this differentiation varies as a function of the economic and familial structure of the particular society (Rosaldo, 1974). Economies based on hunting and fishing and on a reliance on male strength have the most marked sex differentiation in roles and in socialization patterns. In contrast, societies based on animal husbandry and food storage have less marked sex differentiation in roles and socialization (Barry, et al., 1957).

In terms of familial structure, societies with large extended family systems and many people within the family group who share the same tasks tend to have more marked sex-role differentiation than societies with small, nuclear family groupings independent of each other (Barry, et al., 1957). This distinction probably reflects practical necessities arising from group size. That is, if the living group is quite small, then everyone must be able to fulfill several roles if the need arises. In contrast, if the living group is large, then subgroups can specialize in one or two roles and need only fill in for each other within their own subgroup (D'Andrade, 1966).

The specifics of the role divisions vary considerably from culture to culture. For example, in many West African cultures, women market and distribute goods, while in most of western Europe and the United States, men take responsibility for marketing and distribution. Nonetheless, two roles do seem to be universally linked to one sex or the other: child-raiser and warrior-hunter. There are exceptions, but in most cultures women raise the children and men fight the battles. While biological predispositions other than reproductive functions may have influenced this role differentiation, the necessities of survival were also undoubtedly important. Women were needed to nurse the infants they bore. Since reliable contraceptives were not generally available, women had many children and therefore had to spend most of their adult years with infants or young children. Thus it made practical sense to assign them the role of raising the children. Since women were occupied with this role, only the men were available to play the warrior-hunter role.

With regard to other possible biological bases for this role division, testosterone has been linked to aggression in animals (Money and Ehrhardt, 1972; Young, Goy, and Phoenix, 1964) and humans (Persky, et al., 1971). It has been suggested that this link may underlie the male's adoption of the warrior-hunter role. The role of testosterone is discussed at the end of this chapter, but it is possible that both hormonal and survival factors influenced the male's role assignment.

Patriarchy and Male Dominance

In all known cultures, males are dominant over women of equal age and status (Goldberg, 1973; Mead, 1935; Rosaldo, 1974). Men occupy the high-status positions, exercise primary decision-making and political power, and tend to be dominant at interpersonal levels as well (see Chapters 14, 15, 16, and 17). Furthermore, no matter what specific activities men and women engage in, the roles played by men are valued more by society than the roles played by women (D'Andrade, 1966; Mead, 1935; Rosaldo, 1974). For example, in this country the medical profession is characteristically stereotyped as masculine and is regarded as a very high-prestige occupation. In contrast, in the USSR, the majority of doctors are female and the medical profession is not valued nearly as much.

The universality of male dominance suggests that biological factors may be involved. One argument is that a simple, universal sex difference is needed to account for the ubiquity of patriarchy and that a variety of culturally specific explanations would be inadequate. This is based on evidence indicating a link between the sex hormone testosterone and aggressive behaviors. Such an argument would reason that testosterone makes patriarchy inevitable, since their competitive edge over women will allow men always to occupy the majority of high-status, powerful positions. Furthermore, faced with this "biological reality," societies have chosen to socialize the sexes so that they do not compete with one another, with females being socialized into roles that males either cannot play (childbearing and nursing) or would not want to play (low-status positions). In this way, females are protected from inevitable failure. Thus does socialization exaggerate what is a biologically limiting factor (Goldberg, 1973).

Although there is some empirical support for the testosterone argument, this evidence has many weaknesses. As will be described later, research with humans has not convincingly demonstrated a causal relationship between testosterone and assertion or competitiveness, although there is a reasonably clear link between physical aggressiveness and testosterone in animals (e.g., Edwards, 1969). Also, as Chapter 4 emphasized, average sex differences favoring males in any trait or ability do not mean that all males are inevitably better at one activity while all females are inevitably worse. The pervasiveness of role and status differentiation observed in our culture cannot be easily explained by average differences in aggression or competition between males and females, whether or not these latter trait differences have a biological foundation.

A second possible biological argument for patriarchy concerns size and strength differences between males and females. Size and strength are linked to dominance in some species; recent work in nonverbal communication suggests that height alone may be a cue for dominance (see Chapters 7 and 16). In addition, young children in this culture come to associate both positive value and maleness with bigness, and associate power and status with males (Erikson, 1963; Kohlberg, 1966). It is possible that children are responding to the height differential to some extent in ascribing high status to males. Of course it is also possible that the children are responding only to the actual status difference that is apparent in our society and not to the height differential at all. It is impossible in this culture to unconfound the two variables. Yet, it is possible that universal patriarchy might be due, in part, to inferences based on such nonverbal or perceptual cues as height.

Another argument for male dominance in nearly every culture suggests that biology is the percursor of patriarchy only inasmuch as it created the historical necessity of women staying home to bear and raise children in order to provide the best chance for the survival of the children. Since these maternal roles limited women's access to other activities, men by necessity filled the more public roles. In the process of doing this, men also invested these roles with high status (Rosaldo, 1974).

This line of reasoning suggests that as the biological necessities surrounding motherhood are reduced by modern child-care arrangements, both men and women will be freed to take an equal role in both the public and the private domains, and patriarchy could be eliminated. However, many cultures exist, such as the Ashanti, Yoruba, and other West African tribes, in which women play a very active role in the economic system and in which women are extremely mobile. Patriarchy is still the rule in these cultures, despite the blurring of the lines between the public and the private domains. Therefore, it is questionable whether the childbearing role of women alone has destined them to inferior status and whether changes in this role will produce widespread alterations in the structure of patriarchy.

Interpreting Anthropological Research

Anthropological data indicate a number of areas in which biological factors may be involved in producing sex differences. In particular, aggressive and dominant behaviors and spatial skills may involve biological factors. However, we must be cautious in interpreting findings from anthropological research. While there are some very consistent cross-cultural behavioral differences between males and females, there are also some strikingly similar patterns of socialization linked to these differences. For example, while it is true that women are the child-raisers in most cultures, it is also true that most girls are socialized into this role (Barry, et al., 1957). Thus it is difficult to know how much maternal behavior is biologically based and how much is learned. Similarly, while it is true that men universally fulfill the leadership, high-status roles, and that testosterone may affect this phenomenon (Goldberg, 1973), it is also true that self-reliance and achievement are major socialization goals for males but not females in 85 to 87 percent of cultures studied by anthropologists (Barry, Bacon, and Childs, 1957). Other examples could be given, but what is important is the issue this overlap in socialization patterns and cultural universals raises in terms of the relative importance of socialization and biology. Socialization could be producing the differences, or it could be exaggerating a small biologically based difference, or it could be mirroring a powerful biologically determined behavioral system (Goldberg, 1973; Maccoby, 1972; Rosaldo, 1974). Unfortunately, for most behaviors it is not possible to decide which of these, if any, is happening.

There are many aspects of male-female role patterns that are not universal. Many of the specific roles played by men and women vary markedly from culture to culture. In addition, the nature of the relationships between people takes on many different patterns. Kinship systems, sexual patterns, and marital arrangements are as diverse as culture itself. Finally, even the personality dispositions associated with masculinity and femininity vary cross-culturally. Margaret Mead provided the best known examples of this diversity. In her comparison of the Arapesh, the Mundugamore, and the Tchambuli, she clearly documented the flexibility of human behavior. Among the Arapesh, both men and women are expected to be, and are, gentle, nurturant, responsive, cooperative, and willing to be subordinate to others. In contrast, among the Mundugamore, everyone is hostile, suspicious, and extremely aggressive. "Mother-love," as we know it, is virtually nonexistent. Finally among the Tchambuli, men play out what we would consider feminine roles while females exhibit more of those traits we stereotype as masculine (Mead, 1935).

BIOLOGY AND SEX DIFFERENCES

In discussing the influence of biology on "maleness" and "femaleness," one must recognize that these terms have many meanings. The biological concept of sex (male or female) can refer to genetic sex (XX or XY chromosomes), hormonal sex (relative levels of estrogen and testosterone), gonadal sex (ovaries or testes), or genital sex (penis or clitoris/vagina). The psychological or cultural concept of gender (masculine or feminine) also has various meanings: it can refer to other people's reactions to a child and their raising it as a boy or girl, or to one's own sexual identity and sex-role behavior (behaving in ways defined as masculine or feminine). Ordinarily, all of these aspects of maleness or femaleness are highly correlated. The genetic sex normally results in the same hormonal sex, which in turn results in the same gonadal sex, and so on. Occasionally there are inconsistencies among the various types of sex. For example, as a result of hormonal imbalances, a genetic female (XX chromosomes) may be born with masculine-appearing genitalia. Such instances provide the scientist with an opportunity to explore the separate influences of the various possible contributors to the differentiation between boys and girls. The next section will examine the evidence for the influence of biology upon male-female differences which is derived from studies of these individuals who are not consistent in all aspects of their sexual identities. These studies are primarily concerned with the effects of prenatal hormone levels on psychosexual development. Two basic methods have been used: experimental manipulation of pre- and post-natal hormone levels in animals; and correlational procedures with naturally occuring clinical syndromes in humans.

Genes, Hormones, and the Sex Organs

Though the extent of biology's influence on sex differences in *behavior* remains a debatable issue, its impact on the anatomical differences in the reproductive systems of males and females is clear. Biology has its initial input by means of genetic inheritance. Normal humans have twenty-three pairs of chromosomes. One of these pairs determines the genetic sex of the person. For this pair, males characteristically carry an X and a Y chromosome, while females carry two X chromosomes. An embryo's genetic sex determines whether its gonadal cells become ovaries or testes, by means of a mechanism not yet fully understood. If the human embryo carries an X and a Y chromosome, testes are formed approximately six weeks after fertilization has taken place. These embryonic testes then begin the production of male hormones, androgens or testosterones (the most potent form of androgen). If the embryo carries two X chromosomes the gonadal tissue remains undifferentiated until approximately the twelfth week of gestation. At this time, differentiation begins and later during gestation two ovaries form. Further differentiation of the reproductive structures is primarily dependent on the presence or absence of the male hormones which are produced by the embryonic testes. Thus, for about six weeks, the fetus retains the potential to develop along either male or female lines. Complete anatomical differentiation as a male requires the presence of testosterone.

In addition to controlling morphological development, a number of animal studies have indicated that gonadal hormone levels at a particular time early in development have a direct effect on the brain (Gorski, 1968; Goy, Bridson, and Young, 1964; McEwen, 1976). In particular, recent research has indicated that early levels of sex hormones affect the pattern of nerve connections in specific parts of the brain, resulting in characteristically male or female patterns of nerve circuits (McEwen, 1976)

Hormones and Behavior: Animal Studies

The behavioral effects of early exposure to sex hormones, especially testosterone, have been investigated with a variety of experimental techniques and types of animals. The results are quite complex and often depend on the particular technique and species of animal used. One of the most consistent findings concerns effects on sexual behavior. The sexual behavior of most subprimate mammals is heavily dependent on circulating levels of hormones. Male sexual responding is related to high testosterone levels while female responding in animals is related to high estrogen and progesterone levels (see Chapter 11). Alterations in normal hormone levels in adults cause sexual

dysfunctions. For example, if the female hormones, estrogen and progesterone, are eliminated from an adult female rat, by removing the ovaries, she
will not exhibit the typical female sexual posture, though normal sexual
responding can be restored by means of injections of estrogen and progesterone.

The effects of hormone levels on adult sexual behavior can also be dramatically altered by manipulating the animal's early exposure to sex hormones.
For example, the normal sexual behavior of male rats is to mount the backs of
female rats during copulation. Normally, such mounting rarely occurs in
females. However, female rats who have been injected with testosterone
shortly after birth exhibit far more mounting behaviors (of both females
and males) as adults than normal female rats who have not been so exposed to
testosterone (Levine, 1966). Furthermore, in a genetic adult female rat who
received neonatal injections of androgen, the presence of female hormones
does not elicit female sexual behavior. Instead, this female seems to be
responsive only to injections of androgen, which act to elicit masculine sexual behavior such as increased mounting and sometimes even simulated
copulation. Thus, early exposure to androgen or testosterone appears to
result in a male pattern of sexual responding, while absence of testosterone
during this critical period leads to female behavior and responsiveness to
female hormones, even in genetic males (Levine, 1966).

As stated above, early exposure to sex hormones has also been related to
nonsexual behaviors, especially aggression-related activities. Prenatally androgenized female rhesus monkeys exhibit a high incidence of rough-and-
tumble play, a behavior usually characteristic of male rhesus monkeys
(Young, Goy, and Phoenix, 1964). Neonatal administration of testosterone
also increases fighting responses in adult mice (Edwards, 1969). However,
there are a range of animal behaviors that may be labeled aggressive (e.g., at-
tacks, offensive sideways movements, aggressive versus submissive postures),
and only some of these behaviors may be related to early administration of
testosterone (Barr, et al., 1976). Furthermore, such effects are not necessarily
specific to the administration of testosterone. Injections of estrogen into newborn female rats have also been found to increase the fighting behavior of
adult females (Bronson and Desjardins, 1968). Thus, it does not necessarily
follow that when males are more aggressive than females, it is because of sex
differences in levels of testosterone.

In sum, experimental studies with animals do demonstrate significant behavioral effects of hormone levels. Testosterone in particular seems to be
related to aggressiveness and male sexual responding. However, the implications of such findings for masculine and feminine differentiation in humans
are unclear. It is difficult to generalize findings from one kind of rodent to
another, much less from rodents to humans. Similar problems exist in generalizing from apes and monkeys to humans. In addition, as the evolutionary
ladder is ascended, the effects of hormones on behaviors become less dra-

matic, the cortex exerts increasing control, and thus the role of learning and experience becomes ever more important (Beach, 1958). This is especially true of adult sexual behavior, which is largely under hormonal control in lower animals but strongly influenced by attitudes in humans (see Chapter 11).

Hormones and Behavior: Human Studies

A series of studies by John Money, Anke Ehrhardt, and their associates at Johns Hopkins Medical Center have taken advantage of naturally occurring cases of children who have deviated in one way or another from the normal pattern of sexual differentiation. For example, they have studied children with normal and abnormal chromosome patterns and with external genitals partially or wholly inconsistent with their chromosomal sex. In many cases, abnormal levels of prenatal hormones were present as these children were developing.

In an attempt to establish the influence of prenatal hormones on later behavior, these researchers have categorized their cases in terms of prenatal hormonal environment and investigated the behavior patterns associated with these categories. However, the studies reported in this section are based on a small number of clinical cases. The subjects were undergoing clinical treatment at the time of the studies, and consequently, represent an atypical sample which differs from the normal population in several ways. Not only is their prenatal hormonal history atypical and the appearance of their genitalia abnormal at birth, but their membership in a clinical population also gives them unusual life experiences. Given the uniqueness of these individuals, generalizations about all humans must be made with extreme caution. Variations in their behavior patterns could be due to a variety of things: their exposure to the prenatal hormones; their familiarity with the clinical setting; their awareness of their own differences from others; and the reactions of others who know about the patients' unique status.

In discussing these clinical syndromes, one must make an important distinction between the concepts of gender identity and gender-role identity. Gender identity is the awareness and acceptance of one's gender. If a girl knows she is a girl and thinks of herself as a girl, she has an appropriate gender identity. Gender-role identity is the acceptance of the socially defined roles and behaviors associated with being a male or a female. If a girl prefers to play with dolls, wears dresses, and plans to be a wife and mother, she has a stereotypically feminine gender-role identity. It is important to keep these two concepts separate, because the implications in terms of personal adjustment differ considerably between the two. For example, it cannot be said that a girl is disturbed or maladjusted just because she prefers to wear pants or wants a career when she grows up, even though many would define these as male gender-role behaviors. As the roles open to women expand, it is going to become increasingly difficult to say what is an "appropriate" female gender-role identity and, therefore, to say what constitutes a deviation from that role identity. However, most people would view individuals who are confused about their gender (whether male or female) as being somewhat maladjusted. Most people have a strong notion of whether they are male or female which does not depend on particular sex-role behaviors.

Androgenized Genetic Females. The best clinical evidence for the effects of prenatal androgens on human behavior comes from the studies of genetic females born with masculinized external genitalia as a result of prenatal exposure to androgens. There are at least two ways that a human female fetus can be exposed to androgens at the appropriate critical period: her mother can be injected with androgenlike compounds,[4] or her own adrenal glands can malfunction, producing too much androgen.

In two studies, extensive interviews were given to twenty-five fetally androgenized genetic females ranging in age from four to sixteen who had been receiving cortisone since birth and/or who had undergone surgical feminization early in life, so that their genitals would appear more feminine (see Money and Ehrhardt, 1972). On the basis of these interviews, Ehrhardt and Money compared the incidence of certain behaviors and attitudes in the fetally androgenized genetic females with the incidence of these same behaviors and attitudes in a control group, matched to the clinical sample on the basis of similarity of age, socioeconomic background, race, and I.Q. However, the two groups were not matched on familiarity with the interviewers or on experience in the clinical setting. Given the personal nature of many of the questions being asked and given the propensity of people to present themselves as congruent with sex-role stereotypes, the failure to match on these two very important variables makes interpretation of the experimental research work extremely difficult. In addition, the interviewers knew which girls were patients and which were control subjects. This knowledge could have biased the interview process and the interviewers' interpretations of the children's responses (see Chapter 2).

In general, Ehrhardt and Money found that fetally androgenized female subjects showed a higher incidence of interest in masculine-associated clothing and toy preference than the control subjects, and relatively little interest in infant care and feminine-associated clothing and toys. They "considered themselves and were considered tomboys" by their mothers. They reported a greater interest in careers than many girls their age but not to the exclusion of "eventual romance, marriage and motherhood" (Ehrhardt, Epstein, and Money, 1968, p. 166).

These data suggest that fetal exposure to androgens is associated with a higher incidence of "masculine" sex-typed behaviors and attitudes. But, as

---

[4] Once used for some women to prevent a miscarriage, such drugs are no longer prescribed because of negative side effects.

noted earlier, these androgenized girls differed from the control population in several ways, only one of which was the prenatal exposure to androgens. Most importantly, they were more familiar as a group with the cinical setting and with the interviewers. They were also aware of their unique status. Finally, they may have received very different socialization experiences due to their parents' knowledge of their unique status. Thus, it is possible that the results reflect a greater willingness of the androgenized girls to mention cross-sex–typed attitudes and behaviors more than this being a true behavioral difference between the patient group and the control group. This alternative interpretation seems even more plausible after examining the response of the control group. These responses are more stereotypically feminine than would be expected in a random sample of girls in this age group. It is unusual that the vast majority of the control sample preferred dresses, wearing slacks or shorts *only* occasionally; played *only* with dolls and that *none* expressed *any* ambivalence about their female sex role. Data from several sources suggest a higher incidence of wearing slacks, and of playing with toys other than dolls and more ambivalence about their female sex role than normal girls.[5]

There was no greater incidence of physical aggression or fighting in the fetally androgenized population. A higher incidence of physically aggressive behavior in males is one of the few postulated sex differences in children and animals that finds repeated support in experimental studies (Chapter 4). The fact that no significant differences was reported in these studies suggests that prenatal androgens may play a very small role in the origin of masculine aggressiveness in boys or that socialization dictates the expression, or even the emergence, of any potential for greater aggressiveness. Perhaps, instead of physical aggressiveness per se, prenatal androgens predispose the developing organism to a higher level of physical activity, the exact manifestation of which is dependent on socialization.

In sum, the studies suggest that some behaviors and attitudes of the patient population were more "masculine" than the controls. However, these behaviors were still well within the normal range for females in this society. There was no question that these girls had a female gender identity and that their adult sexual preferences were comparable to control samples. Apparently, neither the development of female gender-role identity nor the emergence of stable gender identity is seriously disrupted by the presence of prenatal androgens.

Turner's Syndrome and Androgen-Insensitive Syndrome. What happens when a fetus is not a genetic female but lacks a masculine prenatal hormonal environment? This situation arises usually in one of two conditions. In both cases, the individuals are not genetic females but do have female external

[5] See Brown, 1956; 1957; Hartup and Zook, 1960; Kagan, 1964a; 1964b.

genitals. Neither group is exposed to androgens prenatally. In addition, since female external genitals are present at birth, both groups are generally reared as females. If these groups develop "normal" feminine behavior patterns, then it might be concluded that the feminine behavior patterns are not the result of the possession of two X chromosomes.

One of these groups is comprised of individuals with Turner's Syndrome. These individuals have only one sex chromosome, an X, the second X or Y chromosome having been lost. Recall that two X chromosomes are necessary for ovaries to form and that one Y chromosome is necessary for testes to form. Since these individuals have neither a Y chromosome nor two X chromosomes, they have no gonadal tissue and consequently are unable to produce any gonadal hormones. Since they do not produce prenatal androgens, these X fetuses develop female genitalia. That is, with the exception of ovaries, they develop both the internal and the external reproductive structures of a female. The second group is comprised of individuals who are XY "females." Since they have a Y chromosome they develop normal testes but, due to a genetic malfunction, their body cells are insensitive to androgens. That is, they produce androgens but their cells do not respond to the androgens. Therefore, effectively, they are not exposed to prenatal androgens and, consequently, like the individuals with Turner's Syndrome, they develop the external genitalia of a female.

In a study using a methodology comparable to that used in the study of the andrenogenital syndrome population, fifteen girls with Turner's Syndrome, ten XY androgen-insensitive females, and fifteen matched controls were interviewed. In general, both these patient groups were as feminine in their behavior and interest patterns as the control group or more feminine than the andrenogenital syndrome populations (Ehrhardt, et al., 1970). Thus, the development of a "normal" female gender-role identity is dependent neither on the presence of ovaries nor on the presence of two X chromosomes.

What does seem to be important for the development of gender identity is the assigned sex of rearing (the sex label given by parents and family). In each of these three clinical populations, the children were labeled and reared as females and in each population the children developed a "normal" female gender identity, despite variations in their genetic and prenatal hormonal sex.

Gender Reassigned Cases. Finally, two more cases further emphasize the relative importance of sex of rearing (Money and Ehrhardt, 1972). In both cases, the child was a genetic male who had been exposed to prenatal androgens and was born with male genitals. However, for different reasons, they each had their genitals changed to female and were being reared as females. In the first case, one of two identical male twins was reassigned as a female following a surgical mishap. At seven months, the twin boys were to be circumcised by electrocautery. Due to an electrical malfunction, the penis of one of the twins was totally destroyed. Following the recommendations of their doctors, the parents of this little boy elected to have the boy's sex reassigned. At seventeen months, the boy came to the Johns Hopkins clinic for the necessary surgical corrections to give him female external genitals. Money and Ehrhardt reported that since surgery, the parents have made every effort to raise the twins in accord with their assigned sex—one male and one female. According to the reports of the parents, the two children are developing to fit the role expectations of their assigned sex. The mother described her "daughter's" behavior this way:

> She likes for me to wipe her face. She doesn't like to be dirty, and yet my son is quite different. I can't wash his face for anything. . . . She seems to be daintier. Maybe it's because I encourage it. (Money and Ehrhardt, 172, p. 119.)

Thus, the assigned sex appears in this case to be a more important determinant of behavior than the genetic and prenatal hormonal sex.

In the second case, the male infant did not have fully developed male genitalia. The penis was only one centimeter long and the urinary opening was located behind rather than within the penis. Once again on the advice of doctors, the parents elected to have the child's sex reassigned. In the years following the sex reassignment, the parents have made a concerted attempt to rear this child as a girl. According to their reports she has developed a female gender identity and is adopting the behaviors commonly associated with a female gender role.

In sum, data from the various clinical cases, suggest the conclusion that one's gender identity is not preordained by one's sex chromosomes nor by one's prenatal hormonal history. While prenatal hormones may affect some aspects of gender-role identity, this, too, is determined for the most part by the sex of rearing rather than the genetic or prenatal hormonal sex. In fact, the effect of rearing is so strong that it can and does override, for the most part, the effects of these biological factors if it is established at a young age.

Biology and Cognitive Skills

Recessive Gene Hypothesis. As discussed in Chapter 4, substantial evidence suggests that males, on the average, have better spatial skills than females. Geneticists have suggested that there might be a recessive gene on the X chromosome which has a positive influence on spatial perception. Males have only one X chromosome, so if they received the recessive gene, it would express itself and they would have exceptional spatial perception. In contrast, since girls have two X chromosomes, they would need two recessive genes in order to have exceptional spatial perception. Consequently, since the likelihood of getting two recessive genes is less than the likelihood of getting one recessive gene, it is to be expected that males on the average have a greater chance of having exceptional spatial perception than females. Thus, if it could be demonstrated that spatial perception is influenced by a recessive gene on the X chromosome, it would be reasonable to believe that there is biological basis for the average advantage males have on tasks involving spatial perception (Stafford, 1961).

To test this hypothesis, the intrafamilial correlations of performance on spatial tasks were examined. Since sons receive their X chromosome from their mother and not their father, correlations of performance between sons and mothers should be much greater than the correlations between sons and fathers. Data from several earlier studies have confirmed this prediction.[6] However, three recent studies with very large samples have found no evidence for the X-linked recessive gene bypothesis (Bouchard, 1976; DeFries, et al., 1976; Williams, 1975). Thus, present evidence seems to discount this hypothesis of an X-linked recessive trait of high spatial ability.

Brain Lateralization. Another biological mechanism for the greater spatial abilities of boys being considered today is differential brain lateralization.

The human brain is divided into hemispheres: the right and the left. Recent studies on split-brain subjects (individuals whose hemispheres have been separated) suggest that each hemisphere of the brain specializes in certain abilities: the left hemisphere specializing in verbal abilities and the right hemisphere specializing in spatial perception (Levy-Agresti and Sperry, 1968; Sperry and Levy, 1970). At some point in development, lateralization (the specialization in the functioning of each hemisphere) begins, and one hemisphere, usually the left, becomes dominant in its control of an individual's behavior. It has been argued that the timing of this lateralization may affect the development of both spatial and verbal skills. Since the most consistent sex differences in cognitive functioning are found on tasks involving either spatial or verbal skills, it has been suggested that differential timing of lateralization might underlie, to some extent, these sex differences (Harris, 1976). The reasoning goes something like this: Males perform spatial tasks better than females and females perform verbal tasks better than males. There is lateralization of the brain in relation to these two skills. Lateralization appears to begin earlier in females than males. Perhaps delayed lateralization gives males an advantage on spatial skills.

The sex difference in the timing of lateralization does receive fairly consistent support. Several developmental studies suggest that lateralization begins earlier in girls (Kimura, 1967; Knox and Kimura, 1970) although this claim is still quite controversial (Maccoby and Jacklin, 1974). However, the exact mechanisms responsible for this developmental difference, and the impact of this developmental difference on spatial and verbal skills are unclear at present. Several hypotheses have been advanced, none of which have received unequivocal empirical support.

[6] See Bock and Kolakowski, 1973; Corah, 1965; Hartlage, 1970.

Male Bilaterality for Spatial Skills. Early lateralization might improve verbal skills while adversely affecting the development of spatial skills. Spatial skills require less complete lateralization of, or rather more integration between, the two hemispheres. In contrast, verbal skills are improved by more complete lateralization and by left-hemisphere dominance. Since girls lateralize earlier than boys, they will acquire verbal skills more easily but will not perform as well as males on tasks involving spatial skills. Or conversely, while the delayed lateralization of males may put them at an early disadvantage for language learning, it may give them an advantage later on in tasks involving spatial skills (Buffery and Gray, 1972).

This hypothesis faces several difficulties. First, there is no evidence to support the assumption that weaker lateralization facilitates spatial skills and interferes with verbal skills (Harris, 1976; Sherman, 1977). Second, there is little evidence that delayed lateralization leads ultimately to less complete lateralization or greater bilaterality for spatial skills. Third, the developmental patterns associated with the emergence of sex differences on spatial skills does not mesh with the pattern implied by this hypothesis. Differences on verbal skills emerge early, as would be predicted, but spatial-skill differences do not emerge until adolescence (Maccoby and Jacklin, 1974), by which time lateralization in boys has caught up with that in girls, and may even have surpassed that of girls (Levy-Agresti and Sperry, 1968). Finally, this hypothesis assumes that the development of verbal skills somehow inhibits the development of spatial skills. Developmentally, there is no evidence indicating that children acquire one skill at the expense of the other. Both boys and girls improve on their verbal and spatial skills throughout school (Maccoby and Jacklin, 1974).

Female Bilaterality for Verbal Skills. Another explanation for the possible role of brain lateralization contradicts the above notion that the less complete lateralization of boys gives them an advantage with spatial skills. This hypothesis is that spatial skills require greater rather than lesser brain lateralization (Levy-Agresti and Sperry, 1968). Evidence for this hypothesis is seen in the fact that left-handers, who generally exhibit less complete lateralization, do less well on tasks requiring spatial skills than do right-handers (Nebes, 1971a; 1971b; Silverman, et al., 1966). Since lateralization of verbal and spatial skills may be less complete in women than men, this may account for male superiority in spatial skills.

There are some data to support the conclusion regarding less complete lateralization of verbal skills in females. For example, several studies have reported that the verbal skills of females are less disrupted by left-hemisphere damage than are males. These findings support the notion that verbal skills are being represented in the right hemisphere in females to a greater extent than in males (Bogan, 1969; Lansdell, 1961; 1962). However, there is little conclusive evidence to support specific mechanisms postulated by researchers proposing this theory.

Female Reliance on Verbal Modes. Both of the previous models rely on the assumption that the sexes differ in degree of lateralization and that somehow bilaterality for one skill affects the expression of the other skill. Both of these assumptions are open to question, and the mechanisms underlying the process of interference or augmentation are unknown. Additionally, there is a logical flaw in the reasoning behind both of these models (Maccoby and Jacklin, 1974). Both of these brain lateralization models fail to consider the fact that sex differences are not apparent for other hemispherically localized skills. The left hemisphere, as well as being verbal, has also been characterized as intellectual, analytic, and businesslike, while the right hemisphere has been characterized as spontaneous, intuitive, and experiential, as well as spatially skilled (Levy-Agresti and Sperry, 1968). While girls excel on some verbal tasks and boys excel on some spatial tasks, the pattern of left versus right hemispheric characteristics does not coincide with our more general female versus male sex-role stereotypes (Maccoby and Jacklin, 1974). It would seem that in order for the differential timing of brain lateralization to be a complete explanation of male-female differences on verbal and spatial tasks, then male-female differences ought to exist with regard to these other characteristics as well. Of course it is possible that lateralization in interaction with other biological (such as the sex-linked recessive gene, or prenatal and postnatal sex-hormonal effects) and/or socialization processes could affect verbal and spatial skills without producing comparable effects on these other lateralized characteristics.

The third major model for interpreting possible lateralization effects on cognitive skills does not rely on either of the previous assumptions. Advocates of this model (Rudel, et al., 1974; Sherman, 1971) have posited that the earlier acquisition of language predisposes girls to develop verbal skills at the expense of developing other problem-solving skills. Furthermore, females, more than males, come to rely on the verbal mode and left-hemisphere patterns of problem solving and, consequently, when faced with spatial problems, do not do as well as boys. In this way, social experience could exaggerate a sex difference initially created by a biologically determined maturation rate (Rudel, et al., 1973; Sherman, 1971; 1977).

Hormonal Effects. There have been suggestions that hormones may be involved in cognitive functioning. Two lines of research have suggested that androgens may have a direct effect on spatial ability. Both lead to the conclusion that the expression of the sex-linked recessive gene discussed earlier depends on the presence of some minimal amount of androgen. The relatively low performance of Turner Syndrome (XO) females on spatial tasks was the first set of data which suggested the importance of androgen. Like males (XY), Turner Syndrome females have only one X chromosome, and therefore, also like males, should be more likely to exhibit the recessive trait than females. Instead they do far worse than either males or females on a variety of spatial tasks (Harris, 1976). Androgen-insensitive females (XY) also exhibit this pattern of low spatial skills. These data could be explained if androgen was assumed to be a necessary component in the high spatial response pattern (Bock and Kolakowski, 1973). Both Turner Syndrome females and androgen-insensitive females differ from normal males and females in that they have no functional androgen. Thus if we assumed that high spatial skills depends both on the recessive gene and on the presence of androgen then these two groups would be expected to exhibit low spatial scores.

Lack of Evidence for a Biological Basis for Sex Differences

There are few sex differences that suggest a biological basis for the behavioral sex differences found in older children and adults. The evidence reviewed in this chapter suggests two primary areas for which there may be substantial biological bases for the sex differences in behavioral patterns: aggressive and dominant behaviors in males and differential cognitive functioning. The exact mechanisms mediating these biological effects are unclear, but there does appear to be evidence for these effects. The evidence for biological mediators of other behavioral differences is weak at best.

Roles as well as behaviors are stereotyped. There is little doubt that males and females do play quite different roles in this society (see Chapters 8, 12, 14, and 17). It is also clear that roles vary cross-culturally. Given this diversity of roles, it is debatable whether play behaviors and adult roles are predetermined primarily by biological mechanisms. Socialization is undoubtedly important. Theories regarding the socialization of sex differences in play and other role behaviors are discussed in Chapters 6 and 7. For the time being, it can be concluded that the role biology plays in the development of sex-role behaviors today and the role it played historically in the creation of distinct sex-roles is still an open question.

6 Classic Theories of Sex-Role Socialization

There is very little evidence demonstrating unequivocal behavioral differences between females and males either in adults or in very young children. Thus we concluded in Chapter 4 that socialization is a major factor in sex-role acquisition. In Chapter 5 we demonstrated that gender identity rather than biological sex determines many components of the sex role one learns. Specifically, in a series of recent studies it was found that children whose gender identity differed from their genetic sex acquired sex-role behaviors and attitudes that agreed with their gender identity rather than their genetic sex (Money and Ehrhardt, 1972). In addition, the evidence regarding early behavioral sex differences and cross-cultural behavioral consistencies suggests that of all the behaviors commonly stereotyped as masculine or feminine, only aggression and performance on tasks requiring spatial skills reveal sex differences with any regularity. And even with aggression as the dependent measure, studies do not always find significant sex differences. Based on this review, we concluded, with the possible exceptions of aggression and spatial skills, that there was little, if any, evidence suggesting biological or inborn personality or response differences between sexes.

Instead, the bulk of studies revealing consistent sex differences have focused on sex-role–related behavior such as children's preference for dolls as opposed to toy trucks, rather than response style differences, such as assertive

Jacquelynne Parsons was the primary author of this chapter; she was assisted by Julie Croke.

behaviors as opposed to conforming behaviors. In the majority of these studies, it is clear that both boys and girls, by the age of four, prefer behaviors and objects that are defined as sex-appropriate in our culture.

Experimental evidence indicates that preschool children act out more sex-role appropriate behaviors than sex-role inappropriate behaviors. For example, boys spend more time playing with transportation toys and building blocks while girls spend more time playing with dolls and "working" in the kitchen. In addition, children of both sexes pick same-sex playmates more often than they choose opposite-sex peers (Fagot and Patterson, 1969). This sex bias in playmate choice is apparent regardless of the nature of the play activities and continues until adolescence when cross-sex dating occurs. However, even at this age and into adulthood, friendship patterns still follow same-sex lines.

Does this mean that by three years of age children are already playing two very distinct social roles? No. While it is true that children do engage in a great amount of sex-appropriate behavior, they also spend some time at cross-sex—stereotyped play and all children spend at least half of their time at play which is not sex stereotyped—painting at an easel, riding on tricycles, playing in water, helping the teacher, and swinging or sliding. It does mean, however, that by this age the sexes are already diverging in their interest patterns and in the roles they play.

Adult sex roles also differ tremendously. Men and women, stereotypically, do different things in this society. And while these differences may be decreasing, the strongest, most consistent sex differences still appear in studies focusing on sex-role behaviors rather than personality dispositions. In addition, differences in dress, hair style, and a variety of nonverbal behaviors serve to accentuate the differences in the roles men and women play. Is this division of roles biological? At this point, cross-cultural and historical data suggest not. With the exception of caring for young children, the activities, dress, and interest patterns associated with each sex role vary considerably. Since these role preferences are culturally specific, and since there is so much overlap in behavior between the sexes, it appears that socialization rather than biology is responsible for the bulk of sex differences. The emphasis on socialization is further supported by the fact that the possible biological bases for most sex-typed behavior have not been specifically identified (see Chapter 5).

There are three main theoretical approaches which attempt to explain the processes underlying the socialization of sex-role behaviors: psychoanalytically based identification theory; reinforcement and social learning approaches; and cognitive-developmental theories. In this and the following chapter the focus will be on the utility of each of these approaches for explaining the emergence of sex-typed behavior patterns during the preschool and early elementary school years. Already by this age, sex-role learning is evident. There is little research on the numerous changes which are believed to occur for both sexes in the late childhood years and in early adolescence. Although these changes are a significant area for research, we feel that we cannot attempt to devote much space to the periods of development beyond early childhood because of the paucity of existing data. When appropriate and possible, brief mention will be made of the theoretical and empirical work related to sex-role development in late childhood and adolescence.

IDENTIFICATION THEORIES

The identification theories of sex-role acquisition have their origins in Freudian psychoanalytic psychology. In his efforts to understand the development of the human personality, Freud proposed what was then a rather revolutionary argument. He suggested that children's relationship with their parents, specifically their same-sex parent had a tremendous impact upon their developing personality. "Identification" was Freud's term for a unique learning process through which children unconsciously "mold" their own "ego-ideal" after that of the parent-model. Through identification, the child quite literally incorporates or takes the personality of the model as a goal. Thus, identification was seen as the means by which each child acquires the behaviors which society would require of her or him as an adult—including sex-role behavior. Others, notably Anna Freud, Freud's daughter, developed the psychoanalytic identification theories even further.

Psychoanalytic Theory

Psychoanalytic theory assumes that there are two motivational bases for identification: fear of loss of love and fear of retaliation, each eliciting its own form of identification (Freud, 1925/1974; 1933). Identification based on loss of love is labeled anaclitic identification; fear of retaliation from a powerful figure is called defensive identification. Both identifications require that the child be dependent upon the parent. But while both forms of identification were assumed to induce imitative behavior, Anna Freud argued that the two identification processes result in the child's internalizing different aspects of the same parent and different aspects of different parents. Furthermore, male development is controlled by defensive identification while female development is controlled by anaclitic identification. Consequently, since the processes underlying identification differ depending on the child's sex, Freud concluded that identification could be used to explain the origins of what he assumed to be permanent, global personality differences between males and females. In addition, he viewed identification, especially the differential identification of boys and girls, as biologically based. Sex differences in behavior were seen as the direct, irreversible consequence of perceived and actual anatomical differences. Specifically, psychoanalytic theorists felt that boys experience defensive identification rather than anaclitic identification because they realize that they have a penis and girls do not.

Because the infant is dependent upon the mother for satisfaction of all its physical needs, Freud assumed that all children in infancy form an anaclitic identification with their mothers. Since she gives pleasure, the mother's absence activates a fear of loss of love in the infant. Motivated by this fear, the child tries to recapture the mother by imagining her presence. For example, the child can comfort herself by fantasizing about her mother while she is gone. During this very early period, Freud assumed that the identification process was identical for both boys and girls. When children are about four years old and learn to discriminate between the genitals of the sexes and to experience genital sexual pleasure, Freud stated that the identification experiences of boys and girls begin to diverge.

For the boy, beginning genital sexual awareness initiates the Oedipal complex.[1] He desires his mother sexually and resents and fears his father as a rival. However, the event which forces the boy to resolve his feelings is the sight of the female's genitals—or rather her "embarrassing" lack of genitals! In his childish state of reasoning, the boy concludes that girls have been castrated and that a similar fate threatens him. His fear that he may be castrated motivates the boy to shift his identification to his father. The boy believes that by identifying with his father he will no longer be competing with him but, instead, enjoying his father's status vicariously. Thus, in choosing to be like his father, the boy can keep his penis. The boy, however, may still enjoy his mother sexually, through his father. As a result of this shift in identification, the boy begins to take on his father's characteristics, including his sex-role behaviors. This entire process was not necessarily conscious. In fact Freud assumed that it was probably largely unconscious.

Meanwhile, since the girl has no penis, she *cannot* fear castration, but she can notice the genital difference. According to Freud, this realization affects the young girl's identification experience. He argued that the desire for a penis distorts the female personality, creating a sense of inferiority, a sense of contempt for women, and a "character trait of jealousy." Normally, however, the girl replaces the desire for a penis with the desire for a baby. This causes her to select her father (i.e., men) as the sexual-object choice which will satisfy this need. Thereafter, Freud felt that penis-baby envy supplements anaclitic identification in assuring that the girl will adopt her mother's sex-role behavior, so that she may one day become a mother.

Central to psychoanalytic theory is the conclusion that the female is not motivated by a fear of castration to form a defensive identification with either her mother or father. The female's inability to form a defensive identification and her awareness of her inferior anatomy are seen as the basis for the formation of

---

[1] Following Freud's thinking, the boy's experience is discussed first.

Character traits which critics of every epoch have brought up against women—that they show less sense of justice than men, that they are less ready to submit to the great necessities of life, that they are more often influenced in their judgments by feelings of affection or hostility—all these would be amply accounted for by the modification in the formation of their superego which we have already inferred. (*Freud, 1925.*)

In the absence of defensive identification, the girl continues her original anaclitic identification with her mother. Fear of loss of her mother's love remains her primary motivation for adopting sex-role behaviors and attitudes.

Over the past forty years, Freud's ideas have been reworked into a number of modified theories of the identification process. While these interpretations vary in many ways, they all share certain basic assumptions, having to do with the quality of behavior gained through identification and its cause. Furthermore, while Freud's basic ideas were not derived from empirical data, subsequent research has addressed these basic assumptions. It is to these basic assumptions that we turn now.

ASSUMPTIONS OF IDENTIFICATION THEORIES

Integrated Pattern of Behaviors

First, identification is regarded as the means by which children acquire complete, complex patterns of behavior, attitudes, feelings, wishes, and standards of conduct which constitute a sex-role. But what is meant by a "complex pattern" of behavior and attitudes? Consider the following example:

Mary and Billy watch their mother balancing her checkbook. Their mother sighs and complains repeatedly. Now and then, she stops and starts over again. Finally, she gives up, voicing her disgust for mathematics to Mary and Billy. Later, when Mary and Billy begin to learn mathematics in school, Mary, ordinarily a good student, exhibits her mother's pattern of responses to mathematics. She too struggles and complains. She, too, gives up easily. Moreover, she expresses a similar set of attitudes about math: "I hate math," "I'm no good at math," "Math is for boys." In contrast to his sister, Billy exhibits none of his mother's responses to math.

Identification theorists argue that regular learning theories are not capable of explaining the acquisition of an entire set of sex-role–appropriate responses by Mary but not by Billy (Mussen, 1969). Instead, they maintain that it is because of Mary's identification with her mother—an identification that Billy cannot share—that Mary has come to model her mother so completely.

If the behaviors learned by identification are complex and interrelated, then a child who is feminine in one situation should be feminine in a variety of situations. Thus a girl who has acquired a passive personality by identification should exhibit this characteristic in a variety of situations: in her sexual encounters, in her dealings with repairmen, in academic discussions. Indeed, even if the woman should somehow enter into an activity, say a business career, where passivity can only lead to an adverse outcome (job termination), she should still find it extremely difficult to overcome her passivity. However, empirical evidence does not support this prediction. In fact, sex-typed behaviors vary extensively across situations. A person who responds passively in one situation may well respond aggressively in a different situation (Mischel, 1970; Bem and Allen, 1974).

Similarly, if identification results in the acquisition of broad behavioral dimensions, then the measures of the several specific behaviors constituting this trait should either be found together in people or none of them should exist. For example, if dependency is a global feminine trait, then children, especially females, who are dependent in one situation ought to be dependent in other situations as well. To test this prediction data was gathered on each of the following specific behaviors: amount of negative attention seeking; amount of positive attention seeking; touching or holding; being near or following adults or other children; and seeking reassurance. Contrary to the prediction, however, very little generality of dependency behaviors across situations or measures was found (Sears, et. al., 1965). A similar group of behavioral measures of aggression also yielded very little generality. Out of 132 possible comparisons, only 20 were significant for boys and 6 for girls. In other words, the data strongly suggested that these subjects were not behaving in the uniformly dependent or aggressive manner that an identification theory of sex-role learning would predict (see also Mann, 1959; Heathers, 1953; Gewirtz, 1956; Borstelman, 1961; and Hetherington, 1965).

Stable Behaviors

Identification theorists also assume that behaviors learned by identification are very stable over time. Both because behaviors are learned very early, and thus structure the child's interaction with her environment; and because identification is based on a powerful unconscious motive, behaviors learned by identification are assumed to be very resistant to change.

Data supporting consistency of sex-typed behaviors over time come from longitudinal studies of sex typing. In one of the most extensive of these studies, data based on behavioral observations of children at four different points in their development were compared with interviews of those same subjects in early adulthood. Among other things, the study focused on such sex-role behaviors as aggression, dependency, passivity, and intellectual achievement. Behaviors which were congruent with sex-role standards tended to be stable across one's life cycle. For example, girls who were passive children tended to become passive adults. Behaviors which were counter to the child's sex role were not consistent over the years of the study. For example, boys who were aggressive and overtly sexual generally became aggressive and overtly sexual men. In contrast, aggressive girls did not generally become aggressive women. There were, however, certain behaviors, namely independence and achievement-related behaviors, which were consistent for boys and girls (Kagan and Moss, 1962). A review of similar studies concluded "that sex typing begins very early and becomes crystallized during the first few years of the child's life" (Mussen, 1969, p. 712).

However, while these data generally support the assumption of identification theorists, it is not clear that identification is the process responsible for these behavioral consistencies. It is equally likely that continued reinforcement is responsible for the stability of behaviors over time. If boys are reinforced for doing masculine things they will continue to do masculine things. Consequently, masculine boys should become masculine men. For example, patterns of play were stable for boys from three to ten years of age but not for girls (Fagot and Littman, 1975). Assuming that boys are being reinforced for sex-appropriate behavior across these years, while girls are being encouraged to develop both masculine and feminine interests, these results certainly suggest that the stability of sex-role—related behaviors is dependent more on reinforcement patterns than on the intensity of the identification process. In another study parents reported using this differential pattern of reinforcement of sex-appropriate behaviors for boys and girls (Block, 1977). Thus, while some data support the predictions based on identification theory, it is impossible to conclude that identification is the reason for stability. Reinforcement principles yield the same prediction and thus can be used to explain the data equally well.

Internal Motivation

Identification theorists assume that the acquisition of sex-role behavior is governed by internal motives. That is, identification theories deemphasize the role of the environment in sex-role learning. Instead, they argue that children are stimulated by some internal drive or need to model the parent's sex-role behaviors. These motives are described as unconscious and powerful. They are said to be capable of maintaining consistent behavior even in the face of adverse environmental feedback. For example, Sigmund Freud suggested that sex-role learning is motivated by the Oedipal conflict—fear of castration and penis envy—and Anna Freud suggested that sex-role learning is motivated by the fear of loss of love from one's parents.

Empirical evidence for this is sparse, because of the difficulty in measuring unconscious motives. Several studies have attempted to assess the role of motivation indirectly by examining parental characteristics. For example, based on Sigmund Freud's suggestion that male identification is motivated by fear of one's father, several theorists have predicted that harsh fathers would generate the most fear and consequently the best developed sex-role identity in their sons. Conversely, based on Anna Freud's suggestion that sex-role identification is motivated by fear of loss of love, other theorists have suggested that nurturant mothers (fathers) would generate the most love and consequently the most fully developed sex-role identities in their daughters (sons).

The data on parental factors relating to the existence of unconscious motives in the child are far from conclusive. There is some indication that the parental characteristics of warmth and power may somehow influence the sex-role learning process. Researchers have concluded that their findings are consistent with the predictions of one, two, or all of the identification theories. It has been argued that perhaps no one parental characteristic is so important as that the parent have salience or importance in the child's life (Mussen and Distler, 1959). Thus, it does seem likely that some motivational processes are important in sex-role acquisitions. However, it would be hasty to conclude that the data are supportive of identification theories as opposed to other explanations of sex-role learning. Advocates of the social learning theories have demonstrated repeatedly that nurturance, power, competence, and similarity (e.g., same sex) are all cues which facilitate modeling.[2] Thus, it is equally likely that modeling and the motivational processes associated with modeling account for the data linking these parental characteristics to sex-role learning. In addition, methodological shortcomings clearly weaken the findings and it might just as easily be argued that the fact that the studies provide some support for both Sigmund and Anna Freud's theories indicates that neither of these really represent a total description of the parents' impact upon the child (Mussen, 1969).

Relationship with Same-Sex Parent

It is assumed that identification and, hence, sex-role learning arise from the relationship between the child and the same-sex parent. It is believed that there is a strong emotional tie existing in this relationship which does not exist in the child's other relationships with adults or children. This unique emotional bond is the stimulus which activates the child's motive to identify with or imitate the parent. To return to our earlier example, Mary was motivated to identify with and imitate her mother's math behaviors because of the emotional bond between them. Since Billy could not share this bond, he was not motivated to imitate his mother.

Once again, direct empirical support for this assumption is unavailable. However, indirect support is provided by studies investigating the effects of paternal absences (Biller, 1971). If a strong emotional tie is needed for sex-

[2] See Mischel and Grusec, 1966; Bandura and Huston, 1961; Bandura, Ross, and Ross, 1963a; 1963b; and Bandura, 1969.

role acquisition to take place, then the absence of such a tie should disrupt the acquisition process. Data from the paternal absence studies support this prediction. Boys with no fathers do have more problems with their sex-role identity. They are either less masculine or are overly masculine in comparison with other boys their age. Data on the effects of maternal absence are too sparse to comment on at this time.

But, while the absence of the parent as a source of identification does have some effects upon sex typing, one must consider the interpretations of these results carefully. It has been argued that father-absent children may be less socialized in general; thus, evidence of disrupted sex-role learning may simply reflect a slower rate of or less complete socialization (Mischel, 1958; 1970). When other measures of social behavior are investigated, similar evidence of disrupted socialization is apparent (Biller, 1971). In addition, single parents may treat their children quite differently than the same-sex parent in a two-parent family. For example, a single mother's behaviors may be influenced by a fear that her sons will not acquire the "proper" male sex role. If her expectancies are translated into any of a variety of behaviors, it may be her expectancies that are responsible for the boy's behavior rather than the absence of a male parent. Moreover, the fact that all these parent-absent subjects evidence some sex-role learning indicates that the presence of a same-sex parent is not absolutely essential.

Parent-Child Similarity

The final assumption of identification theories regards the consequences of parent-child similarity. If children are acquiring a sex-role identity by identifying with or incorporating the characteristics of their same-sex parent, the child and her or his model should be similar as a result of the identification process. That is, if the child is acquiring sex roles through identification, the child should be introjecting the same-sex parent. Consequently, once children have completed this process, they should be very similar to their same-sex parent.

Data relevant to this prediction are overwhelmingly negative. For example, in one study, fifth-grade girls did not perceive themselves as any more similar to their mothers than to a generalized feminine model (Fitzgerald and Roberts, 1966). Similarly, other researchers have found that girls were no more similar to their mothers than to any other women (Helper, 1955; Lazowick, 1955). Furthermore, a number of studies have reported that both boys and girls appear more similar to their mothers than their fathers on personality measures (Adams and Sarason, 1963; Byrne, 1965; Gray and Klaus, 1956). These data suggest that the same-sex parent is not the primary source for sex-role learning in children. In fact, peers, nonparent adults, siblings, TV characters, and social organizations, as well as parents, influence sex-role learning (Bandura, 1969; Kohlberg, 1966; and

Maccoby and Jacklin, 1974). Whatever the mechanism, it seems clear that children develop an amalgamated sex role that reflects cultural standards more closely than the sex-role standards exhibited at home.

What then can be concluded about identification as a means of acquiring sex roles? We must agree with the comment that "the evidence for the prevalence or even the sheer existence of these phenomena is extremely sparse" (Brofenbrenner, 1960, p. 38). There is little evidence to support the existence of identification, much less to support the contention that identification accounts for sex-role learning. If parents do have greater influence on their children's sex-role acquisition, then it is probably because the children, in preschool years, are exposed more to their parents than to any other pair of models, and the children perceive themselves as more similar to their own parents than to other adults.

SOCIAL LEARNING THEORY

A second group of psychologists rejected the identification theories and attempted to explain sex-role socialization in terms of the behavioral laws that were being investigated in animal learning laboratories throughout the country. Early in this century, John B. Watson (1919) initiated a new approach to psychology. Objecting to the abstract and largely untestable concepts of most introspective theories—including identification—he stressed the importance of investigating observable behavior rather than covert, unconscious process. His work ushered in the era of *behaviorism*. Innumerable psychologists have since focused their work on establishing behavioral laws to explain the relationship between an animal's behavior and the overt responses of the environment to that behavior. Through the work of scientists like B. F. Skinner, we understand more fully some of the laws governing human and animal behavior. Advocates of social learning theories have used the principles of *reinforcement* and *modeling,* which come from behaviorist orientation, to explain sex-role acquisition.

Comparing Social Learning and Identification Theories

There are several major points of disagreement between the behaviorist approach and that taken by identification theorists. First, identification theorists assume that sex-role learning involves the acquisition of complex patterns of behavior which emerge at one time without a gradual learning process and without reinforcement. In contrast, social-learning theorists have argued that global learning concepts like identification confuse the learning process and that imitation really describes the same process in simpler terms (Bandura, 1969; Mischel, 1970).

Behaviorists maintain that the same process of imitational learning is involved in the learning of both the specific and the complex components of a sex-role: "both concepts [identification and emulation] encompass the same behavioral phenomenon, namely the tendency of the person to reproduce actions, attitudes or emotional responses exhibited by real-life or symbolic models" (Bandura and Walters, 1963, p. 89). Thus, from the social learning point of view, it is only confusing the issue to suggest that there are different factors involved when, for example, a little girl learns to bake a cake and when she learns to enjoy cooking through watching her mother in the kitchen (Bandura, 1969).

This debate regarding the usefulness of a concept like identification continues. Empirical studies have clearly demonstrated that children do learn responses through imitation in the laboratory and that no special emotional attachment is needed for this learning to take place. However, this does not prove that identification does not occur, but only that imitation does occur.

Stability of Sex-Role Learning

Identification theorists assume that once sex-role behavior develops, it becomes a permanent or traitlike part of the personality. This assumption is primarily based on their belief that sex-role acquisition is controlled by internal motives. In contrast, "social learning theorists do not assume that behavior is general or consistent across various situations or across time" (Mischel, 1970).

Because they view sex-role behavior as being maintained by external, social forces rather than internal motives, social learning theorists attribute any consistency which does occur to consistency in the way that society responds to that behavior (Gewirtz, 1969). For example, if a woman exhibits passive behaviors in her business situation, despite the threat of job loss, social learning theory would argue that some strong social pressures must be operating in her environment to maintain her passivity. Perhaps, the men with whom she works are providing sufficient eliciting cues and approval for her passivity. Were they to change their expectations and the basis for their approval to elicit more aggressive responses, her passivity would be expected to disappear.

Age of Sex-Role Learning

Like the identification theorists, social learning theorists assume that much important sex-role learning occurs when the child is relatively young. However, since they do not view sex-role learning as permanent or inflexible, they do not conclude that the child's early learning experiences are unusually formative or irreversible. Instead, the growing child is described as continuing to adopt new behaviors and to alter or eliminate old behaviors from her or his repertoire, as society changes its expectations and reward contingencies for that child. For example, puberty may mark the introduction of a whole new set of contingencies into the life of a developing girl. As other people begin to reward her for expressing greater interest in "feminine" activities, the social-learning theorist would predict that such tomboyish activities as playing baseball and getting A's in math would be replaced by more feminine behaviors such as wearing make-up and playing dumb around boys.

Role of the Same-Sex Parent

The issue on which social learning theory is perhaps most at odds with identification theory is with regard to the hypothesized importance of the parents, or more specifically the same-sex parent, in the sex-role learning process. Basically, social learning theorists do not assume that an emotional bond is a prerequisite for modeling. Instead, they propose that nurturance on the part of the model may facilitate imitation but that imitation will occur even without emotional ties in any situation in which imitation is reinforced. For this reason, social-learning theorists posit that children learn appropriate sex-role behavior through imitation of a wide variety of models, only one of which is the same-sex parent. One such theorist observed that:

> In view of the extensive discrimination training, peer modeling and frequent maternal demonstration of masculine activities at times when the father is absent, it seems highly improbable that a 3-year-old child looks and behaves like a boy primarily as a result of identifying with a 35-year-old man whom he can observe for relatively brief periods. . . . (Bandura, 1969, p. 215).

Children are said to imitate parents, other adults, peers, and heroes in the media according to the particular needs of their ages and the amount of exposure to those models. Each child's role behavior is a unique composite of all his learning experience, rather than a carbon copy of the same-sex parent.

Finally, while social learning theory decreases the relative importance of the parent in the overall socialization process, it does specify additional means by which the parent shapes the child's behavior. Not only do parents provide a model for appropriate behavior, they can also directly reward and punish desired behaviors. Through the provision of sex-typed clothes, toys, and games, and the promoting of same-sex friendships, names, and hair styles, parents also teach appropriate sex-role behaviors.

Motivation for Sex-Role Learning

Unlike the identification theorists, social learning theorists do not posit the existence of any internal motives which cause the child to adopt sex-role behavior regardless of external contingencies. Instead, the incentives to learn are seen as coming from the external social environment. Social learning theorists *do* suggest that after frequent reward for imitation of particular types of behavior or types of models, the child may learn a generalized tendency to imitate (Bandura, 1969). However, this tendency is quite different from the "motive to be like the model" posited by some identification theorists. Social learning theorists explain generalized imitation of a model or models by saying that children imitate many responses when they cannot discriminate between those responses which will be rewarded and those which will not. However, in those situations in which the child is capable of perceiving that the imitation of certain behaviors will not be rewarded, these behaviors will not be imitated. For example, the little girl who imitates many of her older sister's sex-typed behaviors may one day imitate her sister's use of make-up. However, when her parents punish her for this age-inappropriate response (thereby clarifying that the make-up response imitations will not be rewarded), the little girl will be less likely to imitate them again. Therefore, unlike the identification motive, the generalized tendency to imitate proposed by social learning theories remains highly sensitive to variation in the situational contingencies.

Mechanisms Underlying Sex-Role Acquisition

A number of mechanisms are postulated by social learning theorists to explain sex-role acquisition. The simplest and most basic explanation for the acquisition or any behavior is that reinforcement increases the occurrence of the reinforced behavior. Based on this principle, it has been suggested that children perform sex-appropriate responses because they receive direct social and physical rewards for this behavior and avoid sex-inappropriate behaviors because they are punished for them. To be a viable explanation of sex-role acquisition, it must be demonstrated that parents and other socializers differentially reinforce and punish boys and girls in accordance with sex-role standards. For instance, boys on the average are more aggressive than girls. Do parents reward boys more than girls for aggression? Evidence suggests not. Several studies indicate that preschool boys are punished more than girls for their aggressive responses by their parents, especially by their fathers.[3]

Studies focusing on other behaviors also fail to support the hypothesis that parents respond differentially to their preschool children depending on the child's sex. There are few consistent differences, especially during the preschool years. Instead, during these early years parents' behaviors appear to be controlled by the age rather than the sex of the child (Maccoby and Jacklin, 1975).

There is one exception. Boys are spanked and handled more roughly than

---

[3] See Sears, Rau, and Alpert, 1965; Sears, Maccoby, and Levin, 1957; Rothbart and Maccoby, 1966; and Lambert, Yackley, and Hein, 1971.

girls from infancy on. In part, this difference may stem from the belief that girls are more fragile. But this difference may also stem in part from differences in the behavior of the child (Maccoby and Jacklin, 1974). Boys may need to be spanked more because they misbehave more. The fact that boys tend to be more aggressive supports this suggestion.

Even though there are few gender-related behavioral differences, parents do have different expectancies for their children (Parsons, et al., 1976), and clearly defined notions about what behaviors are typical of and appropriate for boys and girls (Lambert, et al., 1971). In addition, both parents themselves and their children feel that parents respond differently to boys and girls (Block, 1977; Maccoby and Jacklin, 1974). One area in which this is clearly expressed is in the purchase of clothes and gifts. Parents monitor their purchases of both clothes and toys in accordance with current sex-role stereotypes. For example, boys get trains and trucks while girls get stoves and dolls.

This process has been called canalization. Children like what is most familiar; by giving girls feminine objects, they will become more familiar with and consequently come to prefer these objects (Hartley, 1960; 1964). This process can be explained in terms of reinforcement. Any behavior which is reinforced increases. But if a child's environment is structured so that sex-appropriate toy choices are much more probable, then the likelihood of being reinforced for sex-appropriate choices increases accordingly. If a girl does not have a truck to play with, she cannot be reinforced for playing with trucks; conversely, if she has lots of dolls, it is very probable that she'll be reinforced for playing with dolls and the incidence of that behavior will increase. Consequently, when given a choice between a truck or a doll, her reinforcement history should bias her choice in favor of the doll. Thus, parents need never punish their children for sex-inappropriate choices. By canalizing their environment, parents insure that sex-appropriate choices will be reinforced more than sex-inappropriate choices. Unfortunately we know of no data testing this hypothesis and consequently cannot evaluate its accuracy at present.

Alternatively, parental purchasing may be under the control of the child's desires. That is, parents may be buying presents that they know the children prefer. Thus it may be the children's preferences that are determining the parental choices rather than the parental choices that are producing the children's sex-typed preferences. While both of these processes are undoubtedly important, to the extent that the child's preferences precede parental choices, the origin of these preferences remains to be explained.

Learning theorists assume that parental attitudes and expectancies are highly important for sex-role learning, but the mechanisms by which these are translated into socialization practices are unclear. When parents are observed, they do *not* consistently differentiate between their sons and daughters for most socialization indices (Maccoby and Jacklin, 1974). This may be because they are being watched. However, parents of older children *do* differentiate more, especially fathers (Block, 1977).

Also, it must be remembered that parents are not the only socializing agents in children's lives. Two studies document the fact that schoolteachers treat boys and girls differently and tend to reinforce stereotypic responses for both sexes (Dweck, 1975; Etaugh, Collins, and Gerson, 1975). Television is also a potent socializing factor which reinforces traditional sex roles (Frueh, and McGhee, 1975).

In summary, one mechanism suggested by learning theorists to explain sex-role acquisition is reinforcement. This view implies that boys and girls are being reinforced differentially for sex-role–appropriate behavior. The evidence for direct differential reinforcements by mothers during the preschool years is very weak. If mothers are creating differential reinforcement histories for these young children, it is occurring at a very subtle level, e.·g., through canalization or in responses to behavioral differences in children. Direct pressures—from peers, parents, and other adults—to conform to sex-role stereotypes may increase as children get older. Evidence with school-age children and college students suggests that this may be true. Consequently, these principles may be more useful for explaining the persistence of behaviors once they are learned. It seems likely that reinforcement does play a role in controlling specific behaviors in specific situations. It is doubtful, however, that reinforcement alone accounts for more general sex-role behaviors like career or life-style choice, or that it can account completely for the acquisition of new behaviors.

MODELING

Two additional mechanisms suggested by social-learning theorists to explain the acquisition of sex-role behaviors are observational learning and imitation. These two processes produce what is called modeling, that is, copying the behavior of others. Advocates of the importance of modeling assume that children can learn from observing the behaviors of others. In addition, they assume that observational learning and imitation are essential to the acquisition of social behavior (Bandura, 1969; Mischel, 1966; 1970; Bandura and Walters, 1963).

In its simplest form, modeling occurs when a child imitates or copies the behavior of some model. However, before modeling can take place, a child must attend to and learn correctly the behavior of the model. The distinction between these two processes—learning and performance—is crucial (Bandura, 1969). Not all behaviors that are learned by observation will be imitated. For instance, a girl may observe a model being aggressive and not imitate that model for any of a variety of reasons. Nor can it be assumed that all imitated behaviors will continue to be performed. Performance is determined not only by prior observational learning but also by the response of the environment to the child's behavior. Consequently, if a child's imitative responses are punished, these responses will decrease in frequency and perhaps cease altogether. Thus, for modeling to affect behavior, a child must observe the behavior to be modeled, and must be motivated to imitate that behavior. If either of these links is missing modeling may not occur, and its utility as a causal explanation for social learning is seriously reduced.

If modeling is to account for sex-role acquisition it must be shown that boys and girls either observe or imitate male and female models differentially. In this section we will discuss theoretical explanations for and empirical evidence of either differential observation or differential imitation.

Observation

For observational learning to account for sex-role learning, it must be assumed that girls are more likely to observe feminine models while boys are more likely to observe masculine models. This assumption would be fulfilled in one of two conditions: one in which the children are exposed to different models or one in which the children are exposed to the same models but attend differentially to these models. If it can be demonstrated that either of these conditions exists, there would be reason to believe that differential observation learning contributed to sex-role learning.

As boys get older there may be a slight tendency for boys to spend more time with their fathers than girls. At least it is part of the common folklore that boys and their fathers play ball, go fishing, and do other "male" things together. If this belief is true, boys may have differential exposure to male models. However, this exposure occurs well after primary sex-role learning has taken place. Thus, it is likely that this differential exposure is the result rather than cause of sex-role learning.

To be an effective cause, differential exposure must occur during the early years of development. However, it seems unlikely that young children are exposed to different models (Maccoby and Jacklin, 1974). If anything, both boys and girls spend most of their time during their early years with female models—their mother, grandmothers, aunts, nursery and elementary school teachers (predominantly female), and female shop clerks and babysitters. Furthermore, fathers, when they are at home, spend an equal amount of time with their sons and daughters (Pedersen and Robson, 1969). Thus, there is little reason to believe that sex differences are the result of differential exposure to male and female roles. In fact, with the disproportionate exposure to female models during the preschool years, it is amazing that both boys and girls do not adopt a feminine sex-role.

Alternatively, even though children are exposed to the same models, it is possible that boys attend more to the behaviors of male models while girls attend more to the behaviors of female models. Thus, children could learn different behaviors while observing the same subset of models. Studies with adults and older children suggest that this may be true to some extent. For example, there is a tendency for seventh-grade children to recall more behaviors exhibited by a same-sex film character than to a cross-sex character (Maccoby and Wilson, 1957). Similarly, "masculine" children of both sexes recalled more behaviors of a male than a female model (Perry and Perry, 1975).

If children do attend differentially to behaviors of males and females, the next obvious question is why? If is possible that children are being differentially reinforced for attending to the same-sex model. For example, Mom may reward Johnny for watching Dad but ignore Mary's attention to her father. Conversely Mom and others may reward Mary for watching females but not for observing males. Unfortunately there are no data available with which to evaluate this hypothesis. An alternative explanation suggests that children pay differential attention to same-sex models because they want information that is consistent with their sex-role identity. That is, children are attending to same-sex models because they have already formed their sex-role identity and are seeking information that will assist their behavior appropriately. This explanation will be discussed more fully in the next chapter (Kohlberg, 1966; Hetherington, 1967).

Imitation

Advocates of a second category of explanations make no assumption about differential observation or learning. Instead they suggest that sex differences emerge from differential imitation. In a classic study, boys, under normal conditions, were found to be more likely to imitate an aggressive model than were girls. However, when told that they would be reinforced for imitating the model, both girls and boys imitated the aggressive model's behavior. Apparently, all children had learned the behavior, but the boys imitated the behavior significantly more often than the girls. (Bandura, Ross, and Ross, 1963a).

To be a viable explanation of sex-role acquisition, it would be necessary to show that children imitated same-sex models more than opposite-sex models. But evidence indicates that children's imitation is controlled by several factors: the model's power, dominance, and warmth, as well as the model's sex. Both boys and girls imitate a cross-sex model when that model controls the rewards (Bandura, Ross, and Ross, 1963a; 1963b). Similarly, children imitate the dominant parent, regardless of sex (Hetherington, 1965). Thus, on the whole, evidence that children do differentially imitate same-sex models is equivocal. In some conditions the sex of model does influence imitation. But in other situations, other cues exert a more powerful influence on modeling. To the extent that these additional cues coincide with sex-appropriate behaviors they should support sex-role learning for one sex or the other. In contrast, to the extent that the cues contradict sex-appropriate behaviors, they should serve to inhibit sex-role learning. For example, in many homes fathers are the most powerful models. In these families, power should facilitate the acquisition of sex-role behaviors by boys but discourage the acquisition of sex-role behaviors by girls. However, children do learn their sex roles; when they reach adulthood the vast majority of them adopt traditional roles.

Furthermore, even for those situations which foster same-sex modeling, it is still important to explain why same-sex emulation occurs. The reinforcement model implies that same-sex modeling occurs because children are reinforced for imitating same-sex models more frequently than they are reinforced for imitating cross-sex models. However, as discussed earlier, evidence for this differential reward is sparse, especially for children in their preschool years.

Alternatively, children may imitate same-sex models because they expect to be reinforced for that behavior, or because they have been vicariously reinforced by observing others being rewarded for that particular behavior (Bandura and Walters, 1963). This hypothesis would also explain why children imitate same-sex models in some situations and not others. But once again this explanation implies that children already know what is appropriate behavior in any given situation. Consequently it is still unclear whether same-sex imitating is the result or the cause of sex-role learning.

Finally, same-sex imitation will produce sex-typed behavior only if the same-sex model is exhibiting sex-role appropriate behaviors. If the primary models are exhibiting a more varied array of behaviors, or if the child is exposed to wide variety of models, then it is to be expected that the child will exhibit less sex-stereotyped behaviors.

There is little doubt that reinforcements are powerful shapers of behavior and, consequently, that reinforcements are responsible for the acquisition of some specific sex-role–appropriate behaviors. Likewise, evidence demonstrates that children learn a variety of behaviors through observation and imitation. However, the manipulation of a variety of independent and dependent variables has revealed such a wide range of results that the interpretation of modeling effects is quite difficult. It seems that modeling may be both the result of sex-role identity and the cause of subsequent sex-role learning. Internal motivational and dispositional factors may be important mediators of social learning (Mischel, 1973b).

Thus, it seems that neither identification theories nor social learning theories are sufficient to explain the role socialization plays in sex-role acquisition. Both of these theories play down the role of the child as an active learner in the process of sex-role acquisition. The cognitive-developmental interpretation of social learning offers one explanation that includes both the child and his social environment. Thus this approach bridges, to some extent, the gap between identification and social learning theories. It is to this theoretical approach that we now turn.

7 Cognitive-Developmental Theories of Sex-Role Socialization

Recently, a new theoretical framework, based on the pioneering work of Swiss psychologist Jean Piaget, has emerged. Early in this century Piaget began his study of the thought patterns and logic of children. Based on this early work, Piaget and other cognitive-developmentalists have carefully outlined the limitations placed on children's reasoning powers at different ages or in different stages of cognitive maturity. In his work on cognition, Piaget has intoduced many important concepts that have added to our understanding of development. Several of these are particularly important for our discussion of sex-role acquisition. First, he suggested that people create *schemata*—mental categories and operations—through their interactions with the world. Once formed, these schemata influence subsequent interpretations of reality. New information is either assimilated into or leads to the accommodation of, or change in existing schemata.

Secondly, Piaget suggested that adaptive functioning, which he called *equilibrium,* reflects a balance between assimilatory and accommodative processes. Thus when one is in a state of equilibrium, one is both modifying new information to fit preexisting schemata and is adjusting one's schemata to fit new information.

Finally, Piaget theorizes that children go through various stages in their cognitive development. Passage through these stages is marked by alternate states of cognitive equilibrium and disequilibrium. During the equilibration

Jacquelynne Parsons was the primary author of this chapter.

state of each stage, the child's thinking is characterized by certain properties which limit the child's reasoning ability and her or his ability to interact with and use information in the environment. Piaget specified four stages: the sensory motor period (0–2 years), the preoperational period (2–6 years), the concrete operational period (6–11), and the formal operational period (11–adult).

During the period of sensory-motor thought, the infant acquires basic cognitive skills that enable her or him to make sense of the world. These skills include the ideas of object permanence, size and shape constancy, primitive conceptions of cause and effect, and rudimentary symbolic and representational thought.

During the second stage—the period of preoperational thought—the child's thinking is self-centered, irreversible, and perception-bound. Because of these properties of thought, the child cannot solve simple conservation problems. For example, if we present the child with two identically shaped beakers filled with equal amounts of liquid, the child will perceive the equality in the two volumes. However, if we pour the liquid from one beaker into a taller, thinner beaker, the child will no longer perceive the volume as equal. She or he will center on one perceptual cue, either height or width, and say that the taller or wider beaker now contains more liquid. The child is apparently not aware that changes in one dimension can be compensated for by changes in the other dimension. Consequently, she or he does not comprehend the idea of conservation of volume, that is, the child is not aware that we can change the peripheral dimension, in this case height and width, without changing the central dimension of volume.

Harvard psychologist Lawrence Kohlberg argues that the same process influences the child's conception of gender. Children may think that changes in peripheral cues, like hair length or style, produce changes in gender. For example, a child might see a woman with short hair and insist that she is a man despite the parents' insistence that she is indeed a woman with short hair.

During the period of concrete operations, the child acquires the cognitive skills necessary for conservation and classification. But her or his thinking is limited to concrete settings. Abstract problems and symbolic reasoning still pose problems. According to Piaget, it is not until the final stage that the child acquires mature cognitive capabilities.

As Piaget's ideas have become more widely accepted, several researchers have begun to extend them to understanding various aspects of social development (e.g., Flavell, 1977; Parsons, 1976a). One of these groups are the cognitive-developmental theorists, who have been concerned with sex-role development. The theories they have developed differ from the classic (Freudian and social-learning) theories outlined in Chapter 6 on two key assumptions. First, cognitive-developmental theorists assume that children play a very active role in their development. Motivated by a desire for competence and mastery over their world, children seek out any information that will improve their interaction with both their physical and social world. Second, cognitive-developmental theorists assume that the children's interaction with and interpretation of their world are limited by their cognitive maturity, which, in turn, is linked to their present stage of development.

Both of these assumptions reflect a much different view of the child and lead to distinct interpretations of the sex-role acquisition process. Several theorists such as Kohlberg have suggested specific interpretations of this process. Before discussing the work of Kohlberg and its possible extension, the major differences between a cognitive-developmental approach and the other two theoretical approaches will be presented.

DIFFERENCES AMONG THEORIES OF SEX-ROLE ACQUISITION

There are several differences between the cognitive-developmental explanation of sex-role acquisition and those of Freudian identification and social-learning theories. Major distinctions among these theories are found in four areas: the motivational basis, the sequencing of the developmental stages, the importance of cognitive processes, and the role of culture.

Motivational Basis

One major difference between cognitive-developmental explanations and the Freudian identification and social-learning theories lies in the motivational basis of imitation. Identification theorists assume that imitation is motivated by fear of separation from a love object. In contrast, cognitive-developmentalists assume a more positive motivational basis for the acquisition of behaviors. They suggest that children imitate same-sex models because they are motivated to maintain a competent, positive self-image and to master the behaviors which they judge to be appropriate for themselves (Kohlberg, 1966).

Similarly, in comparison to the social-learning approach, cognitive-developmentalists have assumed a more active motivational basis for imitation. Advocates of the social-learning view suggest that children automatically imitate certain behaviors because they have been rewarded for doing so either vicariously or directly. In contrast, cognitive-developmentalists assume that the child's primary desire is one of mastery, and conclude that rewards have their effect because they provide useful information regarding mastery and competence.

In terms of sex-role acquisition, cognitive-developmental theorists suggest that rewards serve as cues regarding the appropriateness of various objects and activities. These cues help in the formation of sex-role identity. Once

Box 1   Comparison of the Three Theoretical Positions of Sex-Role
          Development

Freudian-Identification	*Social Learning*	*Cognitive-Development*
Role of Innate Characteristics		
Large role: anatomy is destiny; body structure determines personality	No·role	Small role: cognitive maturation; structuring of experience; development of gender identity
Role of Child in Learning Process		
Active	Passive	Active
Motive		
Internal: reduce fear and anxiety	External: reinforcements Internal: expected reinforcements	Internal: desire for competence
Permanence of Learning		
Very permanent and irreversible	Permanent only if external reinforcements or self-reinforcements maintain behavior; difficulty in changing comes from internalized self-reinforcements and conditioned emotional responses.	Semi-permanent once schemata are stabilized; change depends on presentation of discrepant information and on the child's cognitive maturity.
Sources of Learning		
Parents or parent surrogates	Parents as well as the larger social system	Parents and the larger social system in interaction with the child's cognitive system.
Age of Learning Sex Identity		
By 4 or 5	Throughout life, but early years are very important	Throughout life, but years between 3–20 are most important; years between 6–8 and 16–18 are crucial for change in stereotypic beliefs.

children have categorized themselves as male or female they will strive to imitate behaviors that are congruent with this self-image. If these behaviors are rewarded, so much the better, but the rewards are clearly regarded as secondary. In fact, the child's gender-role identity, once formed, determines what is rewarding. Consequently, it is predicted that children will respond primarily to the rewards for "appropriate" behaviors, tending to ignore rewards for behaviors they judge inappropriate according to their own self-image.

> Our view of the importance of gender identity in psychosexual development is not shared by many social-learning theorists, including Walter Mischel. . . . In Mischel's view, sex-typed behavior and attitudes are acquired through social rewards that follow sex-appropriate responses made by the child or by a relevant model. The social-learning syllogism is: "I want rewards, I am rewarded for doing boy things, therefore I want to be a boy." In contrast, a cognitive theory assumes this sequence: "I am a boy, therefore I want to do boy things, therefore the opportunity to do boy things (and to gain approval for doing them) is rewarding." (Kohlberg, 1966, p. 89.)[1]

There is some evidence to support the cognitive-developmental point of view. Children do seem to selectively attend to and imitate behaviors they see as appropriate and they do this beginning at a very early age (Bandura, Ross, and Ross, 1963a; Maccoby and Wilson, 1957). In a study with eight- and nine-year-old-girls who rated videotaped behavioral sequences and later observed the same tapes again, it was found that the girls imitated behavior they had rated positively significantly more than they imitated behaviors which they had rated less favorably (Hicks, 1971). Similarly, when shown a video sequence of an adult male and female interacting, "masculine" children of both sexes recalled more behavior of the male model than of the female model (Perry and Perry, 1975). In addition, in another study preschool boys preferred "masculine" activities despite greater reinforcement by the teacher for participation in "feminine" activities (Fagot and Patterson, 1969). Taken together these studies suggest that children's behaviors are influenced by their value system and sex-role orientation.

Additional support for the cognitive-developmental perspective comes from a variety of studies investigating the effects of sex labeling on children's preferences and behavior.[2] In summary, these studies show that children prefer objects that have been labeled as sex-appropriate (Liebert, McCall, and

---

[1] A more recent paper by Walter Mischel (1973b) suggests that he has altered his position on this issue somewhat. In that paper Mischel concluded that cognitive interpretations by the individual are important mediators in the process of social learning, and that, in fact, cognitive processes determine to a large extent the reward values of various stimuli.

[2] See Hartup, Moore, and Sager, 1963; Liebert, McCall, and Hanratty, 1971; Montemayor, 1974; Parsons, 1976b; Ross and Ross, 1972; and Thompson, 1973.

Hanratty, 1971; Thompson, 1973); work harder on tasks labeled as sex-appropriate (Montemayor, 1974); resist attempts to reinforce them for sex-inappropriate preferences (Hartup, Moore, and Sager, 1963); and prefer same-sex peers (Kohlberg and Zigler, 1966; Parsons, 1976b).

Thus, it does seem that to some extent children imitate behaviors and develop preferences that are congruent with their sex-role identity. On the other hand, several studies indicate that parental responses and children's expectancies of parental preferences do effect children's sex-role preference. For example, studies of first-grade girls and boys (Mussen and Rutherford, 1963), of third- and fourth-grade girls and boys (Lefkowitz, 1962), and of children ages four to eleven years (Hetherington, 1965), have shown that the quality of the parent-child relationship influences children's preference for their own sex role. Similarly, a study of five-year-olds suggests that children may prefer appropriate sex-role activities because they perceive that parents prefer such sex-appropriate activity (Fauls and Smith, 1956). In addition, inappropriate behaviors have been induced by exposure to older models who perform sex-inappropriate behaviors (Wolf, 1975). Lastly, more data suggest that adult reinforcement of "feminine" activities can influence the behavior of two-year-old boys (Etaugh, Collins, and Gerson, 1975). Thus, it seems that both cognitive mechanisms and social-learning processes interact in sex-role acquisition.

Sequence of Developmental Stages

Another major difference between cognitive-developmental explanations and both social-learning and identification theories lies in the sequence of steps in the acquisition process. A brief summary of the sequence of events suggested by each theoretical position is shown in Box 2. Both the social-learning and identification views assume that the child's sex-typed identity is the consequence of identification or imitation. In contrast, Kohlberg has suggested exactly the reverse, concluding that sex-typed identity is the precursor rather than the consequence of attachment or identification.

In support of the cognitive-developmental approach, much evidence suggests that children know their own sex by age three,[3] that in some cases they are already playing somewhat different sex roles as early as two years of age,[4] and, finally, that children are well aware of cultural sex-role stereotypes by two and a half, and prefer sex-appropriate toys by the age of two.[5] These three lines of research, coupled with evidence that parents are not differen-

---

[3] See Gesell, et al., 1940; Money, Hampson, 1957; and Thompson, 1973.

[4] See Etaugh, Collins, and Gerson, 1975; Fagot and Littman, 1975; and Fagot and Patterson, 1969.

[5] See Brown, 1956; Fein, Johnson, Stork, and Wasserman, 1975; Nadelman, 1974; and Parsons, 1976b.

Box 2   **Sequence of Events in Sex-Role Acquisition**

Freudian-Identification	*Social Learning*	*Cognitive-Developmental*

1. Oedipus complex emerges	1. a. Perception of parent as model
	   b. Differential reinforcement for same-sex modeling and for sex-appropriate behaviors and interests
		1. a. Gender identity
		   b. Valuing of own-sex models

2. Identification with same-sex parent	2. Differential modeling and imitation	2. Sex-role identity
3. Sex-role identity	3. Generalization of behaviors	3. Modeling of same-sex parent, peers, and other adults
4. Imitation of same-sex parent	4. Sex-role identity	4. Attachment to same-sex parent

tially reinforcing children at these ages (Maccoby and Jacklin, 1974), and that modeling has little effect on the children's toy preference (Fein, et al., 1975), suggest that children acquire their sex-role identity and then imitate appropriate-sex models rather than the reverse. But, as noted earlier, this conclusion does not rule out the importance of reinforcement or modeling. Instead it shifts the emphasis from the reinforcer or model to the child as the key person in the process.

Importance of Cognitive Processes

In contrast to both identification and social-learning theories, cognitive-developmentalists assume that the initial emergence of gender as an important social category is the result of the child's cognitive system rather than the result of either psychosexual dynamics or the impact of external models and rewards. Cognitive-developmental psychologists have identified two features of four- to five-year-old children's cognitive systems that would tend to bias them toward seeing gender as an important category with which to classify behavior. First, children's thinking at this age is concrete. That is, they focus on specific, physical cues that can be perceived and understood easily. Gender, race, height, and age are perhaps the most obvious concrete cues children can use to classify people. Each of these four cues is associated with a number of physical cues. For instance, gender is commonly associated with dress, hair length, facial hair, body build, height, other secondary sex characteristics, and the form of the genitals (Katcher, 1955; Thompson and Bentler, 1971). A child can use any one of these physical cues or any combination in classifying by gender. In addition, children's thinking at this age is characterized by the overuse of one cue in making judgments. Piaget has demonstrated that preschool-age children tend to focus on one cue when asked to categorize stimuli. This cue tends to be a concrete cue which the child has used before (Flavell, 1977). Consequently, having once learned the importance of gender, it is to be expected that children will use it as a simple, concrete classification cue for a variety of social behaviors.

The child's culture also reinforces the child's use of gender as a social category. Parents go to great lengths to make children aware of their own gender and the gender of others. People are continually differentiated by gender through the use of pronouns and names. Thus, the child becomes aware that gender is both an obvious and an important cue. Since gender is so obvious in our culture and since the child's social environment does use gender as a basis for categorizing human behavior, the child should make use of this cue to help her or him interpret the myriad of information available.[6] Thus the cognitive-developmental view leads to the prediction that gender will always emerge as a categorical aid and will serve as a basis for early stereotyping of behavior.

The findings that such strong stereotypes exist, develop so early, and are prevalent in every culture support the conclusion that some very basic processes are involved in sex-role stereotyping. Further evidence indicates that very young children will use stereotypes based on gender despite the diversity of roles in their own homes (Emmerich, 1959; Hartley, 1959, 1960, 1964; Smith, 1966). For example, the sex-role stereotypes of father-absent boys are not significantly different from the stereotypes of father-present boys (Smith, 1966).

This brings us to a related issue that can be analyzed within the cognitive-developmental framework: How stable are these categories of male/female behaviors and how can they be changed? It is to be expected that these early stereotypes will continue to be voiced for several years despite efforts to change them. Work by Piaget indicates that children will persist in basing judgments on concrete cues even though their judgments are incorrect. It is not until the children's cognitive system begins to change that they may be motivated to reevaluate the usefulness of these concrete cues. As they enter the stage of concrete operations at the age of six to seven, they begin to use more than one cue and to abstract out more subtle classificatory aids.

Attempts to change sex-role attitudes of preschoolers and first- and second-graders have met with limited success. In one recent effort there was

---

[6] Race is another obvious cue that a child could use and indeed will use unless she is shown that race as a category is not a useful cue for understanding her world.

some success in changing behavior through exposure to stereotyped and sex-role reversal storybooks (MacArthur and Eisen, 1976). On the other hand there has been some difficulty in replicating this finding (Yulish, 1976). Similarly, producing changes in sex-role stereotyping of two- to eight-year-olds was also unsuccessful (Marr, 1974). In addition, stereotyping was found among preschool and elementary school children enrolled in a private school that had the elimination of sex-role stereotyping as one of its major goals (Parsons, 1976b).

Does this mean that stereotypes are impossible to eliminate? No. Data gathered on tasks that involve physical objects indicate that children do come to change their schemata (Flavell, 1968). During the stage of concrete operations (7–11) children gradually accommodate their earlier schemata. For example, in conversion of volume tasks they come to conclude that changes in the shape of a container do not change its volume (see above). They begin to use both height and width cues and become aware that changes in one dimension can be compensated for by changes in the other dimension without changing the volume of the liquid. Similarly, if we persist in giving children information which will force them to question their use of gender as a classifactory cue, then accommodation might eventually take place. In support of this belief, cross-sectional developmental data suggest that, under certain circumstances, children's stereotypes become less rigid with age.[7] However, other studies suggest that children develop more rigid stereotypes with age, especially regarding sex-inappropriate behaviors (Rabban, 1950; A. H. Stein, 1971; Stein and Smithells, 1969). Perhaps a key variable in determining whether children's stereotypic categories will change with age is their exposure to information that is discrepant with their categorical system. While this hypothesis has yet to be tested, some studies indirectly suggest that it might be true. A study of play behavior of children on a kibbutz revealed that older children (six-year-olds) engaged in less sex-typed behaviors than younger children (four-year-olds). It would seem that the younger children selected behavior on the basis of sex-role appropriateness. However, as they got older, the children observed adults of both sexes performing many of the behaviors which they thought of as being sex-typed. Consequently, they changed their schemata regarding what was inappropriate and began to practice those behaviors that were most valued on the kibbutz. Therefore, with age, general sex-role standards were replaced by kibbutz-role standards (Eisenberg, 1974).

Similarly, two other studies investigating the effects of environment on sex-role stereotypes reported results indicating that school-age children living in environments which exposed them to a greater diversity of roles had less stereotypic attitudes than children living in an environment with less

[7] See Atwood, 1969; Bennett and Cohen, 1959; Emmerich, 1961; Hartley, 1964; Shepard and Hess, 1975.

role diversity (Minuchin, 1965; Rabban, 1950). Finally, another study found that children who spent a lot of time watching TV had more stereotypic attitudes than children who spent less time watching TV. To the extent that TV provides a continual source of reinforcement for stereotypic schemata, one would expect high TV viewers not to reduce their stereotypic attitude with age. This is exactly what was found in this study (Frueh and McGhee, 1975).

Thus, a cognitive-developmental approach would lead to the conclusion that gender will emerge as an early classificatory cue, that it will form the basis for stable and persistent stereotypes throughout the preschool and early elementary-school years, and that change in these stereotypes will depend both on exposure of the child to egalitarian models and information and on the child's cognitive maturity. Empirical evidence for the first conclusion is quite strong. Children do use gender as a classificatory cue. This phenomenon occurs quite early and is pervasive. Evidence for the second conclusion is still tentative. There are some data suggesting that stereotypes are common and fairly universal among children ranging in age from four to adolescence. Direct evidence for the third conclusion is not yet available.

The Role of Culture

This brings us to the final distinction—the role of culture. Cognitive-developmentalists believe that it is the child's cognitive organization and not parental reinforcement, modeling, or identification that is the basis for a child's understanding of sex role. It is assumed by cognitive-developmental theorists that a child's conception of his world, both physical and social, comes about through the child's structuring of incoming information into cognitive schemata and then generalizing these schemata to new situations. The child is searching for the patterns in the chaos of sensory inputs. This approach places major emphasis on the child rather than on the socializing agents and the culture. But it does not rule out any significant role for culture in the sex-role acquisition process. While identification theorists play down the role of culture, except as it is indicated through the parents' behavior, and while social-learning theorists place main emphasis on the role of culture as mediated by reinforcement and role models, cognitive-developmentalists emphasize the interaction of the child with her or his culture.[8] Even though cognitive processes structure the categories the child will create, culture dictates, to a larger extent, the variety of sensory inputs available, and thus has an important influence on both the child's categories and her or his generalizations. Furthermore, by providing alternative models,

---

[8] Like cognitive-developmentalists, identification theorists do stress an interaction of the child with her or his parents, but the identification theorists stress psychosocial processes rather than cognitive processes.

culture also provides part of the impetus for change in one's cognitive schemata. Consequently, the system of categories, the nature of the categories, and the extent and rigidity of children's generalizations are inevitably a function of the culture in which they are raised.

An observed interaction between a young boy and a neighbor couple illustrates this point. One day when the boy and his mother were visiting them, the woman offered both her husband and the boy's mother some coffee, which they both accepted. The boy watched as they started to drink and then rushed over to the man, insisting that he shouldn't drink the coffee. When asked why, he replied, "Only mommies drink coffee." In his family, only his mother drank coffee. The parents had never paid any attention to this difference but apparently the boy had. He had incorporated this familial distinction into his categorical system. If both his parents had been coffee-drinkers, he would not have seen coffee drinking as sex-role related.

On a much larger scale, culture structures the data which a child uses to form his gender-role stereotypes. To the extent that a child's family is influenced by cultural norms, one's culture dictates the behaviors of a child's first role-models. Moreover, culture dictates the behaviors of role-models projected in every realm of the mass-media network. Television characters act out the cultural stereotypes. News media point out the consequences for violations of gender-role norms. Storybooks and textbooks depict cultural stereotypes and illustrate both the rewards for conformity and the punishment for deviation. Finally, to the extent that her or his friends are being exposed to similar social information, culture determines the behaviors of the child's peer role-models. The conclusion is clear. Confronted with this pattern of social stimuli, the child will form a gender-role stereotype that conforms to the cultural stereotype. Furthermore, unless the culture provides some diverse or discrepant role-model, there will be no reason for children to question the validity of their stereotype and no reason for them to accommodate their gender-role schemata.

In addition to structuring the social sensory inputs of the child, culture also influences the responses of others toward the child. We have already discussed some of the mechanisms through which the social responses of others can affect children's behavior. But, in addition to reinforcement and modeling effects, social responses also provide the child with a wealth of information about the normative and prescriptive dimensions of sex roles. This social feedback also helps a child to form sex-role schemata.

Thus, culture interacts with cognitive development in the course of sex-role acquisition. Through the behavior of models and through their responses to the child, culture provides the sensory inputs which serve as the basis for the child's stereotypes. In addition, the culture can affect the speed of one's cognitive development. If specific sex roles are obvious and important in a given culture, then a child is likely to form sex-role schemata easily and early. On the other hand, if sex roles are less obvious or less important, then it should be more difficult for the child to abstract out cognitive schemata based on sex. Consequently, she or he should develop less clearly defined schemata and these schemata should emerge at a later point in development. For example, a study of middle- and working-class children ranging in age from three to eight years, found that although children of both classes identify the sex of dolls with equal accuracy, the children of the working class were able to identify the stereotypic characteristics of the doll's sex role earlier than were middle-class children (Rabban, 1950). Data from other sources suggest that masculinity and femininity are more clearly defined by the parents in working-class families than by the parents in middle-class families. It therefore seems likely that this cultural difference works to speed up cognitive awareness of sex differences in working-class children.

KOHLBERG'S MODEL OF SEX-ROLE ACQUISITION

According to Kohlberg (1966; 1969) children pass through three major cognitive steps in the process of acquiring sex-role behaviors. First, they discover that people come in two sexes, and that they themselves are members of one of these two subgroups. Out of this awareness grows gender identity. That is, children come to know their own sex and begin to categorize others as either males or females. With time and cognitive growth, gender identity becomes more stable. In effect, children come to believe that one's gender does not change. As this belief in the constancy of gender emerges, children also begin to categorize behaviors and objects as appropriate for one sex or the other. That is, they use gender as an "organizer" for much of the information in their social world. These categories form the basis for later stereotypes.

Second, based on gender identity, on the categorization of sex-appropriate behaviors, and on egocentric thinking, children develop a system of values for various behaviors and attitudes. Specifically, each child comes to value behaviors and attitudes associated with her or his own sex more than behaviors and attitudes associated with the other sex. As a result of this differential valuing, children begin to imitate sex-appropriate behaviors and to avoid sex-inappropriate behaviors and objects. During this period children begin to model the behaviors of other individuals of their own sex.

Finally, as a result of this differential valuing and differential modeling, each child develops an emotional attachment (identification) with the same-sex parent. This attachment then leads to further imitative behavior and role structuring. But the child's developing sex-role identity continues to be influenced by a variety of outside forces as well.

The Emergence of a Stable Gender Identity

Kohlberg suggested that the first and most important step in sex-role acquisition is the emergence of a stable gender identity. Once formed, this gender identity serves as the "basic organizer of sex-role attitudes," and influences differential valuing of sex-appropriate objects and behaviors (1966). The gradual emergence of a stable gender identity begins at about two and a half to three years of age. In support of Kohlberg's conclusion, a study showed that children are able to classify their own sex consistently and accurately by the age of three (Thompson, 1973). Particularly dramatic evidence for the early acquisition of gender identity comes from studies performed at Johns Hopkins Hospital by John Money.

Money and his colleagues have found that gender reassignment after the age of two and a half is psychologically dangerous. But gender reassignment, with or without surgical corrections, carried out before eighteen months is usually successful, provided the child's social interactants, like parents, accept the reassignment and modify their behavior accordingly (see Chapter 5; Money and Ehrhardt, 1972; Money and Tucker, 1975).

Does all of this mean that children, by age three, have developed a stable gender identity for themselves or that gender will now form a stable category for organizing the child's conception of her or his social world? Kohlberg suggested not, arguing instead that children must be able to identify the sex of others correctly and must have accepted the constancy of gender identity both for themselves and others before gender can serve as a basic cognitive organizer. Since most children cannot correctly label the sex of others until four or five (Rabban, 1950; Thompson and Bentler, 1971), and are not convinced of the constancy of gender identity until six (DeVries, 1969; Kohlberg, 1966), Kohlberg argued that stable gender identity does not develop until five or six. Furthermore, because Kohlberg considers cognitive development to be the causal process underlying the acquisition of a stable gender identity, he argued that a child should not be able to form stable gender identity until she or he has reached the period of concrete operations and is aware that certain central dimensions of objects remain constant despite peripheral changes in less important dimensions.

In other words, Kohlberg argued that the developmental timetable for emerging gender identity corresponds with the developmental timetable associated with the emergence of a child's cognitive-developmental stages as outlined by Piaget. Consequently, Kohlberg predicted that stable gender identity would not be formed until the age of six. Using as criteria for a stable gender identity that children accpet the constancy of gender for themselves and others, two studies revealed that more than 50 percent of five-year-old children asked still believed that people could change their gender if they so desired (DeVries, 1969; Kohlberg, 1966).

What then can be concluded? Children are aware of their own sex by three. But, as Kohlberg suggested, these same children are not yet able to identify the sex of others, nor are they convinced that gender is a constant trait of the individual. It is not until five or six that they have accepted the permanence of gender. This much seems true. However, Kohlberg went on to conclude that children should not be able to use gender as a cognitive organizer until they have accepted the constancy of gender, that is, by age five or six. But data on stereotyping and same-sex peer preferences indicate that children are using gender as a classification cue well before their fifth or sixth year (Maccoby and Jacklin, 1974; Parsons, 1976b). Furthermore, a recent summary of the gender reassignment studies indicated that gender identity is difficult to change after the age of two, suggesting that stability of some kind has been established well before five or six years of age (Money and Ehrhardt, 1972). And, it is unclear that one's willingness to argue that gender might be changeable actually reflects a belief that gender is unstable or very likely to change. A child might well believe that gender could change under extraordinary or magical circumstances (especially if the experimenter offers such a suggestion) and still be reasonably certain that her or his gender and the gender of those around her or him will remain constant. It seems then that gender may be used as a stable cue much earlier than Kohlberg (1966; 1969) suggested and that the emergence of conservation skills in the physical domain are not necessary precursors to the emergence of gender as an important stable social category.

From Acquiring Gender Identity to Stereotyping

Directly related to acquisition of gender identity is the child's sex-role stereotyping of behavior and objects. Kohlberg suggested that having once become aware that people can be categorized on the basis of gender, children would use gender to provide structure for their social environment. For example, it would not be unusual for a son to comment, "Mommies go to school while daddies go to work," if his mother was a graduate student and his father worked for the Veterans Administration Hospital. He would be accustomed to having his mother going to school and his father to work. By using their behavior patterns to form his categories of male (Daddy) and female (Mommy), he would form a schema of what it is to be male or female in this society.

Kohlberg suggested that all children form these schemata. Once formed, these categories provide children with a framework for interpreting what they see and for predicting future behavior. New information is assimilated through these schemata, and children develop expectancies regarding human behavior based on these categories. Empirical evidence supports this conclusion. Preschool children are well aware of cultural stereotypes regarding sex differences by the age of four and use these stereotypes to predict behavior. In virtually every study in which children are asked to predict the behavior or preference of someone else, sex-role stereotypes emerge as a key organizing factor for all children over the age of four (Brown, 1956; Schell and Silber, 1968; Nadelman, 1974).

Given the mass of contradictory evidence regarding sex differences in behavior, this consistency in the research findings on stereotyping is impressive and leads us to believe that the propensity to categorize and to stereotype is indeed a powerful phenomena. Perhaps it is even one of the basic processes of our cognitive development. In our opinion, it is this process, that is, the formation of male and female schemata through categorization, assimilation, and generalization, that is the basis for a child's creation of sex-role stereotypes.

While this process is influenced by cognitive processes, it is also undoubtedly influenced by external socialization agents such as parents, peers, and television. To the extent that parents respond uncritically to children's stereotypic judgments and model stereotypic thinking, children's stereotypes will be reinforced and strengthened. In addition, while these cognitive processes are assumed to be universal, variations in cultural experiences are expected to produce a wide range of stereotypic beliefs.

Sex-Role Preference

For sex-role acquisition to be complete, a child must develop a preference for, as well as an awareness of, the role associated with her gender (Kohlberg, 1966). That is, a girl must prefer the behaviors, objects, and roles stereotyped as female and incorporate these into her behavior if she is to learn her female role. Once children have developed a sex-role preference, they do model sex-appropriate behaviors and respond differentially to rewards for sex-appropriate behaviors. But first, children must come to value their own sex role. Kohlberg suggested that the emergence of this differential value structure is a necessary consequence of certain characteristics of the child's cognitive system. In particular, he suggested that egocentric thought would produce a preference for one's own sex and subsequently for one's own sex role. Egocentrism is one characteristic of the thought of preschool children. They tend to see the world in reference to themselves and to use their own judgments as the standard to evaluate others. A logical extension of these characteristics is the belief that one's own sex is the standard, and therefore good, while the opposite sex is a deviation and therefore not as good.

Some children develop a preference for their own sex, while others, usually girls, express some ambivalence toward their sex. For example, when asked what sex they would like to be, a majority of children from as young as three state a preference for their own sex (Abel and Sahinkaya, 1962; Parsons, 1976b). But girls are more likely to express a desire to be boys than boys to be girls. Similarly, while children of both sexes prefer interacting with same-sex peers, girls are more likely to report friendship with boys than vice versa (Kohlberg and Zigler, 1967; Parsons, 1976b). This sex difference also emerges when children's preference for their sex roles are assessed. Little girls prefer their feminine roles much less strongly than boys prefer their masculine roles (Hartup and Zook, 1960; Kohlberg and Zigler, 1967; Rabban, 1950).

One explanation of this finding is that some girls' distaste for their female role is a reflection of their awareness of the unequal benefits awarded their sex in this society. As was suggested earlier, children form stereotypes to help them understand their world. Furthermore, stereotypes and generalizations along the dimensions of power, competence, prestige, strength, and size are among the earliest to develop (Kohlberg, 1966). Since cultural ideologies attribute men with a greater amount of all of these valued characteristics it is no surprise that girls would be more ambivalent about their sex roles than boys.

Another basic cognitive process is the attaching of positive or negative values to various perceptual cues. Children express an unmistakable preference for big things. Any parent can testify to the frustrations of trying to convince a three- or four-year-old that the biggest present is not always the best. This may predispose children to attribute greater power and status to men. That is, sex differences in height and strength may underlie the greater valuing of males than females (Kohlberg, 1966). For adults as well as children, height is consistently associated with physical attractiveness, perceived power, and actual occupancy of position of power (see Chapter 16).

For the most part, children positively value those individuals who are perceived to possess such traits as competence and prestige (Kohlberg, 1966). So, even though a young girl tends to value her own sex because she perceives that women are like her, she will simultaneously value men because she perceives them to be more powerful. These two opposing tendencies may well cause conflict and make girls ambivalent about their sex role. Furthermore, perhaps this tendency to associate value with size sets the stage for children's universal conclusion that men are better than women, and therefore what men do is better than what women do (Rosaldo, 1974).

An alternative explanation for some of these data suggests that females display a wider range of behaviors, not because they are in conflict about the female sex role but because society condones and to some extent encourages girls to be "tomboys." Advocates of this explanation point out that boys are more likely to be punished for cross-sex behaviors than are girls. For example, one study found that parents expressed more positive attitudes toward boys' sex-appropriate object choices than toward girls' sex-appropriate object choices and more negative attitudes toward cross-sex choices in boys than in girls (Lansky, 1967). Thus, it appears that parents are prepared to respond more negatively to cross-sex behavior and object choices in boys.

Do boys actually get punished more for cross-sex behavior? The original hypothesis was based on the assumption that boys and girls initially exhibit cross-sex behavior with about equal frequency. It was assumed that boys decrease in cross-sex behavior because they are punished, while girls persist in cross-sex behavior because they are not punished. The cognitive-developmental approach predicts that boys will not exhibit much cross-sex behavior for which to be punished, and we could find no evidence contrary to this prediction. From a very early age, boys prefer sex-appropriate behaviors and avoid sex-inappropriate behaviors. In contrast, many girls do engage in cross-sex behavior. Consequently, it seems unlikely that boys are being punished or pressured into a rigid sex role by their parents. Thus, at present, a cognitive conflict model of female development seems to provide the best, although yet unproven, explanation.

Identification

Identification is the result of the acquisition of sex-role identity and is motivated by the desire to be close to and to be like the parent or other adults who share one's sex-role identity (Kohlberg, 1966; 1969). Since it is extremely difficult to measure a concept like identification, and to distinguish it from a continuation of a sex preference and imitation, discussion of this stage will be omitted. Let it suffice to say that people do continue imitating sex-role—appropriate behaviors and same-sex models throughout their lives.

EXTENSIONS OF THE KOHLBERG MODEL

Kohlberg's original model has recently been extended to include an investigation of the development of sex-role concepts and attitudes regarding these concepts from infancy through late-adolescent development (Ullian, 1976). It is now concerned with documenting major stage shifts in children's conceptualizations of and attitudes toward both the descriptive and proscriptive nature of masculinity and femininity instead of just focusing on the acquisition of sex-role identity (see Box 3).

It is difficult to evaluate this scheme since research is still in progress. In similar schemes, children's conceptualizations are assumed to develop from more traditional, rigid, stereotyped sex-role beliefs to more egalitarian, flexible, androgynous beliefs.[9] The progression of psychological theories has also followed a similar sequence. We have come from a period in which sex differences were assumed to be innate (level I) through a period in which sex differences were no longer assumed to be innate but were assumed to be highly desirable (levels III and IV) and finally to the period in which some psychologists are suggesting that androgyny is the goal to be sought after (level VI).

CULTURE, COGNITIVE PROCESSES AND DEVELOP-MENT TOWARD SEX-ROLE TRANSCENDENCE

The evidence is somewhat equivocal for Kohlberg's prediction that one's sex and sex-role valuing would emerge naturally due to the egocentric thinking

[9] See Bem, 1975; Lipman-Blumen, 1975; Rebecca, Hefner, and Oleshansky, 1976.

Box 3   **Summary of Six Levels of Sex-Role Conceptualization**

Stage 1: Biological Orientation

LEVEL I (6 YEARS): Differences between masculine and feminine are expressed primarily in terms of external bodily differences, such as size, strength, length of hair, etc. Social and psychological differences are recognized but are assumed to be the consequence of these external physical differences. Conformity to sex differences is viewed as necessary in order to maintain gender identity and to allow for the expression of innate gender differences.

LEVEL II (8 YEARS): There is a growing awareness that masculine and feminine traits can exist independently from biological and physical features. Emphasis is placed on the ability of the individual to act according to choice, since he or she is no longer limited by physical or biological constraints. Also the role of training, and social conditions are beginning to be recognized. Finally, since children no longer see sex differences as biological necessities, they do not demand the conformity to sex roles characteristic of the younger children.

Stage 2: Societal Orientation

LEVEL III (10 YEARS): Masculine and feminine traits are seen as inherent in the requirements of a system of social roles, and are viewed as fixed and unchangeable. The traits associated with certain adult social roles are assumed to be characteristic of the members of the sex expected to fill those roles. Conformity to masculine and feminine standards is based on the need to satisfy external demands of the social system.

LEVEL IV (12 YEARS): There is a growing awareness that the system of social roles is arbitrary and variable, and may function independently of sex of individual. Stress is put on the individual's freedom to act according to individual self-interest. Conformity is no longer expected.

Psychological Orientation

LEVEL V (14–16 YEARS): Masculine and feminine traits are based on the adoption of an appropriate psychological identity by males and females. These adolescents admit that sex differences are not biologically based and may not be the result of social necessity but these traits are assessed to a central part of men's and women's identities. Deviation is viewed as "sick" or "abnormal," and conformity to external standards is seen as required for maintenance of marriage and the family.

LEVEL VI (18 YEARS): There is an awareness that masculinity and femininity may exist independent from conformity to traditional standards, roles, and behaviors. Sex-stereotyped traits are not assumed to be crucial aspects of personal identity. Principles of equality and freedom are proposed as standards for behavior, and are used to define an ideal model of personal and interpersonal functioning.

SOURCE: Ullian, 1976.

of preschool children. It seems to be true for males. While most girls express positive feelings toward being female and toward the female sex role, there is clear evidence of ambivalence among some females. Does this mean that cognitive-developmental processes play a less important role than Kohlberg suggested? We think not. Instead, what it may suggest is that cultural processes interact with cognitive-developmental processes to influence the acquisition of any behavior and that it is the interaction of both of these forces which determines the final end point of development. If we assume that children are motivated by a desire to be competent and prestigious, it then follows that they will aspire to and model behaviors that are perceived to be competent and prestigious in one's society (Bandura, Ross, and Ross, 1963b). If one's ascribed role (a role gained by virtue of one's sex, age, race, or relationship to another individual) is not considered prestigious, then ambivalence is bound to be the result. Consequently, when a girl's egocentric reasoning leads her to conclude that her sex is the best, but inputs from the society at large suggest that the male sex is best, she will develop ambivalent attitudes toward her sex role and will exhibit as much cross-sex behavior as is permissible by her social group. And, if conditions are appropriate, this ambivalence may motivate development toward a less rigid adherence to sex-role ideologies. This point becomes especially important as a girl enters adolescence. If she happens to be a member of a very stereotypic social group, she probably experiences considerable pressure to conform to the traditional feminine role. In contrast, if she happens to be a member of less traditional subculture, then she may well continue exhibiting cross-sex behaviors and preferences and develop a nontraditional or androgynous sex role.

Here once again is an example of the interaction of one's culture with one's cognitive development. Exposure to discrepant models at crucial points in development can be expected to produce attitude change and accommodation of stereotypic schemata. Entry into adolescence is one such crucial point. According to Piaget, this period marks the transition from the stage of concrete operations to the stage of formal reasoning characterized by an ability to consider concepts in the abstract and to contemplate the possible as well as the actual. It is at this point that children can consider new sex-role systems and can truly question the basis for the division of roles along sex lines that is prevalent in their culture. If they are exposed, at this point or previously, to new models and new ideas, then they may evolve for themselves a new role conception based more on personal needs than role-related restraints (Rebecca, Hefner, and Oleshansky, 1976).

Work in three related areas supports the importance of the adolescent period and to a lesser extent the role of discrepant information in changing sex-role ideas. First, in the realm of moral reasoning, Kohlberg and his associates demonstrated that abstract, principled reasoning emerges for the first time during the adolescent years (Kohlberg, 1969). Second, the political attitude-change literature also suggests that the adolescent period is important (Newcomb, et. al., 1967; Sears, 1969). Also, developmental shifts in both political attitudes and moral reasoning are dependent to some extent on exposure to new ideas or to discrepant models during the late adolescent period. Finally, new work on sex-role attitudes suggests that androgynous attitudes will develop during adolescence, if at all (Ullian, 1976).

WHAT THE COGNITIVE-DEVELOPMENTAL MODEL TELLS US

The major characteristics of each of the three major theoretical approaches to sex-role development were compared earlier in Box 1. On certain issues all three approaches make the same predictions, but for different reasons. For example, all three approaches indicate that sex-role learning occurs early in life. Empirical data support this prediction. Sex roles are acquired quite early, but causal factors are unclear. On other issues the three approaches yield different predictions concerning the motive underlying sex-role acquisition and the roles of the child, society, and biology. On these issues support for the various predictions depends on the particular behavior being examined.

What then can be concluded about the processes underlying sex-role acquisition? First, like all developmental phenomena, sex-role acquisition reflects the complex interaction of many variables and processes. The determinants of one's behavior at any given point in time are many. The factors and processes responsible for the acquisition of and change in responses over time are even more numerous and complex. It is clear that no one theory tells the complete story. Each of the three major theoretical approaches provides son e insight into and explains some subset of the phenomena of sex-role acquisition. The close personal relationship with one's parents is undoubtedly conducive to the adoption of parental standards. Consequently, to the extent that one's parents exhibit clearly defined sex roles, sex-role acquisition will be enhanced by "identification." Similarly, there is no question that reinforcement for sex-appropriate behaviors speeds up sex-role acquisition, and that punishments for sex-inappropriate behaviors both reduce the incidence of these behaviors and lay the foundation for an internal monitoring system that will ensure continued sex-role appropriate behaviors. Finally, since all stimuli must be interpreted by the child before they can have any impact on her behavior, the child's cognitive system inevitably mediates the processes of sex-role acquisitions.

Second, three factors seem of prime importance: the behaviors of the individuals in the child's social world; the child's interpretation of these behaviors and of her or his social world in general; and the reactions of other people to the child's behavior. The role of these three factors in determining behaviors at any one point in time is illustrated in Box 4. Not only do these three factors directly affect the child's immediate behaviors, they also mediate the impact of the cultural milieu and any biological predispositions. Furthermore, changes in the child's behavior patterns are most likely mediated by

Box 4   **Determinants of Behavior**

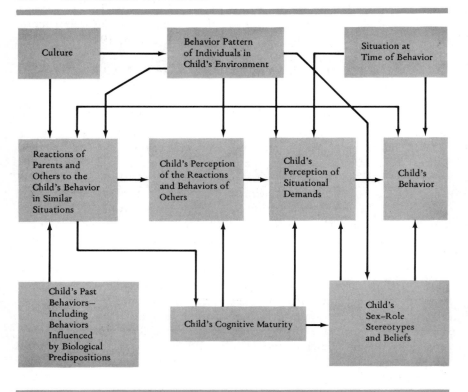

two of these factors: the developmental changes in the child's cognitive system, which alter behavior by inducing changes in the child's perception of others and of situational demands; and shifts in the reactions of others to the child's behavior, which produce changes through reinforcement principles and by altering the child's conception of the situational demands.

Finally, since the cognitive-developmental model represents the most thorough attempt at integrating the role of reinforcement and cognitive development in sex-role acquisition, the cognitive-developmental model seems to be the best framework in which to analyze sex-role acquisition. By elaborating and extending the ideas of Kohlberg and Piaget, the cognitive-developmental model provides a basis for discussing the development of stereotypes and differential valuing of the male and female role, the acquisition of sex-role identity, the emergence of prejudices regarding appropriate behaviors and role and individual capabilities, and the basis for eliminating these prejudices.

Part III

The Roles of Women

8 Changes in Women's Role Participation

Gwendolyn L. Lewis

Women in modern societies are found simultaneously in many different roles. The predominant roles for women are now, as in the past, those of wife, homemaker, mother, and worker. This chapter traces changes in the emphasis placed on each of these roles during this century, some of the reasons for these changes, and expectations for the future.

TRADITIONAL ROLES OF WOMEN

Until the late nineteenth century, women in this country, whether married or single, worked almost exclusively in the home or as unpaid labor in family enterprises. This work involved not only the care of children and the upkeep of the house, but also the cultivation and preparation of food and the manufacture of many of the goods used in the home. Teaching and domestic service were among the very few "outside" jobs open to women. However, with increasing industrialization during the nineteenth century, there was the greater demand for labor, and single women gradually began to leave home to work in factories. Single women were allowed by their families to take jobs in order to be self-supporting (Nye, 1974).

In the early twentieth century, single women began to fill sales and clerical positions and continued to expand their participation in teaching and fac-

---

Irene Frieze collaborated on this chapter with the assistance of Karen Trocki.

tory work. By the beginning of World War II, it had become acceptable for a single woman to work. The expectation, however, was that she would work for only a few years after completing her education, and then would marry and spend the rest of her life caring for her home and family.

By the end of World War II a number of changes had taken place in the relative emphasis placed on women's various roles. Young people started to marry at an earlier age and were more likely to marry. As a consequence, women became mothers sooner, and had more children than in the 1920s and 1930s. It also became more common for both married and unmarried women to work outside the home for various economic reasons. In the years immediately following World War II most young women finished high school and worked full time until getting married. Many of these single women planned to work only for a brief period and were already engaged to be married. They worked to earn money for their weddings, trousseaus, and household goods; after marriage they quit their jobs. The typical woman had her first child after a year of marriage and two or three children over the next few years. It was expected that a woman's life would be focused primarily upon caring for her children and maintaining the home.

Of course, even during the 1940s and 1950s not all mothers were totally occupied with their wife/mother roles. Many women began to work part time when their youngest child entered school. A minority of women worked even with young children. At this time, not only were younger women with children entering the labor force more frequently, but older women were also more likely to work outside the home than in earlier years. During this period children also tended to leave home earlier. So even with more children, parents experienced the "empty nest" syndrome when all their children were gone from home at an earlier age. For the woman this meant a reduction in her roles of mother and homemaker. Women at this age turned to work outside the home, presumably as a means of coping with this role reduction.

A number of societal indicators suggest that changes in the roles of both women and men have come even more rapidly during the 1960s and 1970s. The changes in women's participation in various roles have been caused primarily by three interrelated factors: changes in the economy affecting labor-force participation; changes in the age structure of our society; and changes in values. In the following sections the specific effects of these factors on women's primary roles will be discussed.

Wife

The role of wife is acquired when a woman legally aligns herself with a man through marriage. For most couples, marriage implies that the husband and wife share intimate knowledge of themselves, physical and emotional care, material possessions, living quarters, friends, families, and responsibility for any children. Traditionally, for the woman, this role has been assumed to precede all other adult female roles, and its acceptance has implied acceptance of the related roles of housewife and mother.

Housewife

The housewife's job is one which generally comes to a woman because of her legal relationship to her husband, not through her choice of the work itself. Women are expected to perform household tasks on the basis of love and duty. In fact, the legal marriage bond between a woman and her husband frequently specifies that a wife's legal responsibilities include living in a home established by her husband; performing the domestic chores of cleaning, cooking, washing; and generally caring for her husband and children (Bernard, 1974a). Because of other family needs, the middle-class housewife frequently takes on other tasks, such as taxi service and community welfare projects, if she has the time to do so. Generally, work done in the housewife role is low in prestige.

Not only is the occupation of housewife not freely selected, it also isolates. Women doing housework are cut off from contact with other adults since they have no coworkers. This isolation tends to heighten the housewives' sense of powerlessness and to make these women more susceptible to psychological problems (Bernard, 1974a).

The most positive features of housework are the autonomy and flexibility allowed in its performance. Women doing housework can decide how to structure their time; to some degree they can decide which of their many activities they want to devote most attention to. These characteristics, combined with the variety of tasks involved and the ability of the worker to see the products of her labor, make the housewife job compare favorably with many other jobs that exist in the labor force. Thus, for many women, especially working-class women, the housewife role is a highly desirable one in view of the other work roles to which she might reasonably aspire. Unfortunately, not all women are financially able to exercise this choice.

Mother

The role of mother is unique in that it is taken on by most women because of a biological event: giving birth to a child. However, women also become "mothers" through adoption or other means of taking on the care of children. It is the social definition of motherhood which is important. As the role is currently defined, the mother is the one primarily responsible for supplying physical and emotional care for infants and young children. If the mother cannot provide that care herself, she must arrange for others to do so. This role, like all roles, is also strongly affected by social conventions regarding who should enter this role and when. However, because of the greater availability of diverse and effective birth-control methods on the one hand, and ability to correct problems associated with infertility on the other, the degree of choice over entering the role of mother has been increased.

Labor-Force Participant

One of the important role determinants in any society is the work that people perform. Many types of work important to the functioning of modern societies are not directly remunerated. For example, people frequently participate on school boards, perform charitable activities, belong to boards of trustees, do housework, conduct the business of voluntary organizations, and take care of children for no payment at all. On the other hand, many jobs are conducted as paid labor. People who are in these jobs or who are actively seeking these jobs are considered to be in the labor force.

Historically, women in this country have been working primarily in the unpaid work force. However, as our society has become more rationalized and technologically sophisticated, proportionately more work has shifted to the paid labor force. As a result the number of women in the labor force has increased.

As in the case of the male worker, women workers are to be found in every type of work—from the most respected to the most degrading, from the most demanding intellectual work to the most boring drudgery. Women generally hold less powerful positions than men, they are segregated into occupations primarily held by women, and they do not advance as quickly as men. Many people feel that their work ideally should satisfy the needs of self-actualization, achievement, recognition, and social contact. Because of the conditions of work, as well as the nature of some work, the reality falls far short of this ideal for most people (Agassi, 1975). Self-actualization, achievement, and recognition needs are difficult to satisfy in most jobs. This is especially true of the positions that many women hold. Nevertheless, women have been participating in the labor force in increasingly greater numbers over the years.

CHANGES IN ROLES: PAST AND FUTURE

Societal attitudes toward those roles appropriate to women have been undergoing great changes. Specifically, there have been changes in beliefs about the value of the family, the manner in which child care can best be implemented, the role of marriage in people's lives today, and the possibility of self-expression through work. Along with these changes in attitudes, have come changes in role participation, with more women participating in more diverse roles. As more diversity has been introduced into women's roles, the impact of greater participation in those roles has become more apparent.

Changing Marriage and Divorce Patterns

Two demographic trends have been affecting the predominance of the wife role among American women during the twentieth century: changes in both marriage and divorce patterns. From about the turn of the century until the late 1950s, the age at which American women first married became generally younger: In 1890, the median age of brides marrying for the first time was 22.0; by 1956, it had dropped to 20.1. In 1956, this trend was reversed and the age of marriage for women began to increase gradually, until by 1970 it was 20.8. In addition, the percentage of young women married has recently declined. In 1950, 63.3 percent of women aged 20 to 24 were married. By 1960, the married among this age group had increased to 67.2 percent. However, by 1970 the percentage had declined to 57.9, and the downward trend has continued so that by 1974 only 54.4 percent were married (Sklar and Berkov, 1975). Thus, women are now postponing marriage longer than women did in the 1950s and early 1960s.

Another change in marital patterns has taken place recently. Variation among men's ages at their first marriages has decreased while, at the same time, the range of ages at which women first marry has increased. This has produced a smaller difference between the ages of spouses at first marriage than previously. This trend does not show up in comparing average ages at marriage, but does in more complex comparisons (Current Population Reports, 1975b).

Later marriage for both men and women has also meant larger proportions of single people in the younger ages. In 1975, 49 percent of the women and 67 percent of men were still unmarried by the age of twenty-one. It remains to be seen whether young people of the seventies will be more likely than past generations to remain single for their lifetimes. If past experience is any guide, it seems likely that most will eventually marry. Postponement of marriage and more equal ages of spouses, however, have many implications for the types of marriages that these people will have, especially in terms of the degree of sharing of decision making and other powers within the marriage, the extent to which the wives are likely to work, and the likelihood of the couple having one or more children.

The other major demographic trend affecting both wives and husbands is the increasing number of marriages which end in divorce. During the twenties and thirties the number of divorces for married women age fourteen to forty-four was fairly steady at about ten per thousand (or 1 percent of all married women) per year. During the mid-forties the rate increased to a high of twenty-four per thousand, and then declined to a low point in the late fifties. During the sixties the trend once again was reversed, increasing to a new high of an average of twenty-six per thousand during the period 1969 to 1971. Factors leading to the latest increases were liberalization of divorce laws, decline in the fertility rate, the extensive amount of separation forced on married couples because of the Vietnam war, and the increased ability of women to support themselves financially (Glick and Norton, 1973).

The number of divorces granted has been rising rapidly at a rate of about 10 percent a year, while the number of married people under forty-five, among whom most divorces occur, has risen only 1 percent a year. Because of fewer marriages it is likely that we shall see a decline in yearly divorce rates even though individuals may be more likely to get divorced over their lifetimes. To understand better what future trends in divorce are likely to occur and what this means for individuals' expectations of divorce in their lifetimes, it is helpful to look at the current lifetime divorce experience of women born at different times. Box 1 shows the percentage of women in different age groups whose first marriage had ended in divorce by 1971 and projections of the number who will end their first marriage by divorce. For the youngest group observed—those thirty-two to thirty-six years old in 1976—it is projected that 25 percent will eventually end their first marriages by divorce if they behave over their lifetimes as women were behaving in the period from 1960 to 1965. It is also estimated that approximately 5 to 10 percent of these same women will end a second marriage by divorce.

Although divorce takes women out of the spouse relationship, this can be either a temporary or permanent transition. The remarriage rate of widowed and divorced women has followed a pattern very similar to that of divorce over the last fifty years. The overall trend is one of increasing remarriage. It

Box 1   **Percent of Women Born between 1900 and 1944 Whose First Marriage Had Ended in Divorce by 1971 or May Eventually End in Divorce, by Year of Birth: June 1971**

Year of Birth of Woman	Had Ended in Divorce by 1971	*Percent of Women Whose First Marriage* May Eventually End in Divorce, if Their Future Divorce Experience Is Similar to That of Older Cohorts during	
		1960–65	1965–70
1940–44	13.6	25	29
1935–39	16.8	24	27
1930–34	16.0	21	23
1925–29	16.5	19	21
1920–24	16.7	18	19
1915–19	15.2	16	17
1910–14	13.8	14	15
1905–9	12.1	13	13
1900–4	11.7	12	12

SOURCE: Glick and Norton, 1973.

has been estimated that about 80 percent of women born between 1940 and 1944 who do divorce will eventually remarry (Glick and Norton, 1973). Remarriage is more prevalent among the divorced than among the widowed, although this may be because widows tend to be older. Although there are increasing numbers of divorced people in the population, for most of them this is a temporary condition. Most marry again. Of those who remain unmarried, it is unclear whether they do so by choice or because of the lack of a suitable partner. Researching this question would prove difficult because of normative pressures on most people to say they would prefer to be married.

It is true that divorced men are more likely to remarry than divorced women (Current Population Reports, 1975a). It is usually assumed that this is due to a man's having fewer responsibilities with respect to children and having a wider choice of new partners because of the acceptability of men marrying much younger women as well as women their own age. Also, it is partially because there tend to be more women over thirty than men. In the past, however, remarriage was to some extent limited by the fact that courts frequently held the father responsible for financial support of his children and occasionally of his former wife. More recently, courts have been spreading the responsibilities for physical and financial aspects of child care somewhat more evenly between the divorced pair. Freedom from financial burdens makes it even more likely that divorced men will remarry. But increased physical responsibility for children may also limit men's opportunities somewhat.

The shifting of financial responsibility may result in more divorced mothers finding themselves faced with greater financial burdens. Conversely the shifting of physical responsibility and the increasing availability of day care may free mothers from their total commitment to child care. These two factors are likely to send them into the job market more quickly and to give them more opportunity to meet eligible men whom they might marry if they so desire.

Work in the Home

A number of changes have occurred in the traditional housewife role which have given women working in the home more time on the one hand, and greater needs for money and outside stimulation on the other. Due to appliances, manufactured goods, and prepared foods, housework itself now takes considerably less time than it did even a short time ago. Also there are not as many people in the home to care for. Women are having fewer children and spending fewer years occupied with child care. In addition, it is no longer common for young couples to care for their aging parents, so this responsibility has also been removed from the home.

Women and men differ in the extent to which they perform household tasks, child care, and other daily activities. For example, employed men spent on the average two hours longer per day on work-related activities (including travel time to work) than employed women (7.6 hours to 5.7 hours), but had more free time (4.8 hours to 4.2 hours) than employed women because the women spent much more time on household and family tasks than the men (4.2 hours to 1.8). Not only was the amount of time spent by men and women quite different, the tasks performed were different. "Close to 40% of women's housework consisted of cleaning house; another third was spent preparing food, with the remaining quarter spent on laundry and other house upkeep [repairs, yard maintenance, etc.]. Almost half of men's housework consisted of other house upkeep" (Robinson and Converse, 1966, p. 6).

There is little difference between employed married men and single men in the amount of time spent on household and family tasks (1.9 hours to 1.7). However, employed married women spent much more time on household tasks and family tasks than employed single women did (4.6 hours to 3.5). Employed single women spent over twice as much time on these tasks as employed single men. This may be an indication of both the degree to which women are socialized to perform household tasks and the extent to which they must perform them since they have smaller salaries with which to buy services. Thus, in spite of employment outside the home, married women continued to spend a large amount of time on household tasks in comparison to working men. Apparently work in the labor force for women is added to that which is done in the home.

Women who are housewives have expanded their work roles in many ways other than through participation in the paid labor force. For instance, in the middle class there is the phenomenon of the "two-person" career in which the wife is expected to fulfill certain work roles as an adjunct to her husband's work role (Papanek, 1973). This has been apparent for a long time among people who run small family businesses or farms. It was pointed out in the early fifties as a phenomenon of note among executives' families (Whyte, 1956). Wives were expected to entertain business associates and otherwise help their husbands' careers. Employers have long been aware of the necessary contribution made by the wife in providing social support facilities for the occupation, as well as the ability of many wives to make a direct contribution by performing part of the actual work. In fact, for some jobs the wife is interviewed along with the husband to make sure she will indeed provide the appropriate atmosphere.

In many cases the increased education of the woman and the attitudes surrounding that education have encouraged this expansion of the housewife role to include the helpmate role. The tendency of women to specialize in areas in college which have few employment opportunities, such as the arts and humanities, has contributed to the number of educated women who work primarily in the home rather than in the paid labor force. It also has encouraged the perception of education for women as a luxury which, at best,

Box 2   Average Hours Spent on Various Activities During Working Day by Sex and Work Status*

Activity	Men Employed			Women Employed			Women Unemployed		
	Married	Single	All	Married	Single	All	Married	Single	All
Regular Paid, Working Hours	6.1	6.2	6.1	4.7	4.6	4.7	.1	.7	.1
All Work Related	7.6	7.5	7.6	5.6	5.7	5.7	.1	.8	.1
Household	.6	.5	.6	3.0	1.9	2.6	5.1	3.8	5.1
Personal Care and Sleep	10.0	9.9	10.0	10.1	10.4	10.2	10.6	10.9	10.6
Family Tasks	1.3	1.2	1.2	1.6	1.6	1.6	2.7	2.3	2.7
Educ./Orgs.	.4	.7	.4	.2	.5	.3	.5	1.3	.6
Mass Media	2.5	2.2	2.4	1.6	1.6	1.6	2.2	2.9	2.3
Leisure	1.7	2.0	1.8	1.8	2.2	2.0	2.8	2.0	2.7
Grand Total	24.0	24.0	24.0	24.0	24.0	24.0	24.0	24.0	24.0
Free Time	4.8	5.1	4.8	3.9	4.8	4.2	5.9	6.4	5.9

* Data from Robinson and Converse, 1966.

produces women who can provide only decorative and aesthetic contributions to the family, the husband's career, and voluntary organizations. Education for women has had as its primary goal the creation of better mothers, more interesting companions to husbands, and better helpmates for husbands with high-level careers (Rossi, 1967).

Implicit in the wife's helpmate role is the social value that women should achieve through their husbands. This value previously had its strongest impact upon the most able women. It was considered inappropriate for a young woman to be superior in intelligence or physical strength to her male companions. For the intellectually or physically talented young woman, this was particularly difficult. It was the rare woman growing up in the fifties who did not "play dumb" or "weak" on more than one occasion. Rather than achieving in the outside world in a career or meaningful job, women were encouraged to achieve through their social activities or their husbands and children. Status for young women was measured in terms of the status of their dates and their own interpersonal sensitivity. Married women were judged by the status of their husbands or by the achievements of their children.

Change and the Role of Mother

Lowered Birth Rate. In order to understand the global picture of changing role-emphasis in this country, an awareness of the changes in the number and ages of women who adopt the role of mother is necessary. Throughout the late nineteenth century and into the early twentieth century this country experienced a general decline in fertility. Although women married increasingly earlier during the twentieth century, the estimated number of births for white women decreased from 7.0 in 1800 to 2.1 in 1936. After 1940, family size increased steadily until 1957, when total fertility reached a high of 3.8 for the entire population. Fertility rates then began to decline again.

Declining birth rates have been a continuing historical trend related to lowered death rates of children. The "baby boom" of the 1940s and 1950s which temporarily reversed this trend was initiated by several factors. All were associated with the recovery of the national economy due to our participation in World War II. Initially, a lot of young men were drawn into the armed forces. In some instances this precipitated earlier marriage and consequent childbirth. With the recovery of the economy, many families who had postponed children during the Depression of the 1930s began to have the children they had desired. At the end of World War II the labor market was expanding, and young men, especially since they were better educated than older workers, were drawn into well-paid jobs in the labor force, which allowed the acquisition of homes and made the expense of having children of less consequence. Government assistance to veterans, in the form of FHA loans for housing, assisted in this process. The G.I. Bill, provided support for further education which made it possible for veterans to both attend school and begin families. These factors allowed men and women to marry younger and to begin families earlier. Finally, perhaps because existing situations often become normative, societal values reinforced the idea of early marriage and children. During the 1940s and 1950s marriage was considered to be the only appropriate state for adults. Children were thought to be a natural and joyous outcome of marriage, and a large family was considered desirable. Children were essential for family "togetherness," and many believed that a woman's true fulfillment came only with the bearing and raising of children. Women who did not have children early in their marriages were pitied for their incomplete lives (Hartley, 1972; Tomasson, 1966). Consequently, because both older people, who had postponed children in the thirties, and younger people, who were starting families early, were contributing children to the population at the same time, there was a large volume of births.

However, in 1957 the peak number of births was reached, and a new decline in the birth rate occurred. The decline in births began as a consequence of the fact that the primary candidates for parenthood in the late 1950s were people born twenty to thirty years before, when the number of births was low. Thus, there were fewer people in the prime childbearing ages. The fact that the older parents among these had already had most of the children they wanted contributed further to the decline in births. In the 1960s the impact of this factor became greater, since parents then came

Box 3   **Total Fertility Rates**

Year	Fertility Rate*
1975	1.8
1970	2.5
1965	2.9
1960	3.7
1955	3.6
1950	3.1
1945	2.5
1940	2.3

* The average number of births a woman will have in her lifetime if her future behavior is the same as older women's.

SOURCES: U.S. Department of Health, Education, and Welfare, 1967, Tables I-2, I-6. *Monthly Vital Statistics Report,* 1976, Table 4. National Center for Health Statistics, 1976.

primarily from the very small group of people born in the late 1930s and early 1940s. In addition, beginning with those who came of age in the early 1960s there was a postponement of marriage (Davidson, 1975). The decline in fertility from 1961 to 1973 can be separated into the components of change of marital status and changes in the number of children within marriage (Gibson, 1975). Changes in marital status (through postponement of marriage and separation or divorce) accounted for 14 percent of the decline in births during that period; changes in the numbers of children within marriage accounted for 86 percent of the decline. Postponement of the children born in marriage did not occur during the 1960s, but it has become an important factor in the 1970s, as shown in Box 4.

Delay in Having Children. The data in Box 4 shows that women are waiting longer after marriage to have their first child; they are also spacing their children further apart. Because there were so many more potential parents in the seventies, all the experts had predicted large increases in the number of children born. However delay of marriage and children meant that fewer women who could have been expected to have children were doing so. The fertility rate dropped, as shown in Box 3. However, these trends may reverse. There continue to be more women of childbearing age. Also, there was a slight climb in births in 1974 due to births among those women who were in their late twenties and early thirties but who had never had a child (Sklar and Berkov, 1975). These women are the ones who have kept the birth rate down in the past, but who are now at an age where it is imperative to have children if they ever want to do so. Since it is still the case that most Americans, even among those under thirty, have an aversion to childlessness and even single-child families, one might expect a large volume of births to take place in the next few years (Blake, 1975). However, family size or the average number of births per woman is not expected to increase. Young wives eighteen to twenty-four years old are expecting to have an average of

Box 4   Median Number of Months between Children for Women Who Have Ever Married

	Year of Child's Birth		
	1970–74	1965–69	1960–64
First marriage to first birth:			
excluding births before marriage	19.8	14.9	14.3
First birth to second birth	31.8	28.1	24.7
Second birth to third birth	35.4	31.9	29.0
Third birth to fourth birth	35.1	32.6	29.2

SOURCE: Current Population Reports, 1976, p. 3.

2.2 children each, only slightly above replacement (*Current Population Reports*, 1976). Thus, the extent to which women take on the role of mother is not expected to change much in the near future.

Attitudes about Motherhood. The attitude, widely held during the 1950s and 1960s, that children needed a good deal of care and attention from their mothers strengthened the belief that women should devote themselves to their families. Psychological studies on the adverse effects of "maternal deprivation" through physical deprivation and lack of human contact produced the widespread misbelief that mothers who were not with their children during all or most of their waking hours would do irreparable harm to them. An upsurge in juvenile delinquency and divorce were seen as social ills perpetuated by lack of attention to the family by women. Mothers accepted the responsibility of raising psychologically healthy children as well as caring for their routine physical needs. Women were committeed to spending all their time with their children. The majority of college-educated mothers also felt these responsibilities for their children and expressed the opinion that children were the most important function of marriage. They strongly agreed that the mothers of young children should not work (Westoff and Potvin, 1967).

Although many women still feel that they need to stay home with very young children, those women who do choose to work are not viewed as negatively by themselves or others as they once were (Komarovsky, 1973). In a research study in 1943, 50 percent of college women surveyed said they would prefer not to work after the birth of their first child, especially if their husband had adequate income. In a second study in 1971, only 18 percent gave this response. Sixty-two percent of the women asked said they definitely planned to work after marriage but would stop for a short period during childbearing. In both studies, 20 percent of the women planned full-time careers with minimal time out for child-rearing. The same percentage of women continue to want careers which are uninterrupted by their childbearing, while more women desire to continue with work outside the home after an interruption of that work for childbearing (Komarovsky, 1973).

Even with preschool-aged children, mothers are increasingly spending some time outside the home in labor-force roles. They continue to fill their roles of housewife and mother, but spend less time in these roles than do unemployed mothers. More highly educated women substitute paid help to fill some of their housekeeping tasks but less frequently use others for child care. Mothers with less education, and generally therefore lower income, have less household help. For these women substitutes are generally other family members who take over both child care and household taks when they are available. Because more educated mothers generally choose not to substitute either paid help or family members for themselves in child care, children cause greater competition for the time of these women, which is highly valued in the labor market. This probably reduces more educated women's desire for large numbers of children and additionally implies that there is little incentive for spacing children in terms of their later providing help with younger children (Leibowitz, 1974).

Availability of Child Care. For the time that employed women with young children spend outside the home they must find a substitute means of child care. The predominant means are relatives, paid baby-sitters, and day-care centers. One study estimated that only 10.5 percent of the children of working mothers were in day-care centers (Kahne, 1975). With more women employed outside the home, sources of adult baby-sitters are likely to become inadequate to fill the demand. It would seem that as a result there will be an increasing need for day-care centers. However, as presently practiced, day care is much too expensive for most families to use. Thus, quality day-care centers will become important as a source of child care only if they are subsidized. More informal arrangements with less rigid governmental requirements may be necessary to make institutional day care possible for the families of most working mothers (Lave and Angrist, 1974). This kind of proposal has led to concern about the development of a two-class day-care

Box 5   **Women's Participation in the Labor Force**

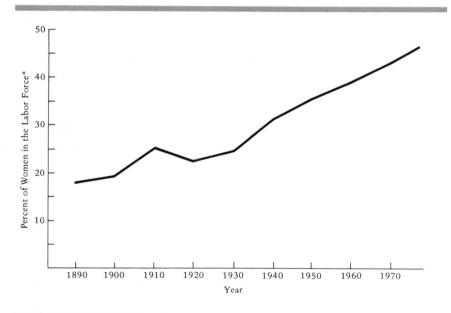

* For 1890–1930 women fourteen years and older; for 1940–1973 women sixteen years and older.
SOURCES: U.S. Department of Labor, 1969b, 1975; Oppenheimer, 1970.

system, where the rich will purchase quality care, the poor will get subsidized quality care, but the middle class will be able to purchase only custodial care.

Women in the Labor Force

Working Outside the Home. The extent of women's participation in the paid labor force has increased steadily during the course of this century. In 1900, 20.0 percent of women over fourteen were in the labor force; by 1940 the percentage of women over sixteen in the labor force had risen to 28.9; and in 1973 the percentage over sixteen participating had reached 44.7 (U.S. Department of Labor, 1969b; 1975). However, these percentages differ for different age groups. The basic pattern of participation for 1900 to 1940 was one of relatively high participation of young women and lower participation of each older age group, so that highest participation was among the young women, intermediate participation among the middle-aged women, and least participation among the oldest women.

The first change in this pattern was manifested in the 1950 census with a dramatic rise in the labor-force participation of women between the ages of thirty-five and fifty-four. At that time there was a slight decrease from the 1940 level of participation by younger women. In 1960 the participation of young women returned to its 1940 level. This upward trend reflected an increasing tendency to work of younger married women, many of whom had preschool children. The increase in participation of older women also continued its rise, surpassing the levels of participation of even the youngest women. By 1970, 50 percent of the married women between the ages of forty-five and fifty-four were working, in comparison to 41 percent in 1960 and 29 percent in 1952 (Ferriss, 1971).

Black Women. Although these labor-force trends are generally true for all women, the rate of increase has been much greater for white than for nonwhite women. Since black women (the largest group of nonwhite women in this country) have often been forced out of necessity to work outside the home, the differential increases for the two groups mean that whites are now beginning to catch up with black women (Gump, 1975). Rates also differ by age. Labor force participation for white and nonwhite women at different ages is shown in Box 6.

Increased Labor Force Participation. The reasons behind these observed changes in labor-force participation are several: changes in the demand for labor, women's competing roles in the home, and the available supply of workers due to past changes in the numbers of people being born. It has been argued that the increase in women workers has been due partly to an increase in the amount of employment available in jobs sex-typed as "female." The sectors in which women have been job-segregated were precisely those with greatest expansion after World War II. With increasing economic development there is characteristically a shift in the demand for labor from manufacturing and farming to service occupations. In this country women monopolized the service occupations by the turn of the century, when they provided 70 percent or "more of the nurses, librarians, telephone operators, stenographers, secretaries, typists and other clerical occupations" (Oppenheimer, 1973). In addition, women have been employed disproportionately as assembly-line workers in the electronics industry which has developed since World War II. It was because these occupations were numerically small in the early part of the century, but grew rapidly, that the demand for female labor grew.

A number of demographic factors affected the supply of women to jobs in the 1940s and 1950s. Because of a declining number of births since before the turn of the century through the 1930s, the numbers of new entrants into the labor market during the late 1940s and early 1950s was reduced at the same time that industry was expanding and requiring more workers. Rises in the proportion of eighteen- to nineteen-year-old women attending school further reduced the pool of young, unmarried women available for jobs. In addition, changes toward an earlier age at marriage caused the supply of young, unmarried women—the traditional labor supply of women—to shrink even further. The response of employers was to hire more older and married women than previously, since there was no other source of labor. Labor force participation has consistently increased for married women with children and has increased even more for older women with no children in the home, as shown in Boxes 6 and 7. Substituting men or machines was not

Box 6   Percent of White and Nonwhite Women of Different Ages in the Labor Force

		Age					
		20–24	25–34	35–44	45–54	55–64	TOTAL (16 years and over)
White	1950	45.9	32.1	37.2	36.3	26.0	32.6
	1960	45.7	34.1	41.5	48.6	36.2	36.5
	1970	57.7	43.2	49.9	53.7	42.6	42.6
	1974	63.8	51.1	53.7	54.3	40.4	45.2
Non-White	1950	46.9	51.6	55.7	54.3	40.9	46.9
	1960	48.8	49.7	59.8	60.5	47.3	48.2
	1970	57.7	57.6	59.9	60.2	47.1	49.5
	1974	58.2	60.8	61.5	56.9	43.5	49.1

SOURCE: U.S. Department of Labor, 1975.

Box 7   Labor Force Participation of Married Women with Children

	1950	1955	1960	1965	1970	1974
No children under 18	30.3	32.7	34.7	38.3	42.2	43.0
Children 6–17 only	28.3	34.7	39.0	42.7	49.2	51.2
With children under 6 only	11.2	15.1	18.2	23.8	30.2	35.7
Children 0–17	12.6	17.3	18.9	22.8	30.5	32.9

SOURCE: U.S. Department of Labor, 1975.

feasible because some of the same demographic factors gave rise to a similar shortage of young men; and the poor pay and opportunities for advancement in "female" occupations made them relatively unattractive to men. Machines were unlikely to be used to displace workers for the kinds of service occupations in which women were primarily employed. Thus, the fastest and least expensive way to obtain more workers was to relax policies discriminating against the employment of older and married women, and this is what happened.

Motivation of Women Workers. It is important to understand the motivations of these women workers. To some extent the above analysis explains why employers sought women to fill jobs. As a consequence of their interest in hiring female employees, increased pay for these positions may have acted as an incentive to women to enter the labor force in increasing numbers. Relative earnings of female employees are shown in Box 8. An alternative explanation is that the opportunity for any income acted as an incentive to women. Other speculation is that these women were dissatisfied with the housewife role, partly because of a reductiion in its demands as a job due to labor-saving devices. However, there is evidence that women who work do not view housewife tasks as more negative than those who do not work (Sobol, 1974). Thus, it does not appear to be dissatisfaction with housework per se which caused women to seek outside work.

The lessening of the housewife role as an explanation for women entering the labor force seems to be especially relevant for older women whose children were grown. The data collected on college graduates of 1961 suggests that older women were motivated to begin or return to work outside the home because they had passed the stages of marriage and childbearing which are the most emotionally satisfying years for the housewife role. For these older women the satisfactions of paid work were greater than those of continuing in the housewife role alone (Rossi, 1967). Another explanation for the increased participation of older women is derived from the finding that there is a relationship between the life-cycle work patterns of women and the life-cycle earnings of men. Women tend to work during periods of family

Box 8   **Median Incomes for Full-Time Civilian Employees***

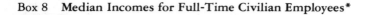

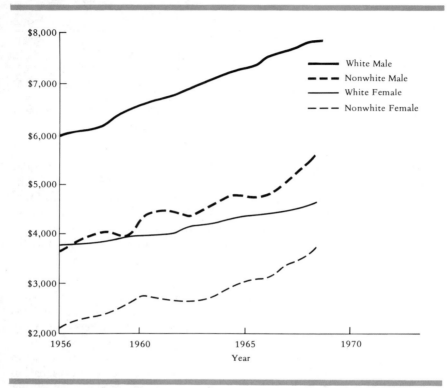

* Median annual money earnings of year-round full-time civilian workers by race and sex (1956–1968).
SOURCE: Ferriss, 1971.

economic stress. For example, peak earnings of male blue-collar and service workers occur relatively early in their careers. Thus, financial stress is likely to increase for these families as the children grow older. Economic necessity then is likely to cause women in these families to begin work in their late thirties and forties. Since professional workers do not reach their peak salaries until much later in their careers, their wives would not have the same economic incentive (Kahne, 1975).

There is another group of women whose primary focus is work. These women established a "deviant" pattern early in their lives, culminating in low involvement in social activities in their adolescence, which allowed them greater opportunities to develop intellectually and to desire self-fulfillment through contributions of some field of inquiry. These women were less likely to marry, and if married, less likely to have children than women not as career oriented (Rossi, 1967).

One wonders whether the beliefs of the fifties and sixties about the importance of a woman attending exclusively to her family and children may not have been a reaction to the perceived threat of more women working. As more women actually enter the labor force, these values may gradually change to a greater acceptance of the childfree state and working outside the home (Bernard, 1976).

Women's Liberation Movement

One factor that might help account for the most recent changes in birth rates and labor-force participation is the increased awareness of women's choices promoted by the women's liberation movement. Although a renewed interest in feminism can be traced back to the early 1960s, with the publication of Betty Friedan's *The Feminine Mystique* (1963, 1974), the media, at least, did not particularly reflect an interest in the movement until the late 1960s. By that time a great many women had become interested, and by the early 1970s the messages of the women's liberation movement had reached most people in this country. Major concerns of the movement have been breaking down sex-typing of jobs; opening job opportunities for women; fighting discrimination against women in terms of unequal pay for equivalent work; and encouraging women to work outside the home. In these areas much has been accomplished. The movement has not only fought legal battles to gain rights for women but has also provided a milieu of social approval for women who are interested in nontraditional activities and encouraged the interest of other women in those activities.

The trend toward women participating in the labor force has continued to grow even though its turn in this direction during the 1950s may have been due to circumstances relatively specific to that time. Women who have never married spend 90 percent of their adult years in the labor force (Mincer and Polachek, 1974). In contrast, married women with children spend less than 50 percent of their time in the labor force, although nearly 90 percent work sometime after they leave school. It is also generally the case that women with the most education spend the most time in the labor force (Kahne, 1975; Leibowitz, 1974). Thus, to the extent that women remain single for longer periods of time and/or obtain more education, we can expect even more participation of women. Family income has a more complicated relationship to women's working outside the home. Wives of men with very high income tend to have little economic incentive to work. In fact, there is reason to believe disincentives exist because of desires for leisure time in which to spend the family income.

FUTURE EXPECTATIONS

It seems clear that changes in women's responsibility for children and home will come about relatively slowly. The downward trend in the size of families will continue, leading to more women entering the labor force, especially as the level of education of women increases. This will lead to greater pressures for subsidized child-care facilities, for the opening of more male-dominated occupations to women, and to instability of traditional marriages. If child care is not available at varied costs and in sufficient quantities, women who otherwise would have entered the labor force will be kept out.

If the number of women working outside the home is to increase further, the question arises as to the availability of jobs. In the past, the expansion of women's employment has taken place primarily through the increase in jobs labeled as "female." Sex segregation of "female" jobs was relatively steady for the first sixty years of the century, but it has begun to decline (Gross, 1971). However, the segregation of "male" occupations has changed very little so far. Female occupations are not expected to expand sufficiently to accommodate both most women and increasing numbers of men (Oppenheimer, 1972). Consequently, we can expect one of three things to happen: a return to the home by women; an acceptance by women of jobs requiring less education than they have; or an increasing pressure from women to break into previously male occupations. The number of openings in the labor market will determine how difficult the barriers to entry into male-dominated occupations will be. The tighter the job market, the more likely we are to have a return to a period of enforced and heightened familism.

9 Women's Adult Development

Esther Sales

"What do you want to be when you grow up?" This question has been familiar to all of us since we were first asked, as preschoolers, to confront the issue of our adulthood. At that point grown-ups were so clearly a different form of being that the question's absurdity encouraged both fantasy and disbelief. Our play became the secure context for trying out the rituals of work and family roles in order to explore the mysterious world of adults.

The pressure to devise some acceptable life plan mounted during adolescence, when we no longer could doubt our approaching adulthood. Our maturing body was an undeniable sign of this reality; we struggled to redefine ourselves as independent people with clear future goals. This struggle, viewed by Erik Erikson (1964) as the central psychological theme of adolescence, involved efforts to establish an identity that would end the role confusions of one's teenage years. But even if we are successful in gaining a sense of ourselves during this period, we commonly enter adulthood with vague, tenuous goals for our future. During early adulthood, work, marriage, and parental roles are seriously explored, as we learn to perform the types of behavior expected for these roles. We often find, to our naive surprise, that our childhood games and experiences have given us little real understanding of these central roles. Although we are eager to master the intricacies of these long anticipated adult roles, they often prove to be more complex than we

Background materials for this chapter were assembled with the assistance of Rosalyn Katz.

had expected. We may suddenly realize how little we knew about them before they were chosen.

A ROLE PERSPECTIVE ON WOMEN'S LIVES

The major points of adult life are marked by role changes. During the early adult period we are likely to take on new roles of paid worker, spouse, and parent, while the later period usually brings about losses of these central roles as children reach their own adulthood, spouses die, and workers retire (Lowenthal, 1971). The roles we choose have many consequences: (1) they define the behaviors expected of us by others; (2) they are major sources of our feelings about ourselves; (3) they expose us to experiences which can affect our later attitudes, feelings, and behavior. Thus, while roles may have been self-selected initially, once chosen, they play a major part in shaping our subsequent experiences and personality.

Because roles define our lives in such central ways, a role perspective will be used to view the changes that take place during the adult years. A *role* is most frequently viewed as the set of expectations that arise from positions in society that one holds—a *position,* sometimes called status, being a collectively recognized category for classifying people (Biddle and Thomas, 1966; Linton, 1936). Some positions are based on personal attributes that are endowed by society with special relevance; gender, age, ethnic group membership, and race are examples of characteristics that affect people's expectations for one's behavior. These *ascribed* positions are different from the *achieved* positions that people hold because of their own effort, behavior, or choice (Davis, 1949).

Ascribed characteristics are visible and are usually important influences on the quality of social interaction. For example, as discussed in Chapter 6, people tend to relate differently to boys and girls from the time they are born. In our society, one's ascribed status can create problems for a person when it conflicts with that individual's achieved status. For example, a young person who holds a position of power and authority, a black who enters a high-status profession, or a woman who pursues a career may be discomforted in having two positions that involve such competing expectations for their behavior. In each case, their work role demands behavior that is incompatible with the submissiveness expected by their ascribed age, race, or sex role. Even if they attain personal comfort in their jointly held roles, they may meet other people who are disconcerted by the inconsistency of their various positions. Currently, this society's laudable efforts to encourage achievement regardless of ascribed characteristics has inadvertently created role problems for many of its members. Thus, when women assume roles that violate the sterotypic expectations for "feminine" behavior, they are placed in a situation that is potentially stressful for themselves and others. This type of conflict often occurs when women enter the work world, although it may begin earlier if a woman excels in her student role, shows athletic skill, or becomes a leader of a coed social group (Komarovsky, 1946).

Role Conflict

Role conflict is defined as any situation in which incompatible expectations are placed on a person because of position membership (Gross, Mason and McEachern, 1958; Kahn, et al., 1964). It creates difficulty for people because it inevitably forces them to violate someone's expectations for them, either by (1) choosing to comply fully with one set of expectations while ignoring others; (2) by seeking a compromise whereby they conform to only a part of each set of expectations; or (3) by avoiding choice through escaping from the situation (Biddle and Thomas, 1966). A woman in a position of power, for example, can ignore her feminine role demands and choose to act "just like a man" in her work role, or she can temper her assertiveness and display the aspects of her feminine personality that she values (or knows are effective in winning over coworkers).

When competing roles are added to a woman's role repertoire, the potential for role conflict mounts (Merton, 1957). A husband socialized in traditional ways may expect his wife to be supportive, respectful of his work obligations, and admiring of his competence. A woman who is herself a jobholder may not nurture her husband's ego as well as a wife whose only contact with the work world is through her husband. Since she is contributing economically to the marriage, she expects more participation in decision making and household tasks (Blood and Wolfe, 1960). It is hard for a woman who is independent and assertive at work to become the compliant wife on her return home.

Role Overload

Another kind of role conflict is based on external time demands rather than inherent contradictions in expectations. When a number of roles demand extensive time commitments, people often experience the unique pressures caused by role overload. In general, the more roles a person assumes, the more logistical problems in time allocation there will be.

Role overload is a common plight of young women who attempt to combine work, marriage, and family roles. Since these roles all have extensive time demands, women who try to meet all the expectations for each role feel excessively burdened (Bernard, 1975; Hoffman and Nye, 1974). They may devise many complex strategies for handling the overload, such as making lists or combining tasks, but these are merely holding actions to stave off imminent disaster (see Box 1). Most people have experienced temporary overload (the end of each term finds most students in this condition), but they can console themselves in the knowledge that it will be of short duration. The working mother of young children has no such consolation. Her efforts to fully satisfy others tax her energies and drain the pleasure from each role.

Role overload can be resolved by a withdrawing from some roles or by renegotiating expectations with role partners. Husbands may be asked to share in household tasks, children may, if old enough, be asked to assume more responsibilities, alternative child care or housekeeping services may be devised, or bosses may be told that their demands are excessive (Merton, 1957). Although these solutions are often difficult to implement, they are the only ways of effectively eliminating the role overload.

Role Discontinuity

Women's adult lives reveal a complex pattern of role changes over time. While young men typically assume work and marriage roles that continue until old age, women's roles and role demands change considerably over time. The patterning is most diverse for women with children. These women typically work until their first child is born. They then reduce or abandon their work roles during their children's preschool years, increasing their outside role involvements as their children enter school. This changing pattern is complicated further by the variations in roles held by different women at each stage in their adult lives. Consequently, social scientists who attempt to study women's adult roles over time must contend with complex role patternings that have little parallel for men (Ginzberg, 1966; Maas and Kuypers, 1974).

These shifting role demands require continued adjustments for women. At each transition point, they have to learn new behaviors that must be meshed with other preexisting role obligations. Role transitions are further complicated when people in one's social network refuse to acknowledge a status change. Parents may continue to expect compliance from their grown children, old friends may be angered when a newlywed no longer has as much time to socialize with them, couples who become parents may find their childless friends bemused by their sudden hesitancy about making social engagements.

If the expectations of a new role are incompatible with the expectations of a previous role, an individual experiences stress in making the transition. This stress is called *role discontinuity* (Benedict, 1938). Role discontinuity is likely to be experienced more frequently by women than by men because of the major shifts in women's role obligations over time. After marriage a woman usually takes on a larger portion of household duties. If she has a child, she is plunged into a new role that demands skills and efforts for which most women are unprepared. At later points of her life, such events as job reentry, the end of her mother role as children leave home, and widowhood may force a woman to radically reorganize her life. Less dramatic changes in

Box 1   Role Overload and Women's Role Performance

People have a variety of ways of adjusting to overload situations (Miller, 1960). These common overload reactions are defined below. Each is accompanied by an illustration of the way in which an overworked housewife-mother might cope with role overload in her daily life.

Overload Reaction

1. Omission: Temporary nonprocessing of demands.

2. Queuing: Delaying response during high overload period.

3. Filtering: Neglecting to process certain types of information while processing others.

4. Cutting categories of discrimination: Responding in a general way to a number of demands.

5. Employing multiple channels: Processing information through two or more parallel channels at the same time.

6. Errors: Processing demands incorrectly.

7. Escape from the task

Mother's Response

1. Forgetting to pick up the cleaning; or not hearing a child's request while talking on the phone.

2. Promising a child that Mother will talk about their problem after dinner; telling someone to call back after the children are asleep.

3. Neglecting household tasks or elaborate food preparation in order to take care of children's needs.

4. Preparing common meals that disregard the food preferences of different family members; having a common bedtime hour for children of different ages; not responding to the unique personality needs of each child.

5. Talking to children or husband while cooking or ironing; changing a diaper while talking on the phone.

6. Confusing the date of a meeting or social engagement; burning the dinner; yelling at a child for something that she/he had gotten permission to do.

7. Going to a movie; falling asleep; leaving home.

Substained overload can lead to demoralization and fatigue. The woman who permits overload to continue while using the coping mechanisms described above is not solving her role problem. Although she is responding as well as she can to her stressful role demands, she does not attempt to restructure her role obligations in ways that reduce the demands on her. Unfortunately, these responses are far more typical of women involved in dual-career conflicts than are attempts to restructure traditional female role obligations. Working women are still reluctant to insist on the reallocation of family and housework responsibilities, opting instead for some form of role juggling that does not place added responsibilities on their husband or children (Katz, 1975).

role performance are required as children develop and role involvements shift over time.

Because role discontinuities seem more common for women than for men during the adult years, it is important to consider ways in which the resulting stress may be reduced. There are at least three ways that role transitions may be eased for an individual. First of all, the person may have developed ability in adapting to changing social expectations. A person who is flexible will find it easier to move into new roles and respond to their demands. Women seem able to respond more readily to shifts in roles because they have been trained to leave options open and respond to the expectations of others rather than their own goals (Angrist and Almquist, 1975).

The person may use available social supports to ease role entrance. Most societies provide formal supports for common role transitions (Brim and Wheeler, 1966). Frequently they structure opportunities for individuals to learn role demands before entering a new status. College orientation programs, premarriage and childbirth courses, and job training programs are examples of preentry introductions to important adult roles. These anticipatory socialization experiences attempt to smooth our transitions into unfamiliar but central roles (Merton, 1957). Sometimes particularly difficult role movements are eased by adding more stages to the transition. Women often become part-time students or workers before reentering these roles on a full-time basis.

In addition, people may informally seek information about new roles from others. Parents and friends may help a person define the expectations for an unfamiliar position. Informal communications among women may facilitate their many role transitions.

Finally, the stress of role transitions is also lessened if there are other valued roles in the person's repertoire (Maas and Kuypers, 1974). One's total life is not so radically changed by the addition or loss of a single role when other aspects of one's life have continuity. Moving to a new city and a new job may be easier for a couple than for a single person, newlyweds may find adjustment easier if their work roles are well established, and women may find it easier to return to work before children leave home than after their departure.

Role transitions resulting in the loss of a valued role may be harder than those which add a new role to an otherwise stable role repertoire. A woman who leaves her job to have a child has to adjust to the loss of work as well as to her new role of mother. She may miss experiencing feelings of competence in her work, the social contacts with workers, or even the seemingly minor pleasures of getting dressed up and out of the house each morning (LeMasters, 1957). The difficulties are even greater when a role loss is imposed by external factors rather than through individual choice. Women confront a number of such losses in later adulthood when their parent role atrophies as their children leave, or the death of their husband terminates their marriage role (Bernard, 1975; Lopata, 1973). These transitions are painful for many women because they may demand major readjustments in living patterns that have been prime sources of gratification during most of their adult life.

THE SOCIAL CLOCK

All societies have norms for behaviors that are expected for its members at various ages. These norms are known to all members of the society, and are communicated to members of each sex during the process of socialization. Regardless of whether one follows or deviates from the role pattern defined by society, one is always aware of the synchronies and asynchronies between our own lives and the "ideal-typical" life we are expected to be living at any age period.

This timetable, or *social clock,* exercises prescriptive as well as descriptive power over our behavior (Neugarten, 1968). When our lives correspond to these age-related role expectations, we are viewed approvingly by society; when we deviate, we risk social criticism. Those who conform to the roles defined by the social clock are able to prepare for transitions and thereby reduce role discontinuity. They also have the support of their social environment when moving into new age-appropriate roles.

Sex-Role Deviation

When people deviate from the social clock, they violate others' expectations for appropriate role behavior. The young woman who is still unmarried by her late twenties knows the extent of social pressure that can be directed at her because she has not embarked on a socially prescribed role, either by choice or by chance. She is viewed as a deviant for violating the normative role pattern of her age and sex. Role conflict is created between others' expectations and one's own behavior. This type of role conflict, based on nonadherence to life-cycle sex-role norms, is a major source of stress for the nontraditional woman. Unmarried women past their middle twenties, childless women past thirty, and mothers who work when their children are young all risk social disapproval for holding nonnormative roles.

People often react negatively to social deviance, both because it often leads them to question their own role choices and because it creates difficulties for their own role performance. A single woman is an awkward intrusion at coupled parties; a childless couple does not understand the young parents' need for careful social planning to accommodate babysitting arrangements. To the extent that strains are experienced by others because of an individual's nontraditional status, interaction between the deviant and significant others becomes more difficult. Parents are deprived of their age-appropriate statuses of in-laws and grandparents, and friends no longer have a companion who shares their experiences. Social deviance may also be threatening psychologically for role conformists.

The nontraditional woman also has to contend with her own internalization of expected life-cycle roles. Aware of her own deviance, she must work at justifying her status to herself as well as others. If her roles are freely chosen, she may have well-reasoned justifications for their selections, but her arguments are often unwanted criticisms to those who have adhered to the social clock. If her nonnormative status is imposed by chance—through not finding an appropriate man to marry, infertility, unwanted divorce, or premature widowhood—she may feel a sense of failure or injustice for being deprived of her age-appropriate roles. In either case the person's awareness of being out of phase with the social clock creates additional burdens for personal adjustment. She has been prepared to expect her life to unfold in the traditional way, and is unprepared for premature role transitions (like widowhood), or for anticipated transitions that do not occur on schedule (like marriage and childbearing). Her personal adjustment is further complicated by the awareness that she has lost step with her age cohort and has entered a divergent life stream with minority status in our society.

Physiological Changes during Adulthood

The social clock prepares us not only for role changes, but also for major physiological changes occurring during the adult years. Physical changes are slower and less visible after adolescence, but they are important determinants of behavior and feelings throughout the life cycle. Changes in physical capacities also require people to change their concepts of themselves. One is forced to redefine oneself as "getting older" when one's body cues different reactions from one's social environments. At some point people stop being envied for their youth, and people are treated more deferentially by those younger than themselves. These social cues combine with one's own perceptions of body changes to signal the need for a new age self-image. For many members of our youth-glorifying society, this forced age redefinition is unwelcome.

THE LIFE-CYCLE PERSPECTIVE

Although most personality theorists still focus on the formative influences of childhood as the sole determinants of adult personality, some have begun to look at personality changes that occur at later points in the life cycle (Levinson, et al., 1974; Gould, 1972; Vaillant and McArthur, 1972). Erik Erikson's (1950) delineation of the eight stages of life-cycle development has had great contemporary impact. However, his description of postadolescent stages is scant in comparison to his full detailing of childhood (see Box 2).

Box 2   Erikson's Eight Ages of Man

Erikson identifies eight central psychodynamic issues that each person must resolve sequentially. Each issue is viewed as having either an adaptive or a neurotic resolution which affects adaptation to subsequent life stages. Five of these eight stages occur in childhood or adolescence; only three are identified for the later years. These stages are defined by the central issues of concern rather than by a clear age parameter.

1. *Basic Trust vs. Basic Mistrust:* In early infancy, children gain security and trust in the world through having their physical needs met lovingly. This early experience develops a positive trust in the goodness of the world. Without such early security, a baby emerges from infancy with a basic mistrust of the social environment.

2. *Autonomy vs. Shame and Doubt:* Beyond the first year of life, the baby can either be encouraged to take control of her or his anal functions, or toilet training can occur in a coercive atmosphere that encourages shame and doubt of one's own capacities.

3. *Initiative vs. Guilt:* The oedipal period (around age 3–5) becomes the background for the development of independent actions as the child seeks to establish gender identification. The child's feelings towards her or his parents at this age can be accepted, or the parents may reject these expressions and make the child feel guilty of them.

4. *Industry vs. Inferiority:* During the early school years that make up the latency period (ages 6–12) the child can invest much energy in learning, if the social environment supports her or his efforts toward competence. On the other hand, a child in an overly critical, demanding environment will emerge with feelings of inferiority about her or his capabilities.

5. *Identity vs. Role Confusion:* During adolescence, the child grapples with the establishment of an identity independent of her or his parents. If such efforts are thwarted by the parents, the child emerges into adulthood without having clarified personal values or goals for the future.

6. *Intimacy vs. Isolation:* The urge to establish meaningful bonds with others becomes central during young adulthood. If one cannot achieve true intimacy and sharing at this time, future relationships will be superficial.

7. *Generativity vs. Stagnation:* Between young adulthood and old age, a person's major energies are directed toward full engagement in major life roles. A feeling of successful contribution is necessary for adjustment during this central adult period. Without the reward of feeling productive, a person experiences stagnation.

8. *Integrity vs. Despair:* In old age, awareness of approaching death leads to a search for the meaning of one's life. If the aged can view their past experiences with pride and satisfaction, they can face the end of their life with acceptance. If they regret their choices and involvements, they will feel a pervasive sense of disillusionment and failure.

Recent research suggests that there may be a complex pattern of psychological changes throughout the life cycle (Clausen, 1972). Each stage of adult life is seen as bringing new central issues, role patterns, feelings, and insights into focus. Personality evolves not smoothly, but in a sequential pattern that has been likened to a series of metamorphoses occurring over the life span (Gould, 1975). Temporary periods of disequilibrium are viewed as necessary precursors to later adjustment. These breakdowns in earlier functioning can provide the basis for new personality growth. Rather than viewing these periods of upheaval as maladaptive, the life-cycle perspective highlights their importance for healthy development.

The developmental perspective rests on at least three basic assumptions about normal psychological growth. It assumes that (1) each stage of life has critical psychological issues that become central focuses for individuals; (2) some stages require major personality restructuring and result in disequilibrium, while other periods show personality consolidation and relative equilibrium; and (3) each stage is sequential, building on preceding stages. Although these assumptions have been generally accepted for the preadult years, they are still only tentatively accepted for later, less studied, life-cycle stages.

The tremendous variability in people's biological, social, and psychological functioning during adulthood may be responsible for the delayed attention to common facets of adult growth. It was easier to see the differences among thirty-, forty-, fifty-, or sixty-year-olds than to observe their common bonds. The problem of identifying developmental patterns becomes even more difficult when we are specifically interested in women's adult lives.

One can assume that women's development does, in many ways, follow the same sequence of highs and lows, equilibrium and disequilibrium, found for men (Gould, 1972; Campbell, 1975). Furthermore, both sexes share the common experiences of marriage, children, awareness of age, and general physiological changes in each age period. However, some aspects of women's development are distinct. For example, motherhood is a unique and central role in most women's adult lives. It involves biological, psychological, and social components that provide a special source of experience. Women's psychological state at each life stage can often be related to the roles they hold or do not hold at that period (Birnbaum, 1971; Maas and Kuypers, 1974). We will try, in this chapter, to explore the impact on personality of women's differing life experiences.

STAGES OF THE LIFE CYCLE

In looking at a woman's adult roles over her life cycle, a number of major themes will emerge with each stage. These include the demands for adaptation created by women's roles; the relationship between expanded role involvements and satisfaction; the decreasing role demands with age; and the psychological growth of women in their later years. Each of these will be discussed in the context of eight stages: (1) young adulthood (ages 18–21); (2) choosing life roles (ages 22–24); (3) role completion (25–29); (4) readjustment (30–34); (5) becoming one's own person (35–43); (6) midlife crisis (44–47); (7) mellowing (48–60); and (8) old age (after 60). These stages have been selected as periods appropriate to women's lives which have some parallel to the stages identified for men's development. Such divisions are necessarily artificial divisions but are necessary for critical analysis. It should also be noted that the age at which an individual experiences each life stage has wide variation. It is the sequence of stages, not the ages, that appears to have the most general applicability.

Like the social clock, the stages of adult development are probably never fully experienced by any one individual. Conversely, each person's life has many points of correspondence with the normative pattern. People all get older, work and/or marry, discover that some roles bring less gratification over time, suffer the loss of roles they value, and share the knowledge of our eventual death. This life-cycle perspective emphasizes the experiences common to people of the same age while fully recognizing the diversities among them.

Young Adulthood

The young adult years (ages 18–21) are the time when most people leave home and begin preparing for their major adult roles. It is a period of transition from lives centered psychologically and economically around parents to lives of independence. Consequently, by the end of this period young adults have recognized their relative removal from their parents' sphere of influence and have begun to assume responsibility for their choices. After this time, they are less likely to see the problems in their lives as stemming from their parents (Gould, 1975).

The adolescent often leaves high school with only a vague idea of later work goals. It is a time of exploration; jobs and college courses are tried in order to arrive at a fit between work options and personal interests and abilities. The college-bound often find the protected college environment supportive of their development. Once there, they engage in activities and peer discussion that aid in discovery of interests, potentials, and self. Five trends in personal growth shown by students during their college years are: (1) stabilization of identity; (2) freeing of personal relationships; (3) deepening of interests; (4) humanizing of values; and (5) expansion of caring for others (White, 1966).

Those who become workers after high school go through the same transition toward full independence without institutional support (Levinson, et al., 1974). They may take a variety of jobs during this period before acquiring skills that insure future employability. Until this state is achieved they are usually supported by family while gaining increasing independence.

This transition period is a difficult one for most people in our society. General life satisfaction is quite low for this age group (Campbell, 1975; Gould, 1975). Standing at the brink of adulthood, young adults may realize their unpreparedness for the major life choices they will soon be making. Our society does little to reduce discontinuity in the transition from childhood to adulthood (Benedict, 1938).

Although both young men and young women face the same developmental tasks during this period, young men seem more burdened by the growth demands placed on them. They report being under considerably more stress than women, and have lower levels of life satisfaction (Campbell, 1975). The pressure for occupational choice is high for men, since this decision is the prime determinant of their adult life-style. It will not only define their work activities, but will also provide the central context for future economic resources, social expectations, and friendship networks.

Women's Special Concerns. The stress of choosing a work role is not felt as strongly by most women. Their socialization has emphasized marriage as their central adult role, with other activities subordinate to, and contingent on, their future family functions (Kuhlen and Johnson, 1952). Work choices are provisional, viewed as temporary, and are not strongly determined by the goal of future economic security. Women are taught that it is the choice of a husband, not a job, that most strongly determines their future (Angrist and Almquist, 1975).

During the young adult period most women maintain a tentativeness in their quest for personal identity as well as in their choices (Lowenthal, et al., 1975). Their sense of self is less clearly defined as they wait until marriage provides a defining context for their lives (Douvan and Adelson, 1966; Erikson, 1965). Since clarification of needs, values, satisfactions, and goals—all central aspects of identity—may increase the likelihood of incompatibilities with prospective marriage partners, continued flexibility may be adaptive by allowing for broader marriage options (Angrist and Almquist, 1975).

Women also retain a stronger dependency on others for support, approval, and direction (Bernard, 1975; Mischel, 1966). For women, the young adult period is frequently viewed as an interregnum between the girl's dependence on parents and her later dependence on her spouse (Bernard, 1975). If women view personal growth as irrelevant to, or even conflicting with, their later roles, they may expend little effort in moving toward autonomy and self-exploration. In this way they avoid the stress of independent decision making felt by men during this period and retain a malleability that may be adaptive for marital adjustment.

Women's activities in pursuit of their marriage goals provide further constraint on movements toward autonomy. Dating conventions encourage passivity and dependence in women. Within the traditional dating situation women are cast in the role of responders, mainly able to exercise veto power on proposals initiated by the man. This normative structure makes it difficult for a woman to view herself as having much autonomy in her relationships with men.

Women who deviate from the norm by actively pursuing work or relationship goals not only experience the same stresses felt by men during this period, but also risk social criticism for their inappropriate sex-role behavior. Parents may disapprove of serious career commitments that may reduce their daughter's marriageability, and young men may rebuff the overtures of an "aggressive" woman. Such pressures are often sufficient to discourage a young woman from taking further steps toward independence and self-realization (Komarovsky, 1946). Only those with strong commitment, competence, and independence may persevere, especially if their parents are sources of support for their nontraditional goals for future (Birnbaum, 1975; Helson, 1972; Ginzberg, 1966). Most young women, however, reach the end of the young adult period without having moved as far as men in clarifying their future life objectives or developing a sense of themselves as autonomous individuals.

Choosing Life Roles

Once young adults gain independence from parents and take responsibility for their own futures, they can begin their initial engagement with adult roles. This period (ages 22–24) is "a time of exploration and provisional commitment to adult roles, memberships, responsibilities, and relationships" (Levinson, et al., 1974, p. 246). The person attempts to structure a life that "provides a viable link between the valued self and the wider adult world" (p. 247). Role involvement is intense as the person makes efforts to master long-awaited adult roles (Gould, 1972).

Central to this period is the development of one's capacity for intimacy. Young people reach out to others in a desire to share their new-found sense of self. This quest for intimacy is the dominant theme of the early twenties, with failure in this goal resulting in future psychological isolation from others (Erikson, 1950). It is during this period that intimacy goals, most fully expressed in love relationships, lead many people to the choice of a marriage partner.

Entry into marriage is a major role transition which is never completely smoothed by the social rituals surrounding it. Although dating, courtship, engagement, and wedding ceremonies may reduce role discontinuity by helping people move toward marriage through progressive stages, the life changes accompanying these new roles are still profound. Socially, the married couple comes to be treated as a stable unit. Schedules, activities, and future plans need to be jointly considered and coordinated. No matter how well acquainted the pair was before marriage, they are likely to face new expectations from each other and from those around them once they enter their new status.

Women and Marriage. In traditional marriages, the new wife has major responsibility for the household. While the husband engages in outside work for their joint benefit, the woman channels her energies into the home. This task division within the family is often represented as a complementarity between the husband's instrumental activities linking the family to the work arena and the wife's expressive functions in maintaining family cohesiveness (Parsons and Bales, 1955). This dichotomy, while sensitizing one to role differences, overlooks the woman's task activities in support of her maintenance role and probably reflects a masculine research bias in family research. That is, men may well see the wife's role primarily in terms of its nurturant, expressive qualities rather than its instrumental, competent qualities. In fact, the wife binds her family together by her competent performance in her traditional role as well as by her nurturant behaviors.

In early marriage the wife appears to thrive in her new role despite its demands. Young married women report levels of life satisfaction that far surpass any other group of men or women at any stage of life. The euphoria of new wives is accompanied by a moderate rise in life satisfaction reported by husbands after marriage. Whereas women show dramatic *decreases* in stress levels after marriage, men *increase* considerably in in their feelings of stress at this time. Married men may feel burdened by their additional economic responsibilities, while married women are freed from their earlier uncertainties about their futures (Campbell, 1975). Our society reflects this discrepancy in the social accolades lavished on the bride while the groom receives warnings of his future responsibilities and restrictions.

For both sexes, however, early marriage is a highly satisfying time, well meriting its status as a "honeymoon period."[1] Adult life becomes more focused once marital choices are made; the couple shares activities and plans for their future. This central role commitment also completes the individual's full entry into the adult world.

While traditional women experience the peak satisfactions of marriage at this time, women with career goals struggle to establish their professional status within a social environment that is often indifferent or actively resistant to their efforts. If the woman is married she must combine the time-consuming role demands of her career with her home responsibilities. If she is single she faces mounting concern from parents and friends as her agemates join the married majority. It is not surprising, therefore, that female careerists have lower self-esteem and more doubts about themselves than their traditional counterparts during this period (Birnbaum 1975; Rossi, 1965).

---

[1] Blood and Wolfe (1960), Burr (1970), Dizzard (1968), and Rollins and Feldman (1970).

Role Completion

The Parental Role. Most life-cycle theorists include the years 25–29 in a single stage characterized by the themes of engagement and provisional commitment to work and family roles. For most women, however, this is the time that they are most completely immersed in their role as mother.

The birth of a child not only plunges a woman into a central new role; it also restructures her entire role constellation. The intense involvement between husband and wife which characterized early marriage diminishes after parenthood (Feldman, 1974; LeMasters, 1957). The birth of a child is also likely to reduce, or terminate, the woman's involvement in her work role. In addition, the couple often finds they have less time for friends or leisure activities. New mothers feel overloaded by child-care responsibilities, and complain of chronic tiredness and confinement to the home. Husbands resent the decline in their wives' sexual responsiveness, and the added economic burdens imposed by the loss of the wife's income (LeMasters, 1957).

The profound changes that occur after childbirth constitute a life crisis for most couples (LeMasters, 1957). Married couples with children under six report the highest stress levels of any group at any point in the life cycle, with the exception of women who are divorced or separated (Campbell, 1975). Although this stress dissipates as children get older, marital satisfaction suffers a decline that continues until children reach maturity.[2]

For women, difficulties of parenthood are counterbalanced by the emotional satisfaction that children provide. Mothers feel consistently more positive about their lives than do women who remain childless (Campbell, 1975). And although fathers of preschool children report more negative feelings about their lives than childless men, they regain their positive feelings as their children mature. At least one major study found couples with one to four children more satisfied than their childless counterparts (Blood and Wolfe, 1960).

Although children seem to add stresses to a marriage, it cannot be concluded that childlessness enhances marital satisfaction. Currently, too few couples remain voluntarily childless to permit comparison with child-raising couples at different life stages. Childless couples are usually grouped into broad age categories, making it impossible to isolate trends in marital satisfaction over time (see Box 3). Many couples may choose to remain childless because their early marriage seems extraordinarily fulfilling. Their higher satisfaction may have preceded their decision not to have children rather than being its consequence. Furthermore, childless couples with unhappy marriages may seek divorce more readily than couples with children (Renne, 1970). More studies are needed to better interpret the positive relationship between marital satisfaction and childlessness.

[2] Campbell (1975), Feldman (1974), Gould (1972), Renne (1970).

Box 3   **Satisfaction and Stresses of Adult Life**

A 1975 survey of married and unmarried men and women presents a profile of the satisfaction and stresses of various adult roles and stages. The following graph indicates the general life satisfaction reported by men and women with different roles.

General Life Satisfaction

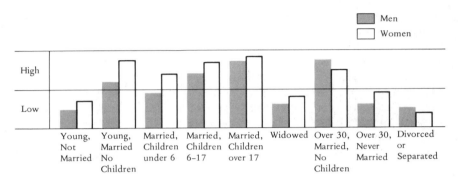

The same people were also asked to report on the amount of stress they felt in their current lives:

Feelings of Stress

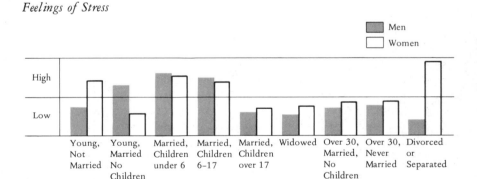

The Working Mother. Most studies of parenting years ignore the wife's work status as a relevant variable in the couple's reactions to parenthood. Yet increasing numbers of women are currently retaining their work involvement throughout child-bearing years, or are returning to work once their children enter school. Thirty percent of women with children under six years old were employed in 1972 (Hoffman and Nye, 1974). When working women were asked why they worked, only 12 percent said they worked primarily for personal satisfaction; most (72 percent) cited financial motives as the main reason for employment. However, many of these women said they would continue to work even if the money they earned was not needed (U.S. Department of Labor, 1971). The woman who works while her children are young adds another demanding role to her already stressful role as mother. On the other hand, she avoids the problems of confinement and reduced income experienced by wives who do not work.

What effect does work have on marital satisfaction during the children's preschool period? The main determinant seems to be whether the woman works out of necessity or choice. Women who need to work are less satisfied with their marriages than nonworking mothers. In contrast, working has little impact on marital satisfaction for women who choose to work (Hoffman and Nye, 1974; Orden and Bradburn, 1969). This dual role choice seems most satisfactory for college-educated women, who have more work options as well as easier access to child care and housekeeping help (Hoffman and Nye, 1974). Working outside the home is most difficult for the mother when the children are in preschool years, since complex and costly child-care arrangements are usually necessary. However, increasing numbers of women are choosing this option (see Chapter 8).

Women who maintain their professional careers during their children's early years can expect to feel role overload during this period. Although they can reduce role strain by hiring others to assist in child care and household tasks, they often feel guilt about their incomplete performance of wife and mother roles (Hoffman and Nye, 1974). Most career-oriented mothers also require cooperation and support from their husbands to handle their multiple role demands. Young couples beginning their careers may have children only if they strongly desire the experience of parenthood, since they usually recognize the complications involved in this choice. Because of these difficulties, they often have fewer children than other couples (Ginzberg, 1966; Hoffman and Nye, 1974).

Working Nonmothers. Although women with children reveal greater positive feelings about their life than childless women, couples without children appear to be higher in general life satisfaction and lower in stress than couples with children (Campbell, 1975). It is likely that the late twenties will find childless women still intensely involved with their mates. Their major problem, in fact, may well be their "deviant" status. Women who are child-free by choice report considerable social pressure from family and friends to have children. Because most of their age-mates are heavily involved in parental roles at this life stage, the childless couple's deviance is very visible. They are often stigmatized by being considered abnormal, selfish, immature, or unhappy because of their decision (Veevers, 1974).

Women with careers may, by this time, be experiencing professional successes that will bolster them against these social pressures. However, they are aware of the fact that their years of easy childbearing are rapidly diminishing. They may therefore feel increased internal, as well as external, pressure to conceive during this period if motherhood is to be part of their life.

The decisions women make during this stage create a life structure that defines their subsequent lives. Some decisions, notably childbearing, are irrevocable; other decisions, like delaying childbearing, or career pursuits, violate the mandates of the social clock and may have negative social consequences. In contrast to men, whose major life choices of work and marriage are made by their mid-twenties, women's choices regarding childbearing lead them to many diverse paths during this period. Yet current life-stage theories do not recognize the later twenties as a critical stage in women's lives.

Readjustment

The excitement of achieving adult status and participating in work, marriage, and family roles subsides by the end of one's twenties. By this time one's adult life has assumed a patterned and familiar form. Confrontation with these adult roles has resulted in "the gradual picking away of magical illusions of omnipotence and omnipotentiality" (Gould, 1972, p. 530). Life is now viewed as providing fewer rewards and somewhat higher demands than one had anticipated. As people begin to feel bound by the structure of their lives, freedom may assume a new value to them.

Around the age of thirty, men and women enter a major transition point in their life cycle (Gould, 1972; Levinson, et al., 1974). Marriages are often strained, children replace parents as centrally important, and work concerns grow more pronounced (Gould, 1972).

The readjustments made during this transitional period (ages 30–34) have major impact on future happiness for both sexes. Men struggle to make firm commitments that replace their earlier provisional role choice. Men who do not make these commitments by the age of thirty-four have a low chance of forming a reasonably satisfying life style for the future (Levinson, et al., 1974). Women also experience a transition point before their mid-thirties. Women who do not develop independence from parents, husbands, and children during this time will probably never develop an independent identity and will remain immature for the rest of their lives (Bernard, 1975).

The woman's rediscovery of her own life when her children enter school can constitute a major identity crisis. No longer preoccupied with the child-care demands of early motherhood, she may experience a kind of initial euphoria in her release. However, when this euphoria subsides she may suddenly realize that she has to overhaul her life, with few ideas for its future directions. Her earlier preparation for wife and mother roles has not prepared her for their short-term centrality. She may also suffer from feelings of not being needed.

Although she may seek her husband's support at this time, he may be preoccupied with his own concerns and interests. Men's work involvement and women's maternal focus during the later twenties have often set them on divergent paths. The distance that has come between them may become clear at this point as both partners resurface from parental preoccupations and confront formerly unnoticed changes in their marriage, each other, and themselves. They are often not pleased by what they see. Marital satisfaction is at its lowest when couples are in their early thirties. Partners find their mates least accepting of them at this time (Gould, 1975). Each partner may have strong need for the other because of the unsettling events of the period but they are often unable to understand each other's concerns.

Going Beyond the Home. As marriage and mothering roles diminish during the early thirties, women may seek new sources of satisfaction to maintain their faltering sense of self-worth. Since they have had little opportunity for role exploration at earlier stages, many options may be considered before goals for the future can be established. A woman may look to work, school, volunteer activities, or sexual affairs as alternative sources of personal fulfillment.

It seems striking that women's exploration of life paths in their early thirties bears strong resemblance to the initial efforts of the young man to establish himself as an adult ten years earlier. While men are now reevaluating their initial life structures and finally committing themselves fully to chosen roles, women are often just beginning their own efforts to establish themselves in the adult world.

These initial efforts toward self-fulfillment often require a woman to first define herself clearly. Her early activities as wife and mother were directed largely by her desires to please others. Her own needs and priorities may finally emerge as she takes independent responsibilities for her own life.

For many women, growth during the early thirties means shifts from dependence to independence, from passivity to activity, from compliance to assertion. A woman may be forced to shed many aspects of feminine sex-role traits in order to pursue her own interests. If her moves toward autonomy draw her away from the home, her children and husband may resent absences. To further complicate the woman's struggle, she may feel guilty about "neglecting" her husband or children.

Many women do manage, despite the difficulties, to extricate themselves to some extent from family-centered role definitions of themselves. Some return to the labor force at this time; there is an upsurge in women's work participation beginning at age thirty (Neugarten, 1968). Not all find gratification from this option, however. A recent national survey revealed that women without college degrees were often dissatisfied by the routine, unstimulating jobs available to them. In contrast, women with college degrees found employment more rewarding than staying at home. It appears that working outside the home may only provide a solution to the identity struggle of more educated women.

Women who attempt to reestablish careers terminated when their first child was born may experience difficulties. They are ten years behind their male age-mates in career development, and may have trouble convincing employers that they are serious in their work commitments. Although age discrimination is not a serious barrier to employment for women in their thirties, these women may be sensitive to the incongruity between their maturity and their status as occupational beginners.

Increasing numbers of women are currently reentering college at this age to complete education terminated earlier. They may also feel discomforted by age discrepancies between themselves and their fellow students and perhaps with faculty as well; they also have to recapture skills that have been unused for a long time.

Other women may find fulfillment in increased participation in voluntary activities. This option permits an expansion of involvements without as many conflicts with home responsibilities. Volunteers often perform needed human services that are challenging and rewarding for the participants. In the process of venturing into such areas of activities, many women gain a new sense of independent self-worth.

Becoming One's Own Person

It is in the mid-thirties that men finally come into their own. This period, which psychologist Daniel Levinson calls BOOM—Becoming One's Own Man—is marked by focused, goal-directed activities, particularly in work roles. Successful men become independent of mentors who have been influential in guiding their earlier professional lives (Levinson, et al., 1974; Vaillant and McArthur, 1972). After this point they will direct the future course of their own development.

The centrality of mentors in men's careers may have a parallel in women's dependence on husbands. Women may have to free themselves from this different, and possible stronger, dependency before becoming their own person (Bernard, 1975).

In 1941 Eleanor Roosevelt, looking back at her emergence from her earlier years as dutiful child, wife, and mother, wrote:

> Somewhere along the line of development we discover what we really are, and then we make our real decision for which we are responsible. Make that decision primarily for yourself, because you can never really live anyone else's life not even your child's. The influence you exert is through your own life and what you become yourself. (Lash, p. 238.)

Mrs. Roosevelt "found" herself by attempting to improve the human condition. Her dedicated efforts sometimes brought her into conflict with her strong-minded husband Franklin, but she had developed sufficient independence by this time to fight for her commitments despite their personal costs. Such a process occurs for many women at this age.

It would appear that, for women as well as men, the mid-thirties are the point when people may finally reach a clarity about their future life direction (Levinson, et al., 1974; Vaillant and McArthur, 1972). Commitments deepen and lose their provisional character, the person constructs a stable life-style reflecting established priorities, and goals established for the future are pursued wholeheartedly. For men, economic security and career advancement are frequently desired goals, with activities directed toward "making it" occupationally (Gould, 1972; Levinson, et al., 1974). There is a corresponding decrease of interest in social activities. Marriages are still low in satisfaction, and parents with adolescent children often find this period the most difficult, least satisfying, life stage (Clausen, 1972).

The source of many of these changes may be found in the fact that people seem suddenly conscious of reaching life's halfway point. The limits of the time left for achieving life objectives is realized, and individuals are less likely to feel that there is enough time to meet all their goals (Gould, 1975). Health concerns also begin to increase.

Despite the problems of the period (ages 35–43), well-adapted older men found the ages from thirty-five through fifty to be the happiest of their lives (Vaillant and McArthur, 1972). However, those unable to make a satisfactory transition into this period found middle life unhappy and yearned for their more youthful years. Thus, for both sexes, the early thirties appear to be a harbinger of future life satisfaction (Bernard 1975; Levinson, et al., 1974). If one attains a clear sense of purpose during the early thirties, one establishes a positive direction for subsequent years.

Involvements outside the Home. Women who have found new and rewarding roles for themselves during the early thirties or women who maintain earlier career commitments may find this period as intensely involving and satisfying as men do. Middle-class women who are not burdened by economic motives for role choices, may also find a great deal of life satisfaction during this time.

Currently, over half the women with school-age children are employed either full or part time. Although many still work from economic necessity, a growing number choose this option when their last child enters school. For these women, work is a satisfying experience that increases self-esteem and adds to marital happiness (Hoffman and Nye, 1974; Orden and Bradburn, 1969). Part-time employment for women with school-age children is related to the highest marital satisfaction for both their husbands and themselves (Orden and Bradburn, 1969). This period also provides psychological compensations for the earlier difficulties of women with careers. They now show significantly higher levels of self-esteem (whether married or single) than their homemaker counterparts (Birnbaum, 1975; see Box 4). While the majority (54 percent) of professional women both married and unmarried, ranked "good" to "very good' in self-esteem ratings in one study, only 14

Box 4   Self-Esteem of Educated Women, Ages 36–46, by Role Choice

| | *Self-Esteem* | | |
	Homemaker	Married Professional	Single Professional
Poor to Average	31%	4%	15%
Average to Good	55%	42%	31%
Good to Very Good	14%	54%	54%

SOURCE: Birnbaum, 1975.

percent of homemakers had equivalent scores. A study of educated women extends this finding to women whose work involvements were less continuous and less committed to career development (Ginzberg, 1966). For highly educated women, work provided a source of ego enhancement that could be obtained within the home only by a very small minority of similar women.

Although these studies do not investigate the effect of work for less-educated women, most women make gains in psychological growth at this time. Women report themselves to be most self-confident during their thirties, with a sense of being in their prime during the latter half of this period (University of Chicago Reports, 1961). Another study, using a standard projective measure, the "draw-a-person" test, found women's self-images to expand during their thirities, reaching a peak around age forty. In contrast, men's self-images began their decline after age thirty (Lehner and Gunderson, 1953).

If one considers the poorly formed identity of women entering adulthood, and the selflessness of their early preoccupations as wives and mothers, it is not surprising that women make identity gains during their thirties when these demanding roles are less salient. Men, however, enter adulthood with a firmer identity and develop greater self-esteem during their early work years. While women expand during the thirties, men may be confronting impediments to their aspirations for the first time.

While there is general evidence that women gain a better sense of themselves during this period, and specific data suggesting that work involvement contributes to enhanced self-esteem for educated women, it is still unclear whether work is growth-enhancing for less-educated females. Nor are there data about whether alternative role options, such as volunteerism, provide comparable growth opportunities. However, it is likely that women who make no effort to seek new roles during their thirties will experience increasing difficulties in their later lives.

Mid-Life Crisis

Theorists agree that there is a point in the life cycle when people experience a major transition into middle age (ages 44–47). As people age they become aware that they no longer look young, may no longer feel attractive, and can no longer rely on their body to function unflaggingly. Their grown children and aging parents also make vivid their own halfway status in the adult life span. No longer able to think of themselves as young, they confront the disquieting prospect of becoming old (Levinson, et al., 1974).

The feeling that time is running out creates a psychological pressure to make the most of one's remaining good years; to seek out desired experiences before it is too late (Gould, 1972). There seems to be a "now-or-never" feeling that underlies decisions made during the midlife transition. Disparities between early expectations for family and work roles and their current form may be sharply discomforting. Stagnant marriages and unrewarding work may be abandoned if more attractive options seem available. By the midforties, people may feel it is "too late to make any major changes in their careers; and that their personalities and lives are pretty much set" (Gould, 1972).

As people examine how their lives have evolved thus far, they may rethink priorities and past role involvements. Unresolved feeling about parents may be reawakened and finally resolved and roles currently held may yield new sources of satisfaction (Vaillant and McArthur, 1972). Marriages may become more comfortably companionate when they are no longer expected to provide total involvement or sexual excitement. Work may offer new opportunities for guiding others as a mentor, and for enjoying increased recognition for one's past achievements. Money and further advancement no longer remain central goals for work after this time (Gould, 1972).

Individuals may achieve a more mature level of self-understanding and more realistic expectations for their future. Although the reevaluation process may provoke depression and disillusionment for some, others achieve a new peace as an outgrowth of the period (Vaillant and McArthur, 1972). One should understand that this transition into middle age need not be accompanied by major disruption. A mid-life crisis period is not inevitable, and many people find increased satisfaction as they move into their later years (Clausen, 1972).

Menopause and the "Empty Nest." The unique female crisis of menopause and the "empty nest" occurs at a life stage when psychological turbulence is already present for both sexes. Most women face a more complete loss of their maternal role while in their forties as children reach adulthood and leave home to establish independent lives. If nurturance and child-care activities have been a prime focus of a woman's life for the last twenty years, she may find that her "empty nest" leaves her with too much unstructured time and few sources of rewarding activities. Role discontinuity can be severe for child-oriented women who lose this mothering role. However, more women react positively to the empty nest. Women whose children have left are more satisfied, less self-pitying, less easily hurt than women whose children are still at home (Lowenthal, et al., 1975). They generally show fewer depressive symptoms when their children are independent of them (Radloff, 1975).

The disequilibrium of this period may be further exacerbated by the onset of menopause which, until recently, occurred in the late forties. Currently, the average age for menopause has risen to the early fifties (Cherry, 1976). The loss of childbearing capacity often occurs close to the point at which child-rearing functions also cease. If a woman believes that reproduction and motherhood define her unique contributions to the world, the juxtaposed loss of these sex-role functions may strip her of her central sources of self-esteem. The feeling that she is now useless, old, barren, and unneeded may trigger a psychological depression that requires therapeutic intervention (Chesler, 1972). These feelings, strikingly similar to those experienced by some men at retirement, testify to the deep impact of role loss on psychological functioning. Many women, however, have already expanded into new areas by this time and adapt well in subsequent stages to their new freedom from maternal roles. Other women approach this age with hopeful expectations for independence and freedom to develop their own interests.

Mellowing

Successful resolution of the mid-life crisis creates a stable, satisfying structure for the years that follow (ages 48–60). Preexisting work and family roles may yield new satisfaction as pressures and responsibilities decline. Their prior devitalization may be overcome by a more mature appreciation of their values. For some, the new role of grandparent is added. Friends become more valued as advancing age threatens the survival of long-standing bonds.

Middle age can be a time of new possibilities. Many people feel really comfortable with themselves as they find they have sufficient experience and self-knowledge to deal easily and competently with life events (Kuhlen, 1964; Neugarten, 1968). People show high levels of life satisfaction, feel only low levels of stress and, in general, feel positive about their lives (Campbell, 1975). Their new maturity enables them to view this period as truly the prime of life (Neugarten, 1968).

Increased contemplation and internal exploration are common outgrowths of the midlife transition. Many investigators have noted the shift to thoughtful self-understanding that occurs at middle age (Neugarten, 1968; Kuhlen, 1964). Actions are more likely to be internally generated rather than being a response to the expectations of others.

A study of a hundred middle-class men and women in their middle years showed them to be enthusiastic about their age status and to exhibit a sense of competence, expertise, and increased self-understanding. They saw themselves as the "norm-bearers and the decision-makers [who] live in a society which, while it may be oriented towards youth, is controlled by the middle-aged" (Neugarten, 1968, p. 93). Very few of the respondents expressed any desire to be young again. Both men and women cited greater maturity and a better grasp of realities as reassuring attributes of being middle-aged and were oriented towards accumulating new accomplishments and satisfactions before life was over.

Although this period can be a very happy one, there are also common problems. The death of one's parents commonly occurs during this time. Although people are largely independent of their parents at this age, the loss of one's status as a child may contribute to one's own sense of aging. Aging parents may also make people fearful of their own entry into old age. Since most American families distance themselves from the responsibility of caring for their aging parents, and may even hope their parents die without prolonged and costly terminal illness, they may feel guilt about aging parents (Kalish, 1969). Such guilt often extends to other instances of perceived neglect or mistreatment during earlier stages of the life cycle.

Despite these feelings evoked by the old age and death of one's parents, the disequilibrium surrounding this is usually not severe. The social clock leads one to anticipate its occurrence around this time. Furthermore, parents in our society cease to play a central role in their children's life after adulthood, so day-to-day living is not disrupted (Kalish, 1969; Parkes, 1972; Reiss, 1969).

Many people may be more unsettled by the upsurge in illness and death among their peers. Even if one's body escapes the direct onslaught of heart attack, cancer, or stroke, the middle-aged person sees increasing evidence of their threat as friends and acquaintances suffer their consequences. Because of these experiences, anxiety over one's health increases dramatically during middle age (Neugarten and Garron, 1959). A national survey found three times more anxiety about physical health was felt by people between ages forty-five and sixty-four as compared to those in the twenty-one to thirty-four age group (Gurin, Veroff, and Feld, 1960).

More personal, though less dramatic, evidence of the effects of aging also contribute to the person's anxiety. Physical signs of age begin to become apparent around age forty (Chown, 1972; Shock, 1960). One may observe declines in reaction time, strength, sensory acuity, and sexual capacity. Chronic complaints such as arthritis, high blood pressure, gallstones, or digestive disorders may become more troublesome at this time, causing serious discomfort requiring change in prior patterns of activities. Weight, cholesterol, and blood-sugar levels may become harder to control and may require dietary restrictions. Breast cancer becomes a major threat for women. Wrinkles, sagging skin, and greying or thinning hair contribute to the loss of youthful appearance. For many people within our youth-oriented society, these cosmetic changes symbolize a loss of highly valued physical attractiveness.

The increasing popularity of efforts to retain youthful image—hair dyes, wigs, face lifts, and hormone treatments—testify to the negative attitude towards aging in our society. People cling to youth not only because of vanity, but because they recognize that age excludes them from many valued spheres of activity. Job possibilities are restricted for middle-aged workers. Age barriers based on the false belief that work capacity diminishes with age, often lead employers to underutilize their older workers—overlooking them for promotions, firing them, or refusing to hire them (Shock, 1960). Age discrimination is a central concern for the increasing number of women who return to the labor market during this time, as well as for the substantial group of men who seek new careers to replace former work that has become unrewarding or stagnant by middle age.

Other reasons for age concealment also exist. Our society has age norms that define many pleasurable behaviors as no longer appropriate in middle age. If people want to maintain earlier involvement in athletics, if they want to remain attractive to the opposite sex, or if they value their enthusiasm and playfulness they may attempt to maintain a youthful appearance so that their behavior remains socially permissible. Although they may not be rebuked directly by being told to "act their age," they find that age norms often impose undesired constraints upon their behavior (Neugarten, Moore, and Lowe, 1965).

Woman's Development during Middle Age. The problems and possibilities of middle age may have more personal impact for women, especially for women who have maintained their traditional role up to this point. The upsurge in mental disturbances among married women during these years testifies to the difficulties some women may have (Chesler, 1972; Lowenthal, et al., 1975). Although women show greater depression than men throughout their adult years, more educated women are less prone to this depression. Interestingly, women whose children have left home show less depression than either childless women or women whose children are still in the home. And, although working women are not, overall, less depressed than nonworking women, women with similar levels of marital satisfaction seem less depressed when they work rather than stay at home (Radloff, 1975). Other data suggest that, in general, "family-centered women (in comparison with their male counterparts or with women who have more involvement with the outside world) are likely to suffer from the psychic consequences of such early deprivation in the later stages of life" (Lowenthal, et al., 1975, p. 240).

Many women, however, seem to gain strength and direction as they meet the challenge of this period. They enjoy the increased time and energy now available for self and their new opportunity to use previously latent talents and capacities (Neugarten, 1968). Having fulfilled society's expectations for child-rearing, they now are free to develop more self-directed roles. During these years, women become increasingly involved in outside activities, while men's activity sphere becomes more limited (Lowenthal, et al., 1975). In general, women show better adaptations than men to middle age (Kuhlen, 1964). Their personalities become more integrated and a positive sense of identity is often first established at this point (Neugarten, 1968). In contrast, men are often conscious of new constraints that restrict their activities in formerly valued role sectors. Men are also more concerned than women during this period about health and body changes (Neugarten, 1968). Women may be aware that they are less likely than men to be subjected to health threats during this period of their lives. They may also have less investment than men in maintaining physical prowess. Furthermore, they may have less discomfort with the dependency situation that possible illness creates. For whatever reason, women are less worried than men by the physical threats of middle age, and show better psychological adjustment during these years.

Changes in Marriage. Women's feelings about marriage also show marked improvement once children have left home.[3] Couples at this point may turn again to one another for the companionship and support that diminished in earlier years because of heavy child-rearing and work demands. Once more they have time for shared activities and communication. Mothers and fathers with older children appear to be happier than their childless age-mates (Campbell, 1975). After the unsettling years of parenting, when marital satisfaction drops markedly, middle-aged couples can look forward to an equivalent number of highly satisfying postparental years. Feelings of companionship and understanding may be quite high for couples at this age.

Women now play a more dominant role in marital decision making than they did at earlier periods. Referred to as "peak wife-dominance," both husbands and wives often consider the wife the dominant partner (Blood and Wolfe, 1960; Neugarten, 1968). This pattern, which is a dramatic reversal of the earlier marital power structure, is further evidence of the increased assertiveness that women show in middle age. They no longer feel as dependent on their husbands for approval, have greater self-direction, and can engage in active effort to gain their desired objectives. For many traditional women, the mid-life crisis seems to culminate in their final unleashing from earlier sex-role personality constraints. They may be aided in this transition by the corresponding decline in their husband's need to play his marital role according to social prescriptions. Both partners, newly comfortable with

___

[3] Burr (1970), Gould (1972), Towenthal et al. (1975), Renne (1970), Rollins and Cannon (1974), and Rollins and Feldman (1970).

expressing their personal rather than sexual imperatives, may reshape their marriage into a more rewarding form.

Working outside the Home.   Women who work during these years may find further enhancement for their marriage. Marital satisfaction is much higher for working wives than for nonworking wives during the postparental period (Rose, 1965), and marital conflict is lessened (Dizzard, 1968). Working couples also share more in decision making, household tasks and leisure-time activities (Blood and Wolfe, 1960). The ability to act independently in assuming a new life role is additional evidence of women's increased self-direction during the middle years.

Although marriages are improved when women hold jobs, women do not choose to work to increase marital satisfaction. Why do women, in ever increasing numbers, enter the work force at middle age?

> . . . women work not only to contribute to the family's funding for goods and services, [but] for greater personal autonomy in spending, for status inside and outside the family, to occupy themselves in an interesting way, to meet people, to have the excitement of being in a contest for advancement, [and] to reduce the amount of housework they do. . . . [While] the jobs most women now have tend to fulfill these desires to a less satisfactory extent than the jobs men now have, they [nevertheless] frequently fulfill them better than staying home would. (Bergmann and Adelman, 1973, p. 512.)

Although women come into the labor market at an age when employers devalue their contributions because of age discrimination and although, as women, their jobs are more mundane and salaries lower than men's, they still gravitate to these new work roles.

Between 1900 and 1970 the work-force participation for women aged forty-five to sixty-five has tripled (Hoffman and Nye, 1974). Women, because of a longer life expectancy and smaller family size, now have a twenty-year period when work is possible once their children are grown. Although at this point a woman cannot expect to equal the career successes of a woman who entered the labor force in her twenties or thirties, she may be content with more modest evidence of her competence. In addition, she assumes the work role at a point when role conflict and overload are unlikely to occur and when work may, as a consequence, seem an unalloyed pleasure.

The woman who choses a career in her early years may, at this point, show diminished work focus that parallels the man's. Her professional confidence and competence are well established by this time, and she may seek new areas for further development. If she is married but childless, her general satisfaction is high, although she feels somewhat more stress at this point than traditional women. If she has never married, her life satisfaction is lower. She may find it harder than the married woman to find companionship during this period when relationships take on new value. However, she maintains a positive feeling about her life, and is better adjusted than unmarried men (Bernard, 1972a; Campbell, 1975).

During the middle years, diversity of role involvements seems to relate to life satisfaction. Working women who are married and have grown children seem, with their broadest role base, to be most satisfied with this stage of life. Women with more truncated role sets may react more strongly to the sex-role losses of the period. Many women, however, attain both personal growth and new satisfactions for this period.

Old Age

When people reach their sixties they enter a new and final stage in the life cycle. At this point they confront the loss of many highly valued roles, the need to establish a new life structure for the remaining years, and the undeniable fact of life's termination. Widowhood and retirement are the central role transitions likely to occur at this time, but the death of friends and relatives also diminishes one's social network. Although people are aware of the inevitability of these role losses as they enter old age, their often abrupt reality may result in severe role discontinuity.

Despite the major problems encountered during this period, new personality growth may occur. Old age is a time for reflections about one's past, new insights into life's meaning, and acceptance of death. If one's past life is viewed positively with feelings of pride and pleasure, then the aging period can bring final conviction about life's values. If, on the other hand, life has fallen far short of one's expectations, its conclusion will be viewed as additional reason for disillusion and despair. Regardless of the outcome, this life stage stimulates a process of life review that leads individuals to a judgment of their worth. The apparent preoccupation with reminiscence observed among the elderly is part of their personal effort to seek new understanding of life's meaning (Butler, 1963; Erikson 1950; Kuhlen, 1964; Neugarten, 1968).

Some theorists believe that acceptance of age only comes with a voluntary withdrawal from prior roles. As one's social network diminishes and one's body offers increasing resistance to physical demands, the aging person may want to disengage from old role and behavioral patterns. According to this viewpoint the disengagement process is a facilitator of successful aging. Better personal adjustment during this life stage is shown by people with more circumscribed role relationships and activities. The aging process is best effected when people's readiness to abandon roles corresponds to actual termination. Problems occur when roles endure after they are no longer desired, or when the person is forced to abandon a role prematurely (Cumming and Henry, 1961). From this perspective, widowhood and retirement may not present inherent problems if they occur when the maintenance of such roles requires too much effort to remain gratifying.

This disengagement perspective has been challenged by other theorists.[4] They suggest that successful aging is related to the maintenance of earlier activities. They found that people with greater life involvement were more satisfied than those with more limited role linkages. Although personality and social factors also influenced the satisfaction levels achieved in old age, activity, not disengagement, was generally associated with better adjustment. Perhaps both patterns exist, with activity being related to successful aging for the healthy vigorous person and disengagement being more appropriate as health deteriorates.

Widowhood. The loss of one's spouse may be the most extreme life crisis one can encounter (Maddison and Viola, 1968; Parkes, et al., 1969). It severs some of the deepest emotional bonds established during one's lifetime. It also requires an extensive restructuring of day-to-day patterns of behavior. The organizing framework of routine, habit, and activities that had shaped one's daily life for most of the adult years is frequently shattered by the death of one's mate. The sense of loss can pervade every aspect of life, since all other role spheres were meshed with one's marriage. The facts and feelings about work and other activities were usually brought into the marriage to share with one's spouse. A spouse's death means that one has lost the person who often knew and cared most about one's life.

Although the death of one's spouse is an acknowledged possibility for most people in their sixties, its actuality can never be adequately prepared for. Grief for the loss of the valued spouse may extend over many months. The grieving process, so necessary to subsequent adjustment, is often hindered by society's resistance to evidence of bereavement (Lindemann, 1944). During this time former friends, discomforted by the mourning process, may withhold beneficial support for the widowed person. Furthermore, married couples may draw away from social contact with their newly widowed friends. Loneliness and social withdrawal are common consequences of widowhood, and are the most serious difficulties reported by widowed women (Lopata, 1973).

Women are likely to suffer extensive reductions in status and social opportunities when their husband dies. Women are often also hindered by their earlier dependence on their husbands for management of finances. Once widowed they find themselves ignorant of their monetary resources, ill-equipped to make financial decisions, and forced to live under drastically reduced income.

Widowhood is a role that women face far more often than men. There are

[4] Kimmel (1974), Maddox (1965, 1970), Maddox and Eisdorfer (1962), Neugarten (1968), Palmore (1970).

five widows for every widower in this country. This imbalance is due to women's longer life span, their husbands usually being older than they are, and the lesser likelihood of remarriage for women (Kimmel, 1974). The average age of widowhood for women is sixty-one, leaving them with approximately sixteen years in their status as widows. Unless a woman is capable of creating a satisfying life on her own, these years can be empty. Women who are middle-class, better educated, and involved in multiple roles are best equipped to cope with widowhood. Some women find new pleasure in the freedom of widowhood, and enjoy new social experiences with the "society of widows" formed in the later years as increasing numbers of women enter this status (Cumming and Henry, 1961). Adequate adjustment to this role, as to most other role changes in the later years, seems to depend upon personal and financial resources developed in earlier life stages.

Retirement. While widowhood is the major role crisis facing women during their sixties, retirement is the central role crisis for most men. Termination of the work role requires extensive adjustment for the person whose entire adult life has been organized around one's job. Retirement means time that needs to be filled, the loss of a central source of self-esteem and competence, a break with work associates who have often been one's major companions in earlier years, and a need to develop new home-based patterns of activity. Often husband and wife resent the intrusion of the other into their formerly independent day-time hours; full-time togetherness creates friction instead of solidarity.

Retirement for many men means the loss of their central male role. They often feel disoriented and useless when they can no longer fulfill their bread-winning functions. These feelings, experienced twenty years earlier by their wives when child-rearing was completed, are hard to overcome. Unless new roles are found that satisfy competence, activity, and friendship needs, the man may withdraw into ruminations about his past satisfactions instead of seeking new outlets for his future (Cumming and Henry, 1961).

Loss of Income and Health. For most people, this period also involves a reduction in income. Income losses after retirement or widowhood force additional constraints on life-style options. Freedom from former roles only become a positive opportunity for expansion when there is sufficient money for recreation, travel, or other leisure-time activities. If income restrictions are severe, as they are for the majority of the aging population, life holds the demoralizing prospect of becoming merely an effort in survival. Health deterioration often imposes additional constraints on the older person. Even without major debilitating illness, the elderly may find that they have less energy for active participation in available role sectors. Their failing bodies may be viewed with frustration as another limiting factor in efforts to maintain past patterns of behavior.

Women's Adaptation to Aging. As in the middle-age period, there is evidence to suggest that women adapt to aging better than men. The disengagement process for women is more gradual than for men, beginning in the early sixties and continuing relatively smoothly as role activities decrease. Women are likely to view role losses in a more positive light, since they often are seen as a "relief" from responsibilities that were becoming somewhat burdensome. In fact, the lowest morale of older women is shown by those who are still most engaged in prior traditional roles (Cumming and Henry, 1961).

Except for widowhood, women may not experience the discontinuity that men often feel after retirement. Women are likely to maintain satisfying bonds with family and friends. Their earlier roles can still provide them with a daily pattern of activity which can continue until physical deterioration is far advanced. Furthermore, their greater comfort in dependency situations may soften the indignity surrounding their declining ability to shift themselves.

Because of their greater comfort with the role changes imposed by aging, women continue their relative gains in ego strength and assertiveness during old age. In one study, participants of both sexes viewed a picture of an elderly couple, and perceived the woman as dominant and the man as submissive. Old respondents, in fact, made these attributions more often than younger groups (Neugarten, 1968). There are some less-healthy manifestations of ego strength that women display as they grow older. Women increase in authoritarianism as they age, while men remain constant (Cumming and Henry, 1961). This authoritarian characteristic, which involves a rigid conviction about the truth of one's beliefs, may be responsible for the increased demandingness that women may also show in later years. Confidence in themselves and comfort in their familiar social environment may lead them to exert increasing domination over others. Their husbands may, after retirement, feel less grounds than ever before for attempting to exert power within the marriage. Carl Jung's observation that men become more feminine and women become more masculine in personality during their last half of life seems to find support in current data (Lowenthal, et al., 1975).

Women who have made nontraditional role choices at earlier points in the life-cycle may show different patterns of adjustment to aging. Nonmarried women may find increased social opportunities as widowhood leaves many women in comparable single status. Childless women may miss support from and interaction with children and grandchildren. Working women may experience some discontinuity at retirement, but unless they were career-committed this event will not cause major disruption. A recent longitudinal study showed that work-centered mothers were highest on life satisfaction of any group of women at age seventy (Maas and Kuypers, 1974). These women were still active and involved with children and friends. Women who were group centered also showed good adjustment at seventy. Other women, who were more exclusively family focused, found less satisfaction in later years. In fact, those who never developed adequate feelings of self-worth, who were relatively inactive, and who found it hard to adapt to life changes showed greatest personality disorganization at age seventy. This suggests that wives and mothers should expand their interests and involvements beyond the circle of the family if their later years are not to become problematic (Maas and Kuypers, 1974). Another study found that the most feminine women of women in their sixties were the most critical of themselves (Lowenthal, et al., 1975).

ADAPTABILITY—A CENTRAL THEME IN DEVELOPMENT

Most women enter adulthood with poorly developed goals for their future. During the college years

> . . . women are open to many possibilities and . . . try to remain flexible and adaptable. They do not peg their plans on a single hook; instead they expect, realistically, to incorporate a number of roles into their adult lives. Such openness helps them cope with the many demands on their lives— marriage, child-rearing, work, community involvement and the myriad other activities they expect to have. (Angrist and Almquist, 1975, pp. 32–33.)

The openness and adaptability that young women show in planning for their future proves to be well founded. Studies of women at later points in the life cycle invariably comment on the complexities of their pattern of role involvements (Ginzberg, 1966; Maas and Kuypers, 1974). They may make tentative work choices before marriage which they later adjust to their new role obligations as wife. If they have children, they are faced with the continued need to adjust to new role demands as their children mature.

Adaptiveness to the changing nature of their lives seems characteristic of women throughout adulthood. At each stage, women attempt to fulfill the external expectations placed on them while building additional roles that may enrich their personal satisfactions. The choices made are often hesitant, since women's realm outside their family roles has never been clearly specified. They frequently select and explore various options—a job, volunteer activities, continued education, social groups—in their effort to arrive at a blend of roles that fits their needs at a specific period in their lives. As their needs change, the process of achieving a balanced life must begin again.

Adaptability has the advantages of allowing women to adjust more easily to changes that occur and to avoid being locked into outmoded behavioral patterns. However, it has the disadvantage of impeding long-range planning, thereby depriving most women of the pleasure of attaining goals that require extended time commitments. Most women experience this type of long-term satisfaction only in their maternal role. Consequently, they often see their child's progress toward maturity as their most substantial contribution to the world. Yet other women are increasingly choosing alternative roles. Future research will reveal both how successfully and how happily they adapt in these new situations.

10 Biosocial Aspects of Reproduction

In the early 1970s a controversy arose when a physician on the Democratic party's National Priorities Committee publicly asserted that women were unfit for high-level executive jobs and government offices because of their physiology, particularly the menstrual cycle and menopause.

> If you had an investment in the bank . . . you wouldn't want the president of your bank making a loan under these raging hormonal influences at that particular period. . . .
>
> There just are physical and psychological inabilities that limit a female's potential . . . all things being equal, I would still rather have had a male J.F.K. make the Cuban missile crisis decisions than a female of similar age who could possibly be subject to the curious mental aberrations of that age group. . . .
>
> . . . it would be safer to entrust a male pilot's reactions and judgments in a difficult in-flight or landing problem than to even a slightly pregnant female pilot. (*New York Times, July 26, 1970.*)

Although few people take such an extreme a position, there is no doubt that beliefs concerning reproduction-related functions are an important factor in discrimination against women. Many believe that it is riskier to employ women than men because of the presumed greater absentee rate of menstruating women or because "women can always get pregnant." The latter

---

Diane Ruble and Irene Frieze were the primary authors of this chapter.

point seems to assume that working and pregnancy are incompatible events.

This chapter will examine what is known about the impact of menstruation, oral contraceptives, pregnancy, and menopause upon the performance and moods of women. The major focus will be the psychological and behavioral changes associated with each biological event. Both biological and social-psychological factors will be considered as causes of these changes.

THE SEX HORMONES

There are three basic hormones or hormone groups which are directly related to reproduction and sexual behavior in women and men. These are androgens, estrogens, and progesterones. Each type of hormone has wide-ranging effects on the body's functioning. These effects depend upon the individual biology of the person as well as upon his or her stage of development. Hormones and other biological factors are responsible for the physical development of the child as either male or female. The relative hormone levels in the fetus determine the form of its genitals as well as influencing its brain development. The prenatal hormone differences between girls and boys will also predispose the adult woman or man to have either a cyclical (female) or acyclical (male) pattern of circulating hormones and to respond more or less strongly to various sex hormones as an adult.

During the childhood years, there are few hormone differences between girls and boys, but with puberty come large hormonal variations. At this time, these sex-linked hormonal variations are responsible for the differing appearance of men and women as they cause their secondary sexual characteristics to emerge. Androgen is often called the male sex hormone, because men produce higher levels of this hormone than do women. Similarly, estrogen and progesterone are often called female sex hormones. Both sexes have these hormones, but women tend to have relatively more estrogen and progesterone while men usually have more androgen. Chemically these hormones are very similar, and within the body they are sometimes converted to one another for particular uses or into common chemical forms. At other times their actions oppose one another.

The Female Hormones: Estrogen and Progesterone

The ovaries are women's major source of estrogen. The ovaries produce varying amounts of estrogen during the menstrual cycle under the influence of the pituitary gland and the hypothalamus in the brain. Estrogen is also produced in small amounts in both men and women by the adrenal glands, located above the kidneys. Male testes also produce very small amounts of estrogen. Estrogen levels rise dramatically during pregnancy, as a result of estrogen production by the placenta, but return to normal levels after the woman gives birth. After menopause, ovarian estrogen production declines so that there are much lower levels of estrogen circulating throughout the body of the postmenopausal woman than at any earlier point in her adult life (e.g., Brown, 1955).

Estrogen is responsible for the development and maintenance of the female sex organs as well as for secondary characteristics such as breast development, fat deposits under the skin which give the adult female body a smooth appearance, some muscular development (although not as much as is produced by androgen), resistance to disease through its action upon the blood, and increased sense of smell. The female hormone estrogen also affects salt and water metabolism and facilitates calcium replacement in the bones.

The second female hormone is progesterone. Progesterone is produced in large quantities by the sac which surrounds the ovum released by the ovary during the midpoint of each menstrual cycle. This sac, called the corpus luteum, remains in the reproductive system for several days after ovulation and continues to produce progesterone. After the corpus luteum degenerates, progesterone production stops until the next menstrual cycle, with the release of a new ovum. However, if fertilization of the ovum occurs, the corpus luteum continues to secrete progesterone for several weeks until progesterone production is taken over by the placenta of the developing fetus. Large amounts of progesterone are produced during pregnancy but after birth this rapidly declines. Progesterone is also produced in small amounts by the adrenals of both sexes and the male testes. Physically, progesterone causes enlargement of the breasts, increased protein metabolism, blocking of the sodium and water retention effects of estrogen, and preparation of the uterus for the implantation of a fertilized ovum.

The Male Hormone: Androgen

The male hormone, androgen, like the other hormones is produced in small amounts in both men and women by the adrenals. In men, however, the primary source of androgens is the testes. The most important of the androgens is testosterone, produced by the testes of the mature male. Often the terms androgen and testosterone are used interchangeably. Testosterone is responsible for the development and maintenance of the male sexual organs and for male secondary sexual characteristics such as muscle development, beard growth, enlargement of the larynx (and thus voice lowering), and chest hair. It may also cause baldness and leads to increased protein metabolism. Men have small daily fluctuations in testosterone levels with peak amounts in the early morning (Luce, 1970).

Androgen Levels and Behavior. Advances in biological techniques have made possible increasingly sophisticated techniques for measuring hormone levels in the body. However, in spite of these methodological advancements, there are still a number of problems. First, the concentration of a hormone in the blood is not necessarily the best indicator of its potency or the best correlate for a given behavior. For example, only a small percentage of the circulating testosterone is biologically active (Doering, et al., 1974). Also, hormones do not operate independently of other physiological activity. For example, a high level of testosterone often inhibits the action of estrogen (Rose, 1972). A second measurement problem is that the hormone concentration in a particular blood sample may not be representative of the average concentration for an individual. Hormone levels vary considerably during twenty-four hours; depending upon the time of the day that the sample is collected, the level may be particularly high or low (Doering, et al., 1974). This daily fluctuation may be especially troublesome in the study of hormone correlates of sexual behavior. Hormone levels present in blood collected at the laboratory may not be at all indicative of levels during sexual activity. Also, individuals differ in their sensitivity to hormones. Thus, it is difficult to fully understand the meaning of the presence or absence of a relationship between hormone levels and certain behaviors.

Although somewhat controversial, some findings suggest that androgen levels are related to sexual and aggressive behaviors in both men and women (Hamburg and Lunde, 1966; Moyer, 1974; Rose, 1972). Most of this evidence is indirect or is based on small clinical samples, but the evidence does come from diverse types of data. First, female sex drive is not significantly lowered after menopause, when estrogen and progesterone levels drop significantly but androgen levels are relatively unchanged (e.g., Masters and Johnson, 1970). Second, levels of testosterone are correlated with self-ratings of hostility or aggressiveness (Moyer, 1974; Persky, Smith, and Basu, 1971), though correlations are not always found or may be very weak (Doering, et al., 1975; Meyer-Bahlburg, et al., 1974). Third, men and women with various abnormal and surgical conditions, which result in lowered levels of androgen after puberty, have been characterized as possessing a low sex drive and sometimes as relatively passive (Bremar, 1959; Moyer, 1974). Finally, treatment of males convicted for violent sex crimes by surgical or chemical blocking of testosterone has resulted in greatly lowered incidence of such crimes (Laschet, 1973).

Many researchers today accept the relationship between testosterone and physical aggressiveness (e.g., Moyer, 1974). The results for sexual behavior are more mixed. For example, in one study, individual men varied widely; sometimes sexual activity across the two-month period was correlated with high levels of testosterone and sometimes with low levels. However, when the data from all subjects was grouped, there was a *negative correlation* ($-.52$) of testosterone and sexual activity (Doering, et al., 1974). It is possible that a minimal level of androgen is needed for normal sexual and aggressive functioning; but once this level is attained, as is the case for normal adult males, additional amounts of androgen have little influence (Rose, 1972). Also, women, whose testosterone levels are generally lower than men's, may be more responsive to these hormones and thus may have equal underlying biological bases for aggression and sexual interest (Persky, 1974).

A final interpretation problem concerns the cause-and-effect inferences that are drawn from a correlation between hormones and behavior. For example, a series of studies on male rhesus monkeys found a high correlation between testosterone levels and the dominance ranks of animals. The questions then pursued were: (1) whether the dominance rank was caused by the level of testosterone; or (2) whether the level of testosterone was a result of dominance. Animals were placed in a variety of situations so that changes in hormone levels could be measured. Testosterone levels were found to rise considerably when the animals had access to sexually receptive females. However, when they were placed with an already established group of males and experienced defeat in aggressive encounters, their hormone levels fell. Thus, it appears that the hormone levels were not fixed and were strongly affected by environmental stimuli (Rose, et al., 1975; Rose, et al., 1971). Clearly, a conclusion that hormone levels caused behavior would, in this case, be misleading, at best. Similar interactions with behavior and hormone levels may well exist for humans.

The relationship between psychological states and behavior and hormones continues to be of great interest to scientists as well as clinicians. However, the issues are becoming increasingly complex. Not only are there difficult biological issues but also, as discussed in Chapter 5, most behaviors reflect a complex interaction of many factors—genetic, physiological, sociocultural. Clearly, previous experience, values, and opportunity are at least as relevant as hormone levels to sexual interest and in determining when sexual behavior is actually engaged in. (This is discussed more fully in Chapter 11.)

THE MENSTRUAL CYCLE

Physical Effects

Menstruation, the flow of blood that occurs about once a month in most women between the ages of twelve and forty-eight, has been the subject of much fear, superstition, and taboo in our society, as well as in most others. Yet menstruation is a natural and integral part of the process of human reproduction.

The menstrual cycle is regulated by changes in hormone levels which are in turn controlled by the hypothalamus and the pituitary gland. The average menstrual cycle is twenty-eight days long, although individual women vary enormously in the lengths of their cycles from month to month, and many women have longer or shorter cycles than twenty-eight days. Box 1 shows how hormone levels vary during the twenty-eight–day cycle. Along with the hormonal variation occurring during each normal cycle, the ovaries develop

Box 1   **Hormonal Fluctuations During the Menstrual Cycle**

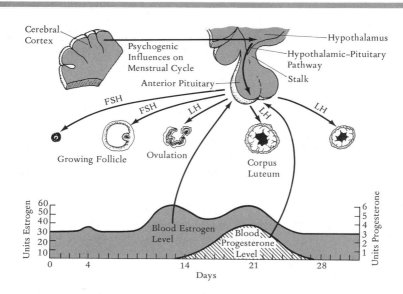

SOURCE: Benson, 1974.

and release an ovum and the uterus is prepared for possible implantation of the ovum if it is fertilized. This lining is shed if fertilization has not occurred, producing the menstrual flow.

Following the standard practice, Day 1 of the menstrual cycle is arbitrarily defined as the first day of menstruation or blood flow. On Day 1, estrogen and progesterone levels are quite low. The uterine lining begins to shed, resulting in approximately three to five days of menstrual flow. This menstrual "blood" is actually uterine tissue mixed with small amounts of blood amounting to a total of two to three ounces of material. As menstruation begins on Day 1, one of the many immature ova in one of the two ovaries begins to mature and the hypothalamus signals the production of more estrogen.

During the next two weeks of the menstrual cycle, estrogen levels continue to rise and the developing ovum grows and matures. As the old uterine lining is shed, a new one begins to develop. By approximately Day 15, estrogen has reached its highest point of the cycle and the ovary releases the ovum, which is now fully mature. This ovum lives for about two days in the woman's body system and can be fertilized by sperm any time during these two days. Fertilization may also occur if sperm is in the reproductive system when the ovum is released. The sperm may have been deposited any time during the preceding two days, since sperm live for about two days in the female body.

After Day 15, estrogen levels drop somewhat, then rise again as progesterone levels rise. Levels of both estrogen and progesterone peak again on about Day 24 and then decline. The rapid decline of these female hormones signals the end of the cycle and the uterus prepares to shed the lining developed during that cycle to initiate a new menstrual cycle (e.g., Segal, 1974).

Along with these changes in the sexual organs and in hormone levels, come a number of other physical changes. Many women report some physical discomfort while premenstrual (Days 25 to 28) or menstruating (Days 1 to 4). Some of the common physical symptoms are cramping, headache, backache, digestive problems and gas, salt and water retention and related weight gain, acne, and breast swelling and tenderness.

Psychological Effects

It is commonly believed that the menstrual cycle exerts a profound effect upon the everyday lives of most women. For example, a recent scientific paper began:

> The menstrual cycle imposes on the human female a rhythmic variability encompassing all aspects of her being, from biochemical to the psychosocial. (Silbergeld, et al., 1971, p. 411.)

Clinicians have labeled the negative symptoms often associated with the menstrual cycle as the "premenstrual syndrome" or "menstrual distress." However, it is not at all clear that menstrual symptoms are as debilitating as is implied by much of the clinical writing, nor even that any strong symptoms are evident in most women or are evident for most cycles in any particular woman. Although much research has suggested that women do experience both physical and psychological changes during their cycles, it is difficult to know how common such symptoms are. Estimates of the prevalence of menstrual symptoms have ranged from 25 to 100 percent (Sherman, 1971). In one study, for example, the incidence of physical or somatic symptoms was higher than the incidence of psychological symptoms (Coppen and Kessel, 1963). Specifically, 45 percent of the women in this study reported moderate or severe pain, but only 23 percent mentioned more than a slight incidence of depression. In some research, significant changes in symptoms across the cycle are not found. In one group of twenty-nine college women, no significant differences were found on six measures of mood, assessed menstrually, at mid-cycle, and premenstrually. Also, the average mood rating were very similar to those obtained from a group of male classmates (Persky, 1974).

In general, most studies have reported correlations with the phases of the menstrual cycle for various psychological factors such as aggression, irritability, elation, activation, and general mood.[1] To the extent that mood changes do occur according to the phase of the cycle, there is a general pattern for negative symptoms to be associated with the premenstrual or menstrual phases of the cycle and positive (or low levels of negative) symptoms to be reported at the middle of the cycle (Ivey and Bardwick, 1968).

Along with psychological and physical fluctuations, women may behave differently when premenstrual or menstruating. For example, during the premenstrual and menstrual phases of the cycle nearly half of the crimes committed by women were done, half of attempted suicides for women occurred, half of women's accidents happened, and half of their hospital admissions occurred (Dalton, 1964). This proportion represented about twice the rate that would be expected if all such events were evenly divided over the cycle. Such data has been interpreted as demonstrating the debilitating effects of menstrual variations on women. However, these data could as easily be interpreted as showing the beneficial effects of female hormones. When female hormone levels are high, women experience very low rates of negative types of behavior. It is only when their hormone levels are relatively low during the premenstrual and menstrual phases that women show some of the same behavioral indicators as characterize men (i.e., high rates of criminal behavior, accidents, and hospital admissions).

Also, a few investigators have described problems interpreting these data. One study failed to replicate the association between attempted suicides and the menstrual cycle and suggested that the association reported earlier could be explained by methodological problems (Birtchnell and Floyd, 1974). Finally, the reported correlations are based on biased samples (Parlee, 1973). The fact that criminal women are more likely to commit their crimes when premenstrual, does not mean that normal women will become criminal when premenstrual, or that they will become suddenly ill, have an accident, or attempt suicide. Instead, they may show increases in more positively valued acts when premenstrual, such as "bursts of creative energy" (Parlee, 1973, p. 456).

Studies which have examined behavioral fluctuations in more typical samples of women have reported fewer findings of impairment in performance of premenstrual and menstrual women. These studies have investigated performance on achievement or reasoning tests, reaction time, time estimation, athletics, and other types of cognitive and perceptual-motor behaviors. Most of these objective measures fail to show an impairment in performance associated with the menstrual cycle (Sommer, 1973). However, 8–16 percent of the women themselves believe that their performance are affected by their cycles. This apparent inconsistency suggests that social-psychological factors are important in interpreting cyclic fluctuations.

---

[1] See Lamprecht et al., 1974; Moos et al., 1969; Reynolds, 1969; Silbergeld et al., 1971.

Measuring the Effects of Menstruation

An important issue in much of the menstrual research is the use of self-report data. In a typical study women were asked to report to the researcher how much or how often they experienced a variety of menstrual symptoms. Some of the problems with this type of self-report data were described in Chapter 4. Specifically, self-report studies relying on memory for past symptoms have problems, since it is difficult for most people to accurately remember details of this sort. When questionnaires relying on memory were compared with daily diary entries, many discrepancies were found (McCance, Luff, and Widdowson, 1937). Self-report measures may also become biased by beliefs about what women are supposed to feel (Parlee, 1974). If a woman believes that normal women experience a variety of premenstrual symptoms, she may report such symptoms because she thinks that this will make her appear normal, even if she does not experience them; or she may discount cramps or irritability that do not coincide with premenstruation or menstruation. Such biases in the reports are particularly likely to arise when the women are aware that the study is concerned with psychological changes associated with menstruation. For example, the subjects may consciously or unconsciously seek to respond according to the researcher's hypotheses.

The biases associated with self-reports were demonstrated in one recent study (Ruble, 1977). Women were told that it was possible, through new scientific techniques, to predict the expected date of menstruation and that their menstrual period was due in a week to ten days or immediately. The women who thought they were premenstrual reported a higher incidence of symptoms, such as retaining more water and experiencing more pain, than women who thought they were intermenstrual. Thus, it appears that thinking she is premenstrual can lead a woman to report a relatively high degree of stereotypically menstrual symptoms.

These potential biases should be kept in mind when interpreting the results of any research dealing with menstruation or other biological events about which there are specific expectations.

Causes of Psychological Fluctuations

In spite of some methodological problems, there does seem to be evidence that there are various psychological and behavioral fluctuations associated with the menstrual cycle. The most common explanation for these fluctuations is that they are caused in some direct, biological way by hormonal variations. However, just because mood changes are *correlated with* hormonal variations, it cannot be assumed that mood swings are *caused by* hormonal variations. There are various alternative explanations based either entirely on social factors or on an interaction of social and biological variables.

Biological Mechanisms. Physiological or biological explanations of cyclical variations assume that hormone levels directly or indirectly affect physical and psychological symptoms. The problem for such explanations, however, is to determine the specific physiological mechanism by which this happens. A number of possibilities have been suggested, but none have been adequately demonstrated to be true (Parlee, 1973; Southam and Gonzaga, 1965).

One explanation concerns the effects of an enzyme called monoamine oxidase (MAO), which is found throughout the body, including the brain, and has been related at least indirectly to depression (Grant and Pryse-Davies, 1968). Its main biological function is to inactivate a group of compounds called monoamines. Changes in levels of estrogen and progesterone during the second half of the cycle are accompanied by an increase in MAO activity, which in turn may increase the likelihood of psychological depression. According to this explanation, negative mood associated with the premenstrual and menstrual periods is "caused" by these changes in neural activity in the brain produced by increased MAO. However, further research is needed to more fully understand these mechanisms.

A second type of explanation is related to levels of some of the other hormones produced by the adrenal glands (Dalton, 1964; 1969). These hormones are important in maintaining several body functions: such as water balance, blood-sugar level, and some allergic reactions. The basic assumption of this explanation is that the balance of adrenal hormone levels is upset in some women during premenstruation because of low levels of other hormones, mainly progesterone. This is supposedly because adrenal-produced progesterone is an essential base to the production of these other adrenal hormones. If, during premenstruation, there is insufficient progesterone in the uterus, then some may be taken from the adrenals. This temporary depletion of progesterone in the adrenals may result in an imbalance here, causing water retention and allergic reactions, resulting in other psychological effects such as depression. Again, the evidence is not adequate to assess this explanation.

Other physiological mechanisms have been postulated, such as variations in nerve excitability or electrolyte metabolism (see Southem and Gonzaga, 1965). However, no physiological explanation has yet been adequately researched. Thus, it is not possible to draw conclusions about the truth or falsity of any of these possibilities. This does mean, though, that there is no adequate basis for saying that there is a clearly understood physiological mechanism for cycle variations in moods or behavior.

Social Psychological Explanations. Other explanations for cyclic fluctuations do not depend upon hormonal or biological changes at all. Women psychologically react to menstruation and the onset of menstruation in ways which are socialized by the culture in which they live. Throughout history, menstrual bleeding has been regarded as an undesirable occurrence and menstruation is frequently the subject of superstition, restrictions on behavior, and other taboos. In the United States, for example, negative attitudes toward menstruation are reflected in Tampax ads, which assert the virtues of being hygienically clean and acting as if menstruation were not occurring. Abstinence from sexual intercourse is another taboo practiced by many couples in this country. Some women also feel they cannot swim or bathe during menstrual flow. The term "the curse" aptly summarizes the nature of traditional attitudes toward menstruation (Ernster, 1975). Given all this, it is not surprising that women may be anxious or irritable premenstrually or while menstruating.

Recent work suggests that women have several different types of attitudes about menstruation. These include the beliefs that menstruation is debilitating and that it is bothersome. Other attitudes focus on the necessity of planning for and the anticipation of menstruation. Others believe that menstruation is a positive reaffirmation of femininity, or they believe that it has no real effects (Brooks, Ruble, and Clark, 1977). Depending on the attitudes of the woman herself and those around her, each of these might be related to specific reactions to menstruation.

A woman who has negative attitudes about menstruation may expect to feel irritable or depressed when premenstrual. Because of these expectations she may unconsciously behave in this way in order to meet her own and others' expectations. Another related possibility is that since women and men "know" that premenstrual women are irritable and depressed, when a women acts in a negative way, she and others are likely to label her behaviors as a premenstrual reaction (Koeske and Koeske, 1975). Other cultural factors such as religion may also affect attitudes and reactions to the menstrual cycle (Paige, 1973). This suggests that an extremely complex set of sociocultural variables influences a woman's psychological response to her body.

Yet another reason for premenstrual distress is concern over pregnancy. Nearly every woman who is engaging in sexual intercourse has some degree of uncertainty over whether she is pregnant each month. For many women, the onset of menstruation is a time of relief or disappointment, depending on whether she desires pregnancy or not. But, in either case, her concern could be a nonhormonal reason for premenstrual anxiety or irritability.

Psychophysiological Interactions. Cyclic psychological fluctuations may also be the result of women's emotional reactions to the physical symptoms associated with being premenstrual or menstrual. A woman might well be hostile or irritable because of unpleasant or painful cramping. The actual menstrual flow is usually viewed as inconvenient, and having to be concerned with preparations for menstruating could also cause irritability or anxiety. For example, in one study, premenstrual anxiety in women was related to the intensity of the menstrual flow (Paige, 1971). Thus women with more incon-

Box 2   Attitudes towards Menstruation and Possible Reactions
           to Menstruation

Negative Attitudes	*Possible Reactions*
Menstruation is debilitating.	Attributions of irritability, depression or tiredness to being premenstrual or menstrual; lower activity rates; less sexual activity.
Menstruation is bothersome.	Anxiety over preparation for menstrual flow; irritability.
Menstruation requires planning.	Attributions of irritability, depression, or tiredness to premenstrual biological symptoms.
Neutral or Positive Attitudes	
Menstruation is a positive reaffirmation of femininity.	Little anxiety over menstrual flow.
Menstruation has no real effects.	No premenstrual or menstrual symptoms.

venience reported more negative affect. Sexual abstinence was also less common for women with lower flow intensities. Having to abstain from sexual activity, at a time when many women report highest levels of sexual arousal could also be a contributing factor to negative affect (Bardwick, 1971). Women may also be anxious premenstrually because of acne or weight gain—common physical symptoms. Thus, there are a number of ways in which the physical symptoms associated with menstruation may indirectly lead to negative affect.

Not only may physical changes affect psychological changes, the reverse also appears to be true in some cases. That is, socially mediated psychological reactions, such as anxiety or stress, may lead to changes in hormone levels which may create physical symptoms. For example, watching stressful movies may result in increased excretion of certain adrenal hormones, whereas relaxing movies lower excretion rates of these hormones (Levi, 1968). In general there is often an increase in adrenal activity when an individual is in a disturbing situation or even a novel situation (Gibbons, 1968). These findings imply that the coinciding fluctuations of some hormones with mood and physical state may be due, in part, to a third factor (a woman's social and stressful reaction to the event of menstruation). In addition, symptoms associated with stress—headaches or cramps—are very similar to the symptoms reportedly associated with menstruation, indicating that the "premenstrual syndrome" may, in part, reflect a psychological stress reaction to menstrual bleeding.

There are many explanations for cyclic fluctuations experienced by many women. Hormonal explanations, although the most direct, do not explain all of the social data. On the other hand, explanations relying solely on social psychological factors fail to recognize that there may be some very real physiological mechanisms affecting these fluctuations either directly or indirectly as women react to biological changes. Presently there is insufficient evidence for any theory to draw definitive conclusions.

ORAL CONTRACEPTIVES

In 1960, the Food and Drug Administration first approved the use of oral contraceptives by the general public, and since that time the use of the "pill" has become widespread throughout the world. Oral contraceptives consist of synthetic hormones which have some effects similar to estrogen and progesterone. However, the synthetic estrogens and progesterones are structurally different from the natural hormones and thus do not act in precisely the same way. Because manufacturers use different synthetic estrogens and progesterones, the pills vary in their specific effects.

There are two major groups of pills: sequential and combination. For both, the user takes a tablet a day for twenty or twenty-one days and then stops for seven or eight days. However, for the sequential pills, the first fifteen or sixteen tablets contain an estrogen only and the last five contain both a progesterone and an estrogen. For the combined pill, all tablets are identical, containing some combination of estrogen and progesterone (Segal and Atkinson, 1973). Combination pills are taken for twenty-eight days, but the last seven pills are placebos (which may contain iron). Most pills now on the market are combination pills. Sequential pills are slightly less effective and appear to have more side effects and, therefore, most of them are no longer for sale in this country.

Although oral contraceptives are nearly 100 percent effective in preventing pregnancy, the exact mechanism producing infertility is not known. Not only do the pills prevent ovulation, they also change the chemistry of the uterus and the cervix, making fertilization more difficult. Nevertheless, it is clear that the use of synthetic hormones affects much more than reproduction. Oral contraceptives cause changes in many physiological processes throughout the body (Segal and Atkinson, 1973). These synthetic hormones have extensive metabolic affects and may elevate blood pressure, affect blood clotting, cause liver tumors, and produce other changes in the circulatory system. In addition, a number of negative side effects, such as nausea, headaches, and skin discoloration, have been attributed to the pill. Psychologically, pill-takers sometimes report lowered sex drive which may result from the high female hormone levels counteracting the effect of the unchanged androgen levels (Seaman, 1972).

Use of oral contraceptives may also have positive side effects, like a lower incidence of premenstrual and menstrual symptomatology (Herzberg and Coppen, 1970; Moos, 1968). For example, in one study, only 18 percent of the women taking oral contraceptives complained of moderate to acute cramps, as compared to 30 percent of the non-pill group (Moos, 1968). Mood and emotional symptoms, such as depression and irritability, may be similarly affected, though some studies have reported an increase in depression among oral contraceptive users (e.g., Winston, 1973).

The mood changes associated with oral contraceptives are often attributed to elevated or stabilized levels of sex hormones (e.g., Bardwick, 1971). However, social psychological factors, such as increased freedom from pregnancy, may also be important. In addition, the hormone effects of the pill may have an indirect influence on mood. For example, the reduced menstrual flow associated with oral contraceptives, may lower the inconvenience associated with menstruation and thereby reduce anxiety and irritability (Paige, 1971).

PREGNANCY

Pregnancy involves a number of dramatic biological changes in a woman. Her normal menstrual cycle is interrupted, as the uterus accepts the fertilized egg and develops an elaborate system to protect and nourish the child. Approximately nine months after conception, the uterus will expel the fully developed child through a process of strong contractions initiated by hormone changes. During pregnancy, female hormone levels increase rapidly—as much as several hundred times their levels in nonpregnant women. Although hormone levels do vary during the course of the pregnancy, they are always well above normal. Then, just before birth, hormone levels in the mother drop quickly to below their usual levels when the woman is not pregnant (Heap, Perry, and Challis, 1973). This extreme change is the greatest change in hormone levels which the woman will ever experience in her lifetime; it is compressed into a period of at most a few days (Hamburg, Moos, and Yalom, 1968).

As might be expected, these hormonal variations are also correlated with mood changes and changes in behavior. Unfortunately, as with the fluctuations that accompany the menstrual cycle, it is difficult to separate out the effects of physiological changes *per se* from the many social psychological factors which are also operating during pregnancy and shortly after the birth (Parlee, 1978). For example, women reported large increases in life changes, such as changes in sleeping and recreation habits, during the period of pregnancy—enough to be classified as experiencing major life crisis (Williams, et al., 1975). In addition, relative to menstruation, there is little research on hormonal or psychological correlates of pregnancy so there is even less relevant literature upon which to base our conclusions.

Physically, pregnancy is accompanied by weight gain, enlargement of the stomach, swelling of the breasts, and changes in metabolic, digestive, circulatory, and eliminative systems. Many of these are physically uncomfortable and may well be associated with negative psychological reactions to the pregnancy. On the other hand, pregnancy can also be a pleasant experience. A woman can be excited and happy over the upcoming birth. In either case, the woman may also be concerned over how she will be able to care for her child and whether the child will be normal. The birth itself may be anticipated with either dread or excitement, or a combination of attitudes.

Many investigators report that emotional changes do occur during pregnancy, but there is little consistency between reports about the nature of the changes. They range from "crisis state" to "sense of well-being" to "lazy and cowlike" (Sherman, 1971). However, there is sufficient evidence to suggest that mind and body states interact in complicated ways to determine how positive an experience pregnancy will be for women. The type of emotional and physical changes reported appear to be related to the state of pregnancy—the most negative physical symptoms occurring during the first trimester, the most positive emotional state occurring in the middle, and increased tension occurring toward the termination of pregnancy—though these associations appear to depend on the type of mood being assessed and previous pregnancy history (Lubin, Gardener, and Roth, 1975). The stage-related changes may be attributed to hormone levels which shift during the stages of pregnancy, but it is also possible that concerns about the pregnancy are greatest initially and just before the birth.

As mentioned earlier, the hormone changes associated with the birth process itself are quite extreme. Additionally, the psychological reactions to the birth of a child may also lead to increased upset over one's adequacy as a mother or worry over the mechanics of caring for a young infant. Thus, it is not surprising that many studies report that women experience a period of depression immediately after the birth process. The symptoms accompanying this period, often described as the "postpartum blues" resemble a state of mild depression and include crying spells, restlessness, fatigue, and irritability (Hamburg et al., 1968; Hamilton, 1962). Estimates of the incidence of such symptoms range from about 30 to 60 percent (Sherman, 1971). Many investigators attribute the cause of these symptoms directly to physiological changes. However, such a direct link has not to date been empirically demonstrated, and there exist many possible social psychological causes (Parlee, 1978).

MENOPAUSE

The term "menopause" technically refers to the cessation of menstruation, while the broader range of menopause symptoms, often associated with the gradual ending of ovarian function, is called "climacterium." Some accounts of the climacterium imply that all of the positive aspects of being a woman are now ended; many women perceive this to be the case.

Menopause normally occurs to women between the ages of forty and fifty-five, although technically menopause can also occur earlier if the ovaries begin to malfunction. This leads to declining levels of progesterone and estrogen, although there can be temporary increases of these hormones as the pituitary attempts to have the body compensate for the lower hormones produced by the ovaries. Gradually, though, the hormones achieve a stable, but very low level, menstrual cycles stop, and ova are no longer produced. This gradual decline in hormones begins in the late twenties although the final cessation of menstruation does not generally occur until the forties or fifties. After menopause, estrogen levels are on the average about one-sixth of that of a premenopausal woman and production of progesterone also shows a substantial drop. Androgen levels, however, are relatively unaffected, although they show a gradual decline.

A wide range of physical and emotional changes have been associated with menopause. Box 3 lists many such symptoms and their relative self-reported incidence in a study of women from thirteen to sixty-four years of age (Neugarten and Kraines, 1965). It is clear from Box 3 that the group of menopausal women report a relatively high number of physical symptoms such as hot flashes and cold sweats. However, menopausal women did not report a consistently higher incidence of psychological symptoms. Although for some symptoms the percentages listed for menopausal women are very high (e.g., 78 percent report depression), the percentages are essentially no higher than those listed at most other ages. In fact, adolescents reported the highest incidence of many psychological symptoms commonly attributed to women experiencing menopause.

It is difficult to assess how general the percentages reported in Box 3 are, but other studies, too, report various physical and psychological associations with menopause. After menopause, women exhibit a variety of body changes, but it is unclear if such symptoms are a result of having undergone menopause itself or if they reflect the effects of aging. Among these effects are: drying of skin tissues; weakening of muscles; decreased immunity to disease; bones becoming more brittle; shrinking of the breasts; and thinning of the vaginal walls. Also, even though sexual functioning is affected (the vaginal walls become thinner and thus more prone to infections and vaginal lubrication necessary to sexual intercourse is reduced), many women report feeling continued or increased interest in sex (Neugarten, et al., 1963). Finally, some women react to menopause with depression, though the risk of

Box 3   Percentages of Women Reporting Menopausal Symptoms

Symptoms	Age of Woman					
	13–18	20–29	30–44	45–54		55–64
				Pre-menopausal	Post-menopausal	
Physical						
Hot flashes *	29	6	24	28	68	40
Cold Sweats *	19	6	13	16	32	4
Weight Gain *	47	30	40	41	61	38
Cold Hands and Feet	53	40	36	31	42	17
Numbness and Tingling	18	14	27	37	37	17
Breast Pains	20	28	31	10	37	6
Constipation	28	50	36	24	37	31
Psychological						
Irritable and Nervous	76	90	82	71	92	48
Depression	79	88	62	56	78	46
Excitable	66	64	51	47	59	20
Crying Spells *	58	50	36	38	42	6

* Most associated with menopausal group.
SOURCE: Neugarten and Kraines, 1965.

developing an affective disorder during menopause does not seem to be as high as many think (Winokur, 1973).

The symptoms associated with the climacterium, as with the correlates of the menstrual cycle and pregnancy, can be attributed to a variety of biological and psychological factors. Along with the hormonal changes of menopause and the general effects of aging, middle age is time when mothers find their direct maternal role is over, with the adulthood of their children being reached. It is also accompanied by fears of loss of beauty and concern over the deaths of parents and other loved ones. Marital difficulties may also emerge. All these factors may also be causal elements in the depression so often related to menopause, as well as some of the physiological symptoms (Bart, 1971).

One of the major theories of the underlying cause of postmenopausal and menopausal symptoms is that they are produced by the withdrawal of estrogen from the woman's body. Many of the physiological symptoms discussed earlier can be seen as opposites of the general effects of estrogen upon the body. Also, some research suggests that postmenopausal symptoms can be relieved by the administration of estrogen (R. A. Wilson, 1966; Wilson and Wilson, 1973). It does seem plausible that direct physiological symptoms could be aided with hormone therapy, but this will do little for psychological symptoms. It is less clear that a depressed middle-aged woman should be given estrogen when the possibility of negative side effects has not been ruled out and when depression could well have psychological rather than biological reasons. These are complicated issues and there are no easy answers. The estrogen might well have the effect of making a woman look and feel younger, which might in turn relieve her depression, but are the risks worth this possibility? The medical profession is currently in controversy about the increased risks of cancer as a result of estrogen-replacement therapy.

THE IMPACT OF HORMONAL CHANGES

To what extent do reproductive functions affect the everyday lives of women? While there are physical and psychological changes associated with menstruation, pregnancy, and menopause, the relative impact of these changes must be placed in proper perspective, for there are many events—biological, social, and environmental—that affect health and mood. A change in weather or illness of a loved one may have just as great an impact on daily functioning as these biologically based functions. This was observed in a study of college students where general environmental effects, such as midterms, accounted for more mood changes in both sexes than menstrual cycle variation (Wilcoxon, et al., 1975). In addition, there are many cyclic phenomena unrelated to female reproduction that affect men as well as women. These cycles may be grouped under the general rubric of "biological rhythms." The menstrual cycle is only one of these rhythms.[2]

Reproduction and Psychological Changes

We began this chapter by describing a newspaper article in which a physician made some derogatory comments about women's fitness for high government office. In a later article, these charges were countered by another physician, Dr. Estelle Ramey, who pointed out that cyclic phenomena may affect the performance of male presidents.

> If a man has a peptic ulcer, should we let him be president? Peptic ulcers are cyclical, too.
> John Kennedy had Addison's disease (slow destruction of the adrenal gland, the gland which secretes the stress hormone adrenalin) and chronic back problems. Thomas Jefferson had periodic migraine headaches all of his

[2] See Luce, 1970; Doering, et al., 1975; Richter, 1968, for discussions of other biological rhythms.

life. Abraham Lincoln had periodic depressions. Do these things make them unfit for public office? (*Los Angeles Times,* February 21, 1972.)

Dr. Ramey suggests that we may consider reproduction-related changes as only one of many fluctuations in mood and behaviors that both men and women experience. Most of these fluctuations are viewed as natural processes of life that we adapt to and accept. Yet, fluctuations associated with female reproduction have generally been viewed with negative connotations, as if we assume these changes are much harder to cope with than others.

Why is there an apparent negative bias associated with rhythmicity in female reproduction? There may be many reasons. First, reproductive events are more overt or noticeable than many other internal or external causes of psychological fluctuation. That is, the onset of menstruation, pregnancy, and menopause have clear physiological signs; while the psychological effects of daily biological changes may be less noticeable and thus less easily associated with emotional changes. In a sense, reproductive events may dominate the perceptual field so that other factors are discounted in explaining mood (especially negative) changes (e.g., Koeske and Koeske, 1975).

A second possible source of the negative bias associated with female reproduction is the sociocultural view of women and characteristics associated with women. Much recent research has suggested that women's traits and abilities are generally regarded as inferior to men's (Broverman, et al., 1972). Also, beliefs about female reproductive events are heavily surrounded by fear, superstition, and taboo. It is thus not surprising that psychological changes associated with female reproduction would themselves take on a negative valence—a kind of guilt-by-association phenomenon.

In sum, research on psychological changes associated with reproduction have tended to focus on and magnify the negative features. As such, it has served as partial justification for discrimination against women. There is, however, no adequate basis for excluding women from any endeavor on the basis of reproductive events. It would be absurd to discriminate against an individual because he or she has small daily mood or performance fluctuations, and there is no reason to expect that the effects of reproduction are any greater than these daily rhythms. Future research should serve as a means for men and women to learn about the relationship between mind and body, not as a rationale for continued discrimination against women.

11 Sexual Roles of Women

Sexual attitudes and behaviors in this country have been undergoing rapid change in this century. Each succeeding generation has been exposed to new values about what constitutes "proper" sexual activity, and each generation has tended to disagree with both the values of their parents and their children. This has resulted in continued interest and debate over the sexual activities of various groups in our society. Recently, feminists have become involved in analyzing some of the assumptions implicit in our sexual attitudes and morals. All of these trends suggest that a discussion of the sexual roles of women and men is particularly important for understanding the psychology of women.

Corresponding to, and perhaps reflecting, the increasingly open interest in sexuality evident in the general public is the growth of research into the topic of human sexuality. Psychological interest in sexuality was greatly stimulated by the writings of Freud in the early twentieth century. Freud felt that sexual drives were the underlying force for human behavior of all kinds. He wrote that civilization was based upon the repression of sexual desire and the channeling of sexual energies into socially acceptable behavior. Although many psychoanalytic theorists—such as Adler, Jung, and Horney—criticized Freud for his extreme emphasis on sexuality, most psychologists today would acknowledge that sexual needs are important for everyone.

Irene Frieze was the primary author of this chapter. Background materials were assembled by Theresa Christerson Mason.

Although they acknowledge its importance, not all theorists see sexual desires as fundamental to all behavior nor even as one of our primary motives. There is also research which suggests that sexual behaviors are strongly influenced by other motives (e.g., Gagnon and Simon, 1973). People may engage in sexual activities because they are lonely rather than aroused, or they may have sex with someone in hopes of gaining money or other benefits such as status. Concern about one's career or a friendship may also inhibit sexual activity. Thus, psychologists disagree on which motives are more basic.

Sexual behavior is based upon a complex interaction between biological factors such as hormone levels, general health, energy levels, and the motivational state of an individual at a given time (see Boxes 1 and 2). Along with these internal factors, the particular situation or environment and the previous learning and values of an individual are also important in determining

Box 1   Determinants of Sexual Activity

A number of factors interact to determine whether or not a person is sexually aroused and what type of sexual activity, if any, they engage in. People differ in the degree of importance attached to each factor.

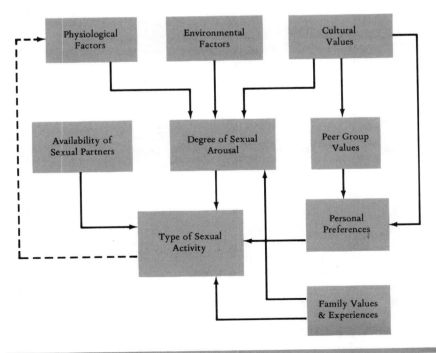

Box 2   **Factors Influencing Sexual Activity**

Type of Factor	Increased Heterosexual Activity
	Unlearned
Physiological	High androgen/estrogen ratio
	General physiological arousal
	Good general health
	Lack of physical aches and pains
	Stimulating drugs
	No alcohol
	Learned
Environmental	Protected location
	Privacy
	Soft lights
	Music
	Nudity
	Comfortable setting
Cultural Values	Culturally acceptable partner
	Sexuality generally encouraged
	Religious prohibitions not strong
	Belief that sex is fun
	Use of birth control accepted
Peer Group Values	Belief that both sexes enjoy sex
	Status associated with increased heterosexual activity
Personal Preferences	Preferred physical characteristics in partner
	Preference for opposite-sex partner
	Other
Availability of Partners	Presence of opposite sex

what sexual feelings are present. No matter how seductive the situation nor how much enjoyment a person has had engaging in sexual relations with her current companion, if she feels very ill she will not feel like having sex. Similarly, even given interest and a receptive partner, few people would engage in sexual behavior in locations they had been taught were inappropriate for such activity. As humans, our beliefs about what constitutes proper sexual behavior is also of special importance and can override both internal factors and the impact of external stimuli. Indeed our sexual values and attitudes are probably the single most important factor in analyzing when and with whom we engage in sexual behavior. It is unlikely that we would engage in sexual behavior nor even feel sexually aroused toward an attractive person if he or she happens to be a close relative or someone we have been taught is "taboo" as a sexual partner. Both societal values and personal attitudes influence sexual response.

Attitudes influence not only the timing of sexual activities, but also our definitions of what is sexual and what is not (Gagnon and Simon, 1973). While in many cultures, kissing and hand-holding are interpreted as signs of friendship, in others such behavior is a sign of romantic involvement. There are no universally understood sexual activities. Each culture defines what it considers to be sexual. Even sexual intercourse may not be perceived as sexual if performed by children or within the context of a religious ritual.

Along with definitions of what is sexual, our cultural values also give us a set of beliefs about the sexual natures of women and men. For example, the close relationship in our culture between the concepts of masculinity and sexual prowess results in the expectation for men that they should always be interested in sex and sexually aggressive with women. However, if the woman does accept his sexual advances, the man is expected to please her and cause her to finally enjoy love-making. Thus, one of our cultural assumptions is that every woman needs to be made love to by a "real man" and men are anxious to demonstrate that they can fulfill this function. Other attitudes contradict this belief. One of these is that only "bad" women can enjoy sex or experience sexual pleasure. Although our sexual attitudes are undergoing change, such assumptions still underlie many of our beliefs today.

SOURCES OF SEXUAL ATTITUDES

Many of our attitudes come from religious teachings. Changes in these attitudes have been stimulated by the writings of Freud and, more recently, by the human potential movement, which stresses self-actualization and enjoyment of life. Research into human sexuality has also shaped many of our attitudes as we gain more information about our sexual activities. Because of these varying sources of our attitudes, they are often contradictory. In cases where historically based assumptions are being shown to be false in light of recent research, much confusion results as people begin to question values they had been taught and had accepted without question for many years.

Religion

Some of our most pervasive sexual attitudes derive from the Judeo-Christian tradition. For the Hebrews, the inferiority of women was firmly established. Women were possessions, necessary for bearing children, although deep love between "man and wife" was possible, as demonstrated by the Song of Solomon. Women's bodies and female bodily functions were considered unclean, and a large number of purification rituals were associated with menstruation and pregnancy (Hunter, 1976; Juhasz, 1973).

In the writings of early Christian leaders, women were seen as temptresses and seducers of men. These men believed that women's concerns with earthly matters and children kept women from the absorption in spiritual matters necessary for salvation. A woman's basic sexual nature was also considered to be a constant threat to the salvation of men since women distracted men into thoughts of sex rather than God. By necessity, good women, idealized in the Virgin Mary, were not interested in sex and did everything possible to keep men from viewing them as sexual partners. Most women, however, were thought to be seductive and sexual, and were therefore morally inferior to men. Marriage was accepted as necessary for most men and women but true purity and holiness was associated with celibacy (Hunter, 1976; Juhasz, 1973).

The basic Christian emphasis on chastity and the association of evil or sin with open sexual expression has been evident in the United States since its Puritan beginnings. Such beliefs were at their peak during the nineteenth century (Barker-Benfield, 1976). At this time "good" women only tolerated sex within marriage as one of their conjugal duties. It was considered an insult to these women to suggest that they might derive pleasure from sex. Men, on the other hand, were considered highly sexed. They sought prostitutes as sexual partners since frequent sex with "good" women such as their wives was considered improper. Men were viewed as innately polygamous, showing interest in any attractive woman. Only a few questioned this double standard of encouragement or acceptance of the sexual activity of men and the strict prohibition of either expression of interest or of actual sexual behavior for women.

These views began to change in the nineteenth century. Marriage manuals of the mid 1800s saw women as having no sexual desires, but by the late 1800s, sex *in marriage* was advised as a good thing. However, men were still viewed as innately polygamous and highly sexed, while women were seen as monogamous; their sexual natures could be developed only by a man they loved (Gordon and Shankweiler, 1971).

Freud's Influences

Coming from this Victorian tradition and reflecting many of the basic beliefs of his time was Sigmund Freud. Also a major influence for change, however, Freud wrote, contrary to the beliefs of his time, that both sexes experience sexual desire, although he felt that women were "sexually" motivated primarily by the desire for a child while men experienced sexual desire more directly. (For a thorough discussion of the Freudian theories of sexual motivation, see Chapter 3).

Freud has had an enormous impact upon the beliefs of our society. The sexual attitudes implicit in his writings have in many cases supported and strengthened the sexual attitudes found in the Judeo-Christian writings. Freud believed in the basic inferiority of women (stemming from their lack of a penis) and the orientation of their sexuality toward children rather than the desire for sexual pleasure alone. His writings supported the historical belief in the greater sexual aggressiveness of men and the passivity of women. Freud was also responsible for suggesting a definition of normal, mature feminine sexuality which many women had trouble meeting—the concept of the "mature" vaginal orgasm as compared to the "immature" clitorial orgasm. Although research has since demonstrated the biological impossibility of complete sexual response for women without sensations in both the vagina and clitoris and the necessity of clitorial stimulation for many women to achieve orgasm, this Freudian view of vaginal orgasm has persisted. Many women have and do feel inadequate because of their need for clitorial stimulation to reach orgasm. Another Freudian view which current research has contradicted was that postmenopausal women had no sexual desires since they were no longer capable of bearing children. While recent data suggest the opposite, this view is still widely held and many people have difficulty believing that older women can enjoy sex.

Although much of Freud's work gave scientific support to traditional religious ideas, Freud was also responsible for helping people to accept the idea of sexual feelings in normal women and men as well as in children. Perhaps partly because of Freud, people have shown increasing openness since his time to the discussion of sex and the view that "good" women have sexual interest and achieve sexual pleasure just as men do. One result of Freud's insights about the negative effects of repressing sexual feelings has been a growing belief that sexuality should be encouraged for everyone.

Research on Human Sexuality

Another important influence on current sexual attitudes has been research into human sexuality. The work of Alfred Kinsey and his collaborators (1948; 1953) and William Masters and Virginia Johnson (1966; 1970) has had a major impact on people's views of sexuality, especially female sexuality. Although some of the results of these studies confirmed what people had thought all along, others were quite unexpected and tended to be disbelieved. However, both of these studies are now accepted as primary sources of information in an admittedly difficult-to-research field.

The Kinsey research was based on a series of interviews of over ten thousand people begun in 1938. Questions assessed nearly every aspect of people's sexual behaviors. The results are shown in Boxes 3 and 4. Kinsey found that males reported more overall sexual activity than females at all ages but that the form of activity and frequency varied for different ages. In general, men tended to have increasingly frequent sexual activities until their early twen-

Box 3   Frequency of Sexual Outlets for Women and Men

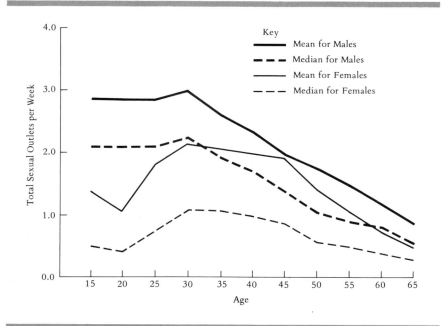

SOURCE: Modified from Kinsey, et al., 1948, 1953.

ties but declined thereafter. Women, on the average peaked in activity at thirty and remained at this high level until about forty-five and then declined. Although the male average was always higher, the differences were least between the ages of forty and forty-five. There was also enormous variability and many females reported being as active as the most active male.

The sexual outlets represented in Box 4 summarize all types of sexual activities for women and men. The most frequent sexual activity resulting in orgasm was masturbation for single women and marital intercourse for married and divorced women. For men, only the younger single men reported masturbation as their most frequent outlet. For older single men and married men, sexual intercourse was most common. Kinsey also reported that more men (92 percent) had masturbated than women (62 percent) although masturbation, particularly through clitorial stimulation, was the most successful means of orgasm for women, with 95 percent of the women who did masturbate reaching orgasm through this method.

Looking at other forms of sexual outlet, petting was an important activity for teenagers of both sexes, with over 80 percent having engaged in genital petting by the age of eighteen. Also, premarital intercourse had been a part of the sexual experiences of 68 percent of college men and 60 percent of college women. This experience was related to education level. Thirty percent of women who did not go beyond grade school and 98 percent of these men had had premarital intercourse. Thus, the double standard was much more prevalent in the less-educated group, while college-educated men and

Box 4   **Types of Sexual Experiences Resulting in Orgasm**

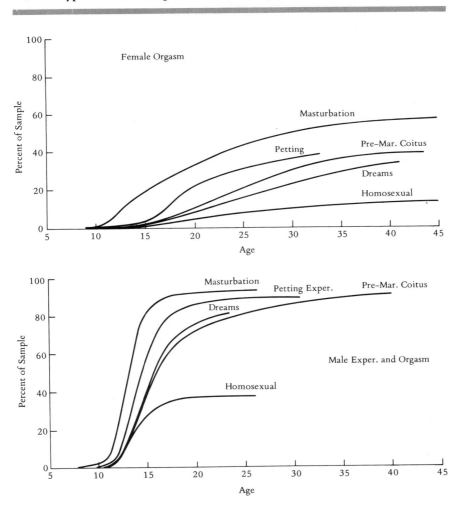

SOURCE: Kinsey, et al., 1948.

women were relatively equal. Kinsey also found that the use of prostitutes was greater for the less-educated men (as might be expected, since less of the women in this group were engaging in sexual intercourse). These results for premarital intercourse, coming from the 1940s, may seem higher than many younger people of today might expect. More recent studies show that premarital intercourse is becoming more common for all groups of women (Hunt, 1974).

Kinsey's data regarding marital sex suggested that married couples rarely engaged in oral or anal sex but did employ manual stimulation of each other's genitals during foreplay. Sexual intercourse itself had an average duration of only one to two minutes, although 45 percent of the women reported experiencing orgasm 90 percent of the time. Kinsey also reported that some women experienced multiple orgasms, a report which was widely ridiculed until the later work of Masters and Johnson demonstrated conclusively that females could experience multiple orgasms. The double standard was again seen in Kinsey's data that nearly 50 percent of the husbands engaged in extramarital affairs while only 20 percent of the women did so. Although Kinsey's samples were known to overrepresent homosexual males, figures corrected for this bias suggested that 10 percent of men over fifteen and 1 percent of the women were exclusively homosexual. However, a much larger percentage (25 percent of the men and 3 percent of the women had had an overt homosexual experience).

Although Kinsey's work was highly criticized, it has been widely read and cited. People were able to read the results of these studies and evaluate their own sexual behaviors for perhaps the first time. This led to a greater openness about sex and perhaps to greater experimentation. More recent data indicates greater variety in the sexual activities of married couples (Hunt, 1974).

A second major study of sexuality which has had great impact on public thinking is that of William Masters and Virginia Johnson (1966; 1970). Coming from a medical background, their work was the first comprehensive scientific study of what actually happens during sexual arousal and orgasm. By bringing couples into the laboratory, they were able to measure precise bodily changes during sexual activity. Their work showed that for both men and women, the breasts, skin (sex flush), muscles (muscular tension), rectum, heart (heart rate and blood pressure), and lungs (increased breathing) are all involved in any complete response. In addition, women show changes in the clitoris, vagina, uterus, and labia, while men have changes in their penis, scrotum, and testes.

Both sexes have four basic phases of sexual response, although the lengths vary greatly from person to person as well as with one person on different occasions (see Box 5). The first phase—excitement—brings feelings of sexual and physical arousal through vasocongestion (swelling of the blood vessels) in erogenous zones and increased muscular tension. Breathing increases, as does heart rate, and the skin becomes flushed. Other changes during this phase

Box 5   Sexual Response Cycles of Women and Men

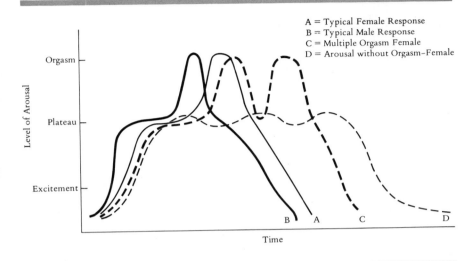

A = Typical Female Response
B = Typical Male Response
C = Multiple Orgasm Female
D = Arousal without Orgasm–Female

SOURCE: Modified from Masters and Johnson, 1965.

begin in the sex organs themselves, as shown in Boxes 6 and 7. The excitement phase is followed by the plateau phase, experienced as intense sexual arousal. This stage may be very brief or quite prolonged. Many men learn to prolong this phase and delay orgasm in order to increase the pleasure of their female partner, since it generally takes longer for women to reach orgasm than men. The third phase is the orgasm phase. During orgasm the entire body becomes rigid. For men there is a sense that ejaculation is coming and then an explosive feeling of pleasure with sudden discharge of muscular tension throughout the body. For women, the feeling is more a momentary sensation, followed by a peak of intense sensation in the pelvic area which may then spread to other parts of the body. During the resolution phase, for both sexes, the rhythmic throbs associated with orgasm become progressively less intense and frequent as the entire body relaxes.

This detailed analysis of the human sexual response has added significantly to our knowledge of human sexuality. This research has also contradicted a number of cultural beliefs and has been a major impetus for changes in these beliefs. Probably based on the idea that women were not sexually interested nor generally responsive was the disbelief in the idea of multiple orgasms for women. Although many women have never experienced multiple orgasms, Masters and Johnson feel that they are possible for any woman given appropriate stimulation. Masters and Johnson also demonstrated that failure to reach orgasm has biological consequences for women. When a woman be-

Box 6 **Female Sexual Responses**

Area of Response	Stage of Arousal			
	Excitement	Plateau	Orgasm	Resolution
Breasts	Nipple erection / Increased breast size	Reach maximum size	No change	Slow decrease in size and nipple erection
Skin Flush	Begins at stomach, neck, and throat	Spreads over body	Intensity correlates with orgasm	Disappears in reverse order
Muscle Tension	Begins throughout body	Increases / Contractions in hands and feet	Many contractions	Rapid decline
Rectum	Irregular contractions	Contractions	Strong contractions	—
Heart rate, blood pressure, breathing	Increased	Continues to increase / Hyperventilation	Increases more	Slow return to normal / Sweating over body
Clitoris	Some enlargement	Glans pulled back	?	Return to normal
Vagina	Lubrication / Inner ⅔ enlarges	Contractions	Strong rhythmic contractions	Slow return to normal
Uterus	Irregular contractions	Elevates	Rapid irregular contractions	Very slow return to normal
Labia Majora	Lips separate (effects differ for women with and without children)	No change	No change	Return to normal
Labia Minora	Enlarge	Color change	No change	Return to normal

SOURCE: Modified from Masters and Johnson, 1965.

Box 7 **Male Sexual Responses**

Area of Response	Stage of Arousal			
	Excitement	Plateau	Orgasm	Resolution
Breasts	Nipple erection	More erection of nipples	No change	Slow return to normal
Sex Flush	Begins on stomach	Spreads	Intensity correlates with orgasm	Rapid fading in reverse order
Muscle Tension	Begins	Increases Contractions all over body	Very strong	Total relaxation
Rectum	Some irregular contractions	Contractions	Rhythmic contractions	—
Heart rate, blood pressure, breathing	Increased	Markedly increased	Increases more	Return to normal. Sweating in palms and feet
Scrotum	Contractions	No change	No change	Return to normal
Testes	Elevate	Strong elevation	No change	Reduction in size
Cowper's Glands	—	2–3 drops fluid secreted	—	—
Penis	Erection	Stronger erection	Rhythmic contractions and ejaculation	Rapid initial loss of erection; slow decrease after this

SOURCE: Modified from Masters and Johnson, 1965.

comes aroused, the associated vasocongestion and muscular tension persists for several hours if there is no release through orgasm, and physical discomfort may result. This contradicts the belief that women do not need orgasm and that only men need sexual release after long periods of arousal.

A third belief overturned was Freud's notion of the "mature" vaginal orgasm. With their precise recording instruments Masters and Johnson found that *any* orgasm involves not only the vagina *and* the clitoris, but also a number of other areas in the body, as shown in Box 6. In fact, stimulation through masturbation or any other form of sexual stimulation results in the same bodily responses. The only necessity for orgasm is adequate stimulation. Many women experience their most intense orgasm through masturbation, probably because this allows them maximum control over the stimulation they receive. Thus, sexual intercourse is only one of many potentially fulfilling forms of sexuality.

These results suggest a different picture of female sexuality than the traditional image of women wanting sex only for purposes of procreation or of women being relatively disinterested in sex as compared to men. Certainly women have the capacity to fully enjoy sex and in fact are potentially able to enjoy sexual stimulation more frequently or longer than men because they do not experience a period when further stimulation is impossible which men often do after ejaculation. Some writers have elaborated on this idea and have projected an image of women as being highly sexed (Sherfey, 1972).

Another myth Masters and Johnson exploded is the idea that a larger penis always means a better sexual partner for a woman. First, nonerect penis size is not related to the erect size. Second, within the normal size ranges, the vagina will expand to fit the erect penis. Although very small penis may not give sufficient stimulation, very large penises may be very painful for some women, especially those whose vaginas are small. Most women would agree that sexual technique is far more important than penis size.

Masters and Johnson demonstrated that withdrawal was *not* a reliable birth-control technique since the male secretes a few drops of fluid during the plateau phase which may contain sperm. They were also able to show that intercourse during pregnancy was not harmful except during the last few weeks before birth. Finally, they demonstrated that older people do have sexual interests. They found people in their seventies and eighties who thoroughly enjoyed sex and performed quite adequately.

Sexuality and Birth Control

Today, there are several relatively safe and easy methods of birth control (see Box 8). Although many of these methods are risky, the risks are less than those associated with pregnancy or abortion, and they represent a major advance for the woman who wants to limit or space her children. Most of those methods are the primary responsibility of the woman, giving her the choice and the burden of avoiding pregnancy. Modern means of birth control allow women to engage in sexual relations without fear of pregnancy. This also means, however, that for some women, the choice to remain celibate is no longer an option. Virginity for adult women is gradually becoming negatively rather than positively valued (Schaefer, 1973). And, by putting the entire responsibility on the woman, men are more free than ever to engage in sexual relations without concern over possible pregnancy.

Current Sexual Attitudes and Behavior

Many of the sexual attitudes derived from religious traditions and psychoanalytic thinking are still held by many people. However, general sexual attitudes and behaviors have changed quite dramatically since the nineteenth century. Freud, Kinsey, and Masters and Johnson have all implied that both women and men should be more open about sex and express their sexual feelings more in their behavior. Many other writers have contributed to this increasingly popular viewpoint. As a result, people are becoming more oriented toward enjoying sex and experimenting with various forms of sexual behavior, rather than associating sex primarily with reproduction or "sin."

Women, especially, are becoming more sexually active; the classical distinction between the "good" woman and the "bad" woman is beginning to disappear as more and more women engage in premarital sexual behavior. Women, too, are experiencing more sexual pleasure in marriage and both sexes have become more concerned with women achieving maximum sexual pleasure. Many writers have discussed the effects of such changes on women and have suggested a whole new set of sexual values for women (e.g., Firestone, 1970; Francoeur and Francoeur, 1974). Marriage manuals are becoming more accepting of nonmarital sex for women and of noncoital sexuality. There has also been more open discussion and acceptance of sexuality in older couples (Gordon and Shankweiler, 1971).

Some of the specific changes in sexual behavior were demonstrated by Hunt (1974) in a replication of Kinsey's study, and the *Redbook* survey (Levin and Levin, 1975). Hunt's data was collected from over two thousand people in 1972 using random sampling procedures. The *Redbook* survey was based on the responses of a hundred thousand women to a questionnaire in the magazine in 1974. Using results of both studies, several conclusions can be drawn. Although men show slightly increased rates of masturbation, far more women are using masturbation as a sexual outlet than in Kinsey's study. Also, more women (55 percent) and men (70 percent) engaged in premarital petting. Premarital intercourse was also more common, with 68 percent of the women and 97 percent of the men having done this by the age of twenty-five. Women are also having premarital intercourse at earlier ages.

People are experimenting more with various forms of sexual expression. Incidences for oral sex rose greatly, especially among the college educated,

Box 8   Birth-Control Techniques

Technique	Person Responsible for Use	Effectiveness	Possible Medical Side Effects
Birth-Control Pill	Woman	Excellent	Nausea, weight gain breast enlargement, blood clotting, liver tumors, cancer
Intrauterine Device (IUD)	Woman	Excellent	Heavy menstrual bleeding, irregular bleeding, cramps, uterine puncture, infection
Diaphragm and Contraceptive Cream or Foam	Woman	Very good	Minor irritation from cream or foam, interference with rectal and bladder function when worn for long periods
Spermicidal Foam, Cream, or Jelly	Woman	Good	Minor irritation
Condoms	Man	Very good	———
Withdrawal	Man	Fair	———
Rhythm	Woman	Poor to Fair	———
Douche	Woman	Poor	Irritation to vagina

with oral sex now being very common for both men and women. Anal intercourse was also practiced more but frequencies for this are still relatively low. Extramarital sexual affairs showed little change, except that more younger women reported them than older. Even with the younger wives, their husbands were still twice as likely to have an affair. Hunt also found a decrease in the use of prostitutes as compared to Kinsey's data. Homosexual activities were about the same, with a slight increase in female homosexual behavior.

Major changes in frequency and duration of marital intercourse have also occurred. The average time spent in intercourse itself, not counting foreplay

Psychological Advantages	Psychological Disadvantages
Clean, easy to take, not related to sex act	Must be remembered every day; loss of sex drive
Nothing to remember except check string	May be felt during intercourse
No medical side effects	Interference with sex act; messy to insert; must be available when needed
No medical side effects; easy to obtain; no prescription needed	Interference with sex act; messy; must be available when needed
No medical side effects; easy to obtain; no prescription needed	Reduced sensation for male
No medical side effects; no cost	Requires great will power for male; may reduce enjoyment for both sexes
No medical side effects; no cost	Requires long periods of abstinence, especially if woman has irregular cycles
Inexpensive	Interferes with sex act resolution

or afterplay, has increased from one to two minutes to ten minutes. As might be expected, more women reported experiencing orgasm. The majority of the women in the *Redbook* survey reported that the sexual aspect of their marriage was good or very good, although women who had been married longer were less satisfied than those married a shorter time. Religion was not related to satisfaction with marital sex, in fact, more religious women reported more satisfaction. Very few women (4.7 percent) felt that intercourse was too frequent. Sexual satisfaction for all of these women was highly related to general marital happiness and personal happiness.

Summarizing these results, both attitudes and behavior are more permissive. People are spending more time in sexual activities and using more variations in foreplay and positions for intercourse. Women, especially, are becoming more similar to men in their sexual activities although there are still some differences. More women are experiencing orgasm. There is little change, however, in extramarital sex, homosexuality, or in the general belief in the importance of a good emotional relationship as being important for a good sexual relationship.

With all these changes, many people still have many of the sexual attitudes described earlier. Women are regarded as less interested in sex than men, and are expected to put limits to inappropriate masculine advances, while men are trained to be sexually aggressive. This is in spite of data showing ever increasing sexual interest in women. At the same times women are expected to be attractive to men and to use sex as a weapon for "catching a man." These attitudes have implications for a number of issues related to the double standard—the view that different sexual rules apply to men and women.

SEXUAL EXPECTATIONS AND THE DOUBLE STANDARD

As stated above, our society views female sexuality with different standards and expectations than male sexuality. Women are expected to respond to the advances of men rather than to initiate sexual activity themselves. They are considered generally less interested in sex, especially when the sexual activity is not with someone they love. People expect that men will always be interested in sex, regardless of the emotional context of the situation, and that they will be able and willing to perform sexual intercourse if given the opportunity. These general beliefs are manifested in numerous ways in the sexual behavior of women and men.

Are Women Disinterested in Sex?

Stereotypes about men (active, aggressive) and women (passive, dependent) in general and about male and female sexuality more specifically would certainly suggest that women have lower levels of sexual interest than men. Marriage manuals over the last hundred years have implicitly or explicitly stated this and many aspects of our society reflect this belief (Gordon and Shankweiler, 1971). Advertisements, for example, frequently employ sexual appeal directed towards men (use of an attractive woman in close association with a product being sold); rarely is there an analogous appeal with an attractive man being used to sell a product to women. When men are employed in advertisements for women's products, they are frequently protrayed as experts rather than sex objects (see Chapter 15).

Another indicator of women's apparent sexual disinterest is the lower level of sexual activity in women as compared to men. Although the differences are lessening, women are still less likely than men to engage in premarital or extramarital sexual intercouse (Gagnon and Simon, 1973; Hunt, 1974; Kinsey, et al., 1953). They also masturbate less and tend to express guilt over masturbation when they do do it (Barbach, 1976; Schaefer, 1973). Since the incidence of homosexuality also appears to be lower in women than men, this means that combining over all sexual outlets, women engage in sexual activity less than men (Gagnon and Simon, 1973; Hunt, 1974; Kinsey, et al., 1953). One conclusion is that they are less interested either because of cultural conditioning or because of biologically based differences in sex drives.

In spite of their greater capacity for orgasm, women also appear to be less sexually responsive than men. Although modern marriage manuals suggest that a woman's potential level of sexual desire is equal to that of a man, they also point out that women tend to become aroused less quickly than men and that prolonged sexual foreplay is needed for most women to achieve orgasm on a regular basis (Gordon and Shankweiler, 1971). Although most would agree that women appear to be less responsive, several writers have denied that their slower response to sexual stimuli is caused by biological differences. Masters and Johnson (1966; 1970) did not find a sex difference in their subjects, but this group was very sexually experienced. Others suggest that women must learn to be sexually responsive—to overcome cultural conditioning which has caused them to inhibit their sexual feelings (Sherfey, 1972; Barbach, 1976; Schwartz, 1975; Sherman, 1971). Kinsey found that women with premarital sexual experience were more likely to report having orgasm during marital relations. Other studies have shown that women without early sexual experience tend to "catch up" and also become more orgasmic as they become familiar with sexual activities (Sherman, 1971). Regardless of the sources of these differences women do appear to be less interested and slower to respond to sexual stimuli than men.

Sexual Dysfunctions

The above patterns are reflected in the typical patterns found for female and male sexual dysfunctions. Although women may experience a variety of difficulties surrounding sexual intercouse, their major problem is orgasmic difficulty or inability to experience orgasm. This problem is treated by clinicians as a psychological problem related to sexual inexperience or feelings of fear, shame, or guilt about sexual feelings. Treatment generally involves a series of relaxation exercises and sensual explorations of one's body in a supportive, relaxed environment (Barbach, 1976; Masters and Johnson, 1970).

Thus, women may need help to overcome earlier sexual repression (Schwartz, 1975).

For men, the major psychologically based dysfunctions are premature ejaculation (ejaculation more than half the time before their partner is satisfied) and impotence (the inability to maintain an erection). These problems are also believed to result primarily from feelings of shame or guilt about sex or bad previous experiences with sexual intercourse. Premature ejaculation has been described as an extreme manifestation of the rapid arousal expected of men. Men also build up anxieties about failure to perform as an adequate sexual partner which could also result in impotence. All of these difficulties are treated with the same type of relaxation therapy used with women (Masters and Johnson, 1970).

Attitudinal factors are not the only source of sexual dysfunction. Physical problems can also account for sexual difficulties. Women may experience painful intercourse because of undiagnosed vaginal infections, too much douching, allergic reactions to vaginal deodorants or birth-control products, or tearing or improper healing of the vaginal tissue after childbirth. Vaginal areas may also become painful after menopause if there is insufficient estrogen to maintain the tissues at their normal state. Pain resulting from any of these problems can be treated medically. Most sexual dysfunction programs include a detailed physical examination so that difficulties resulting from nonpsychological factors can be ruled out. However, even these medically based problems may lead to psychological difficulties if the woman develops an expectation that sex will lead to pain rather than pleasure.

Problems for men can also have a physical basis. Impotence can result from drinking too much, sickness, or physical tiredness. As is the case with women, however, if a man experiences temporary impotence because of physical problems, but does not realize the source of the difficulty, he may then develop a psychological fear of inadequate performance which persists after the precipitating physical problem has disappeared. Often, couples who seek sexual therapy have a joint problem: the women are nonorgasmic and the men ejaculate prematurely or are impotent, problems which intensify one another and make sexual adjustment increasingly difficult for both (Masters and Johnson, 1970).

Women as Sex Objects

Physical Attractiveness. Women in our society are expected to be physically attractive. Even successful professional women are often described in terms of their appearance in newspaper or magazine stories. Although appearance is considered important for men as well as women, a much greater emphasis is placed on a woman's attractiveness (Schwartz, 1975).

One important reason for the importance of attractiveness for women may be that men expect them to be attractive. If a woman's status is derived primarily from the man she marries, and physical appearance is a major source of attraction for men, it logically follows that women would be concerned with appearance and would socialize their daughters to be similarly concerned. There is much experimental evidence that men do use physical attractiveness as a major criterion for determining whether they want to date a woman or not and that attractiveness is more important for men than women (Berscheid, et al., 1971; Stroebe, et al., 1971). The high or low attractiveness of a man's "date" either enhances or detracts from evaluations made of him, while the attractiveness of a woman's date has little effect on the evaluation made of her (Bar-Tal and Saxe, 1976). Thus, the fact that men are judged by the attractiveness of "their women" may be one reason for attractiveness being so important to men. In any case, it again documents a double standard in judging men and women.

Women are aware of the importance of their attractiveness and may use this as a base of power over men, indirectly offering sexual favors in exchange for other things they want (see Chapter 15). However, women who have relied heavily upon their appearance to influence men and for their own self-esteem may be especially distressed as they become older and are no longer considered as attractive (Schwartz, 1975).

Rape

The issue of rape is a complex one which relates to many of our stereotypic beliefs about men and women (Brownmiller, 1975; Medea and Thompson, 1974). Box 9 points out a number of commonly held myths about rape.

First, there are a number of myths about the victims of rape. Built on the idea that women have an enormous power over men by being able to arouse them is the belief that rape occurs when a woman tempts a man too much. For no other crime is there so much suspicion about the truthfulness of the victim. Victims of burglary are not treated with the skepticism of the rape victim, even though both crimes are private and frequently have no witnesses (Curtis, 1974). Questions about the victim's clothing are considered relevant in rape trials, the assumption being that if a woman is too attractive, a man will be overcome by desire and if rejected in his sexual advances will be "forced" to commit rape. Stores are not blamed for marketing their goods attractively if someone then shoplifts something, nor are wealthy people held responsible for displaying their wealth if someone robs them. It seems strange that women are blamed for being too attractive, especially since many other pressures in the society are simultaneously being placed on women to be as attractive as possible.

Rape happens to all types of women in many different circumstances. Although dark alleys do have their "share" of rapes and the press is always eager to expound upon the evils and terrors that await the female hitchhiker, a large percentage of rapes (anywhere from 35 to 55 percent) occur in a resi-

Box 9   Fact and Fantasy about Rape

Are the following items true or false? The correct "answers" appear in the text.

The Victim

If a woman is raped, she provoked it.
Most rapes occur in dark alleys and to women who hitchhike.
No normal, healthy woman can be raped.
Every woman really secretly wants to be raped.
A woman cannot be raped by her husband.

The Rapist

A rapist is a sexually unfulfilled man carried away by a sudden uncontrollable
  sexual urge.

Rapists are generally "sick," perverted men and should be pitied.

Most rapes involve black men raping white women.

Most rapists are strangers to their victims.

---

dence—the woman's home or some other residence. Some would suggest
that the solution to rape is to have women stay off the streets after dark. Such
a tactic would put too much of a constraint on the woman who lives alone,
supports herself, and desires free movement. Similarly, it is fruitless to argue
the efficacy of such a solution, as it clearly reflects the prevailing attitude that
women should depend on men for protection, transportation, and economic
security.

That no woman who resists can be raped is an old "ploy" (fortunately inadmissible now) used by defense attorneys to show the physical "impossibility"
of raping a normal, healthy woman. What this myth fails to take into account is that women may be unable to resist. Many women who have been
raped relate that their greatest fear was that they would be killed or harmed if
they resisted. In fact, 85 percent of rapes are accompanied by violence or the
threat of violence. Further, women in our society are rarely encouraged or
taught to utilize physical power or violence to protect themselves and as a
result are rarely a match for a man who has, among other things, the element
of surprise on his side.

Another myth is that every woman secretly wants to be raped. Underlying
this is the notion that sexual nature of women is to be the passive recipient of
male sexual prowess. There is a corollary attitude which posits that when a
woman says "no," she really means "yes," and therefore the resistance a
woman displays is further proof of her desire to be raped. Though many
women admit to having "rape fantasies," the element of *control* (over who,

how, and where) is what is missing for the victim of the rape. It is ludicrous to suggest that a woman could enjoy sexual *attack* by a man she is not attracted to under conditions she did not agree to and at a time she did not choose.

There are also a number of myths about rapists. One mentioned earlier is that they are victims of female temptation or of misunderstanding a woman who says "no," assuming she really means "yes." Many rapes are planned in advance and are committed by married men who have otherwise normal sexual relationships, which would tend to contradict the idea that rape involves uncontrollable sexual urges on the part of unfulfilled men. Rapists appear psychologically normal on most dimensions, differing from other men only in their tendencies to express violence and rage. They do not appear to be "sick" within the usual definitions. Rapes generally involve people within the same racial group; rape of white women by black men is relatively infrequent. Rapes often involve strangers, although as many as 40 percent of reported rapes are between people who are at least casually acquainted. Many rapes are not reported to the police because of the difficulties women have in being believed by authories. This is especially true when the rapist is known to the victim.

Rape again perpetuates the stereotypes of men as sexual aggressors and woman as passive recipients. Women who are raped are often blamed for their role in the act, based on the belief that good women are not interested and therefore do not have sex except with their husbands. Legally, a women cannot be raped by her husband since a husband legally has sexual access to his wife. This is reflected in the divorce laws of many states which allow the refusal of sexual contact as grounds for divorce.

LESBIANISM: WOMEN LOVING WOMEN

Differential standards and beliefs about sexuality underlie many attitudes about lesbianism. The lesbian is first of all a woman. She experiences all the socialization pressures common to women and holds many of the attitudes held by women in general. This fact is often overlooked in discussions of lesbians, producing a very distorted image of the lesbian as manlike and totally preoccupied with her homosexual preference (Gagnon and Simon, 1973). Lesbians are more similar to heterosexual women than they are different. Since most research on homosexuals has tended to focus upon male homosexuals and upon clinical populations, there is little data about the origins and characteristics of lesbians. This may partially reflect the societal belief that women's sexuality is primarily in response to men, with a consequent denial that women are lesbians, unless they are severely disturbed.

It is still not well understood why certain women become lesbians. In one of the few studies with a nonclinical population, lesbians were often found to have been tomboys as children, but the frequency for the lesbian group was not significantly higher than such tomboyish behavior for heterosexual girls (Saghir and Robins, 1973). One of the primary determinants of lesbianism seems to be initial sexual experiences. Either a very good sexual experience with a woman or a very poor one with a man may result in a woman becoming a lesbian (Hyde and Rosenberg, 1976; Rosen, 1974). However, most lesbian writers express a strong positive attraction to women rather than a dislike for men or an inability to attract a man (Abbott and Love, 1972; Bengis, 1972). However, the question of the origins of lesbianism remains unanswered. Hormonal and psychoanalytic explanations are widely held, along with explanations focusing on early childhood learning and experiences. Currently there is not enough data to conclusively support any of these theories.

Just as women and men differ, so do homosexual men and women. Lesbians tend to have more long-term love relationships than do male homosexuals (Saghir and Robins, 1973). They also place more emphasis on the emotional and romantic aspects of their relationships (Gagnon and Simon, 1973; Hyde and Rosenberg, 1976). Lesbians are more frequently bisexual and have had more sexual experiences with men than male homosexuals have had with women.

Although lesbianism is becoming somewhat more common, the incidence of reported male homosexual behavior is still higher than that for females (Kinsey, et al., 1953; Hunt, 1974). This may reflect actual differences or it may be that fewer women admit to being homosexual. It is still unclear if the increasing sexual openness of women will mean that eventually there will be as many open female as male homosexuals. The incidence of male homosexuality does not appear to have changed over the last few decades. This may be taken as evidence of underlying biological factors which have remained constant, or it may simply reflect the fact that changes in all sexual practices have been much greater for women than men over these years.

More research is needed to understand lesbians and lesbian relationships. Are sexual attitudes of lesbians different from those of other women? What is the effect upon children when raised by a lesbian mother? Once questions such as these can be answered we will understand women who love other women far better than we do now.

The issues in this chapter all point to the importance of societal beliefs and attitudes about sexual behavior in determining how we handle our sex lives. Many of the beliefs from earlier centuries are still prevalent in our society although in modified forms. Men still appear to be more sexually expressive than women and although women are becoming more expressive they are still different from men in their sexual attitudes and behaviors.

A number of explanations have been given for these sex differences in sexual behavior. There is some evidence to suggest that men are biologically more oriented towards sex than women because of higher hormone levels. As discussed in Chapter 10, men tend to have higher levels of androgens than women. Other research has implied that there is a direct relation between androgens and sexual interest or drive. This would lead to the conclusion that men are inherently more interested in sex than women. However, this argument can be criticized on several grounds. First, it is not at all clear if any significant portion of human behavior is hormonally based. Although it is very possible that hormone levels do affect basic levels of sexual interest, cultural effects are so important that this basic level of sexual interest may have little or no effect upon behavior. Also, there is some evidence that environmental influences or emotional states may affect hormone production (Bermant and Davidson, 1974). However, it seems unlikely that women would ever have more androgen than men since androgens are responsible for secondary male sex characteristics as well as sex drive and aggressiveness. All this suggests that the hormonal argument has not really been proved or disproved. We would conclude that androgen levels are one of the determinants of sexual activity, although a relatively unimportant one (see Box 2).

As equally strong argument for differences between men and women in overt sexual interest is that both sexes have high levels of biologically based sex drives, but that women's natural levels of drive are suppressed by cultural teachings. As discussed earlier, there are a number of cultural beliefs in our society which state that women do not and should not feel strong sexual interest (Schwartz, 1975; Sherfey, 1966). There is good data that expectations influence behaviors in a variety of settings (Frieze, et al., in press). If women are not expected to act overtly sexual, they may not label their arousal states sexual, while men may be inclined to overlabel various sorts of perceived stimulation as sexual (Valins, 1966). Because women are not expected to display open sexual interest, they may be embarrassed to tell other people about their feelings or to act upon their desires because of the shock or disapproval they anticipate receiving from others for their "deviant" behavior.

A third reason why women may not engage in sexual behavior as freely as men might relate to fears of pregnancy or physical harm. Sexual intercourse can always potentially result in pregnancy; in our society, as in most societies, it is the woman who assumes responsibilities for the child which might result. This is a large burden, especially for a young or unmarried woman. These practical considerations, then, might be a further explanation for why women do not appear as eager to participate in sex as men.

How these differences will change in response to changing attitudes is totally a matter of speculation.

12 Achievement and Nonachievement in Women

ACHIEVEMENT AND MEN

The people of the United States have traditionally been oriented toward personal achievement for themselves and have valued it in others. Men, especially, have been socialized to desire success in their work and other areas, such as sports, college, and politics. Social prestige is generally awarded to men on the basis of their success in their work or other areas. Perhaps because of the strong social value attached to the work men do, men's personal sense of worth has also often been strongly tied to their work. Along with the central role of work achievement in their lives, men have also tended to be highly motivated toward doing things well and many of them display high levels of what psychologists have labeled "achievement motivation."

The traditional roles assigned to women further help men in their efforts to be successful. Women are socialized to encourage their husbands and to assist in their success in every way that they can. The traditional wife cares for the daily needs of the husband as well as helping him in other ways such as entertaining business associates. She may also aid him in secretarial or clerical work if that is needed. Women are expected to be emotionally supportive of the efforts of their husbands, not only in their jobs, but also in their other achievement efforts (Papanek, 1973).

In addition to receiving support from his family, a man is also helped in

Irene Frieze was the primary author of this chapter.

his achievement efforts by society in general. Men are expected to be competent and much interaction serves to maintain this competent "face" for men (Broverman, et al., 1972). Men are expected to perform better than women in most jobs and these expectations change only very slowly (e.g., Feldman-Summers and Kiesler, 1974). Such stereotypes, once formed, are highly resistant to change.

ACHIEVEMENT AND WOMEN

Although women have been as exposed as men to the general achievement orientation of our society, women have not been as encouraged to succeed in those areas traditionally defined as male. While society aids and encourages men in thier achievements, women are discouraged from achieving outside the home. Women are judged on the basis of the success of their husbands, and women who are more successful than their spouses are often the basis for joking and ridicule. Men may be threatened by successful women and few men are pleased by the idea of a woman earning more money than they do. Women who are married and working are expected to perform the usual homemaking roles expected of nonworking women. They, themselves, lack the supports provided by the traditional wife. Instead, these women are often expected to perform these support functions for their husbands as well as for themselves. Thus, for the married woman, career success means success in both work and homemaking roles.

Women as a group have not been as successful as men in the fields which have traditionally been labeled achievement areas. Even though more and more women are working in jobs outside the home, women continue to earn lower salaries than men (Bernard, 1971). This is true even when the effects of factors such as differential experience and training are statistically eliminated (Levitin, Quinn, and Staines, 1971; Treiman and Terrell, 1975). Women are also less likely to be hired in many fields traditionally defined as male (Centra, 1974; Epstein, 1970) and they tend to occupy the lower levels of nearly every occupation in which they work (Bernard, 1971; Epstein, 1970). Since income and type of job are often equated with excellence in performance as well as with social prestige, these discrepancies are important because of their implications for our perceptions of the capabilities of women as well as for their inherent inequality. On other indices as well, women perform at lower levels than men. Fewer women attain advanced college and professional degrees, fewer women are in political positions of any sort, and women are especially missing from major decision-making positions. Until recently women have also been systematically excluded from professional sports, another field in which successful performance is highly regarded in our culture (McHugh, Duquin, and Frieze, 1977).

Why do women have these lower levels of achievement? Several explanations have been offered. Many have focused on internal-psychological factors which could inhibit women from career achievement. All share the characteristic of attributing the causes of women's failures to achieve to internal deficiencies in the women themselves. Such an emphasis ignores external factors which could also determine the behavior of both women and men. Hence, the rest of this chapter will look at these two sets of factors: the internal-psychological and the external.

PSYCHOLOGICAL BARRIERS TO ACHIEVEMENT

There are three major explanations for women's lower achievements which focus on psychological factors. The first is that women differ from men in having different underlying motives or values in their lives. A second is that both women and men are motivated to be successful, but that women define success differently than men do. That is, they look upon achievement as being successful in feminine fields rather than in traditionally masculine fields. A third major viewpoint is that women's beliefs about their abilities and their perceptions of why they succeed or fail reinforce a pattern of nonachievement for them.

Motivational Factors

Achievement motivation. Motives are defined as unconscious psychological forces which excite and direct the actions of the individual. We experience our motives as things we want or which are important to us. Some of the motives which have been extensively studied are a desire for close friendships (affiliation); a desire for recognition and control (power); a desire to harm (aggression); and a desire to do things well and be successful (achievement motivation). Research on achievement motivation should be especially relevant for understanding achievement-oriented behavior and its lack in women. Unfortunately much of it tends to be focused primarily on understanding males and male achievement behavior (Alper, 1974).

Numerous studies over the last twenty-five years have established that there is a relationship between achievement motivation levels in males and a number of behaviors which tend to maximize performance levels. Males with high achievement motivation are more likely to have confidence in their abilities, prefer intermediate risk situations, have realistic aspirations, persist when working on achievement tasks, be active in college organizations while in school, and be more successful in business. In general, given equal ability, the person with high achievement motivation does better in school, works harder on tasks he feels are important, is motivated to try harder when he fails an achievement task, and is more able to delay gratification in seeking long-term goals (Atkinson, 1964; Weiner, 1972). These results, though, have not always been consistent, perhaps because of measurement difficulties (see Weiner, 1972).

In trying to understand the research on achievement motivation, it is important to know how this motive is measured. The standard measurement of achievement motivation is the Thematic Apperception Test or TAT. The test consists of a series of ambiguous pictures depicting either men or men and women. Subjects look at each of these pictures briefly and then write a short story about each of them. The assumption underlying the TAT is that people will project their own motives and desires into these ambiguous situations and express them in the stories they write. Thus, if someone is highly motivated to be successful, it is assumed that this person will write stories about people who are also motivated to be successful and that their stories will concern people striving for excellence and concerned with failure and success.

When male college students were told that their stories would be used to judge their intelligence and potential for future success, their achievement scores tended to be much higher than when they were not given these "arousal" instructions (McClelland, et al., 1953). Women's scores became higher when they were told that their stories were indicative of social skills (French and Lesser, 1964; McClelland, et al., 1953). The fact that males and females reacted differently to TAT instructions led researchers to conclude that the female scores were not valid. The fact that early researchers also found that their female college students scored very high on the tests may have also been disconcerting, since it was assumed that female scores should be low to explain their lack of achievement.

This failure of the female subjects to respond as expected led researchers to conclude that the scores were not valid for females. However, there is no real evidence which can be used to conclude with certainty that male scores are more valid than female scores.

In addition to the differences between females and males in their reactions to the type of instructions given, men and women also differed in their responses to TAT pictures involving males as compared to females (French and Lesser, 1964; Lesser, Krawitz, and Packard, 1963). These problems in the measurement of achievement motivation have led researchers to develop other measures of this motive (French, 1958; Mehrabian, 1969). These measures have sometimes been successful at predicting achievement-oriented behavior in women (Baruch, 1967; Reid and Cohen, 1973; Shelton, 1967), but overall, the results with any of these measures (including the TAT) are equivocal for women (see Alper, 1974; O'Leary, 1974).

Anxiety or Fear of Failure. Early work with achievement motivation suggested that achievement behavior was a function of both desire for success or achievement motivation and anxiety or fear of failure (Atkinson, 1957). Fear of failure was a tendency to feel shame given nonattainment of a goal, and was believed to be an inhibitory factor which kept people from attempting achievement activities because of the possibility of failure. Fear of failure was measured empirically with anxiety scales, most commonly the Mandler-Sarason Test Anxiety Questionnaire (Mandler and Sarason, 1952). An achievement-oriented person was not only high in achievement motivation, but was also low in fear of failure. On the other hand, someone who typically avoided any achievement activity would be low in achievement motivation and high in fear of failure (Atkinson, 1964; Weiner, 1972).

Although there was little research with women because of the problems with measurement of female achievement motivation, other research has indicated that high levels of anxiety are indeed debilitating for successful achievement behavior, in either sex. For example, by the third grade, more anxious boys and girls tended to score lower on intelligence tests, presumably because their high anxiety tended to interfere with their concentration while taking the test (Montanelli and Hill, 1969). In fact, anxiety may be especially debilitating for girls (Stein and Bailey, 1973). There is a negative relationship for girls between various indices of achievement and anxiety (Maccoby, 1966). Academic performance is also negatively correlated with anxiety measures (Maccoby and Jacklin, 1974). The fact that girls and women typically do score higher on anxiety scales may therefore suggest that anxiety in women is one of the reasons for their lower achievement (Hill and Sarason, 1966; Maccoby and Jacklin, 1974). Although this explanation does appear to have validity, the issue is not entirely clear. For example, there are problems in the measurement of anxiety and in the interpretation of sex differences in anxiety (Maccoby and Jacklin, 1974). Also, there are situations when a little anxiety may be motivating so that the relationship may be curvilinear rather than direct. This possibility of anxiety as an explanatory factor in understanding female achievement does deserve further research.

Fear of Success. Much of the recent research surrounding anxiety as an explanation for the nonachievement of women has tended to focus not on anxieties about failure, but instead on anxieties about being too successful. This "fear of success" motive was conceived of as resulting from girls and women being afraid of social rejection and loss of their femininity if they were to become highly successful (Horner, 1972). Much of the research on fear of success was based on the original conception that fear of success was a stable motive acquired early in life in some women and that this motive was especially aroused in competitive situations when the competition was with men. Fear of success is assessed by a projective instrument using verbal cues rather than TAT pictures.

Although an enormous quantity of research has been generated by this popular conception, many of the original conceptions of fear of success have not been supported by empirical data. For example, fear of success does not appear to be a stable motive evident only in women (Condry and Dyer 1976;

Tresemer, 1974). In fact, fear of success is becoming more and more common in men. A review of forty-six studies revealed that the percentage of subjects showing fear of success in their stories ranged from 11 to 88 percent in females, with a median of 47 percent, and from 33 to 86 percent in males, with a median of 43 percent (Tresemer, 1974). Thus, even if the motive were a valid motive, it does not appear to be a motive experienced only by women and therefore cannot be easily used as an explanation for differential achievements in men and women.

Fear of success is best defined as a set of "realistic expectancies about the negative consequences of deviancy from a set of norms" (Condry and Dyer, 1976). It is possible that the increasing incidence of fear of success in men does represent a change in values in our society where achievement is no longer valued for men in the way it formerly was. New data that achievement motivation in males is declining in the United States lends support to this idea (McClelland, 1975). Thus, fears of being too successful or too dedicated to work may keep both men and women from attempting achievement activities. Since the research has not consistently demonstrated, though, that fear of success scores are directly related to avoidance of achievement, no firm conclusions can yet be made about fear of success as an explanatory factor for the lesser achievements of women.

Achievement in Feminine Fields

Other research has suggested that women do experience motives to achieve but that their achievement strivings are directed toward the home and other areas related to the traditional female role (Stein and Bailey, 1973). Women are socialized to value close interpersonal relationships and interpersonal skills such as empathy, nurturance, personal expression, and interpersonal communication. Thus, it would not be surprising if women decided to achieve in these areas instead of having careers. For example, as stated above, women are more likely to write TAT stories with high levels of achievement imagery if they are told that their stories are measures of social skills.

Another study asked women what types of things in their lives they considered as accomplishments or achievements. In this study, women mentioned successes in interpersonal relationships as well as career or school achievements (Lipinski, 1965). Thus, high achievement-motivated women may redefine success and failure in terms of traditional female values rather than desiring to succeed through careers or work in masculine fields. Also, parenthood is often defined as an achievement situation by college-educated women (Veroff and Feld, 1970).

Redefining women's goals for what constitutes success and failure may result in some negative consequences. What this pattern of redefining achievement goals means is that the woman is attempting to satisfy her achievement needs in a way in which there are few objective criteria for success. Research with men has consistently demonstrated that the high achievement-motivated man strongly desires feedback on his performance (see Atkinson, 1964). By directing achievement only to interpersonal areas, the woman never has the opportunity to evaluate herself objectively and must instead rely on emotional feedback from others. One reason women are returning to the labor force in such great numbers is their desire for objective indices of their successes and failures (Astin, 1975). Also, maintenance of self-esteem for women is dependent on their involvement in major adult roles other than or in addition to their wife/mother role (Birnbaum, 1975).

Along with achieving in homemaking and interpersonal roles, some women may also direct their achievement needs to vicarious achievement through their husbands or children (Birnbaum, 1975; Tangri, 1972). There are a number of reasons a woman would choose to achieve indirectly through others rather than directly for herself: if she is discouraged from achieving because of fear of negative consequences; if she is too successful (fear of success); if she further realizes that it will be difficult for her to get a good job or to be recognized for her accomplishments—all of these would indicate a decision to help her husband and children instead of directing her efforts toward personal achievement. This course of action would also be socially acceptable and expected of her as part of her traditional wife/mother role. In addition, she would receive direct economic benefits from her husband's accomplishments. However, by achieving through others, she would never be able to develop a strong sense of her own ability to achieve.

A pattern which seems to combine the best of achievement within the traditional feminine role with the experience of a personal sense of accomplishment, is to first achieve in the wife/mother role and then turn to achievement outside the home. In one study, women's achievement-motivation scores varied according to the stage of their life (Baruch, 1967). Women who scored high on achievement-motivation scales were likely to return sooner to paid employment, especially if their children were old enough to be in school. Older women in graduate school were also found to have higher achievement-motivation scores than younger female graduate students (Lubetkin and Lubetkin, 1971). These older women, having fulfilled their feminine role, may have been less conflicted about achievement outside this role, and thus scored higher on the TAT.

This pattern of women first achieving in the femine role does have disadvantages. All too often, when a woman is in her thirties and ready to return to school or work outside the home, she is far behind others (male and female) of her own age in career advancement. If she goes to work outside the home, her training and skills are likely to be outdated and allow her to take only a low-status position. Even if she gets further training, many employers would rather hire younger people, especially for jobs with opportunities for promotion. Thus, the woman returning to the work force in her thirties or forties is unlikely to make the contribution that she would have been capable of if she had had a continuous work pattern. However, the woman who has this discontinuity has had the personal and societal benefits of fulfillment of her feminine role (Ginzberg, 1966).

Other women may redefine feminine achievement and appear to express their achievement in following the pattern which has typically character-ized men. These women have high career aspirations and tend to be nontradi-tional in a number of ways. For example, rather than being concerned about appearing too competent, they express guilt over sometimes wanting to ap-pear more competent than they really are (Stewart, 1974). This, of course, could also be indicative of their low self-esteem which does not allow them to realize how competent they really are. Although it seems obvious that women differ from one another, this has not been explicitly noted in the research looking for motivational explanations for women's lack of achieve-ment. Much of the ambiguity in early research on achievement motivation and anxiety might be explained by more realization that there are several dif-ferent orientations toward achievement in women that also may or may not be different from men (McHugh, 1975).

Cognitive Variables

Thus, most of the work dealing with psychological reasons for women's lack of achievement has been based on the assumption that nonconscious motives, such as achievement motivation, are the key variables in understanding achievement behavior. Unfortunately, nonconscious motives are difficult to measure, so that much of the reasoning is speculative.

Recent work in an area called attribution theory has suggested that per-ceptions about the causes of events and expectancies for success may be a useful and interesting way of analyzing human behavior of all types and especially achievement-oriented behavior. Such variables are conscious and more easily measured than motives. People engaging in achievement behav-ior have ideas and beliefs about what they are doing. One type of belief is an expectation about the likelihood of their being successful or not. Such expec-tations influence people's choices of future activities and the level of their subsequent performance (Frieze, 1976; Frieze, et al., in press). In addition to such expectations, people also make judgments about why particular events occur. These judgments are also an important predictor for future be-havior.

Research oriented toward a cognitive approach to understanding sex dif-ferences in achievement behavior has focused on three major areas. First, numerous studies have documented that, in our society, higher expectancies for personal success are held by men and boys than by women and girls. Sec-ond, several studies suggest that men and women habitually make different causal attributions or judgments about the causes of their own successes and failures. Finally, attributions made by other people depend upon the sex of the person being observed.

Expectations for Success and Failure

Expectations for success or failure have been shown to affect behavior in a variety of achievement situations. Several studies have demonstrated that people with high expectations for success actually tend to perform better on achievement tasks (e.g., Battle, 1965; Feather, 1966). This effect may be the result of a favorable past history of success for those with higher expectations, if people with high expectations are indeed more competent. However, the expectancy effect is also found in studies which have led people to believe they will do well or poorly in the future on a particular task independent of their past performance levels.

Differential expectations for success and failure in males and females have been well documented. A series of studies demonstrate the generally low expectancies of girls and women in a variety of tasks, ages, and settings (Crandall, 1969). These results have been found for elementary-school children, who gave expectancy estimates for their performance at new intellectual tasks; for eighth-graders who were asked to state how well they expected to do at a matching task; for college students estimating their grades; and for college-aged people who guessed their performance at a geometric task. Consistently, males had generally higher initial expectancies than did females. Moreover, when objective ability estimates were available, males tended to overestimate their future successes relative to their ability level, while females tended to underestimate their future performances. Thus, both sexes were inaccurate but in different directions, although girls tended to be more accurate overall.

Other researchers have replicated these findings with a variety of age groups and tasks (see Frieze, et al., in press), but a few studies have indicated that these sex differences in expectancies are not always clear cut. Some of the discrepancies in the data may be the result of trying to separate the expectation from the specific task (McHugh, 1975). A distinction between generalized and specific expectancies could clarify this. That is, generalized expectancies are held in situations in which an individual has had little or no prior experience, while specific expectancies develop out of past experience in a particular situation (Rotter, 1954). For women there appears to be a major difference between generalized and specific expectancies. Given our sex-role stereotypes that men are more intelligent, achieving, and competitive than women, it is to be expected that females would have lower generalized expectancies than males in our culture. Theoretically, females' specific expectancies should not be as influenced by cultural sex stereotypes and might be high for some tasks, on which they had done well in the past (McHugh, 1975).

Many of the studies demonstrating lower expectancies in females have used tasks in which the subjects have had little or no experience. These studies may be tapping generalized expectancies, since people would have no way of really knowing how well they might do. Those studies which have not found differential expectancies have tended to use more familiar tasks for which expectancies are known on the basis of previous experience.

Since expectations are important for determining what types of tasks or activities a person will attempt, the generally lower expectancies of girls and women may well represent another barrier to high levels of achievement for women. While expectancies are another psychological explanation, they do appear to have a rather direct connection to traditional sex roles for women and, thus, may be more easily changed than the more stable personality traits or motives suggested by other researchers.

Attributing the Causes of Success and Failure

There are many possible reasons or causal attributions for why a particular success or failure might occur (Heider, 1958). The four most studied causes of achievement outcomes are ability, effort, luck, and task ease or difficulty (Weiner, et al., 1972). Thus a person may succeed at a task because of her or his high ability, trying hard, good luck, or the fact that the task was relatively easy. Failure may result from low ability, not trying hard enough, bad luck, or task difficulty. More recent work has indicated that other causal factors are frequently employed to explain the causes of successes and failures. These include stable effort or consistent pattern of diligence or laziness, other people who may aid or interfere with performance, mood and fatigue or sickness, having a good or poor personality, and physical appearance (Elig and Frieze, 1975; Frieze, 1976).

A three-dimensional system for classifying these causal attributions is summarized in Box 1. Some causes have to do with factors in the person; these are *internal* causes. Other causes are *external* to the person, because they are causes involving either the environment (luck, the situation) or other people. The location of the cause along the internal/external dimension is related to the affect experienced by the person undergoing success or failure. If a person perceives that her successes are due to factors internal to her, such as ability or effort, she will feel more pride than if the cause is external to her. A second dimension along which attributions can be classified is stability. Some causes can be expected to continue unchanged in the future, while others will vary. Luck, for example, is highly variable, as is effort, but abilities are relatively stable. The stability dimension has been empirically related to expectancies. If a person succeeds and attributes her or his success to a stable cause, the person will expect to continue to succeed in the future. If the attribution is made to an unstable cause, the person is then uncertain about future outcomes. The third dimension is intentionality. An attribution is considered to be intentional to the degree that the person is perceived to have control of her or his actions. Thus, ability and personality are factors within the person over which that person has little control, and events attributed to these factors would be unintentional. However, the person is perceived to have control over the effort she or he exerts, so that attributions to effort are intentional (as well as being internal). The intentionality dimension appears to be related to reward and punishment (Elig and Frieze, 1975; Weiner, 1974).

It is hypothesized that in many cases people have well-established patterns of making causal attributions. People with self-esteem would tend to make internal and stable attributions for success and external or unstable attributions for failure. This would perpetuate their feelings of pride and lessen any feelings of shame. It would also lead to high expectancies for themselves in future activities. Although these patterns of perceiving success and failure may perpetuate self-esteem, other data suggests that maximum achievement striving is associated with slightly different patterns. High achievement-

Box 1   **A Three-Dimensional Model for Classifying Causal Attributions for Success and Failure**

	Internal	
	Stable	**Unstable**
Intentional	Stable effort (Diligence or laziness)	Unstable effort (Trying or not trying hard)
Unintentional	Ability Knowledge or background Personality	Fatigue Mood
	External	
	Stable	**Unstable**
Intentional	Others always help or interfere	Others help or interfere with this event
Unintentional	Task difficulty or ease Personality of others	Task difficulty or ease (task changes) Luck or unique circumstances Others accidentally help or interfere

SOURCE: Modified from Elig and Frieze, 1975.

Box 2   The Low-Expectation Cycle

Initial Expectation	Out-come	Cognitive State	Causal Attribution	Future Expecta-tion
Low Expectation	Success	Cognitive inconsistency	External and unstable (good luck)	Low expectation
Low Expectation	Failure	Cognitive consistency	Internal and stable (lack of ability)	Low expectation

SOURCE: Modified from Jackaway, 1974.

motivated men tend to attribute their successes to both high ability and effort while they perceive their failures as due to lack of effort. The attribution of failure to lack of effort would lead to greater subsequent trying when they do poorly. This attribution pattern explains the motivating effects of failure for high achievement-motivated males (Atkinson, 1964; Kukla, 1972; Weiner, 1972).

Given the low initial expectancies of women generally, certain attributional patterns can be predicted from the attribution model discussed above. If a woman expects to do poorly but succeeds, she is likely to attribute the outcome to an unstable cause such as luck. This means she will not change her expectancies and she feels no pride in her success if the attribution is made to the external element of luck. When a female with low expectancy fails on a task, an expected outcome, she tends to attribute it to lack of ability. This attributional pattern perpetuates a Low Expectation Cycle by minimizing the positive effects of success and maximizing the negative effects of failure as shown in Box 2. Some research has supported these predictions that women would attribute success to luck and failure to lack of ability.[1]

However, much of the current research does not find this hypothesized attributional pattern in women. Many studies have, instead, found a general pattern of externality on the part of the female. Some studies have found that females rate tasks as easier than do males in both success and failure conditions (Bar-Tal and Frieze, 1977; Croke, 1973; McMahan, 1972). Other research has indicated that women make greater use of luck attributions for both success and failure (Bar-Tal and Frieze, 1977; Feather, 1969; McMahan, 1972; Simon and Feather, 1973). By employing either of these patterns, women reduce the value of their successes and take less responsibility for them. Women employing these patterns would also experience relatively little pride in achievement situations.

[1] See Dweck and Reppucci, 1973; Nicholls, 1975; Crandall, et al., 1965; McMahan, 1972.

Although research has established that there are some patterns of attributions which appear to be more common for women than men, recent thinking has indicated that women (like men) differ from one another in many ways which would affect their attributional patterns or how they respond to attribution questionnaires (Frieze, et al., in press). Some women may be reluctant to state that their ability is responsible for their successful performances. Others may be afraid of appearing too successful because of fears of social rejection. Women, as has been noted earlier, differ from one another greatly; it may well be that future research will verify a number of attribution patterns for women. Along with individual differences in attributional patterns among women, there are also a number of situational factors which affect attributions.

Training Women for Nonachievement

Given our different traditional expectations for the future roles of boys and girls, one is likely to find socialization processes pushing boys and girls in different directions. Children soon learn what activities are considered feminine and which are considered masculine (see Chapter 7). These sex-role definitions affect task performance, especially for children who most strongly hold to male or female sex preferences (Dwyer, 1972; Milton, 1959; Stein and Bailey, 1973). Traditionally, girls have known that regardless of their particular interests or talents, they will be expected to spend a major share of their adult lives as wives and mothers. Boys realize they have more freedom to choose an occupation which will then be their major adult focus (Bem and Bem, 1970).

In general, girls tend to be more protected than boys. Although girls do perform well in elementary school, their performance is often attributed, even by themselves, as resulting from a desire to be good and please others (Birnbaum, 1975). They are frequently discouraged from being too far from home and are encouraged to develop interpersonal skills rather than assertiveness and independence (Block, 1975; Hoffman, 1972).

General sex differences in achievement are directly related to socialization. For example, parental interest and involvement in children's achievement activities are important, as is having a positive view of the child's competence and setting realistic but challenging demands for her or his accomplishments (Maccoby, 1966; Smith, 1969; Winterbottom, 1958). These attitudes are more typical of parents of boys than girls, but they have been observed in the backgrounds of successful career women (Angrist and Almquist, 1975; Birnbaum, 1975; Ginzberg, 1966; Rossi, 1967).

Evidence for the general attitude of encouraging achievement in boys and discouraging it in girls is also visible in the increasing sex differences in achievement as children get older. For example, the ratio of female to male underachievers increases with age. At young ages there are far more male underachievers, but by the college years there are more girls who fail to achieve at their potential (Raph, Goldberg, and Passow, 1966; Shaw and McCuen, 1960). There is also a general decline in IQ found for girls during childhood and adolescence but not found for less strongly feminine-identified girls (Dweck, 1975; Maccoby, 1966). Parents also differentiate more sharply between their children on the basis of sex when the children are older—with the maximum sex differentiation being during high school (Block, 1975). Teachers are more likely to criticize girl's performances in school than boys, perhaps because little boys are expected to have other interests. Thus, teachers may be reinforcing the low expectancies girls have of themselves (Dweck, 1975).

Beyond direct reinforcement of parents or other socializing agents such as schools and churches, children also learn behavior by modeling adult behaviors, especially the behaviors of same-sex models (see Chapters 6 and 7). Career-oriented women have frequently had employed mothers who served as models for their daughters. Also, many successful working women have mentioned the importance of having close relationships with a teacher or other professional person as influential in their professional life (Almquist and Angrist, 1971; Ginzberg, 1966). These people, too, may have served as role models. Although in the situations just mentioned, role models encouraged girls to adopt nontraditional roles, the situation is usually the reverse. Most mothers in the past have not worked and have thus been models only for traditional roles. Television, another strong modeling influence, tends to show few successful employed women; those who are shown are typically unmarried or unhappily married (Manes and Melnyk, 1974). Many women have become successful in careers. The experiences of these women are unusual in one or more ways, as shown in Box 3.

EXTERNAL BARRIERS TO ACHIEVEMENT

Along with the various personality factors which may lead to women being less achievement-oriented than men, women must also cope with a variety of external barriers to their achievement outside the home. These barriers include the discriminatory attitudes of employers as well as the disapproval of family and friends. Successful achievement is not only unexpected for a woman, it may also be considered unfeminine, both by herself and others (Hoffman, 1972; Horner, 1972). Men may be threatened by a woman who earns more or is more successful than they are. For women who marry, they are often responsible for household tasks to a much greater extent than their husbands, even if they both work (e.g., Bem and Bem, 1970). For women who do not have to work for financial necessity, there is always the socially approved option of giving up their job if they encounter too many difficulties or feel discouraged and returning to the traditonal wife/mother role. Because

Box 3   **Characteristics of Successful Women and Women with High Career Aspirations**

Family Background
Supportive father
Mother who is happy in a career or who is unhappy as a traditional homemaker

Marriage/Children
Husband who supports the idea of the woman's career
Late marriage or single
No children or children after the career of the woman is established
Early return to work after having children

Personality Characteristics
Nontraditional values
Enjoy solitary activities such as reading
Discuss goals with female friends
Tomboy as a child

Other Influences
Female role models

SOURCES: Angrist and Almquist, 1975; Ginzberg, 1966; Parsons, Frieze, and Ruble, 1976; Rossi, 1967.

of this option, these women may not be as motivated to fight the discrimination and disapproval they encounter.

Employment

Employers adhere to a number of beliefs about women which serve to reinforce a pattern of nonemployment and nonpromotion for female employees. Some of these are listed in Box 4. For example, many employers feel that women only work for extra, nonessential money and, therefore, that their jobs are not essential; this leads to the conclusion that men should be hired or promoted rather than women. Data indicates, however, that 40 percent of employed women are *not* financially dependent upon others and that one-third of these women are the sole wage-earners in their households (Chafetz, 1974; Crowley, Levitin, and Quinn, 1973).

Some employers believe that women are not really motivated to hold jobs outside the home and, therefore, that women are unreliable, do not take their jobs seriously, and will quit whenever the financial necessity forcing them to work is alleviated. Data would tend to contradict this belief as well. In one study, working women and men were asked: "If you were to get enough money to live as comfortably as you would like for the rest of your life, would you continue to work?" It was found that 74 percent of the men and 57 percent of the women said they would continue to work given this situation (Crowley, et al., 1973). Since many women, unlike men, do have a well defined and socially approved role (being a full-time wife and mother) they could perform if they quit their jobs, it is especially surprising that so many women would continue to work outside the home. Their jobs are clearly fulfilling needs for them other than economic ones.

More and more college women are looking forward to having careers for intrinsic interest. Seventy percent of a recent sample of college women expected to work outside the home all or most of their adult lives (Frieze, Parsons, and Ruble, 1972). Statistical evidence for the large percentage of women in paid employment would also support the belief that women are taking their jobs seriously (see Chapter 8). Even more interesting is that there are few differences in the ratings women and men attach to the importance of various facets of their jobs. Both sexes rated having friendly and helpful coworkers and a competent supervisor as very important. The major-

---

Box 4   Myths about Women Workers

1. Women only work for "pin money."
   It's true that women do not earn as much money as men *but* many women work out of economic necessity. For married women, their income as well as their husband's is necessary for comfortable support of the family. As divorce rates go up there are more and more female-headed households.

2. Women are not worth hiring or training for skilled jobs since they just get married and pregnant and quit.
   Turnover rates are higher in low-skilled jobs and since women work in more of these low-skilled jobs they do quit more *but* when job level is held constant, there is no difference. Women do cite family reasons more as a basis for quitting; men leave more often to take a better job elsewhere.

3. Women are often sick on the job and miss work especially when premenstrual or menstruating.
   Female and male workers have about the same number of missed work days. Women have more short-term illness while men have more chronic illness. Of course, women may report sick time when it's actually their children who are sick. In spite of this, women average no more sick time than men.

4. Things are getting better for women workers.
   Although barriers are going down in many fields, the majority of women workers are still in very low-paying jobs. Women's wages are rising less than men's are so that the differences are getting bigger all the time.

SOURCES: Chafetz, 1974; Laws, 1975.

ity of men and women also wanted clearly defined responsibilities and free-dom in deciding how to do their work (Crowley, et al., 1973).

Employers also believe that married women with children are more com-mitted to their home responsibilities than their jobs. It is true that women see such aspects of the job as having good hours and a convenient location as being more important than men do, but there is no convincing evidence that women do not perform as well as men in their work or that they are less mo-tivated to do well (Crowley, et al., 1973).

One reason that actual performance is difficult to assess is that there are so many conscious and unconscious beliefs about the competence of women held by our society (see Chapter 14). An example of this is seen in early resesrch on creativity which assumed that women were not as creative as men in spite of test results to the contrary (Helson, 1975). Women are expected to do more poorly than men at numerous achievement tasks. For example, in one study, researchers reported that they were unable to find any occupation in which females were expected to outperform males. For all the professions they used—which included pediatrician, writer, child psychologist, surgeon, dancer, diagnostician, clinical psychologist, and biographer of famous women—males were expected to be more successful than females (Feldman-Summers and Kiesler, 1974). These lower expectations for women might well affect the original hiring and training of women for these jobs. These expectations may also directly affect the performance of women. That is, when people are randomly assigned to high and low expectancy groups, the high expectancy group tends to perform better than the group to which low expectancies were assigned (Rosenthal and Jacobson, 1968; Tyler, 1958).

Causal attributions for performance also differ according to the sex of the person being evaluated. When both male and female college students were asked to evaluate another's performance at finding hidden objects in a com-plex design, males were expected to do better when the task was described as a masculine task. When given information that the person had succeeded at the task, males' successes on the "masculine" task tended to be attributed more to ability while females' successes were more likely to be attributed to luck. However, when the task was described as feminine, women were ex-pected to do better. There were no differences in subjects' perceptions of the causes of success on the feminine task. Attributions were intermediate be-tween ability and luck (Deaux and Emswiller, 1974).

The causal attributions made about a person have important implications not only for the affect and expectancies of that person, but also for the rewards given that person by others. People are constantly being evaluated by others for their achievements. The kinds of attributions made by the decision-makers have major consequencws for those being judged. An ex-ample of this process is the reaction of an employer to a poor performance by an employee. If the employer perceives that the poor performance was due to circumstances over which the employee had no control (such as being given a difficult assignment) or which might be expected to change in the near future (the employee had been sick and is now better), the employer will be more likely to give that employee a second chance. If, however, the employer felt that the poor performance was the result of the employee being lazy or generally incompetent, the employer might well fire the employee.

Although there have not been a great many studies in this area, those studies which have been done suggest that female successes are more likely to be attributed to unstable factors such as luck or effort while male successes are more often attributed to the stable internal factor of ability. Such patterns, if they generalize, would imply that even when women do succeed, since their successes are attributed more to unstable factors, they would not be expected to continue to be successful.

A model relating initial expectations and causal attributions suggests that when making a prediction about the future performance of an individual, the perceiver considers both the individual's most recent performance and the expectations which the perceiver had before that performance (Valle and Frieze, 1976). The question is, when making predictions for the future, how much importance will be given to this recent performance and how much to initial expectations. This model suggests that the amount of importance given to a previous performance is related to the attributed cause of that performance. If the performance was attributed to stable factors (e.g., ability or task) the previous outcome would be weighed heavily. If, on the other hand, the outcome was attributed to unstable factors (e.g., luck or effort) it should be weighed less heavily. In addition, the type of attribution made will be dependent upon the difference between the actual outcome and the intitial expectations. If the difference between is small there will be a tendency to attribute the outcome to stable factors. As the difference increases, the tendency to attribute the outcome to unstable factors will increase (see Box 5).

Consider an example of a manager who expects a new female worker to do poorly. If the worker performs well on her first assignment the manager will probably attribute this unexpected performance to an unstable characteristic of the situation, such as luck. Since the manager attributes the performance to luck, he will not consider this performance important in determining how well she will do in the future and will continue to expect her to do poorly. On the other hand, if the performance had been poor, the manager would consider this expected performance to be the result of the low ability of the worker (or some other stable attribute) and this poor performance would confirm his initially low expectation. In neither case would the manager be likely to recommend her for promotion.

Male managers, therefore, have negative views of women in management. Female characteristics in general are believed to make them more suited for low-level clerical jobs than higher-level management or professional jobs (O'Leary, 1974). Thus, women are not expected to perform as well as men.

Box 5   **Attributional Mediation of Expectancy Changes**

Initial Expectancy	Performance Level	Causal Attribution	New Expectancy

High
— High → Ability or Other Stable Internal Factors → Very High
— Low → Bad Luck or Lack of Effort or Other Unstable Factors → High

Low
— High → Good Luck, Special Effort or Other Unstable Factors → Low
— Low → Lack of Ability or Other Stable Internal Factors → Very Low

SOURCE: Valle and Frieze, 1976.

Once they have been hired, there is also evidence that women's performances are not rated as highly as those of men. Several laboratory studies have shown that male performances are rated higher than female performances when they are held constant (Deaux and Taynor, 1973; Goldberg, 1968; Pheterson, Kiesler, and Goldberg, 1971). Also, women are less likely to be promoted than men, given similar job performances (Rosen and Jerdee, 1974a; 1974b).

All this would indicate that women are discriminated against in employment. The model in Box 5, which may underlie this process, is pessimistic, since it suggests underlying causes for discrimination against women which may be difficult to change since they are largely nonconscious. However, it may also allow for greater change if these mechanisms are better understood.

SOCIAL BARRIERS TO ACHIEVEMENT

Along with direct or indirect discrimination in employment, women must also contend with negative attitudes in friends and family if they become too successful. Having the supportiveness of husbands or boyfriends for their careers has frequently been noted as an important factor for successful achievement of women. Many women have said that they would not pursue career plans over the objections of their husbands; however, aspirers to nontraditional careers are characterized by having male friends who support their aspirations (Birnbaum, 1975; Hawley, 1972; Horner, 1972).

Single professional women report that men are often threatened by a woman who is more successful than they are. For a highly successful women this may severely limit the pool of men she can socialize with, to either those more successful than she is or those who are not personally threatened by successful women. Perhaps for this reason, it is more often the most successful women who are likely to remain single, while the opposite tendency is true for men—highly successful men are more often married and the least successful males do not marry (Bernard, 1972a). Fears about this phenomenon are common in women who score high in fear of success (Condry and Dyer, 1976; Horner, 1972).

Married women must also cope with societal disapproval for working, although this may be diminishing. Gallup Poll data from 1945 and 1969 indicates that both sexes are becoming more supportive of working women. To the question, "Do you approve of a married woman earning money in business or industry if she has a husband capable of supporting her?", 18 percent responded yes in 1945, and 55 percent were favorable in 1969. However, even with this change, a large proportion of people do not approve of women working. Some of these people are likely to be coworkers who will express their disapproval to the working woman in subtle or nonsubtle ways and make her job more difficult. Women report having trouble establishing the informal contacts with coworkers so important to successful job performance for many types of jobs (Epstein, 1970). Such disapproval is even more prevalent for married women with children (see Hoffman and Nye, 1974).

WHY SHOULD WOMEN ACHIEVE?

With all the internal and external barriers to women achieving outside of the home, why should women bother to try? Although many people ask this question, the data on the number of women, especially young women, in the job market would alone imply that women want to work outside the home. Although it is clearly true that some women enjoy being full-time wives and mothers, this role does not allow personal recognition for many women (Astin, 1975). Studies also indicate that working women, especially professional women, tend to have very high self-esteem and life satisfaction fifteen to twenty-five years after graduation from college while comparable women who had been housewives for most of their adult lives had the lowest self-esteem of any of the women (Birnbaum, 1975; see Chapter 9). These types of studies indicate that women do find their jobs meaningful and important for their lives. Women should have a real option about how they decide to live, and helping those who want achievement can only increase these options. Also, many women do work out of necessity and these women should not have their job of supporting their families made more difficult than it already is.

13 Psychological Disorders in Women: Indices of Role Strain

Jeanne Marecek

Women's roles are currently undergoing rapid change. The ultimate goal of the movement for change is more freedom, satisfaction, and personal fulfillment for women and men. But, the *process* of change may produce conflict and uncertainty for those involved in it. For instance, some women may feel guilty when their career role detracts from their maternal role. They may have absorbed the belief that growing children deserve instant access to their mother; however, they may also have been educated to aspire to a challenging job. Other women may find that their choice of career, life-style, or sexual orientation estranges them from their parents or friends. They may be forced to choose between frustrating their own needs and losing the esteem and support of others. Still other women may find culturally approved roles personally distasteful, yet perceive no other options. This seems to have been the case of Sylvia Plath. In Plath's autobiographical novel, *The Bell Jar* (1971), Esther, a college student, speculates about marriage:

> . . . one of the reasons I never wanted to get married [was that] the last thing I wanted was infinite security and to be the place an arrow shoots off from. I wanted change and excitement. . . . I hated the idea of serving men in any way. I wanted to dictate my own thrilling letters . . . (p. 62 and p. 68–69).

Later, in her own marriage, Plath struggled to write poetry while running a household and raising children. Eventually, physical exhaustion, feelings of isolation, and depression led her to take her own life.

To describe women's psychological disorders is to describe the conflicts those women experienced and the social experiences that generated those conflicts. Much of the discussion that follows is drawn from the reports of women undergoing psychiatric treatment. Unfortunately, this fact may be a source of bias. Not all women (or even most women) resort to professional help in personal crises; instead, they may rely on the support of family, friends, or clergy. In particular, the data are probably biased in the following ways: (1) they may overrepresent women who are affluent enough to afford treatment; (2) they may omit certain areas of conflict for which women are reluctant to seek treatment; and (3) they ignore the many women who manage personal crises without professional help and, in doing so, overlook women's strengths and inner resources. Thus, caution should be exercised in drawing conclusions from the following discussion. Information on women in psychiatric treatment may not shed enough light on the condition of women in general.

WHAT IS A PSYCHOLOGICAL DISORDER?

There is also the thorny question of terminology. Terms like "mental illness," "abnormal behavior," "problems in living," and "psychological disorders" are often used interchangeably. In fact, each term implies a different set of assumptions about the nature, causes, and, sometimes, treatment of the behavior under scrutiny. For instance, "mental illness" implies a disease process that is analogous to that of physical illness. Proponents of this viewpoint might recommend such treatment as drugs, hospitalization, and professional care. There is no evidence that all psychological disorders involve a physical disease process. Many disorders have no biological cause, but rather result from various environmental and interpersonal stresses. In some disorders, a biological predisposition is present, but it is not expressed behaviorally unless the individual is under stress. In this chapter, attention is focused primarily on the effects of environmental and interpersonal stress, not biology. Hence, mental illness is not an appropriate term for our discussion.

What about "abnormal behavior"? On the positive side, it eliminates the notion of sickness and any implications of medical treatment. On the negative side, however, it implies that there are absolute and unambiguous standards for evaluating behavior. This is simply not the case; standards of normality can change dramatically with time, place, and circumstances. Consider marijuana use, a practice that has evoked a broad range of judgments, ranging from condemnation to tolerance to approval. At present, there is less condemnation and more tolerance for marijuana use than there was ten years ago. However, people's attitudes toward marijuana vary with their cultural background and socioeconomic status. Furthermore, in judging a particular drug-user, information about his or her age, background, and motives for using the drug would affect the evaluation of normality. Most of us would be more concerned about marijuana use in a nine-year-old child who rarely attended school than in a college student on the honor roll. We might also be less concerned about a college student who "got high" on Saturday night with friends than one who needed to get "high" to be relaxed enough to attend classes. The point is that behavior always occurs in the context of numerous cultural, situational, and personal elements. The ever-changing face of this context makes the formulation of absolute and clear-cut standards impossible. The term abnormal behavior implies a certainty of judgment that we may never reach.

The label "problems of living" was coined by theorists who believe that social or interpersonal factors underlie all psychological disorders (Adams, 1964; Szasz, 1960). Although this chapter highlights social pressures and interpersonal problems that bring women into treatment, problems in living is misleading in one important respect. It glosses over the contribution of biophysical factors to certain disorders. Thus, like mental illness, problems in living is not all-inclusive enough to fit our needs.

In the preceding passages, three labels, each reflecting a particular theoretical viewpoint, have been discarded. Only the term "psychological disorder" remains. It, too, is not a completely neutral term. For instance, disorder may have a medical connotation similar to that of illness. However, that connotation is not intended here. Rather, psychological disorder is meant to signify problems which originate from either social, interpersonal events, or from the combination of a biological predisposition and social stresses. These problems involve combinations of behavior, feelings, and thoughts that trouble individuals or seriously interfere with their daily living. This is not a very precise definition, but the current state of our knowledge does not permit great precision.

Psychosis and Neurosis

There is one additional point of terminology to clarify. In the pages that follow, the terms psychosis and neurosis will occasionally appear. Psychosis refers to a class of psychological disorders which involve a loss of contact with reality and, consequently, are quite serious. Persons who have psychotic disorders may be oblivious of their surroundings part of the time, experience hallucinations, or be convinced of delusional ideas. These extreme symptoms probably reflect a brain malfunction; however, situational conflict or stress is generally the trigger for this malfunction.

Neurosis, on the other hand, refers to psychological disorders in which contact with reality remains intact, although strong feelings of unhappiness, depression, anxiety, etc. may be present. Although most neuroses are problems in living, interpersonal or environmental stresses may be complicated by biological malfunction. In general, the more specific diagnostic terms identifying types of psychosis and neurosis will be avoided. For one thing, these terms do not have clearly agreed-upon meanings; different professionals use them to mean different things. Furthermore, the disorders that many individuals now experience are not reflected in the traditional systems of classification. For example, crises of self-identity or severe feelings of alienation are not officially recognized as psychological disorders, although they cause many individuals to seek therapy.

The basic issues of this chapter can now be presented. First, basic information will be described: What is the incidence of psychological disorder among women? What kinds of disorders occur most frequently among women? What life circumstances promote or prevent women's psychological disorders? Then, some interpretations will be offered: What experiences are responsible for the growing incidence of psychological disorders among women? Why is depression more common to women than men? Why might marriage seem to have a negative effect on women's psychological well-being? Finally, therapy will be considered: What are the goals of treatment for women? Have therapists adapted their methods and goals to the changing needs of their female clients?

WOMEN'S PSYCHOLOGICAL DISORDERS

What is the evidence concerning rates of psychological disorder among women? Are there patterns reflected in these rates that might reveal sources of social or interpersonal conflict? The evidence concerning rate of psychological disorder in our culture underscores the importance of this topic. The number of people seeking psychiatric help has more than doubled over the past twenty years; and the proportion of women has increased consistently. Various trends in the incidence of women's psychological disorders provide a starting point for our speculations about the stresses in women's lives.

Rates of Psychological Disorder

Superficially, taking a census of those suffering from a psychological disorder may seem like a straightforward job. In fact, it is far from simple. Much of the available information concerns only those who have entered psychiatric hospitals for treatment. But, of course, many people seek treatment from outpatient clinics, private practitioners, family physicians, counselors, and friends. Thus, statistics reporting hospital populations underestimate the total number of people with psychological disorders. There is another bias in the treatment statistics which is more serious. In many cases of psychological disorders (especially milder ones), the decision of whether to seek treatment is made on subjective and highly personal grounds. These personal grounds may vary systematically among groups of people. For instance, women may find it easier than men to share emotional concerns (Aries, 1974; Carlson, 1971). Thus, they may be more inclined than men to seek psychotherapy, which involves relating one's experiences and feelings to another person. People from the lower social classes may be less likely to believe that psychotherapy can produce changes in behavior and feeling. Hence, they may not make contact with psychiatric institutions except when a disordered behavior can no longer be controlled or tolerated by the community. These and other sources of bias require that only tentative conclusions be drawn from the statistics on treatment use.

National surveys of patients in psychiatric treatment suggest three trends in treatment (Chesler, 1972). First, the number of people using psychiatric facilities is increasing. This increase could be due to increased acceptance of the idea of psychological treatment and greater knowledge of available facilities. The growing rates may also be indicative of increasing stresses in daily living. The second trend in use of treatment facilities is that women have been increasing their use of psychiatric facilities much more rapidly than men. It would be difficult to argue that attitudes and knowledge about psychiatry are changing faster in women than men. Instead, it is more plausible to argue that a rising amount of stress and conflict in women's lives is responsible. The third trend in treatment usage is the decline of hospitalization as the major type of treatment and the rise of outpatient services. This trend reflects a national mandate, the same one that has led to the creation of community mental health centers. Dual goals of cutting costs and sparing patients needless isolation from their families and community are at the heart of this policy.

Patterns of Psychological Disorders

A look at the available statistics on women in psychiatric treatment reveals some striking patterns. Women in certain life-styles and in certain age ranges appear to be more likely to have psychological disorders than other women. In addition, women are more likely to experience certain types of disorders than other types. These patterns provide some clues about what factors contribute to psychological disorder in women.

Married women are more likely to seek psychological help than married men, but single women are better adjusted than single men (Bernard, 1971). In fact, married women form the most heavily represented group in psychiatric treatment. They use both hospitalization and private psychotherapy more than any other group.

The age at which women are at particularly high risk for psychological disorders provides another clue to what experiences might be stressful. Although there are people of all ages in psychiatric treatment, there are especially large numbers of women in their late thirties and forties and of men in their early twenties.

Finally, women appear to be more likely to seek help for some disorders more than for others. The feelings and behaviors prevalent among women in treatment tend to fall into the category of "turning against the self" (Phillips and Rabinovitch, 1958). Women are more likely to experience depression, feelings of inadequacy and inferiority, and excessive guilt. Anorexia, a disorder involving self-starvation, is exclusively a female disorder. Suicide attempts are between six to ten times more common in women's lives than men's. By comparison, the disorders prevalent among men typify "turning against others": antisocial behavior, low control over violent impulses, and breaking social conventions by abusing drugs and alcohol. What causes this difference between men and women? Lacking biological evidence, we must look instead to the social and situational context of men's and women's lives.

Determinants of Psychological Disorders

An understanding of the causes of psychological disorders requires consideration of diverse aspects of human experience, including environmental events, interpersonal relationships, physiological dysfunction, psychological conflicts, role conflict, and personal values. The effects of some elements, notably physiology, are not yet thoroughly studied. The effects of other elements (for example, relationships or role conflict) may never be completely analyzed. They are embedded in a complex of experience and feelings that is unique to each individual, not entirely in conscious awareness, and constantly changing. It is an individual's life history that gives meaning to current events. Because of this individuality, a fully adequate theory of the causes of psychological disorders may never be developed.

Box 1 illustrates a common sequence of events preceding the onset of a psychological disorder. It is a sequence with many stages. The likelihood is very high that a stress will be resolved by the individual before the appearance of an overt disorder. The reason for describing this sequence is to emphasize the interplay between the occurrence of the stressful event, the individual's understanding of it, and the responses that are intended to deal with it. At the first stage of the model, an event occurs. "Event" as used here means practically any experience in a person's life. Many events, of course, are not stressful and do not provide any particular problem for the individual. On the other hand, some events may engender psychological stress, in the form of anxiety, depression, or guilt. Because subjective meanings of events differ so widely from person to person, any event can evoke a wide spectrum of reactions from different people. For example, an abortion may evoke feelings of guilt from some women and feelings of relief from others. There are also differences in how people behave under stress and in how effective these behaviors are. For example, a woman in a marital crisis might suffer in silence, initiate divorce or separation proceedings, threaten domestic violence, or seek counseling with her husband. Whether or not any of these actions resolved the crisis would depend on a complicated set of situational and personal factors. The model in Box 1 suggests that a psychological

Box 1   How Psychological Disorders Develop

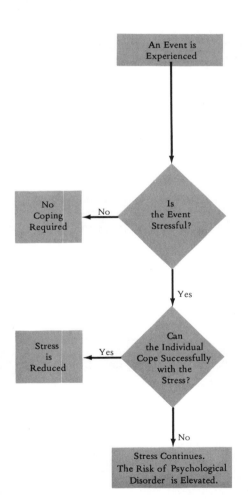

Some Events
Typically Producing Stress:

Physical: chronic fatigue, poor
    nutrition, illness
Relational: death of a loved one,
    marital crisis, birth of a child
Environmental: low social status,
    natural catastrophes
Psychological: loss of identity, role
    conflicts, feelings of powerlessness.

Some factors that Make
an Event Stressful:

The "cultural meaning" of the event
The learned personal significance
    of the event
Lack of anticipation or preparation
    for the event
The amount of stress the individual
    is under due to previous events

Some Factors that Lead
to Successful Coping:

Availability of support from others
Cultural approval of the behaviors
    needed to reduce the stress
The behaviors necessary to cope are
    in the individual's repertoire

disorder results from a combination of actual events and the responses to them.

As can be seen, each stage shown in Box 1 is necessary but not sufficient to produce psychological disorder. For instance, the occurrence of a catastrophic event does not invariably produce a psychological disorder. However, if the event triggers psychological stress *and* the stress cannot be resolved, the individual has a high chance of developing a psychological disorder. Likewise, an individual who lacks the resources to cope with stress or who is prevented from using the resources she does have could minimize the risk of psychological disorder by adopting a minimally stressful life-style. However, the more intense or prolonged situational stress is, the less likely the individual is to be able to manage it. Factors leading to psychological disorders interact with one another.

Many theories of psychological disorder focus on only one aspect of experience and attempt to explain all disorders in terms of this one factor. For instance, adherents of the medical model attempt to explain all disorders as consequences of faulty genes, physiology, or biochemistry. Such explanations leave no room for variations in one's life roles and expectations. Adherents of psychodynamic models (e.g., followers of Freud and other psychoanalytic theorists) place a great deal of emphasis on responses to stress which are learned in early childhood, minimizing the role played by the very real conflicts in the person's adult life. A theorist whose view of the causes of psychological disorder focuses solely on external events or situations runs the risk of ignoring the individual and the personalized strengths and weaknesses that she or he brings to the situation. Theories about the causes of psychological disorder will be more complete and more accurate if they take a broad view of human experience.

STRESS-PRODUCING EVENTS

Stress can occur in nearly any area of human experience. It is likely that all of us will experience many stressful events during our lifetime. Physical events such as illness, injury, aging, or chronic fatigue can be psychologically stressful. Interpersonal factors such as disruptive relationships or the loss of a loved one may produce stress; social roles that are incompatible with an individual's aspirations and abilities may also produce stress. Stress-producing conflicts may be completely intrapsychic (that is, literally, within the individual's mind), as is the case when two sets of values are irreconcilable or two desired goals are mutually exclusive. However, objective realities such as economic hardship, racial or sexual discrimination, and even national political events may also be psychologically stressful. These stress-producing events may be either single crises or protracted situations. Some (for instance, fatigue) can be prevented or controlled by the individual; others (such

as death or natural disasters) cannot be eliminated, controlled, or even predicted.

The types of stress that people encounter are to some extent determined by
their sex, as well as such characteristics as race, socioeconomic status, and
age. For example, black Americans may experience job discrimination and
heightened fears of violence or criminal attack. The poor are at high risk for
disease and poor physical health based on inadequate nutrition and medical
care. The aged must endure the deaths of their close friends and relatives.
The physical and psychological stress of childbirth is an experience limited to
women. Women are also considerably more likely to experience the death of
a spouse than men are. Men bear the increased risk of physical illness such as
cancer, heart disease, and hypertension.

In addition, an individual's sex role strongly determines the subjective
significance of stressful occurrences. Sex-typed interpretations of life events
are particularly likely to occur in areas of experience where the culture holds
rigid prescriptions for appropriate sex-role behavior. For example, in our culture, marriage often has a different meaning to the husband and the wife,
such that wives may be more attuned to and distressed by marital discord. A
turbulent and unhappy marriage may produce considerable anxiety for the
wife, based on her feelings of failure and lowered self-esteem and her realistic
fears about starting an independent life. Her husband, on the other hand,
may regard the marital situation with much less concern since his primary
source of self-esteem and self-definition may be his work rather than his emotional relationship to his wife and family. Responses to biological events—
which are universally experienced—may also be sex-typed. A woman may
react to the passing of her fortieth birthday with depression because she
believes that her beauty and attractiveness are fading. For a man, the psychological significance of being forty years old may focus on concerns about
his sexual prowess or his career advancement. Although a man and a woman
may encounter the same objective situation, one's subjective experience of it
may be very different from the other's.

There are four common components of women's experiences: marital roles,
aging, socioeconomic status, and female physiology. The specific events associated with these components are generally quite common occurrences.
Marriage and childbearing, for example, are normative in this culture.
Aging and menopause are biological givens. The vast majority of women
pass these hurdles without developing a psychological disorder, but a small
percentage do not. Those who do not develop a disorder may not experience
the event in a stressful way or they may have opportunities or resources to
resolve the stress they feel. A good example is the departure of grown children from home. Women suffering clinical depressions often report this leave
taking to be a major source of stress. What about women who don't become
depressed over this occurrence? For some, the leave taking may not signify
the loss of their purpose for living, but rather freedom from responsibility,

more flexibility, pride, and so on. However, a more common pattern probably entails a sense of loss and emptiness when the last child leaves the house, since, for many women, children are their raison d'être. Those women who are able to involve themselves in volunteer work or to return to work or school can reduce their sense of loss and purposelessness and, thus, lower their risk of psychological depression. Thus, although the categories of experience discussed below raise the risk of psychological disorder, the majority of women cope successfully with this risk and avoid actual disorder.

Marital Roles

Surveys of the clientele of psychiatric treatment facilities show that the incidence of psychological disorders is higher among married women than married men, and lower among single women than single men. Why does marriage make women more vulnerable and men more protected? One possible hypothesis is that women who are less able to tolerate stress are more likely to marry. However, this explanation lacks empirical support since the evidence shows that, among women who were once married (but subsequently divorced or widowed), the occurrence of psychological disorders is as low as it is among single women. Thus, the coping abilities of women who marry cannot be responsible for their rates of psychological disorder. We must look instead to the marital situation.

Critiques of marriage abound in feminist literature (e.g., Chesler, 1971; Friedan, 1963; Mainardi, 1971). It is important to make clear from the outset that research literature provides no grounds to condemn all marriages, or marriage per se; rather, specific requirements, expectations, and obligations of women's traditional marital role appear to be sources of psychological stress. This section examines four such aspects of the role of wives: (1) loss of autonomy and independence; (2) lack of differentiation and diversity in roles; (3) stresses of motherhood; and (4) loss of status and function.

Loss of Autonomy

In most marriages, both partners sacrifice some autonomy and independence to achieve harmony and mutuality. However, it is primarily the wife whose sacrifice entails her psychological autonomy and her selfhood. Longitudinal studies of marriage generally show that wives make more concessions and modifications of their values and personal qualities than do their husbands (Barry, 1970). Both husbands and wives agree that wives make the greater adjustment in marriage. Indeed, the cultural norm has been that, upon marriage, the husband maintains his daily living routine with little if any modification (Burgess and Wallin, 1953). Unfortunately, this situation is not a psychologically healthy one. Although superficial inquiries may show that husband and wife usually view their marriage as equally happy, more pointed

questioning often reveals dissatisfaction, frustration, bitterness, or even des-
peration on the part of the wife (Bernard, 1971a; Friedan, 1963). In many
marriages, the wife's task encompasses adjustment to her husband's personality and values, and adaptation to the life-style demanded by her husband's
occupational, educational, and socioeconomic status. The toll of this sacrifice
of individuality and self-determination seems high. There are some indications that nonworking wives run the highest risk of psychological disorder:
they may enter therapy most frequently (Bart, 1971); they are most likely to
use prescribed tranquilizers or stimulants (New York Narcotic Addiction
Control Commission, 1971); and they have an elevated rate of suicide
(Shneidman and Farberow, 1965). Wives who work maintain more autonomy and self-determination vis-à-vis their husbands and this may protect
them from psychological stress (see Chapter 9).

Role Differentiation

Nonworking married women generally have fewer major roles than their husbands. At the most simplistic level, husbands play two roles, one that
centers around their occupation and another that centers around their family
life. Until recently, the culture has prescribed that married women hold only
a family role. The psychological significance of the number of separate roles a
person plays derives from the power of roles as sources of identity and self-
esteem (Gergen and Marecek, 1976). Women who perceive their lives to be
lived within a single role may suffer paralyzing blows to their self-esteem
whenever they experience a failure or a disappointment in this role. On the
other hand, if an individual perceives life to be comprised of multiple roles,
shortcomings can be compensated for by the successful aspects of other roles.
Playing multiple roles allows one's psychological outlook to be more balanced and stable.

One of the major roles of traditional married women is the role of mother.
Having children is a major source of satisfaction for many women, as well as
the focus of a number of problems. Some of these problems may arise from
the fact that the primary responsibility for the welfare of her children is
placed on the mother. Many women feel ill equipped to raise children, since
they have little prior skill or education in child-rearing and often do not
know what to do with their children in a variety of circumstances. Also, to
the extent that popular psychology emphasizes the effects of early childhood
experiences on the later adult personality, the mother may hold herself
responsible for her children's intelligence, career, and marital success.

There is one more consideration about women's marital role that is relevant here. The role of housewife is *ascribed* to a woman when she marries
rather than *achieved* by her. Occupational roles of both men and women, on
the other hand, are achieved roles. People in ascribed roles are expected to
perform them competently. Because of this expectation, competence or suc-

cess is not well rewarded and failures are dealt with harshly. In the case of achieved roles, there are lower expectations about role performance. Thus success is heavily rewarded, while punishment for failures may be moderate or light. Married men in our culture generally have both an achieved role (in their job) and an ascribed role (in their family). This duality may protect them from anxiety about failing in their family role and from others' criticisms if in fact they do fail as fathers or husbands. The same reasoning may apply to women who hold both a work role and a family role: success in their work may reduce their anxiety over their competence as homemakers, mothers, and wives. Women who have only an ascribed role, on the other hand, may be more anxious about failure in that role because they have no other responsibilities that would excuse a poor performance.

Motherhood

Bringing up children is a third source of strain on married women. It is not that children *per se* are usually sources of anxiety or discomfort. Rather, it is the cultural values and beliefs about raising children that are the source of strain. Bringing up children is a job for which most women are not trained. Furthermore, much advice on raising children is either contradictory or too general to be put into practice. Despite this vagueness, popular opinion places a heavy burden of responsibility for the child's development on the mother and many women fell compelled to curtail their self-expression, career development, and self-actualization "until the children are grown." The years when a woman's children are very young probably encompass the most psychologically stressful aspects of motherhood. Young mothers describe the birth of their first child as a time of radical personal change, in which they must shift from satisfying their own needs to satisfying those of the newborn. Many mention "overwork," being "tied down" to the infant, and constant physical demands and fatigue. For the woman with preschool children, the problems of isolation from adult company and lack of mobility are reported as sources of stress (Lopata, 1971).

Despite the negative aspects of raising young children, most women find deep satisfaction and pleasure in motherhood. Although there are stresses, few mothers seek help from the mental health profession. Furthermore, recent changes in women's roles provide mechanisms which can reduce some of the strains of motherhood. For example, some women maintain their occupational role throughout the period when they are raising children. Also day care and nursery schools are more available for those women who can afford them and who want to spend some time away from their children. There are more labor-saving devices used in the home, which reduce the amount of time spent on the additional housework which comes with children. Finally, husbands are being more encouraged to share in child-rearing activities, thus freeing some of the mother's time and reducing her isolation.

Loss of Status

Another strain on married women comes from reductions in the requirements and status associated with the traditional mother and housewife roles.
The responsibilities, satisfactions, and status of the traditional feminine marital role have been gradually diminishing over the past twenty-five years
(Gore and Tudor, 1973). First, the time spent in child-rearing is shorter,
due to increased community support services, changing social patterns, and
couples' decisions to have fewer children (see Chapter 8). Organizations,
school activities, and youth centers keep older children away from home.
Furthermore, the number of years when there are children living in the home
has diminished as family size has decreased. Along with this decline in the
work allocated to the housewife role has come a decline in its perceived importance and prestige, as documented by a survey of urban and suburban
middle-class housewives (Lopata, 1971). This devaluation of the traditional
feminine role may result in lowered self-esteem, feelings of worthlessness,
and bitterness among women in this role. More positively, many women
react to their loss of status by choosing to return to work or school. In addition, changes in the economy such as inflation, high unemployment, and
economic depression may revive enthusiasm and respect for the homemaker
role. Such functions as budgeting, bargain-hunting, sewing, and gardening
stretch family finances and expand the importance of the housewife's role. If
low status and diminished responsibilities cause psychological stress in nonemployed housewives, then an economic crisis may *reduce* their risk of psychological disorder.

Marital Roles and Social Class

In an effort to present a clear picture of various role strains in marriage, the
discussion thus far is oversimplified in a major respect. It has largely ignored
the differences in experience, attitudes, and values that membership in different socioeconomic classes may produce. In particular, wives with different
class backgrounds have somewhat different conceptions of their marital roles.
Working-class women are likely to emphasize those aspects of their marital
roles that entail concrete responsibilities and obligations. They are more
likely to evaluate their lives in terms of the jobs they perform (e.g., taking
care of the house, raising the children) rather than their emotional satisfaction or their degree of self-actualization in the marriage. Conversely, middle-
and upper-class women are more likely to require that their marital roles are
emotionally fulfilling and intellectually satisfying. (Lopata, 1971).

Differences in attitudes and values lead to differences in reactions to
various stressful events. There is no direct evidence concerning women's class
background and the role strains leading to psychological disorder. However,
for working-class wives, the risk of psychological disorder may be elevated if

they believe they have failed in their responsibilities to their husbands or children. Middle- and upper-class wives, on the other hand, may be at higher risk for disorder when they feel thwarted in their personal ambitions or emotionally unsatisfied by their relationships to their husbands and children. Values and ideology determine which events or circumstances are sources of stress for various women.

Aging and Psychological Disorders

Statistics on psychological disorders consistently show that women over forty have a higher incidence of disorder than men of the same age or younger women. Among the many possible reasons for this disparity, two seem most crucial: loss of self-esteem due to the physical effects of aging, and role loss associated with children's departure from the home.

Physical Beauty and Self-esteem. Contemporary American culture values feminine youth and physical beauty very highly. Attractive young women advertise nearly every commodity imaginable, from cars and computers to vacation trips, food, and medicine. Women are trained to regard beauty as a vital personal quality and the means to achieving personal goals. The dual message that beauty is a woman's most important asset and that only youthful women are beautiful can be devastating to older women. The more a woman's physical appearance is perceived as the major source of her identity and self-worth, the more stressful will aging be to her.

Just as increased diversity and differentation among women's marital roles can promote psychological well-being, so the greater a woman's realization that her physical appearance is merely one of the multiple aspects of her self, the more comfortable she will be with growing old. As discussed in Chapter 9, most women do respond well to aging and are able to accept themselves and their bodies as they age. In addition, experiences such as consciousness-raising groups often enable women to understand the origins and consequences of the youth-and-beauty cult, and, thus, to reject its values.

The "Empty Nest." One of the most stressful events that older women face is, paradoxically, also one of the most common. This is the departure of grown children from the home, an event encountered by nearly all women who bear children. A survey of women patients showed that the incidence of depression (versus other diagnoses) was highest among women whose lives were most child-centered. These women viewed child-rearing as the single focus of their lives. When their children grew up, they lost their major role and, therefore, their lives lost much of their meaning (Bart, 1971). Box 2 describes this situation for one typical child-oriented woman.

Depression due to loss of the parent role is not a universal occurrence. It rarely occurs in men; it is not universal in women across cultures. In our own culture, it is linked to sex, race, social class, and occupational status; white,

Box 2   The "Empty Nest" and Depression: A Case Report

Mrs. S. is a forty-three-year-old housewife who was admitted to a mental hospital after she took an overdose of tranquilizers. She has a daughter who married and moved out of state two years ago, and a son who just entered college. Mrs. S. explains her current situation in the following way:

> When Jimmy [her son] moved away, there wasn't anything to do with myself. I didn't have enough to keep me busy at home and I don't care enough about shopping and playing cards to do that all the time. It's a very lonely day and most of the time, I feel like no one cares whether I'm alive or dead.

Mrs. S. attended an elite women's college. She dropped out before she completed her studies, got married, and supported her husband through law school. When her husband completed law school, she stopped working and bore two children in rapid succession. She spent the next twenty-odd years completely involved in her role of mother:

> When the kids were home, there was always something to do. I was a den mother, scout leader, PTA President, and football fan. I sewed all my daughter's clothes, even her prom dress. My son could bring his friends home any hour of the day or night and there'd be homemade cookies for them. In those days, there was a place for me. My children needed me and I felt useful. My family appreciated me—they couldn't have gotten along without me.

What does Mrs. S. see as her future goals? She appears to be at a loss about her future.

> Well, my therapist says I have to start learning to think about myself—to put my own needs first. He says I should start thinking about my strengths. Well, frankly, I'm not sure I have any. My husband says I should get a job, just to take my mind off things. I guess he's right, but I just don't see the use of it.

Mrs. S. clearly has a lot of unlearning to do before she can put her own needs first or overcome her depression and sense of loss. Her sense of self-worth is at low ebb. Her relationships with her children were so central to the meaning of her life that she cannot accommodate to their departure. Although she may be angry at her children or her husband for their lack of attention, she does not feel that she can express her anger, or demand changes in their behavior. Her therapy will probably be long and difficult, as Mrs. S. has many long-standing patterns of feeling and behavior that need to be worked through and altered to fit her new role.

---

middle-class, nonemployed housewives are the most vulnerable group. These women focus their energies primarily on their children, to the exclusion of their personal satisfaction or their relationships with their husbands. When the maternal role has been a woman's source of identity and self-worth for twenty or more years, its loss can precipitate severe psychological stress. Unless alternative sources of identity, self-esteem, and emotional gratification can be substituted, a psychological crisis is likely to occur.

The advantages of role diversity and role differentiation seem quite apparent in the case of maternal role loss. Women who hold diverse roles—both inside and outside the home—probably have the easiest readjustment period when their children leave home. They may expand their occupational, educational, or recreational activities or devote more time to relationships and social activities. It is the woman who sees her entire married life as a child-raising enterprise who is at highest risk for disorder when her children leave home. The increasing flexibility in the definition of women's roles and the influx of married women into the work force each lower the risk of psychological disorder following maternal role loss.

Social Status and Psychological Stress

Throughout history, women have had fewer legal rights and lower social status than men. This inequity has led to a number of negative consequences for women: economic hardship; loss of self-esteem; feelings of powerlessness; lowered control over external events, etc. It is not difficult to see that social and economic discrimination can make women's lives more difficult. But what evidence is there that discrimination and lower status raises women's risk of psychological disorder?

A study of the relationship between the incidence of stressful life events and the role of psychological symptoms among men and women provides some answers to the question above (Dohrenwend, 1973). Respondents from various ethnic and class backgrounds were interviewed about recent life stresses they had undergone and about any psychological symptoms they were experiencing. Life stresses were defined as events that were associated with major life changes or disruption of usual activities, including: change in marital status, change in occupation, change in place of residence, illness, birth of a child, death of a loved one, etc. Psychological symptoms included two kinds of items: psychosomatic symptoms (e.g., headaches, digestive disturbances, trembling hands) and mood symptoms (feelings of depression, worrying, etc.). The results showed that the women in the sample reported significantly more life stress during the year preceding the interview than did the men. Life stresses have previously been shown to produce psychological symptoms (Dohrenwend, 1973; Ricks, Thomas and Roff, 1974); in the present study also, life-stress and symptom level were positively related to one another. Further analyses suggested that, for women, psychological symptoms were most strongly associated with events that they could not control. For men, however, the issue of control did not seem to be an important determinant of psychological distress.

Therefore, several important points can be made. First, like other low-status groups, women face more stressful life events than their high-status counterparts. Second, these stressful life events produce symptoms of psychological distress; thus, women have more symptoms than men. However, when the contribution played by life events is held constant, both sexes have comparable rates of psychological symptoms. The third point is that women are not "weaker," less able to cope, or more reactive to external stresses than men.

Two reservations about these data need to be mentioned. First, all the respondents in the study were heads of households; this is a somewhat unusual role for women and the high incidence of stressful life events may be contingent on that role. Also, the study indexes fairly mild and transient symptoms in people who have not sought psychiatric treatments, rather than acute symptoms requiring attention. However, despite these drawbacks, this study points up the importance of women's lower social status as a factor leading to their greater experience of psychological disorder.

Physiology and Psychological Disorders

Women's biochemistry is different from that of men. Women's unique capacity to bear children is accompanied by a complex hormone cycle. Hormonal changes during a woman's monthly cycle affect several physiological systems, including the brain. The effects of these fluctuating hormone levels on mood states and on behavior is still poorly understood, although their effects may have been overemphasized (see Chapter 10).

The most common psychological effects of the menstrual cycle occur immediately preceding the menstrual period and include depression, restlessness, and tension. Many women report such mood alterations, but most find them to be of little consequence. However, clinical case reports on the effects of the menstrual cycle paint a much more serious picture. Typically, these reports studied the menstrual histories of women in crises such as suicide attempts, accidents, or psychiatric emergencies (Dalton, 1959; Glass, et al., 1971). The timing of these psychological crises was closely correlated with the premenstrual or menstrual phases of the patients' cycle.

How can the statement that most women find menstrual symptoms quite trivial be reconciled with these reports? The two sets of data are not necessarily mutually incompatible. Instead, they are representative of two different groups: the general population of women in the first instance, and women with psychological disorders in the other. The data suggest that women who are already more likely to experience psychological disorder will be even more likely to experience this disorder during their premenstrual phase. When the stress of hormonal changes is added to already existing stress, tolerance limits are exceeded and an overt disorder develops. Thus, hormone fluctuations do not *cause* psychological disorders, but only influence their *timing*.

Pregnancy and childbirth also bear some relationship to psychological disorder. There is some suggestion that women's risk of psychosis is lower during pregnancy than at other times (Silverman, 1968). However, the period following childbirth is marked by an elevated risk of psychological disorder. Childbirth is accompanied by abrupt and extreme changes in the levels of estrogen and progesterone. Some have suggested that these abrupt changes may trigger brief psychotic depressions (known as postpartum psychoses) which typically occur very soon after delivery and are short in duration. In addition, women are more likely to experience neurotic disorders in the year or so after they have given birth; this higher risk is probably due to the many (often unanticipated) changes in life-style and social relationships that motherhood produces. Neither psychoses nor neuroses need be interpreted as an unconscious "rejection of the child" or "rejection of femininity," explanations that are quite common in the psychoanalytic literature. A woman's feelings toward her child and her identity as a woman may be genuinely positive and accepting, even though she suffers postpartum depression. The causes of her disorder may be temporary biochemical upset, fatigue, or anxiety resulting from her feelings of inadequacy as a mother.

Another time at which women are more likely to experience psychological disorder is during menopause. So much has been written about menopausal depression that it may seem as if every menopausal woman becomes depressed. This is simply untrue. Although menopausal depression can be caused by decreases in estrogen, not every woman reacts to this hormone decrease by becoming depressed. Psychological factors discussed earlier which center around the empty-nest experience may also provide a source of depression during these years. For those women who do become depressed as a result of hormonal decreases, estrogen replacement therapy is usually successful in relieving these symptoms. It cannot, however, relieve psychologically based symptoms.

RESPONSES TO PSYCHOLOGICAL STRESS

Thus far, the discussion has focused primarily on sources of stress in women's lives. But many of the circumstances that were described are extremely common and relatively few women develop psychological disorders: What determines whether stresses will lead to successful coping or to psychological disorder? Consider the following contrast: The psychological disorders prevalent among women encompass passivity, guilt, low self-esteem, and feelings of inadequacy or helplessness; on the other hand, impulsivity, aggression, and disregard for social conventions typify the disorders prevalent among men. It could be said that women and men with psychological disorders exhibit behaviors which are exaggerations of the stereotypes of femininity and masculinity. What do these stereotypes suggest about the characteristics of people or situations which are most conducive to psychological disorder?

The first line of reasoning is one that was adopted by many of the clinical personality theorists described in Chapter 3. They hold that patterns of behavior evidenced by women and men in treatment reflect exaggerations of "normal" or universal personality traits. Thus, masochism, anxiety, passivity, and guilt, all figured predominantly in psychoanalytic and neo-Freudian views of women. However, the supposition that behaviors or traits prevalent among disordered women will also be prevalent among women in general is not true. Much of the research described in Chapter 4 failed to demonstrate that women's personalities were different from men's. Specifically, sex differences in dependence-independence, passivity-activity, nurturance, and self-esteem failed to clearly emerge when groups of normal children and adults were tested. Therefore, it seems likely that sex-role extremes are associated with psychological disorder and not reflective of the general population.

A second explanation of the sex-stereotyped pattern of psychological disorders suggests that differences in the stressful situations faced by each sex lead to the disparity in men's and women's responses. For instance, women are members of a low-status group. In addition, women often have less power than men in interpersonal relationships, in political life, and in occupational roles. Some psychological effects of low status and low power are lowered self-esteem or feelings of worthlessness, feelings of powerlessness, submissiveness, and suppression of anger. Comparing these behaviors to the symptoms of depression (a disorder which is twice as common among women as men), we find a remarkable similarity. Depression entails low self-esteem, sadness, feelings of helplessness, dependency, and loss of initiative and energy. Helplessness, of course, is very much like powerlessness. Those who feel helpless or incapable may rely on others and stop trying to accomplish things independently. This would suggest that either sex might react to powerlessness and low status by developing the symptoms of depression. However, situations of powerlessness and low status occur much more frequently among women than men and therefore depression is found more in women.

A third line of reasoning holds that the difference between people who cope successfully with stressful situations and those who develop psychological disorders lies in their capacity for dealing with stress. People who use ineffective or limited ways of dealing with stress will be more likely to develop psychological disorders than others.

One common limitation of possible behavior is based on sex-role stereotypes. We might hypothesize that people whose behavior conforms to rigid sex-role expectations will be less capable of coping with a broad range of stressful situations. This hypothesis would explain why women and men with psychological disorders tend to conform more to sex-role stereotypes than the population at large. Their conformity to stereotypes places them at higher risk for psychological disorder. For example, people who hold extremely masculine or feminine self-perceptions performed poorly in situations which required more flexibility in behavior (Bem, 1975). Also, people with very masculine self-concepts lacked spontaneity and nurturance in playing with a kitten; and those who were extremely feminine were more likely to conform to others' opinions in a task requiring independent judgments. Although there is no direct evidence as yet concerning people whose behavior in stressful situations conforms rigidly to sex stereotypes, such individuals may be severely handicapped by their rigidity.

Three possible models to account for differences in responses to situational stress have been proposed. The first model, which views different responses as a consequence of universal personality differences, can be rejected on the basis of empirical evidence. The other two models focus on the nature of the situational stresses occurring in men's and women's lives and the possible vulnerability to stress caused by rigidity in sex-role expectations. Although both these models are plausible explanations of the variability in responses to psychological stress and the sex-typed patterns of psychological disorders, neither model has been adequately researched as yet. The task remains for future researchers.

WOMEN AND PSYCHOTHERAPY

Most types of psychotherapy rely upon a fairly long-term relationship between the therapist and the client, during which the client's actions, feelings, and attitudes are discussed and interpreted according to the training and biases of the therapist. Generally this involves the client talking about her problems under the guidance of the therapist. The trust of the client for the therapist is considered to be highly important. Often there is a focus on early childhood determinants of current psychological difficulties and a good deal of time is devoted to talking about early memories. Releasing previously unconscious thoughts or feelings is a major goal.

There are a number of reasons to question how well this traditional therapy deals with the problems of women. First, surveys of private practitioners and outpatient clinics usually find that the majority of psychotherapy clients are women. The numbers of women receiving this type of treatment makes it more important that its effects are growth-producing for women clients. Second, as described in Chapter 3, the traditional personality theories espoused by clinicians are neither accurate nor flattering in their portrayal of women. To the extent that psychotherapists work out of their theoretical backgrounds, they may be prejudicial toward their female clients. Finally, there is reason to be concerned that psychotherapy may distract women from the true sources of their problems, and thus prolong their discomfort and unhappiness. If our analysis of women's psychological disorders is correct, then therapy which looks for sources of disorder in the client's early childhood or in her unconscious fantasies will not be successful. At its worst, such therapy may generate feelings of self-blame and low self-worth which intensify the original problem. At best, it may be an interesting, but expensive waste of time. In the discussion of psychotherapy that follows, some empirically demonstrated biases in therapists' beliefs and behavior toward women are described. Subsequent to that discussion, the Feminist Therapy Movement, with its unique goals and values concerning women will be considered.

Psychotherapy ideally attempts to replace maladaptive patterns of behavior, thought, and feeling with ones that are more positive, more socially acceptable, and more growth-enhancing. The choice of specific goals of therapeutic change for individual patients is strongly influenced by the therapist. Therefore, the question of therapists' sex biases is an important one. Several studies of therapists have demonstrated that, as a group, their image of women conforms to traditional stereotypes and is somewhat negative. An early study in this area gave clinicians a list of adjectives and asked them to indicate which adjectives characterized a "healthy adult male" and a "healthy adult female." Their answers were highly differentiated, with the male being described as more logical, more independent, and less emotional than the female. Those adjectives personifying a "healthy male" were also used to describe a "healthy adult," while those used to describe a "healthy female" were also used to describe a "mentally ill individual." Male and female clinicians concurred on their ratings: both saw the two sexes as highly differentiated and viewed women in a negative way (Broverman, et al., 1970). Several other studies have been done following similar formats and each has come to similar conclusions: by and large, therapists (like the general public) hold negative stereotypes about women (Broverman et al., 1972; Nowacki and Poe, 1973; Fabrikant, Landau, and Rollenhagen, 1973).

How do these negative sex-role stereotypes operate in actual therapist-client relationships? Here the evidence is very sparse. Psychotherapy is a difficult subject for study because it is highly unstructured, it is private, and it takes place over a long (and indeterminate) span of time. In addition, therapists' goals and values tend to be implicit rather than explicit, and may be conveyed to the client by nonverbal cues or by implication or nuance. In view of the difficulties of studying the therapy process, some investigators have chosen instead to study psychological testing situations.

Psychological tests are often given prior to therapy and are used to formulate diagnoses and assess the clients' particular strengths and weaknesses. The evidence for sex biases in the administration, scoring, or interpretation of these tests is well established (Harris, 1974). However, the bias is not systematic and sometimes depends on the sex of the tester, the age or education of the client, and the nature of the client's responses. Nonetheless, evidence that therapists may shift their evaluations of clients' behavior or personality according to the clients' sex should alert us to possible sex biases in the therapeutic interactions as well.

There are many other facets of psychotherapy relationships in which sex bias is likely to occur. Therapists' acceptance of clients' anger, their criteria and timetable for improvement, and their willingness to establish an egalitarian relationship with their clients may be affected by their sex-role beliefs and the sex of the client. The area of sex bias in psychotherapy is one in which more research and thought is clearly needed. The limited evidence to date also suggests that individuals—both therapists and clients—need to monitor therapy sessions conscientiously in an effort to identify and modify sex-biased transactions.

The need for raised consciousness concerning sex bias on the part of therapists has triggered the Feminist Therapy Movement. Feminist therapists are practitioners (usually women) who evidence their special concern about sexism by careful scrutiny of their own attitudes and behavior toward women clients, by research or political action aimed at raising consciousness about sexism in the mental health professions, or by educational efforts aimed at improving women's awareness of the detrimental effects of sex bias in their lives. Feminist therapists hold many different therapeutic philosophies, but they share an explicit nonsexist value system and a commitment to explore the impact of rigid sex roles and sex-biased social institutions on clients' lives. Another thrust of many feminist therapists concerns maximizing the power allocated to women clients in therapy in order to increase women's feelings of self-determination. One form this takes is the encouragement of leaderless consciousness-raising groups and other kinds of groups designed to deemphasize the power of the therapist. Other feminist therapists have focused on ways of providing low-cost therapy so that poor women in need of therapy may have access to help. The Feminist Therapy Movement is a young and growing one, but it has already captured attention in the psychotherapy establishment. In the long run, the movement may not only offer women alternatives to traditional therapy but also improve the quality of all therapy.

Part IV

Women and Power

14 Prejudice and Discrimination

MR. X: Women shouldn't be promoted into the managerial ranks of M.C. Industries because they can't be trusted to stay with the company—if they're not married, they'll quit when they get married; if they are married, they'll get pregnant and leave.

MR. Y: But data from the personnel office indicate that women are actually slightly *less* likely to leave M.C. than men who hold equivalent jobs.

MR. X: That's why we can't hire women in the higher ranks—they never leave, and it's hard to get rid of them, even when they do poor work.

MR. Y: But our efficiency manager found that women are somewhat more productive than men, and make less errors in their work.

MR. X: That's the problem with women—they're uncreative, plodding workers.

This hypothetical conversation between Mr. X and Mr. Y points out the most important features of prejudice. What is compelling about this "discussion" is the tenacity of Mr. X's prejudice. He is obviously willing to engage in some pretty slippery thinking to maintain it. Facts and figures in no way affect his view of women workers   (*Allport, 1954*).

Gail Zellman was the primary author of this chapter.

PREJUDICE

Prejudice has been defined as ". . . an antipathy based upon a faulty and inflexible generalization. It may be felt or expressed. It may be directed toward a group as a whole, or toward an individual because he is a member of that group. . . . The net effect of prejudice, thus defined, is to place the object of prejudice at some disadvantage not merited by his own misconduct" (Allport, 1954). There are three basic elements in this definition that bear further discussion. The definition states that prejudice involves negative feelings; that the judgment or judgments upon which the prejudice is based are erroneous, that is, that these judgments are formed prematurely on the basis of incorrect or incomplete information; and that prejudiced views are inflexible and not readily changed, even in the face of new and contradictory information.

A basic mechanism underlying prejudice is categorization, which involves grouping people into classes. Categorization is necessary in order for people to handle the complexity of the environment, but it may have negative aspects. When continuous characteristics such as intelligence are separated into nonoverlapping categories, there is a tendency to exaggerate differences between groups on the characteristic in question, and minimize differences within groups (Tajfel, 1969). In the case of intelligence, categorization might result in viewing all members of one group as very bright, and all members of another group as slow. The process of categorization results in stereotypes, which are traits or characteristics attributed to large human groups (Tajfel, 1969). Stereotypes are not causes of prejudice, but are images invoked by the prejudiced individual to justify the prejudice he already has. The same traits that we consider to be virtues in members of liked groups are often seen as vices when observed in members of disliked groups. For example, people admire Abraham Lincoln because he was thrifty, hard-working, eager to learn, ambitious, and successful. But thrifty Jews are stingy, miserly, and uncharitable. Hard-working Japanese have a sweatshop mentality. Chinese who are eager to learn are cunning and crafty. Ambitious blacks are ruthless (Merton, 1957).

It is similar with women: an ambitious and assertive man is admired by all. The same traits in a woman are viewed less positively: she is aggressive rather than assertive, and castrating rather than ambitious.

Through selective perception, stereotypes become more widely and deeply accepted. Women have long been accused of much lower job stability than men ("They're always quitting to get married or have babies"). The facts indicate that women are only slightly more likely to quit than males (Bergmann and Adelman, 1973), and this higher quit rate is largely accounted for by the different kinds of jobs men and women hold. Skill level of the job, age of the worker, and tenure on the job are all better predictors of stability than sex (Women's Bureau, 1969a; Stevenson, 1973). Since women tend to fall disproportionately into low-status jobs, their high turnover is understandable without considering sex. In spite of these facts, stereotypes remain, and a woman who leaves to get married or have a family is more likely to be remembered than a man who leaves to take another job. Often in the process of categorizing, noticeably different and sometimes contradictory traits are assigned to members of a category. This is very clear in the case of women. Can one group really be conniving and feather-brained at the same time? Or frigid and sexually insatiable? Contradictory trait descriptions provide ammunition against facts, and allow prejudice to be maintained in the face of compelling evidence.

Stereotypes are also maintained by admitting only supportive evidence. A woman who is a poor administrator is likely to be long remembered by someone whose "male-female" category includes the stereotype that men have managerial skills while women have none. Evidence of a woman who is a competent manager is either ignored entirely or withers under "yes-but" assaults.

A good example of the "yes-but" approach to contradictory information occurred when women in the Washington, D.C., police department were sent out on patrol with male partners. A follow-up evaluation of the program revealed that many of the men who had had women partners were satisfied with their own partner's performance, but were no less likely than other officers to feel that "it would be a mistake to hire large numbers of women" (Milton, 1972). What they were saying was, *Yes,* my partner's ok *but* she's an exception (for a variety of reasons). Other women still have all the negative attributes of my 'women as police officers' category."

In summary, prejudice is a negative attitude toward a group of people. This attitude is not based on facts, but is highly resistant to contradictory evidence.

Is There Prejudice against Women?

One way to determine if people are prejudiced against women is to insure equal performance of males and females experimentally, and then measure the evaluations subjects make of males and females. In situations where no actual differences in performance exist, any differences in evaluation are evidence of prejudice.

Are women prejudiced against women? In one study a number of papers were selected from the professional literature in six academic disciplines: two from areas rated "feminine"—elementary school teaching and dietetics; two from sex-neutral areas—linguistics and art history; and two from "masculine" fields—law and city planning. The articles were edited and abridged to be of approximately equal length and were combined into booklets. The crucial manipulation concerned the sex of the author. Each article was written by a person identifiable as a "male" for half the subjects, and a "female" for the other half. Thus each of the 140 female subjects received a set of six articles, three written by "males" and three by "females." Subjects were asked to read the articles and rate the authors in terms of writing style, professional competence, professional status, and personality. Articles were also rated for value, persuasiveness, and profundity.

Papers supposedly written by males were rated more favorably than "female" papers, not only in masculine fields but across the board. Since the articles differed only in terms of author's sex, the evaluation of "male"-authored articles as superior was clearly a distortion based on prejudice. The female subjects were obviously sensitive at some level to the author's sex and judged "women" authors more harshly (Goldberg, 1968). Such bias on the basis of an author's sex alone has been labeled the Goldberg paradigm.

Several years after Goldberg's study,[1] this type of prejudice seems to have diminished. Identical papers attributed to male and female authors have been rated equally in more recent studies. It is possible, however, that this apparent nondiscrimination was due to subjects' feelings that prejudice against women was now inappropriate, rather than being based on a real lack of prejudice (Baruch, 1972; Leon, 1974).

The interpretation that prejudice against women still exists does have support. In a recent study, subjects received descriptions of five high-status professions—architect, college professor, lawyer, physician, and scientist. Each profession was described on an information sheet. Half the subjects were told that the percentage of women in the profession would remain stable and low over the next twenty-five to thirty years. The other half were told that the percentage of women in the profession would sharply increase over the same time period. Subject ratings of the professions revealed a consistent tendency for each profession to be rated lower in prestige when subjects expected an increasing proportion of women practitioners (Touhey, 1974).

Cross-cultural data clearly validate these findings. While tasks described as "women's work" vary tremendously from culture to culture, the value placed on women's work is almost universally lower than the value placed on the work men do (Rosaldo, 1974).

It is not only the *work* of women that is devalued, but women themselves. A consistent finding is that when respondents are asked if they ever wished they had been born a member of the opposite sex, virtually no males reply "yes" (generally, less than 3 percent) while 25–30 percent of female respondents answer in the affirmative (Erskine, 1971). This finding is maintained across cultures. Puerto Rican respondents were asked what sex they would choose to be if they came to life after death. Sixty-seven percent of the women would choose to be male, whereas only 7 percent of the men said they would like to be female (Sanchez-Hidalgo, 1952).

---

[1] See also Pheterson, et al., 1971; Deaux and Taynor, 1973; and Kiesler, 1973.

In America, male children are clearly preferred over female children. Women who had only daughters were happier about a new pregnancy than mothers who had only sons (Sears, Maccoby, and Levin, 1957). When the first child was a boy, the interval before a second child was conceived was longer than when the first child was a girl (Westoff, et al., 1961). These results could not be explained by the fact that male babies are generally more difficult to raise. The birth of a female child was found to be associated with a higher incidence of postpartum depression (Gordon, Gordon, and Gunther, 1961). Recent data indicate that people of all groups still prefer boys, especially as a first child (Markle, 1974).

Experimental evidence also demonstrates that men and women devalue women. In one study, subjects used adjective checklists to describe their real and ideal selves, an ideal member of the opposite sex, and an ideal member of their own sex as perceived by the opposite sex. Based on this data, it was revealed that (1) women's real selves were less favorable than men's; (2) women's real selves conformed more closely to "female" adjectives than men's real selves did to the "male" cluster; and (3) women's perceptions of men's views of the ideal woman were much more sex typed than men's perceptions of women's views of the ideal man. These data suggest that men feel better about themselves than women do, and feel freer to deviate from prescribed sex-role categories (McKee and Sheriffs, 1957; 1959).

These findings of negative views of women shared by women and men are not surprising, given that the studies were conducted in the fifties, a time when women were not viewed as participants in the world outside the home (Friedan, 1963). However, a number of studies that use a methodology very similar to that of the earlier studies report similar findings (Broverman, et al., 1972; Rosenkrantz, et al., 1968).

Briefly, in these later studies, college-student subjects were asked to list all personality characteristics which they considered to differentiate men and women. Any item listed more than once was included on the list. They took the resulting list and made 122 scales, one for each adjective. For example, aggressiveness became a scale that looked like this:

Not at All Aggressive						Very Aggressive
1	2	3	4	5	6	7

All subjects were told to "imagine you are going to meet a person for the first time and the only thing you know in advance is that the person is an adult male" (Rosenkrantz, et al., 1968). Subjects were told to mark on the scales the extent to which they expected each item to characterize this adult male. After completing the questionnaire, subjects were asked to go back through it two more times, first to describe an adult female, then themselves. (To control for order effects, half the subjects were given the male/female order, the other half the female/male. All subjects rated themselves last.)

These studies find that men and women agree about what typical men and women are like.[2] The college samples had little problem assigning differing characteristics to men and women. Additionally, stereotypically masculine characteristics were rated (by different subjects) as socially desirable significantly more often than stereotypically feminine characteristics. The greater valuation placed on masculinity was found to be due to a considerably larger number of male than female traits being positively valued (see Box 1).

Box 1   **Positive Stereotypic Traits**

Positive Traits Associated with Men

Aggressive	Feelings not easily hurt
Independent	Adventurous
Unemotional	Makes decisions easily
Hides emotions	Never cries
Objective	Acts as a leader
Easily influenced	Self-confident
Dominant	Not uncomfortable about being aggressive
Likes math and science	Ambitious
Not excitable in a minor crisis	Able to separate feelings from ideas
Active	Not dependent
Competitive	Not conceited about appearance
Logical	Thinks men are superior to women
Wordly	Talks freely about sex with men
Skilled in business	
Direct	
Knows the way of the world	

Positive Traits Associated with Women

Does not use harsh language	Interested in own appearance
Talkative	Neat in habits
Tactful	Quiet
Gentle	Strong need for security
Aware of feelings of others	Appreciates art and literature
Religious	Expresses tender feelings

SOURCE: Rosenkrantz et. al., 1968. Traits listed in this table were rated by at least 75% of subjects as more typical of males or females, respectively, and were rated as socially desirable by independent raters.

[2] Rating-scale methodologies tend to produce more stereotypic thinking than free-response data (Frieze, 1974).

Finally, the results indicated that both males and females tended to rate themselves in a way that conformed to the stereotypes. That is, males placed themselves closer to the male pole, and females to the female pole, though neither group rated itself as extremely as it had rated the typical male and female.

The reasons for this self-stereotyping seem clear. Self-ratings were done after the ratings of the typical male and female. Subjects may have been biased by these earlier ratings. It is likely that self-ratings would conform more closely to typical ratings of one's own sex under these conditions. For this reason, it would have been preferable methodologically for each subject to have made only *one* set of ratings.

The lower level of self- as opposed to stranger-stereotyping was predictable from the theory of stereotyping which indicates that stereotyping is a way of handling new situations or people about which little is known. In strange situations, people draw most heavily on prior experience. Thus, when asked to "describe" a person about whom nothing was known but sex, highly stereotypic responses would be probable. On the other hand, people know most about themselves. Therefore, the motivation to stereotype self-descriptions would be reduced. Also, stereotypic thinking may be less prevalent when other cues are available or when subjects have more leeway to respond to ambiguous stimuli.

The conclusion is, therefore, that males and females share stereotypes about men and women, and that the male stereotype is considerably more favorable. Both men and women describe themselves as being fairly close to their respective sex-role stereotypes, so that men are more valued by themselves and society than women are.

DISCRIMINATION

While no one likes to be disliked or judged negatively, if prejudices were not acted upon, prejudiced attitudes would not be a serious social problem. But usually, prejudice is acted upon to produce some form of *discrimination*. Discrimination is "the differential treatment of individuals considered to belong to a particular social group" (Williams, 1947). It is often referred to as prejudice in action, and considered to be a natural outgrowth of an attitude of antipathy towards a particular group. Prejudice need not, and does not invariably lead to discrimination, but it happens often enough that the amount of discrimination that members of a group suffer is the clearest and most commonly used index of prejudice directed toward the group.[3]

---

[3] Prejudice may not be acted upon in some circumstances. For example, no situation may occur in which a prejudiced person and his target meet. You may have a strong prejudice against Cloanians, but since you have never met one, your prejudice has remained unexpressed. Or, situations may arise in which prejudice might be expressed, but situational con-

Women have been routinely and legally discriminated against in our society since its inception. At one time, women were not allowed to vote, practice law, demand custody of their children, sit on juries, or manage their own financial affairs. Many jobs were closed to women. Married women and divorcees still have trouble getting credit or loans in their own names, though the new federal Equal Credit Opportunity Act should ease credit problems. Such discrimination is less evident today, but overt as well as subtle discrimination may still be found in both law and practice. Overt legal discrimination against women is decreasing, especially in employment, under the impact of legislation such as Title VII of the 1964 Civil Rights Act, which states that discrimination on the basis of race, color, religion, sex, or national origin is an unlawful employment practice, and the Equal Pay Act of 1963, which requires equal pay for equal work regardless of sex. Neither want ads for jobs, nor jobs themselves can be declared the property of one sex or another. Women must legally be paid the same rate for the same job, and be given the same fringe benefits. Employers may not bar special categories of women (e.g., mothers of preschool children) from any job unless they prohibit men in a similar situation (here, fathers of preschool children) from the job (Edwards, 1973).

While legal discrimination is still being legislated away, prejudice against women remains and therefore discrimination against women still occurs. Now, however, such discrimination must be more subtle in order to get around the law. When equal pay for equal work became the law, many employers renamed jobs and gave men slightly more to do in order to justify paying them more. However, the courts declared that all that was required for equal pay was *substantially* the same work.

Employers have generally justified discrimination by claiming sex as a *bona fide occupational qualification* (BFOQ). That is, job requirements demand abilities women are presumed to lack. In one case, a company's rule that women could not lift or carry more than thirty-five pounds barred them from a number of jobs. Such a rule, based on "generally recognized physical capabilities and limitations of the sexes" was declared discriminatory and hence illegal. In general, the courts have construed BFOQ very narrowly. The employer has the burden of proving that he had reasonable cause to believe that "all or substantially all" women would be unable to do the job. To justify sex as a BFOQ a characteristic of all or substantially all women must be factually proven to be true rather than just a stereotype or assumption about women.

Exclusions cannot be made on the basis of prejudice. Stereotyped characterizations of the sexes and views about the proper role of women cannot be

---

straints prohibit such expression. Typical is the prejudice workers have toward fellow workers from other groups. Their negative attitudes remain unexpressed because noncooperation or a show of hostility is likely to cost a worker her or his job.

a basis for discrimination. Instead, an employer must judge each applicant as an individual with unique and determinable capabilities (Edwards, 1973; "The Mandate of Title VII," 1970). Currently, the only conditions under which sex has been accepted as a BFOQ are in jobs which require authenticity, such as being an actress ("The Mandate of Title VII," 1970). The fact that women as a group may cost an employer slightly more in fringe benefits or may be slightly more likely to leave a job has not been found to be legal ground for justification or discriminatory practices, including lower pay or denial of employer-sponsored training (Bartnoff, 1973).

In spite of these laws, more subtle forms of discrimination occur routinely in the workplace. In these cases, women are not denied jobs on the basis of assumed female attributes, and rarely is sex even mentioned. But discrimination occurs in the equal administration of apparently sex-neutral rules and policies. Typical of this type of discrimination are rules that ignore the different life experiences of men and women (Zellman, 1976). For example, men are much more likely than women to have a history of military service. Policy in one organization required demonstrated leadership skills in successful candidates for its management development program. The company accepted military service of any type as evidence that the candidate possessed leadership skills, but did not recognize experiences more likely to occur in women's lives (e.g., teaching). As a result, the likelihood of women being accepted into the program was reduced (Bartnoff, 1973).

This record suggests strongly that much of the motivation for discrimination lies in prejudice against women. Until prejudiced attitudes are changed, people will continue to try to find ways to treat women differently.

EFFECTS OF PREJUDICE AND DISCRIMINATION

A minority group is any group of people who, because of their physical or cultural characteristics, are singled out from others for differential and unequal treatment, and who therefore regard themselves as objects of collective discrimination. The definition has two essential parts. The first is the more objective, and refers to the presence of discrimination; i.e., there is considerable discrimination against women. The second part is subjective, and requires that women perceive themselves as members of a group against which discrimination is directed. Women have largely avoided such awareness. It is far more comfortable to see oneself as part of a privileged class than an underprivileged one. Reluctance to recognize their own oppression might be expected to be strongest in middle- and upper-class women, who do experience secondary gains from their low status. But lower-class women are equally likely to ignore discrimination.

Lower-Class Women

Many lower-class women have largely been left out of the struggle for change. This is due primarily to their strong allegiance to their roles as wives and mothers. Generally, they perceive the women's movement as derogating, and even trying to eliminate such roles.

For someone with little education, "liberation" often means taking a job in a factory or as a file clerk. These people know that these jobs often provide little personal satisfaction. They are also sensitive to the low status of such jobs. One lower-class wife in her forties, who had begun her first job—as a file clerk—a month earlier, had this to say:

> Well, I know it's not much of a job in the eyes of anyone else. Even the secretaries look down on file clerks. . . . But to me the job is something. . . . I never went to college. I never worked before I was married, and I don't really have the training for anything more. (Jacoby, 1973, p. 42.)

Anxiety and insecurity are characteristics of many lower-class women. They generally do not believe that they have any power to change the course of events (Seifer, 1973). At the same time, real inequities exist which could bring these women into the movement for change. Those lower-class women who do work (and, since the probability of a wife working increases as her husband's income decreases, many do) suffer from being both women and mothers. The difference between men's and women's salaries in 1970 were greatest in those occupations that are most likely to employ lower-class women: service and sales workers, and assembly-line workers (Seifer, 1973). Women on "mother's shifts" of six hours a day earn less per hour and are usually denied seniority and fringe benefits. Additionally, these women tend not to have had technical training and thus hold the lowest-paying jobs, which are also the ones most likely to be eliminated because of automation or cutbacks (Agassi, 1972).

Black Women

The women's movement has been largely a white middle-class phenomenon. Black women have generally not played a prominent role. Indeed, some blacks argue that black women should not devote their energies to combating sex discrimination and promoting feminism as long as discrimination against blacks remains. Many black women feel that they must continue to take a supportive and submissive role vis-à-vis black men who have been badly scarred by racism (Hare and Hare, 1970). Because of this, the whole issue of differential treatment on the basis of sex may be of less concern to black women. Recent data suggest that black women may not experience as much discrimination on the basis of sex as white women do. Black women are also less likely to experience self-hatred and dislike of other women. Black professional women are self-confident and do not derogate other professional women, as white professional women tend to do (Epstein, 1973).

However, in some ways, black women suffer most from the current system which incorporates both sexism and racism. They are more likely than white women to work outside the home and to earn less than black or white men, or white women with the same education. Indeed, some blacks maintain that women's liberation is necessary to insure the success of the black movement and all other movements whose goals are to eliminate unequal treatment on the basis of group attributes (Chisholm, 1972).

Recent survey data indicate that black women are sensitive to the problems they face as women (Harris, 1972; Roper, 1974). In 1972, in a national sample, black women were substantially more supportive of efforts to strengthen or change women's status in society than white women (62 percent versus 45 percent). And they were nearly twice as supportive of the efforts of women's liberation groups (67 percent versus 35 percent). In 1974, 67 percent of black women reported themselves to be supportive of efforts to strengthen or change women's status; the figure for white women was 55 percent.

Reactions to Oppression

While few women perceive or report themselves to be members of an oppressed group, women have adopted a variety of behaviors that can be described as reactions to oppression. Such reactions include denial of membership in one's own group, obsessive concern with one's minority status, withdrawal and passivity, slyness and cunning, self-hatred and in-group aggression, strengthening of in-group ties, sympathy toward the oppressed, and aggression and revolt (Allport, 1954; Pettigrew, 1964). These reactions fit into two categories: those that reflect extropunitiveness or punishment of others, and those that reflect intropunitiveness or self-punishment. Two in particular—identification with the dominant group and aggression against one's own group—are found frequently in women.

Several studies have shown that women tend to share men's feelings that women as a group are inferior. Ratings by men and women of the extent to which 122 items characterized the adult male and the adult female were almost identical (Broverman, et al., 1972). Ratings of the value of these traits showed similar high agreement. Many more masculine than feminine traits were valued by subjects. Men and women seemed to agree both about what men and women are like, and that men are better. Additionally, it was found that the self-concepts of the male and female subjects were close to the respective sex-role stereotypes, indicating that women hold themselves in low valuation relative to men. Other studies reviewed earlier also showed that women rated the work of women as inferior to that of men.

Another form of self-hatred may not include oneself, but may describe one's feelings for other members of one's group because they possess the qualities that the dominant group devalues. This behavior is common among professional women, particularly those who achieved high status before the women's movement became a salient factor. These women, who have made it, or are trying to make it in a masculine, often hostile environment, look with scorn at traditional women as the cause of men's antifemale attitudes. These successful women often feel that they had to fight hard to get where they are, and are proud that they did it on their own. Women who are trying to achieve success may feel that identification with the less desirable group—women—may impede their progress (Lewin, 1948). These women often feel that women who are sitting at home waiting, or crying "discrimination" should be ignored. Sadly, such women tend to be in high positions where they could help other women if they were willing but instead may sabotage younger women (the "queen bee" syndrome). At the same time, women who select the domestic life often resent and deride those of their sex who have careers, or broader interests than their homes.

There are other, more positive reactions to oppression than self-hatred. One is to develop a special solidarity and group loyalty which is an essential factor in improving the status of a devalued group. In general, this has not been a common reaction among women, in part because they live separated from each other.

DEVELOPMENT OF PREJUDICE TOWARD WOMEN

It is clear that there is prejudice toward women. How does this prejudice develop? Theorists who have studied ethnic groups have attempted to describe the causes of prejudice. While one must be cautious in comparing the oppression of women with that of ethnic groups, it is possible to make three basic statements about the development of intergroup attitudes. First of all, ethnic attitudes are learned. Second, ethnic attitudes are multiply determined. Third, ethnic attitudes are usually functional to the goals of the individual and often to the goals of the society which fosters such attitudes.

Learning of Attitudes

The notion that attitudes are learned seems intuitively obvious. Most theorists agree that all attitudes are developed through learning and experience (Chein, 1948; Doob, 1947). While some argue that attitudes like racial prejudice may have a genetic component in biological differences in levels of aggressiveness, the notion that specific antipathy to blacks, Jews, or women could be genetically determined is generally rejected by social scientists (McGuire, 1969).

One of the earliest group identifications children make is a sexual one. By age five children appear to have a stable gender identity as a boy or a girl. There are a number of theories of sex-role development but they all involve the notion that children learn to associate their sexual identity with sex-appropriate behaviors (see Chapters 6 and 7). At the same time that they are learning what is appropriate behavior for members of their own sex, they are also learning what is not appropriate because of the fact that it "belongs" to the other sex. There is evidence that children also learn in these early years that being a boy is better. This lesson is learned when the child's own cognitions are reinforced by cultural beliefs.

Factors Determining Attitudes

Given that attitudes toward women are learned, the notion of multiple determinism implies that these attitudes are a result of a number of factors varying in strength and salience to the learner. The diagram in Box 2 shows how numerous the potential causal factors are and which factors lead to attitudes of prejudice toward women.

Box 2 expands on an important social psychological equation: behavior is a function of the actor's psychological predispositions and the environmental influences that impinge on him. In other words, both our environment and our personal characteristics influence attitudes and behavior.

Historical and Sociocultural Factors. These are aspects of the social environment that the average person does not experience directly. Included here are both historical and contemporary features. Our history is one of inequality of treatment for women. It was only fifty years ago that women gained the right to vote, and even today, women are still fighting to achieve economic and political equality. Men have most of the power in virtually every area of society except those they specifically delegated to women, such as domestic management. Women are physically capable of doing nearly all jobs in our increasingly mechanized factories, farms, and offices. Yet prejudice and discrimination remain.

Continued prejudice toward women serves those who have power in a variety of ways. There may be an economic explanation for its tenaciousness (Amundsen, 1971). Prejudice toward women provides society with a reserve labor force who can be hired in time of need, and fired in time of oversupply. Women can, after all, always return to "home base." During wars, when the labor supply is sharply reduced, women are employed in factories. More generally, women's "roles" provide men with an enormous supply of unpaid domestic labor. Were women to be paid for housework, a massive redistribution of wealth might occur (Benston, 1971).

Box 2   **Factors That Relate to Prejudice**

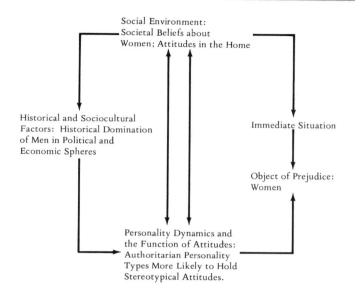

Social Environment:
Societal Beliefs about
Women; Attitudes in the Home

Historical and Sociocultural
Factors: Historical Domination
of Men in Political and
Economic Spheres

Immediate Situation

Object of Prejudice:
Women

Personality Dynamics and
the Function of Attitudes:
Authoritarian Personality
Types More Likely to Hold
Stereotypical Attitudes.

SOURCE: Adapted from Allport, 1954.

Social Environment. It is in the context of individuals' immediate social environments which extend from birth through adult life, that their psychological dispositions and attitudes are developed. Other people constitute an individual's social environment. For example, through a process of direct socialization, children learn what their parents think about women through their words, their deeds, and particularly the way the parents act—both toward each other and in regard to the outside world. If the mother and father have a stereotypic relationship, we would expect the children to develop stereotypic attitudes about women. Some evidence for this comes from a survey of college women in which it was found that whether or not a woman's mother was employed was strongly related to career orientation (Almquist and Angrist, 1971). Women whose mothers were employed during the time their daughters were in college were much more likely to be career-oriented themselves. Children of working mothers also have less stereotypic views of men and women generally (Broverman, et al., 1972).

Another theory of socialization suggests that what parents socialize are not attitudes per se, but personality dispositions. The notion here is that people with certain personality traits tend to express these traits in their attitudes. For example, the findings in a study of the relationship between

authoritarianism and anti-Semitism seemed to indicate that highly prejudiced subjects tended to have a more rigid personality than the more tolerant. These personality traits were found to be related to early childhood experiences in a family setting characterized by harsh discipline, conditional
love, and a hierarchical family structure (Adorno, et al., 1950).

This theory of the acquisition of prejudiced attitudes is consistent with
the repeated finding that although children do learn from their parents,
they do not always agree with their parents. For example, only 59 percent
of parents and their children (high-school seniors) shared a political party
preference (Jennings and Niemi, 1968). This low level of agreement (given
the limited number of likely choices for political preference) may be largely
due to ignorance on the part of children of their parents' views (Sears,
1975). Level of ignorance would be likely to be especially high with regard
to parental views on "the woman question." For one thing, although it is
more and more discussed, it is not a salient or recurring political issue, as is
party affiliation. For another, it is largely nonconscious (Bem and Bem,
1970).

As one matures, one's social environment is increasingly populated by
peers. Peers serve as models of sex-appropriate behavior; they convey information about women, and on the basis of this information, transmit group
norms. Group norms are an important factor in attitude formation and stability. It has been found that people who value a group such as their family
or sex group and want to be accepted by it tend to conform to existing
group norms and, therefore, will accept the attitudes and values of the
groups with which they identify (Festinger, Schachter, and Back, 1950).
Group norms seem to affect attitudes toward women. In a sample, attitudes
toward women's liberation groups varied substantially by age, marital status, and level of education. Young single men and women, blacks, and
those with college educations were most supportive of women's liberation.
Older whites, and particularly those with little education who lived in rural
areas of the South were least supportive (Harris, 1972). These data point to
the existence of norms about women's proper roles that vary across population groups. Data at a more individual level indicate that a woman's boyfriend or husband has a substantial influence on her attitudes and behaviors
(Horner, 1972). Women whose boyfriends are less prejudiced against
women and are supportive of women's achievements are more likely to be
planning for a career during college.

Personality Dynamics. The functions that attitudes may serve for a given individual, and the way that personality traits predispose people to hold certain
opinions are called personality dynamics. The notion that attitudes serve psychological functions for individuals makes the study of prejudice complex.
The same prejudice may serve different functions for different people. For example, one person may be prejudiced against blacks because his father is, and

he wants to identify with his father. A second person may hate blacks because by thinking blacks are sexually promiscuous, he can rid himself of any guilt about his own sexuality. Therefore, different individuals are likely to respond quite differently to attempts to strengthen or change their prejudiced attitudes. The functional approach serves as a reminder that we must be aware of the function a given attitude serves for a given individual if we are to successfully modify it (Katz, 1960).

Prejudice toward women may also serve a number of functions. For many insecure men, viewing women as dependent and weak serves to make them feel more independent and strong in contrast. Men are socialized to be especially fearful of appearing emotionally weak, and are not supposed to cry or show anxiety. Both of these are "feminine" behaviors, permitted or even encouraged in women. A man with some doubts about his masculinity need only look at (or better yet, comfort) a weeping woman to be assured of his superiority. Analogously, a man who doubts his ability as a good provider may reduce these doubts by viewing women as too scatterbrained to hold responsible jobs. Such men may also insist that their wives stay home.

For men who may be frightened of their own sexuality, viewing women as temptresses and sexually insatiable may be useful. Such men can look down on women for their "lust," and avoid any responsibility for sexual contacts with them.

Holding certain attitudes may serve to bring a person closer to other individuals or to a group. Attitude similarity has indeed been found to be an important determinant of liking (Triandis and Davis, 1965). "Male" may be a desirable in-group, and men in the group are quick to point out similar qualities and attitudes they share. Such a function is positive, but frequently the in-group gains solidarity at the expense of a rejected outgroup. Being a male and glad of it does not necessarily mean believing that being a woman is bad, but this is frequently a companion attitude. Differences between males and females are exaggerated in these cases, and individual differences *within* groups are obscured.

The Immediate Situation. It is sometimes useful to think of attitude and situation as being in a kind of push-pull relationship: the stronger the attitude that is pushing a certain action, the less need there is for situational support for the behavior to occur. Conversely, a somewhat weak attitude may be acted upon if the situational stimuli are strong (Greenstein, 1969). Imagine a women's club where a feminist speaker requests women to come forward to sign a petition that urges passage of the Equal Rights Amendment. No one moves. There appears to be little support in the group for the ERA. In a nonsupportive environment like this, the first woman to step forward probably has stronger feelings for ERA than the others. Let us now imagine that that first signer encouraged others to come forward, and that nearly all of the women present have signed. Not signing at this point is a strong statement of nonsupport. In the last few minutes, the social environment has begun to exert substantial force on those who have not signed. Those who are mildly or even slightly pro-ERA are likely to sign. Only those who are really opposed are likely to resist.

Sometimes attitude and situational constraints may be pushing for inconsistent behaviors. The acting out of a strong attitude in these instances will be inhibited by strong situational constraints. This often occurs in regard to ethnic and racial prejudice. Consequently, not all prejudice leads to discrimination. Frequently, the constraints of a situation require a prejudiced person to behave in a nondiscriminatory way. A classic study demonstrates this point. The author traveled across the United States with a Chinese couple for an extended period of time. The threesome stayed at many motels and hotels and ate in thousands of restaurants, diners, and coffee shops. They were refused service only once. After the trip, each establishment they had patronized was sent a letter asking if they accepted "members of the Chinese race as guests in [their] establishment?" Ninety-two percent of the restaurants and cafes and 91 percent of the hotels, auto-camps, and tourist homes replied "No." The remainder replied "Uncertain; depends on circumstances" (LaPiere, 1934). One of the reasons for the apparent inconsistency between attitude and behavior was situational factors. It was apparently hard to refuse to serve a well-dressed Chinese couple travelling with a European in a face-to-face setting (Campbell, 1963). Proprietors may have felt embarassed, or did not want to provoke a scene. In a face-to-face situation, such factors as cleanliness or apparent wealth are more important than race. When answering a letter, environmental constraints and personal information are both lacking and prejudiced attitudes are expressed (LaPiere, 1934).

A similar phenomenon—actions that are inconsistent with beliefs—is occurring with increasing frequency with regard to women. New laws and affirmative action programs are creating employment situations in which the pressures against discrimination are growing. In spite of an employer's personal views about women, and his wish that they would either work for "pin money" or stay home, he must welcome them to the firm, give them advanced training (if they qualify) and pay them as much as men. In spite of the prejudiced attitudes he may express to other males, he must behave in a nondiscriminatory manner or face fines, lawsuits, and harrassment.

It is likely that alterations of the immediate situation will have the most direct and rapid impact on women's equality and advancement. Prejudice is hard to change because it is learned early, reinforced by peers and group norms, and may express or maintain an important part of a person's personality. However, if one can alter the force of an immediate situation, prejudice may, for all intents and purposes, become irrelevant. When situational constraints are strong enough, only the most prejudiced will behave in a discriminatory manner.

Nondiscrimination may also reduce prejudice. When one is forced to treat people as equals it may become uncomfortable to regard them as inferior. For example, men on a work crew may violently oppose putting a woman on the crew. Once she is there, however, and the men are forced to cooperate with her to get the job done, it may be more and more dissonant to view this person with whom they work and upon whom they depend as inferior and incapable.

Situational constraints are probably not the *best* way to bring about lasting, across-the-board equality, however. If people have prejudiced attitudes, every situation must be designed to provide sufficient constraints to ensure that discrimination will not occur. This is a slow process and cannot be accomplished in every case. It would be far better to bring about change in attitudes, but such change is difficult; many factors operate to maintain prejudice.

THE MAINTENANCE OF PREJUDICE

Many of the factors which maintain prejudice toward women differ little from those which produced those prejudices in the first place. Most Americans are socialized by parents, peers, and society to a common set of conventions and norms which provide a basis for highly resistant attitudes in later life (Sears and Whitney, 1971; 1973: Zellman, 1973). One of these conventions is the place of women. Many men and women claim to believe in equality, yet feel that it is right that women not participate equally with men, and that their concerns should center on the home and being help-mates to men. Such conventions are resistant to change in part because of tradition.

What is familiar tends to *become* a value, whether or not it was valued at first (Allport, 1954). That is, we come to like the people and customs with which we have grown up simply because we *did* grow up with them. Support for this idea was found in a study in which Turkish words were inserted into two college newspapers over a period of several weeks. Words were inserted from one to twenty-five times. Subjects whose college newspapers had carried the Turkish words were later asked to choose the words they liked best. The results showed that subjects liked the words that had appeared most often, although they had no idea what the words meant or why they were in the paper. Thus, repeated exposures alone made the words more likeable (Zajonc, 1968).

The relevance of this point to women is clear. All of us are most familiar with women in the roles of wife and mother, because most women *do* occupy these roles, if not exclusively, certainly primarily. Thus, we come to value the idea that women *should* be primarily wives and mothers, and are disinclined to favor any other arrangement of roles.

People also maintain their prejudices by associating only with people who agree with their own beliefs. This de facto selective exposure tends to produce a great deal of attitudinal consistency over time (Sears and Freedman, 1967). Another factor that tends to make prejudices resistant to change is the very prejudgment they incorporate. If both the prejudiced person and target of prejudice share certain beliefs about the attributes of the target group, any interaction will reinforce the prejudice. This occurs commonly in male-female relationships. Both men and women in America have been taught to believe that women are illogical and somewhat helpless. Because of these beliefs, men and women "play the game" in encounters (Pettigrew, 1964). A man will rush to a woman's aid in a situation where, for example, a woman is trying to find her direction by using a map. His help is readily accepted, because she feels she cannot perform the task by herself. The job accomplished, the man leaves the scene, his prejudice reinforced.

What is perhaps more interesting and alarming is the role that women themselves play in the maintenance of the sexual status quo. While one might expect that women, who are oppressed and discriminated against, would be agents for change, recent data indicate that less than half of all women report having any sympathy with the efforts of women's liberation groups. Young, single, college-educated women are most sympathetic. Women over thirty with less than college education and middle-class incomes are least supportive (Harris, 1972). These variations in level of commitment are a response to changing cultural norms in some groups, and are also linked to the secondary gains that middle-class women accrue in the present sex-role system.

These secondary gains include considerable amounts of leisure time, a guaranteed annual wage, and few demands for achievement (Epstein, 1970). Women seem to be sensitive to these benefits. In a recent survey, women who felt that women had a better life than men in this country were much less supportive of the Equal Rights Amendment than women who felt men had it better (Gallup, 1975). Two points should be stressed here. One is that lower-class women are as supportive of the system as middle-class women, though they are not, by and large, receiving these secondary gains. Their support stems from a wish to one day have leisure time and not need to work. Fighting the system means abandoning those dreams. Second, these gains really are secondary, and are often purchased with a woman's independence and sense of self.

Many men and women do not perceive their beliefs about women to be prejudice, but an accurate reflection of "natural differences." The nonconscious nature of these beliefs contributes to the maintenance of the sexual status quo. The goal of such things as consciousness-raising groups and women's studies programs is to make conscious these assumptions and beliefs. Implied in this goal is that once conscious these assumptions will clash head-on with the egalitarian ideals of our society and be discarded. Some recent data support this view. Participation in women's studies courses increased perceptions of discrimination against women and led to more non-stereotypic beliefs about women (Ruble, et al., 1975).

CHANGING ATTITUDES

A number of factors contribute to the maintenance of prejudice against women. Early acquisition of attitudes and beliefs, support for such beliefs by peers and society, and strong vested interests tend to reinforce and maintain prejudice. There are ways to bring about change, however. One way to change attitudes is to change *behavior* first. A good way to change an attitude is to persuade the person who holds the attitude to engage in behavior or perform tasks that are inconsistent with the attitude. When the task is completed, the person feels uneasy for having done something counter to his beliefs, particularly if there was little or no force used to get him to perform the behavior. They fact that he did something he did not believe in without a really good reason may produce dissonance between belief and behavior. In these instances, the person's attitude is likely to change (Festinger and Carlsmith, 1959).

Change in attitude may result from performing new behaviors. Engaging in a new behavior or experiencing a new situation that is discrepant with a long-held attitude may sometimes result in new perceptions and views. Probably the best example of this latter phenomenon occurred during World War II, when women performed well in jobs previously considered "masculine." Their success made it hard for people to continue to believe that women could not handle such work. This kind of attitude change may occur even when the new behavior occurred *only* because of real force, such as a threatened fine or lawsuit, or because munitions workers were desperately needed. The fact that new behaviors often result in new attitudes suggests that legislation which requires compliance—that is, the performance of behaviors that are inconsistent with attitudes, will produce attitude change. The sense of inevitability that legislation frequently produces has been found to decrease prejudice against blacks.

This seems to be the direction that change is going. Recent legislation, most of which concerns employment, such as Title VII of the 1964 Civil Rights Act, has made employment discrimination against women illegal. No matter how they feel about women, employers must now treat women in a nondiscriminatory manner. The Equal Rights Amendment, if ratified, will require equality of treatment in all realms, not just employment. Equality of treatment will foster greater and more equal participation of women in society. Such participation is likely to quicken the demise of prejudice.

THE EQUAL RIGHTS AMENDMENT

The Equal Rights Amendment (ERA) has been gathering dust in Congress for nearly fifty years. The amendment is simple, but reactions to it are not.

Sec. 1   Equality of rights under the law shall not be abridged or denied by the United States or by any state on account of sex.

Sec. 2   The Congress shall have the power to enforce, by appropriate legislation, the provisions of this article.

Sec. 3   This amendment shall take effect two years after the date of ratification.

First introduced in 1923, this amendment seemed to its writers a logical sequel to the suffrage amendment (Kraditor, 1968). It has been introduced in each Congress since 1923 and has been repeatedly reported out favorably by the Senate Judiciary Committee. It finally passed Congress in March 1972, and must be ratified by thirty-eight of the states by 1979 for it to become law. Within four months of its passage, twenty states approved it. At this writing, it has been approved by thirty-five states, and needs approval of three more by 1979 for ratification. The prospects of this are poor. Unless Congress takes the unusual step of extending the deadline beyond 1979, ratification is unlikely.

The amendment was written in order to provide equal rights for women beyond the realm of electoral politics. The ERA would give women constitutional protection against laws which discriminate against women just because they are women, and would guarantee that women and men be treated equally under the law. The important words in the amendment are "under the law"; the ERA will not directly affect social customs or personal relationships between men and women, nor will it affect those laws that are based on purely physical differences between the sexes, such as rape laws.

Supporters argue that the amendment is necessary because while some laws (e.g., the Equal Pay Act of 1963, Title VII of the 1964 Civil Rights Act) have been interpreted to include equality for women, the process of gaining full legal equality without a constitutional basis is too slow, too piecemeal, and too uncertain.

A good example of the problem comes from Congress itself. A recent survey found that women employees on congressional staffs are paid significantly less than men performing comparable tasks. However, Congress has specifically exempted Capitol Hill staff members from the provisions of the Civil Rights Act of 1964.

As a result, women employees have no legal means of appeal (Newsweek, 1976). This could not happen under ERA. Ratification of the amendment would provide constitutional protection against the passage and implementation of discriminatory laws, or, as in the example above, would prohibit waiving the protection of laws guaranteeing euality. Legislators would more closely monitor laws covered by a constitutional amendment. Laws which appeared to discriminate would be more likely to be challenged in the courts and the courts would have a more substantial basis for rendering decisions which fostered equality.

Opponents claim that the ERA will send women into combat, break up homes, legalize rape, and require men and women to share public toilets. These arguments are exaggerated and largely untrue. The ERA *will* affect laws about military conscription and the family. Any law which makes a distinction between the rights and responsibilities of men and women will be invalid. It is expected that, in general, where previous legislation restricted the freedom of one sex (e.g., to obtain credit), such laws will be declared unconstitutional; and where previous laws conferred a privilege on one sex (e.g., a wife's right to alimony), these laws will be extended to apply to both sexes (Schwartz, 1973). When the criteria governing who goes into combat are applied equally to both sexes a few women may indeed be part of the group. Some women *want* to share this responsibility with men.

At present, of course, there is no draft; all military recruits are volunteers. The Equal Rights Amendment would enable women to volunteer on the same basis as men (currently women must meet higher and more stringent standards), and require restrictions on assignments and promotions to be lifted, thus opening to women many military and veteran's benefits now available only to men, including education loans, housing, health, employment, and job training.

Should the draft be reinstated, women would be subject to it—and to the same exemptions and deferments, physical and moral, as men. Men with families have often been exempt from the draft and the majority report of the Senate Judiciary Committee states that "the fear that mothers will be conscripted from their children . . . is totally and completely unfounded."

PROSPECTS FOR CHANGE

Prejudice against women affects all aspects of women's lives. The remaining chapters in this part discuss some of the direct results of women's lower status and lack of power. Women have less power in interpersonal relations and in the larger political structure. Chapters 15, 16, and 17 outline how these power differences are expressed and some of the factors which subtly maintain the status quo. However, they also point out areas where change has occurred and can occur in the future.

15 Women and Interpersonal Power

Our society has fixed ideas about how men and women are and are not supposed to use power to influence each other. Many of these ideas have persisted from earlier times (e.g., Ellis, 1913). Power and influence are part of everyday life, from the small requests we make of other people to the big demands made by government. How power is expected to be used by men and women can certainly affect both their everyday relationships and the kinds of positions they have in society.

Many of the ideas people have about power and influence are part of the sex-role expectations society has developed. Since these expectations regulate both how we behave and how we evaluate the behavior of others, they affect how people use power and how people react to power used by others. For example, the stereotypes of women as less competent and aggressive and more warm and emotional than men have implications for our expectations of sex-role appropriate behaviors. According to these stereotypes any behavior like aggression or competitiveness is out of role for a woman. These expectations and the differing opportunities for power acquisition and use produce actual sex differences in influence behavior. Furthermore, some react to the behavior of others partially in terms of how well they play their male or female roles. If these roles are not played out according to expectation, the reaction may be quite negative. These differential expectations and opportu-

Paula Johnson was the primary author of this chapter.

nities for power use, actual ways in which power is used, and the consequences of power use for women will be examined in this chapter.

WHAT IS POWER?

Power has been used interchangeably with a variety of concepts such as force, authority, strength, control, and influence (Bernard, 1972b). It is an important component of such diverse behavioral domains as leadership, social roles, communication, interpersonal and intergroup relations, and emotional adjustment. Power has also been viewed as an aspect of the personality, either as a need for power or feelings of powerlessness (McClelland, 1975; Minton, 1967; Winter, 1973). In this chapter, power will be viewed as an aspect of interaction in a social relationship (Cartwright, 1959).

Interpersonal power is the ability to get another person to think, feel, or do something they would not have ordinarily done spontaneously. If one possesses the means to affect another, one has *power* vis-à-vis that person. If one uses one's power, it is called *influence*. If one's influence is successful, it is called *control* (Cartwright, 1959).

Power, influence, and control are a part of every person's life. Most power is not even noticed because it is built into our norms for social interaction. For example, we influence a clerk to give us the merchandise by handing the clerk the money—an example of reciprocity norms. Or we follow the directions of a policeman directing traffic since our norms give him the power to do this. Students are often well acquainted with how to influence others when they ask their parents for money. There are many ways a student could go about this—emphasizing direct reasoning, dropping hints, referring to the closeness of the relationship, mentioning her or his helplessness in being unable to produce the funds alone, pointing out the needs of all college students. In a recent interview study, one student informed his father that he was certain a stereo system for his apartment would reduce the tensions of studying. One female reported that she often confides in her mother first on a *personal* matter and then asks for money; another female used an indirect approach with her father. She said, "I subtly hint around about whatever I want to do but never come out and say it." A third woman reported smiling and apologizing a lot—a helpless rather than a competent approach. While men, too, reported using these indirect approaches in dealing with an authority figure, women tend to use these helpless, personal, and indirect modes more widely than men do (Johnson, 1976). As well as using these direct and indirect verbal approaches, people can also express power nonverbally.

Television provides clear examples of verbal and nonverbal power usage, and television is especially helpful for demonstrating the close relationship between sex roles and power usage of men and women. Since behavior on television is often exaggerated for comic or dramatic impact, everyday events become magnified and more clear cut. For example, what does Lucy do when she wants Desi to take her Hawaii? Does she ask him directly? No. She puts travel brochures all over the house—in Desi's socks, in the refrigerator.

A THEORY OF POWER USE

Study of power has led to the development of a typology of kinds of power to which people may have access, and which differ in their consequences when used. Most social influence derives from one or more of six power bases: reward, coercion, referent, legitimate, expert, and informational (French and Raven, 1959; Raven, 1965). The term "power base" refers to the particular nature of the relationship between the influencer and influencee, which is the source of the power (Raven, 1965). These aspects of the relationships are as follows: one person can theaten the other with punishment, *coercion;* promise a *reward* to the other; appeal to similarity and liking between herself or himself and the other, *referent;* act in terms of one's right to influence and the other's obligation to comply, *legitimate;* use superior knowledge or skills, *expert;* or persuade the other with new *information* about the outcome of the other's compliance. The study of why people choose these bases of power and the consequences of their choice can provide a framework in which the effects of sex-related expectations and opportunities for power use can be examined.

DETERMINANTS OF POWER USE

Why might an influencer choose one kind of power over another? There are three basic determinants of power choice (Raven and Kruglanski, 1970; and Cartwright, 1965). First, influencers estimate just how effective a particular power base will be and how much time, money, or effort it may take to use. This may be done consciously or nonconsciously. For example, the students who were asked how they got their way with their parents often began their explanation by describing what would not be effective. For example, one said, "emotional outbursts just won't work with my dad," and proceeded to explain what would be effective.

Second, the influencer evaluates the possible reactions of others to the choice of power behavior. How others see influencers and react to them is partially based on their position and roles. People also choose a particular form of influence consistent with their roles, since people are motivated to achieve societal rewards given for complying with the role expectations.

Finally, personal wishes and needs can effect the influencer's choice of power. The way a person looks at the world (e.g., as good or evil) and her or his other interpersonal goals (such as one-upsmanship) may lead to particular power choices. Both a person's general personality patterns and the specific content of the situation can be related to these needs. For example, a person might view people as basically not very altruistic and thus in need of incentives. This person might use coercion with a person she or he wants to get even with, and at the same time might use reward with someone she or he wants to do something nice for. Since research has not come to consistent conclusions about sex differences in personality (see Chapter 4), and the specific situations involved may be infinite, this third consideration may be less sex linked than the first two considerations.

The first two determinants of power use—effectiveness and evaluation by others—often affect male and female influencers differently. One's estimates of the effectiveness, the costs, and possible evaluation by others can be affected by sex-role–linked expectations and opportunities for power use. For example, if a woman were to try to get another person to do something through threat of withdrawal of resources, she might be effective but disliked and avoided. Indeed, it has been found that a woman who has control over resources *is* seen as out of role. For example, adult women who controlled resources (toys, cookies, etc.) were criticized by children for not giving them away to an adult male (Bandura, Ross, and Ross, 1963a and b). The opportunities open to women and the expectations for appropriate behavior will now be examined and related to choice of power modes.

OPPORTUNITIES FOR POWER USE

Four factors have been suggested as important determinants of how much power a person can have and use: status, concrete resources, expertise, and confidence (Tedeschi, et al., 1972).

Status

Every human society assigns value to certain characteristics. A person comes to have a certain status depending on how much of the valued characteristics she or he possesses (Brown, 1965). Status, therefore, is a hierarchy of inferiority and superiority on some dimension or set of dimensions. Societies vary on what dimensions are important. Typical ones include physical strength, various skills, position in the kinship system, sex, lineage, occupation, wealth, and roles in an organization like the army or church (Brown, 1965).

Two things happen when a person has high status. First, the high status itself can form a base of power with which the person can influence. This is a form of legitimate power. Second, high status can give people greater leeway in how they influence others. "Idiosyncrasy credits" refer to the ability of a high-status person to get away with the same behavior which would have negative consequences for a low-status person. As long as one's high status is secure, one does not have to be too careful about what one does, because almost anything, even idiosyncratic behavior, is acceptable (Hollander, 1958).

High status also affects other evaluations of the influencer by third parties. Whatever a high-status person does, she or he is liked better than a low-status person who does the same thing (Ditties and Kelley, 1956). Sometimes high status and high power are synonymous, since high-status people often possess the other determinants for power use: resources, expertise, and confidence. However, status itself allows more and varied use of power. High status thus gives an individual greater access to all power sources or combinations thereof.

Status is socially defined. It is a question of value, and anything can be valued. In our society it is most often those positions and accoutrements that males have which are valued (see Chapters 12 and 14). For example, income or education are often a determinant of status. Men have the higher incomes and educations that give them status (as well as concrete resources and expertise) (Bird, 1968). Position can also be a determinant of status. Men have the highest positions in all military, industrial, technical, scientific, intellectual, and political institutions in our society (Millett, 1970). Women can acquire status through their role as mother, but this status is generally effective only in the immediate family.

However, even if women do have status through wealth, education, or a professional job, they do not acquire power along with their status in the same way a man would. At least for young women, their primary source of status is their physical attractiveness. A women who is attractive can often get men to do things for her, thus, she can have power over a man who is attracted to her. However, this type of power is temporary and has definite limits. For example, it is generally effective power over only one man at a time. It also is not available to many women of any age and usually does not last beyond the age of forty even for the most beautiful women.

Second, other than youth and beauty, a woman's status is usually measured by the status of the man she marries rather than her own achievements. Women are expected to marry, and when they do, they take on the status of the men they marry. In our society the ideal match is the young, beautiful woman with the rich, successful professional man (Rubin, 1973). Both have the high status associated with their own sex. An attractive woman gives status to a boyfriend or husband, but an attractive man does not enhance the status of his female companion (Bar-Tal and Saxe, 1976). Thus, women can use their attractiveness for "getting a man," but cannot generally use this status as direct power.

The third problem with a woman realizing the benefits of status is that being male in itself means higher status. In this society, the male is the norm, and male characteristics are more valued in most societies (see Chapters 3 and 14). Many professional women, for example, frequently feel this lack of status in everyday interactions with people who accord status only to males of the same age and rank. A woman is then more limited in her power use simply because she is a woman. A related problem for professional women is that in order to be a competent professional she must exhibit "malelike" characteristics in her work. Since these are out of role for her, she may face criticism or even overt hostility, both of which make it more difficult for her to exercise the power normally associated with her position.

Within many mariages, women have less status, not only because they are female, but also because they are younger, less educated, and earn less money than their husbands (Bernard, 1972a). All of these factors are related to relative power within marriage. For example, wives with less of these external status indicators than their husbands have less influence in the couple's long-term and short-term plans (Wolfe, 1959). Thus a woman's status has a pervasive effect on how she may use power in her everyday life.

Concrete Resources

Resources include time, money, other material possessions, physical strength, and other personal resources, such as sexual favors and warmth or affection. These resources may be drawn upon directly to reward or coerce a person into doing something, or they can be indirectly used to back up other kinds of influence attempts. For the direct use of resources to be effective, the influencee must have a need (i.e., desire to avoid pain or a need for money) and see the influencer as able to satisfy this need. Resources are important when an influencer is considering the costs and effectiveness of power. The more resources a person has, the more one may be able to offer, and the less relative cost per expenditure there would be. Back-up resources are needed for many influence attempts.

In our society, males tend to be in control of the resources. For example, a small number of men control most of the money of this country, with women being only peripherally involved (Domhoff, 1970). Even if a woman has resources, it is often assumed that she is not able to control them. For example, there are stereotypes that she cannot balance her checkbook, or she is not objective or realistic enough to deal in high finance. Indeed, one study found that children often did not even *perceive* females as really controlling resources even when they did. If a female had valued resources, the child assumed they actually belonged to the male. For example, "He is the man and it is all his because he is a daddy. Mommy never really has things that belong to her" (Bandura, et al., 1963, p. 533). Thus it is often difficult for a woman to use the resources she does have as a power base.

On the everyday level, the relationship of resource control to power can be seen in a study of married couples (Wolfe, 1959). Wives who had control over the financial resources of the family (e.g., they had an income or paid the bills) were more likely to have more say over other activities. It is also possible that outside work allows the wife to have her personal needs met by more contact with the world. Thus, her power may come from having fewer needs as well as from having more resources.

Expertise

How one uses power is also affected by one's expertise. An expert possesses special resources—knowledge, information, or skills. The doctor who prescribes medicine is believed to know best, so the patient is influenced to take it as directed. However, a person is usually an expert in only one area or set of areas. A physician may have expertise to influence beliefs about the health of the human body, but not much influence on one's other beliefs. However, status, wealth, and confidence may make the physician a successful influencer in other areas, too.

In our society, men are the acknowledged experts in nearly every field. There are certain areas in which a woman may be granted expertise—cooking, child-rearing, sewing, education, art, and literature. However, even in these areas, the top authorities tend to be males. Men are expected to perform better generally and to be more skilled at almost all tasks (see Chapter 12).

As was the case with status and concrete resources, even women who have expertise have difficulty exercising influence. An expert woman may be perceived as having less expertise not only because there are few opportunities to acquire expertise, but because we do not expect a woman to be an expert. This is demonstrated in Box 1. What makes the riddle in Box 1 so difficult is that we do not expect a woman to be in an expert position.

Box 1

A well-known riddle goes like this:

> A man and his son were driving down the highway and had an accident. The man was killed instantly, and the son was rushed to the hospital in critical condition and prepared for surgery. The surgeon arrived, and looked at the boy and said, "I can't operate; that's my son!" Who was the surgeon?

The answer should be plain to you in this context—the surgeon was his mother. The role of doctor-expert for women is so unusual that many people cannot answer this riddle.

Self-Confidence

Possession of high status, concrete resources, and expertise can all lead to greater self-confidence. Confidence is a "generalized expectancy of success" and a self-confident person is one who feels sure "he is competent and will succeed at tasks he undertakes" (Tedeschi, et al., 1972, p. 299). Such feelings are much more common in men than women (Chapter 12). People with confidence do indeed attempt to influence more. The self-confident person expects his influence to be both more effective and to have lower costs because there will be less resistance (Tedeschi, et al., 1972).

Lowered confidence in women (or anyone) has the effect of lessening their expectations for success and causing them to choose modes of influence which would have less risk of receiving a negative evaluation by a third party. Thus, women would be less likely to attempt to exercise direct power than men would.

All this suggests that women do not have as much access to the major determinants of power use—status, concrete resources, expertise, and confidence. This lowers the power of women. In addition, even if women possess one or more of these determinants, they often face difficulty in using them effectively.

WOMEN AND MANIPULATIVE POWER

In what ways *are* women allowed to use power? Stereotypes indicate that women are supposed to act as if they are *not* using power when in fact they *are:* Women are expected to be less direct than men and more sneaky. This implies that indirect, or manipulative, rather than direct forms of power are viewed as more typical of women (Broverman, et al., 1972).

Basically, manipulative or indirect power can be defined as occurring when the influencer acts as if the person on the receiving end of the influence is not aware of being influenced. Indirect power is not just one of several modes equally open to women, rather it is the primary mode that women are able to use.

It is clear that culturally and socially, women are brought up to use power manipulatively. Culturally the feminine woman is supposed to be "delicate, dainty, passive, nurturant and emotional"; "to be feminine is to be weak, and although women are not weak, feminine women are." Consequently, ". . . since femininity is the norm to which females are supposed to conform, they do their best. They are punished by rejection if they do not. Women, in brief, are rewarded for being weak, punished for being strong." So if a woman is strong, it is expedient for her to appear weak, that is, to use manipulative power so no one knows she is really strong and powerful (Bernard, 1972b).

Manipulative power has several negative implications for a woman in terms of the position of power or powerlessness she finds herself in, how others view her, and how she views herself. First, manipulative power may be quite successful in the short run—a person may be able to get exactly what she wants. However, if a woman is really successful at using manipulative power, the other person will not realize that an attempt to influence has been successfully made. Thus, the influencer will not be seen as being powerful and will not be able to build a basis for future influence. Also, the influencer will get no credit for her contribution to the situation. For example, when a woman makes indirect suggestions for her husband to improve at something, it is he who gets the glory that comes from the achievement. On the other hand, if a woman is not subtle enough in her manipulations, she may be perceived as being too pushy. Thus, people are likely to see her either as helpless or pushy and sneaky. In turn, she is not likely to view herself as a direct or strong person if she uses this type of power, and thus is not likely to develop confidence. Instead she may develop a rather distorted image of herself as a person who must be indirect and sneaky if she is to get what she wants.

THEORY AND PRACTICE OF POWER USE

In order to examine the ways in which power is used, the bases of power—reward, coercion, referent, expert, legitimate, and informational—will now be considered. These are briefly described in Box 2.

The interplay of sex-role expectations and opportunities can be illumi-

Box 2   Bases of Social Power

Power Type:	Influencer Has:
Reward	Ability to provide positive sanctions or rewards
Coercion	Ability to provide negative sanctions or punishments
Referent	Similarity and likableness which lead to identification
Expert	Superior knowledge or skills and trustworthiness
Legitimate	The right to influence based on position, prior obligation of others or helplessness
Informational	Ability to provide explanation for why it would be to the other's benefit to change

SOURCE: Adapted from Raven, 1965.

nated by imagining each type of power as it is actually used in a *real* relationship between two people. Imagine, for example, a student who is studying and a neighbor who is playing a stereo so loud that it is distracting the student. Would male and female students be likely to use different power bases to influence the offending person to turn down the volume? In what different styles would males and females use the power? Are there expected or actual sex differences in these kinds of power use?

Reward and Coercion

The student could attempt to solve the loud stereo problem by threatening to turn her or his own stereo on at 3:00 A.M. (coercion) or promise to pay for the neighbor to go to the movies (reward).

Reward power is power based on giving the other person something valued in return for compliance. Thus, to effectively employ reward power, the influencer must have resources and the confidence to use them. Reward power is an effective power base which can be used directly or indirectly. Coercion involves the withdrawal of rewards or threat of punishment for noncompliance. Coercion is effective only if the person attempting to carry out the threat has the power to actually do so. Thus, coercion is often used by mothers over children, employers over employees, or husbands over wives (see Box 3).

Both reward and coercive power are generally considered to be types of influence more commonly used by men than women, and use of these power bases is considered masculine. For example, in one study students were asked to imagine that they were to present one of two topics to a class. A classmate would present the other. One topic was interesting and one was boring; one presentation was to be in four days and one in two weeks. The hypothetical teacher leaves it up to them to decide who will do which topic and when. The student then gets one of several possible messages from the classmate

Box 3   Wife Abuse: An Example of Physical Coercion

Physical violence or the threat of such violence is one form of coercive power that men exercise over women. Although cases of wife-beating are often guarded secrets, more and more attention is being given to the problem of women who are suffering such abuse and who cannot easily leave their marriages—either because of lack of money and alternative housing or fear of reprisal (Pagelow, 1977). Although there are various theories about why men beat their wives, much of the data suggests that these men use coercive power either because they do not know how to use other forms of power or they choose not to (Frieze, 1977).

trying to influence her or him to do the more boring topic. For example, two messages were, "If you do not do the more boring topic, I will speak at the later date" (coercion); and "If you do the more boring topic, I will speak at the earlier date" (reward). Both reward and coercion messages were rated as masculine on attitude scales regardless of whether the sender was supposed to be a male or female (Dunn, 1972). Similar ratings of reward and coercive power attempts as being more masculine have been found in other research (Johnson, 1976).

Along with this data on greater perceived use of direct reward and coercive power by men, one can also look at which power types are typically used to influence males and females. We have norms against using coercion with a woman, unless she behaves too badly. Indeed, research reveals that nonphysical coercion is seen as used by males with males but not females; and reward is slightly more likely to be used with females. (Johnson, 1976). Little work has been done with physical coercion although it is clear that men do use more physical violence than women and sometimes direct this against women (see Box 3) as well as other men. Within the family, more men than women use physical violence to enforce their wishes (Frieze, 1977; Pagelow, 1977).

People can use reward and coercive power either directly or indirectly. Indirect use of these power bases is called "reinforcement control" (Tedeschi, et al. 1972). Using reinforcement control, the influencer does not make an overt threat or promise but uses what amounts to operant conditioning techniques—shaping of behavior by subtle rewarding of desired responses and punishing of undesired responses. For example, many are familiar with the story of students reinforcing the professor by being very attentive when she or he is on one side of the class and unattentive when she or he is on the other side. Soon, the professor spends more and more time on the reinforced side, unaware of how her or his behavior is being influenced. Indirect use of reward or coercion is much more correspondent with sex-role expectations for women than the direct use of these powers.

Direct reward or coercion can also be based on personal resources. Personal resources such as showing affection or giving attention or approval are often stereotypically associated with women (Broverman, et. al., 1972). When a woman does not have the status or concrete resources for influence, she may well influence others by filling needs to be liked or by threatening withdrawal of love. The use of personal reward and coercion is perceived as feminine by others and is in fact more used by women than men. Personal coercion is seen as feminine, but not as feminine as concrete coercion is masculine. Thus, males are permitted to use personal coercion more than females are allowed to use direct or concrete coercion (Johnson, 1976).

By relying primarily on use of personal resources as a power base, it appears that women may limit the sphere of their influence to those affected by the personal nature of the techniques and to those situations in which personal relationships are possible. Finally, this type of power also conjures up the stereotype of the glamorous but evil woman who uses love or sex to achieve power through association with her husband or lover.

Powerfulness is related to the influencer's ability to control reinforcements for oneself as well as for those who are being influenced (Stogdill, 1959). Women are trained to give love and affection and approval to others and sometimes to use it covertly to get what they want. Their negative self-concept, however, may make it difficult to give these kinds of rewards to themselves (Bernard, 1972b).

Referent Power

When two people have similarities and like each other, they may share enough feelings of common identity that one can influence the other by appealing to this identity. "Because we are friends . . ." or "Because we are in this together . . ." are two ways in which a person can attempt to influence another through referent power. The student might influence the neighbor to turn down the stereo by appealing to the fact that they are friends or are both hard-working people, or any other similarity or relationship they might have. Referent power is based on the psychological process of identification, or a feeling of oneness, between two people or between a person and a group. In order for one person to have referent power, the other must see him or her as likable and similar.

Referent power is one base that may be open to a female because she may be similar and likable to an acquaintance, friend, or husband. It would certainly be "in role" for a female because she does not have to be aggressive. She may just rely on her similarity and likableness for the other person to identify with. Referent power is a likely base for female use and possibly more likely for females than males. In one study, when asked to select the means of influence most typical of their spouses, respondents said that their spouses tended to emphasize the fact that they were part of the same family and should "see eye to eye" on most matters. Additionally, this referent power base was found to be even more likely for wives to use than husbands, suggesting that referent power is appropriate for females as well as males, and perhaps even more so. (Centers, Raven, and Rodrigues, 1971). Elsewhere it was revealed that referent power was not stereotypical as either masculine or feminine, and was rated as only slightly more likely for women to use than men (Johnson, 1974).

Because of its reliance upon perceived similarity, referent power is often used by women over other woman and men over other men. However, referent power can be used for any two people who identify with one another—students, family members, professional colleagues. However, sex is a major component of similarity, and professional relationships may not be salient enough to overcome male-female differences. It may be difficult for some men to identify with some women due to the different, if not negative, traits ascribed to successful women, making referent power an unlikely source to be used by women with some men. Thus, women executives and other professionals have difficulty using referent power with male associates (Epstein, 1970). As women tend to devalue women, there may be additional barriers to the use of referent power by women—the requisite similarity and liking is not always found between women. Nevertheless, referent power is one of the few power bases that is readily open to women.

Expert Power

One can use expertise itself to influence others. For example, if the student with the noisy neighbor had some expertise in physiology of the human ear or optimal functioning of stereo systems, she or he could tell the neighbor, "I know best, turn it down."

Men are more likely to be in the expert positions in our society. The use of expertise to influence should, then, be seen as out of role for women. For example, wives see their husbands as using expert power much more than husbands see their wives as using it (Centers, et al., 1971). In addition, expert power is rated highly masculine and significantly used more by men than women (Johnson, 1974). In this same study, when students received a message using expertise from a woman ("I've worked on this sort of thing before"), she was seen as quite aggressive (Johnson, 1974). Thus, expert power was seen as out of role for women and was not used by women as much as by men.

Legitimate Power

The student could ask the neighbor to turn down the stereo because, as a fellow neighbor, the student had a right to request a reasonable noise level in the environment. The neighbor should feel an obligation to comply. In this case, the student would be using *legitimate* power. Legitimate power is the most complex form of power as it is based on one's prior learning of influence norms—rules for who has the right to influence whom. Often, legitimate influence is built into the position a person holds in society, such as neighbor, professor, sergeant, or employer. Thus, for example, the professor has a right to influence a student on some matters. Such roles have built-in power relationships.

Women have less access to legitimate power than men and in fact use very little legitimate power. First, women do not usually hold the formal positions which would give them a right to influence. Additionally, a woman's sex role can override her professional role, making her less likely to choose to use her power (Epstein, 1970). A woman using legitimate power based on her position of authority is rated as highly aggressive by college students

(Johnson, 1974). However, one of the roles in which women do have legitimate power is the role of mother. But, even here, the father may have the ultimate legitimate power in the family.

Another example of the use of legitimate power is based on the norm of reciprocity: "If I do something for you, you are obligated to do something for me." Legitimate obligation (mentioning that it was "only fair" that one person do this because of things the other had done for the person in the past) is seen as highly masculine (Johnson, 1974).

There is a type of legitimacy that is hypothesized as characteristic of females. This is legitimate helplessness (Raven and Kruglanski, 1970), which appeals to the norm of social responsibility. Through helplessness, low-power people can get others to do things they cannot do themselves. A classic example of helplessness is the woman standing by the side of the road with a flat tire "influencing" someone to stop. All in all, helplessness is in role for women since it is considered a passive type of influence and by definition involves dependency, two characteristics stereotypic of women.

Helplessness is indeed more effective for women to use than legitimacy of position. In one study, a situation was set up where a student arrived for a psychological experiment to find a note from the experimenter asking the student to do a task. The absent experimenter was either a male or female as evidenced by various articles in the room and either made a straight legitimacy request relying on position or a helplessness request in the note left on the door. The female was more successful with the helpless request than with a legitimate request. Males were more successful with either request, and more successful than the legitimate female. A helpless female was only slightly more successful than a helpless male. So it seems that helplessness does work for women, at least in the short run, and that using legitimate position is out of role for females, even for those in a position to use it (Gruder and Cook, 1971). Even though helplessness is typically perceived as a feminine means of gaining power, it is still acceptable for males to use (Johnson, 1974). For example, males appear to be especially helpless in the kitchen or when attempting traditional feminine tasks.

While the use of helplessness may be successful in the short run, it is hypothesized to have the consequences of maintaining the influencer in a low power position and in fact lowering self-esteem even though being successful (Raven and Kruglanski, 1970). It does not build up a continuing influence base for the person who uses it. If a woman uses helplessness, she often cannot use any of the other powers because she has, in effect, admitted that she is weak, or knows nothing.

Informational Power

Another way to influence people is to say *why* they should do something. If the information seems sound, and the influencer is seen as credible, then they may be persuaded. This kind of power is called *informational* power. It differs from expert power in that the influencer does not just say she or he knows best, but explains why. The influencer attempting to use reward or coercion may inform the other about gains or losses that may come from following or not following the advised course of action. However, people using these

Box 4

The following example of one result of differing expectations for power use by males and females is called "the doctor-nurse game":

> The medical resident on hospital call is awakened by telephone at 1:00 a.m. because a patient on a ward, not his own, has not been able to fall asleep. Dr. Jones answers the telephone and the dialogue goes like this:
>
> "This is Dr. Jones," (an open and direct communication)
>
> "Dr. Jones, this is Miss Smith on 2W. Mrs. Brown, who learned today of her father's death, is unable to fall asleep." (This message has two levels. Openly, it describes a set of circumstances, a woman who is unable to sleep and who that morning received word of her father's death. Less openly, but just as directly, it is a diagnostic and recommendation statement; i.e., Mrs. Brown is unable to sleep because of her grief and she should be given a sedative. Dr. Jones, accepting the diagnostic statement and replying to the recommendation statement, answers:)
>
> "What sleeping medication has been helpful to Mrs. Brown in the past?" Dr. Jones, not knowing the patient, is asking for a recommendation from the nurse, who does know the patient, about what sleeping medication should be prescribed. Note, however, his question does not appear to be asking her for a recommendation. (Miss Smith replies:)
>
> "Pentobarbital mg 100 was quite effective night before last." (A disguised recommendation statement. Dr. Jones replies with a note of authority in his voice:)
>
> "Pentobarbital mg 100 before bedtime as needed for sleep; got it?" (Miss Smith ends the conversation with the tone of grateful supplicant:)
>
> "Yes, I have, and thank you very much doctor."

In this example, the nurse is expected to communicate a recommendation without appearing to do so. She must, according to the norms, take an indirect, manipulative approach so as not to challenge the authority of the doctor as a male and as a physician. She knows what should be prescribed, but it is contrary to her role as a nurse and as a woman to be direct about it. Nurses are, in fact, taught how to mask their power of having exclusive information. We can also see how the doctor-nurse game may be found not only going on between doctors and nurses, but between males and females everywhere.

SOURCE: Stein, 1971b.

power bases also have direct control over the relevant resources. The influencer using informational power does not have control over the resources. So, "If you do not move your car off the railroad tracks, the 7:07 will demolish it," is an example of informational power.

Women do not have access to information to the same extent that men do. They are not perceived as being as logical or as competent as men, and therefore are not expected to use informational power. If a women does have information available, as is the case in many daily, interpersonal activities, then she would be able to use it. However, it would be out of role for her to do so directly. Informational power is generally seen as masculine and used by males (Johnson, 1976).

A woman often arouses hostility in a man by telling him why he is wrong or showing him she has "too much" information. One study (Zellman and Connor, 1973) found that a woman was seen as more negative when she was transmitting information directly rather than when she was presenting it in a more stereotypically "feminine" manner (soft voice, smile, hesitation; see Chapter 16). A male, however, was more positively evaluated in the direct role. The situation was set up so a male and a female gave a speech to different groups of people, each playing a "masculine" and a "feminine" role. The most effective at changing attitudes were the "masculine" roles, but the "masculine" woman was seen as unhappy.

Thus, a woman can use information in an unobtrusive, indirect manner and not be seen as out of role. The doctor-nurse game, described in Box 4 is one example of how it is normative for information to be used indirectly by women.

Personal reward and coercion, referent, helpless, and indirect forms of power were rated in several studies as more typical for women to use than men, but men were not denigrated for using these forms. Concrete reward and coercion, expert, legitimate, and informational power were seen as almost exclusively used by males. Thus, females appear to be restricted to power based on personal, helpless, and indirect modes: hypothesized to keep women in dependent positions and to reinforce the image of women as incompetent (see Box 5).

POWER USE FOR WOMEN

Women who use the traditionally assigned power bases are at a disadvantage in both their personal relationships and the outside world. Yet those women who do not follow the traditional expectations are subject to negative evaluations from others. The "damned if they do, damned if they don't" set of expectations is an example of the double bind intrinsic to female sex roles (Broverman, et al., 1972). That is, if a woman acts traditionally she is judged weak and ineffective, yet if she acts nontraditionally she is criticized

Box 5   How Power Bases Are Perceived

Form of Power	More Associated With
Reward	Males
Coercion	Males
Referent	Females
Legitimate	Males
Helpless	Females
Information	Males
Indirect Information	Females
Expert	Males
Ingratiation	Males and females
False Information	Females
Nagging	Females
Sexuality	Females

SOURCE: Modified from Johnson, 1976.

for acting "like a man." It is important to find power use which leaves women with a truly equal social status and in a balanced psychological state.

Consequences of use of power in traditional and nontraditional ways may be examined in several life settings. Most women are either married or working, or both (see Chapter 8). How power is used in marriage and work are particularly important issues as so much of women's lives are spent in these areas. Other interesting areas for looking at power use are mother-child and woman-woman relationships, but these have been studied very little thus far.

Power on the Job

A woman's position in society may be affected by the way she attempts to influence her coworkers, supervisors, and employees. Advancement in work may depend on her walking an ill-defined line between what is stereotyped as being too masculine (direct, aggressive, knowledgeable) and feminine (weak, warm, emotional). As women take more jobs with titles which connote power (e.g., assistant vice-president rather than executive secretary), the traditional feminine forms of influence may not suffice and other power bases must be developed.

If a woman were to approach her boss to ask for time off or to make a suggestion for changing a work procedure, and attempted to get her way by offering some form of personal reward, she might achieve her immediate goal. In addition to the extent that competence is required in a job situation, such a personal approach may mask it. Use of personal reward power stresses the salience of the relationship rather than the woman's competence. The disadvantages of indirect and helpless power are even more obvious: Through using such "power" one is not known as a person who can present ideas directly, or even worse, one is known as incompetent.

In reality, women may not have much of a chance to be concrete, direct, and competent in their low-status, low-paying jobs. Or, on the other hand, because women are expected to be indirect, personal, and helpless, they may be judged to be competent to perform only low-status jobs. In either case, if women are to achieve more in the work world, their power use and job opportunities both need improvement.

Marriage

Marriage has been defined as an enforced economic dependency which leaves women with a narrow range of behavior and minimal functioning therein. Narrow range refers to limited personal growth and minimum functioning refers to the limiting of women's experience to the home sphere of activities (Reeves, 1971). Involved in this situation is the confounding of emotional ties with economic dependency for women. Though marriage does not necessarily have these results for women, it often happens this way in our society (Bernard, 1972a).

In marriage, or in any personal relationship, both individuals need some power or some ability to get others to do things, if each partner is to have some control over her or his own life and the nature of the relationship. Many situations can be imagined in which husband and wife may need to influence each other. For example, there are some issues that might lead to the use of power in everyday family life (Centers, Raven, and Rodrigues 1971): one partner might want the other to clean or repair something; to change a personal habit; to see a doctor; to go somewhere on an outing; to change the television channel. In each case the first partner will look for a way to influence the other. In addition to these daily power uses, there are larger decisions and long-range goals.

In marriage one can find both normative (rule-following) relationships and spontaneous relationships that may even be counternormative. The traditional rule in our society is that the husband has the right to make most decisions in most areas of family life (Wolfe, 1959). In some countries this norm is part of the legal code. Italy, for example, in 1975, replaced a century-old law that gave the husband the right to make all key decisions in the family with a new law giving wives full legal equality with their husbands. Custom, however, may take longer to change. But in Italy as well as here, the wife may in some cases actually be the more powerful member of the family due to individual characteristics regardless of norms. Such wife-dominant marriages are in the minority, as are true egalitarian marriages (Bernard, 1972a). Most of the dominance-versus-egalitarian classification made by the researchers who report these results are based on who in the marriage makes decisions, who initiates ideas, who receives most agreement, and who participates most in discussions. Commentators on this research have noted that these measures do not make clear the concepts of egalitarianism or dominance, and what is needed is the conceptualization of the processes by which power is exercised (Bernard, 1972a; Zelditch, 1964). Hopefully, these processes would tell us more about the ability of women to achieve full function and range.

The concepts of direct-versus-indirect, personal-versus-concrete, and helpless-versus-competent power, along with the six power bases, are a step toward such a conceptualization. Norms alone do not produce nonegalitarian marriages; how the norms are acted out is even more important. Thus, the women who seek to mask their power (consciously or nonconsciously) by using it indirectly, by helplessness, and by personal appeal may reinforce dependency or threaten a relationship.

Box 6   Using Power Effectively

Smoke gets in your lungs: You are at a public meeting in a large room. A man enters the room and sits down next to you, puffing enthusiastically on a large cigar. The smoke is very offensive to you.

Alternative Responses:
A. You suffer the offensive smoke in silence, deciding it is the right of the other person to smoke if he wishes.
B. You become very angry, demand that he move or put out the cigar and loudly assail the evils and health hazards of the smoking habit.
C. You firmly but politely ask him to refrain from smoking because it is offensive to you, or to sit in another seat if he prefers to continue smoking.

The first alternative is an example of a submissive response; the second is an overly aggressive response; the third is an assertive response. The assertive response (C) is more effective in the long run, since it is not as likely to anger or hurt the other person and provides a direct informational approach, along with implicit legitimate power (norms of our society stress that we should not make others uncomfortable if we can easily avoid it). Response (A) allows for no relief of the offensive situation, while response (B) relies upon coercive power but lacks the underlying power base which is necessary for the effective use of coercive power.

SOURCE: Alberti and Emmons, 1974.

Changing Power Relationships

What then should a woman do in work or marriage if she wants to express her own needs, get her own way some of the time, and maintain good relationships with the people involved? The direct use of informational, expert, legitimate, reward, and coercive methods may lead to conflict and perception of the woman as aggressively out of role. Yet types of power that do not show strength may leave their users in low-power positions or may even backfire (see Box 6).

For a good marriage or work relationship it seems to be a necessity that there be direct communication, that personal relationships are not constantly changed and used as a means to other needs, and that each individual has an adequate amount of confidence in herself or himself. Conflict may also be an acceptable part of relationships. In a situation in which a woman desires to influence, there may be real conflict of interests and the conflict can be dealt with directly without necessarily augmenting it, but without distorting it into personal terms or putting oneself in a helpless position.

Is there a philosophy of power use without submissiveness or aggressiveness? Such use would be based on the idea that everyone has a right to meet his or her wants and needs, but without hurting others. Perhaps this type of legitimate right can be called human legitimacy, as it is not based on position, obligation, or helplessness but on each human's rights. (Alberti and Emmons, 1974).

16 Being Feminine
or Masculine—Nonverbally

The separation of people in our society into females and males is one of our most basic divisions. At a very young age boys begin to learn how to "act like boys" and girls learn to "act like girls." This difference in male and female behavior includes a whole set of nonverbal behaviors. Boys and girls learn to sit and stand differently, to gesture in certain ways, to use facial expressions more or less extensively, and to occupy space in different ways. These nonverbal behaviors are strengthened through continuing socialization, so that by the time children have grown into adulthood, they think of these actions as instinctual and natural. Many people assume that "feminine" women automatically sit and stand in certain ways, and rarely are these nonverbal behaviors questioned, unless someone acts in a way considered sexually inappropriate.

NONVERBAL COMMUNICATION

We communicate with one another in many ways, both verbal and nonverbal. Face-to-face interaction involves not only words, but also various types of nonverbal signals which modify or intensify the meanings of spoken language. The tone of voice we use and our facial expressions, gestures, and body positions all are interpreted by the people around us. One learns about

Irene Frieze was the primary author of this chapter.

the feelings of others by interpreting their nonverbal behavior. We are consciously or unconsciously "communicating" with others on a nonverbal level any time we are in view of other people or when they can hear us speaking. This nonverbal communication is not communication in the sense that we decide to tell someone something and then do it. Instead, our nonverbal behaviors communicate because our culture and perhaps, to a lesser extent, our evolutionary history have assigned meanings to these behaviors. Thus, if we sit in a certain way or wear a particular type of clothing, other people interpret this on the basis of what they know about us and our culture. We may not intend that others receive the messages they do. Much of nonverbal communication is nonconscious; we do not realize what messages we are sending and others do not *consciously* interpret our nonverbal behaviors. People often respond to nonverbal messages without realizing they are doing so.

There are many channels for nonverbal communication. Some of these are:

Body Size and Shape: Our height, weight, and strength communicate our potential dominance over others. We are less likely to respond aggressively to someone who is bigger than we are.

Style of Dress: The type of clothes we wear can reveal our status in the society, our age and subgroup identification, as well as the type of activity we are engaged in.

Use of Space: People of high status tend to occupy more space and better space than low-status individuals. This is seen very clearly in how office space is assigned, but is also evident even in temporary occupation of space in waiting rooms or other public places. Also, people have personal space around their bodies; how close we sit or stand next to others is dependent upon personal space needs.

Body Position and Gesture: High and low status is communicated by body relaxation. Men and women have very different ways of sitting and standing and have distinctive styles for gesturing.

Use of Touch: Touching can indicate either emotional warmth and closeness or it may be a dominance indicator. By touching someone who does not or cannot reciprocate, we violate the personal space of that person. Reciprocated touching usually reinforces feelings of intimacy.

Eye Contact: Looking at someone within the context of interacting with that person is a sign of liking or approval. A stare unaccompanied by other friendly gestures is an aggressive threat which is universally understood among primates.

Smiling: Smiles can be indicators of happiness, approval, liking, or submissiveness depending upon the context in which they occur.

Other Face and Head Gestures: Nodding, looking up or down, frowning, and other facial movements all have clearly understandable meanings.

Other Body Movements: The way we walk and other body movements appear to be highly expressive, but these patterns have not been investigated extensively by social scientists.

Voice Tone and Loudness: Talking in a loud or soft voice has a very different impact upon the listener, as does the harshness or smoothness of the voice tone and the voice pitch.

Nonverbal communication is possible because of a shared nonverbal "language" in which certain behaviors acquire specific meanings within a cultural group (Faltico, 1969). Within our own culture, some of the most commonly understood nonverbal messages have been incorporated as idioms into our language, as shown in Box 1. The meanings associated with various nonverbal behaviors are probably learned through observation and modeling rather than through direct tuition. People in every culture learn to act in an appropriate nonverbal way but rarely are people directly taught how to stand or smile or use their eyes. Particular nonverbal expressions are associated with specific cultural groups. Part of our socialization is the acquisition both of appropri-

---

Box 1   Nonverbal Expressions in Spoken English

The importance of nonverbal behavior and the general understanding of certain nonverbal "communications" has been acknowledged by the incorporation into our spoken language of many nonverbally based expressions. We all know the meaning of the following expressions:

Use of the eyes	*Costume*
Catch her eye	Wear the pants
Look down at	Dress to the teeth
Look down your nose at	
Look up to	
Admiring gaze	
Look ahead	
Forward looking	
Don't look back	

Mouth	*Other*
Grit your teeth	Sick to his stomach
Friendly smile	Land on your feet
Smile of satisfaction	Run in circles
Stiff upper lip	Keep at arm's length
Bare your teeth at	Get your hands on something
Grin and bear it	Hold tight
	Too close for comfort

ate nonverbal behaviors and of related interpretive skills. In addition to cultural variations in nonverbal expression, there may also be some universally understood nonverbal behaviors. Certain dominance behaviors such as the direct stare are understood as aggressive gestures not only by people from diverse cultural backgrounds, but also by our primate cousins. Other nonverbal signals, such as smiling, are also understood cross-culturally (Ekman, 1973; Hall, 1959).

Although nonverbal behaviors have commonly understood meanings, one must remember that nonverbal cues always occur within a particular context. Just as words and phrases must be considered in context for full understanding, so must any nonverbal sign. In some cases, for example, a smile is a gesture of warmth and liking, while in others it may represent ridicule or anger. Eye contact may be friendly if it occurs within conversation but a stare usually invites aggression or withdrawal.

In general, nonverbal channels of communication are of major importance for perceiving emotion (Auger, 1969). Experimental studies have demonstrated that when films of people participating in normal conversations are shown without soundtracks, raters are highly accurate at judging the emotions portrayed in the film (Faltico, 1969). Even though most people rely extensively upon nonverbal behavior to understand emotions, people do differ in their ability to interpret the nonverbal messages of others; this process is known as decoding. Similarly, some people encode or express their feelings nonverbally more clearly than others do (Buck, et al., 1972; Gitter, Black, and Mostofsky, 1972; Zuckerman, et al., 1975).

SEX DIFFERENCES IN NONVERBAL BEHAVIOR

Nonverbal patterns of behavior differ not only from culture to culture, but also between groups within a culture (Goffman, 1967; Hall, 1959). Various ethnic groups within the United States have unique patterns of displaying affection or demonstrating emotional feeling. Older people and children may act differently than adults between the ages of twenty and sixty. With all these variations, it is not surprising that women tend to show consistent patterns of nonverbal behavior which are not shared by men. This chapter will focus on these differences and will attempt to analyze the resulting nonverbal messages being communicated by women and men.

Two major types of nonverbal messages are those indicating dominance or status and those communicating emotional warmth and expressiveness. These seem to be of particular relevance for the study of sex differences, since these are the types of nonverbal behavior which most clearly differentiate men and women (Frieze and Ramsey, 1976.) Men are generally more dominant and display higher status on a nonverbal level, while women show more liking and warmth. These differences are in agreement with traditional sex-role stereotypes as discussed in earlier chapters. The typical adult male is stereotypically perceived as competent and assertive while the typical adult female is seen as less competent and assertive, but as demonstrating warmth and expressiveness (Broverman, et al., 1972).

Not only are the pervasive differences in female and male nonverbal behavior in accord with stereotypic views of personality differences between the sexes, they also agree with existing power differences. Thus, nonverbal behaviors may serve to maintain and perpetuate the higher power and status associated with males. As research relating to specific sex differences is reviewed, it must be remembered that this data applies only to white, middle-class Americans unless otherwise noted. However, the general implications of these differences may be applicable to other cultures or subcultural groups with similar power relations between women and men.

Situational Effects

Differences in nonverbal behavior occur not only as a function of the sex (or other group identity) of the person, but also as a function of the sexes of the people around that person. There is some informally gathered evidence that women behave in less stereotyped and more "masculine" ways when they are interacting with other women, especially women friends, than they do when there are men present (Bardwick, 1971; DeBeauvoir, 1952). Conversely, sex differences are maximized when flirtatious or sexually motivated behavior is occurring. For example, women seem to smile less when with other women than when with men in whom they are sexually interested.

Although women seem to be more likely to behave "in role" with men, we are not certain when men display "masculine" nonverbal behavior. Some men are certainly most "masculine" in all their behavior when with other men. They are likely to be aggressive and to display high-status or dominant behaviors when with men. However, these behaviors may be even more typical of men in mixed-sex groups. Some men report being able to display their tender, affectionate, and dependent feelings only in the presence of women. However, other men say they feel ill at east and uncomfortable expressing any deep feelings when interacting with women.

Since formal studies have not systematically investigated situations which maximize and minimize sex-role–related nonverbal behaviors, we do not know how the majority of men (or women) act in the company of different groups of people. One hypothesis is that studies will show sexual interest to be an important element in producing highly "feminine" and "masculine" behavior. Men and women who are attracted to one another will tend to act in the most conventionally "masculine" or "feminine" ways. Some recent research suggests that both sexes perceive themselves as less stereotypically feminine or masculine when in the presence of members of the other sex (Ruble and Higgins, 1976). However, sexual interest was not manipulated in these studies. Also, the relative status of men and women may be important for understanding apparent sex differences in mixed sex groups. Behavior in general is more formal and stereotyped when people of different statuses make up a group than when all the group members are peers. Since men and women have generally differed in their levels of power and status, these differences may interact with the sexual composition of various groups. People of higher status are more relaxed in a group situation when lower-status people are present (Mehrabian, 1972). This would suggest that men would appear more relaxed than women in mixed-sex groups.

DOMINANCE AND HIGH STATUS

Use of Space

One of the clearest nonverbal messages of dominance or high status is the use of space. Space in the form of territory is associated with high-status individuals. Larger and better space is associated with higher status and power. This is seen in the fact that job promotions often mean receiving a bigger or more pleasant office. Also, within public places, people who frequently occupy a certain chair or other space come to think of it as their own and resist violations through stares and other aggressive gestures (Goffman, 1967). In the home, space in the den is frequently associated with the father while the kitchen is more often associated with the mother. Children think of their bedrooms as belonging to themselves and may even have clearly marked areas within shared rooms.

Territory is associated with an individual and permission is needed for someone else to enter this territory. Knocking with an associated "come in" may be a means of obtaining such permission. It may also be obtained through nonverbal signaling or verbal conversation. Violations of territory occur when someone enters or otherwise uses the space without permission. Such violations are met with verbal hostility or threatening nonverbal signs such as a direct stare or frown unless the other person is an intimate friend or lover (Hall, 1966; Sommer, 1969; Stratton, Tekippe, and Flick, 1973). Public space for which no permission is needed to enter is space which is not controlled by an individual.

Along with physical space in our environment, a given amount of space around our bodies exists which is referred to as personal space. We all have certain distances at which we feel comfortable sitting or standing next to another person. These distances may vary according to the situation and with the people we are near, but within every situation we have definite comfort zones. If we are closer than we would like, we feel uncomfortable or "hemmed in." Conversely, if the distance between us and other people is greater than we would like, we feel overly formal and "distant." Definitions of close and far distances for comfortable interaction vary from culture to culture (Hall, 1966). However, within each culture, four basic degrees of distance or boundaries of personal space can be identified even though the specific measurements associated with these regions may differ:

> *Intimate Distance:* Direct contact to thirteen inches. We feel comfortable at an intimate distance only with close friends, relatives, or lovers. Often this intimate distance is not considered appropriate in public. At intimate distance, we are intensely aware of the other person, perhaps to the extent that they "fill our entire space."

> *Personal Distance:* Thirteen inches to four feet. Although close enough to casually touch the other person at the close extremes, the degree of contact and intensity is not as great as within intimate distance. Personal distance is most comfortably used with close friends.

> *Social Distance:* Four feet to twelve feet. Social distance is normally employed for conversation in social and business situations. The further extremes of social distance are used in more formal gatherings and for people who work together and have intermittent social interaction.

> *Public Distance:* Twelve feet and more. Public speakers and very prestigious individuals function at public distance from others.

Just as territorial violations are met with aggression, so are violations of personal space. If the other person appears to have purposefully come too close, we react by withdrawing or with aggression if the person is of equal or lower status. We allow higher-status people to "violate" our space by coming too close since we cannot challenge their right to do this. High-status or more powerful individuals can and often do violate the personal space as well as the physical territory of lower-status individuals since they need not fear reprisal. Thus, for example, the boss may come quite close to his secretary to give her an order, but she would never come close to him and ask him a question (Henley, 1970). High-status individuals may be unaware that they are violating the space of others but would know immediately if their own space were violated. In cases where close contact is unavoidable, such as in elevators or on buses, we generally respond by ignoring the people around us— treating them as nonpersons.

Much of our understanding of how dominance signals operate nonverbally comes from ethological studies. Among mammals and some other types of animals, a frequent manifestation of dominance within a group is the amount of territory controlled by an individual. The more dominant individuals have a larger space in which to hunt food and/or have greater choice of food and sexual partners within the group. Dominant animals also appear to have larger personal space around their bodies which functions as an extension of their physical body. An animal cannot enter the personal nor controlled territory of another adult animal within the group without initiating threats of or actual violence (Moyer, 1974). However, lower-ranking group members may

vacate their feeding, sleeping, or walking space when a higher-ranking animal approaches them (Eibel-Eibesfeldt, 1970). Thus, actual physical dominance is ultimately necessary for most animals to maintain territory. Within
animal groups, females generally occupy the lowest positions in dominance
hierarchies (Exline, 1972; Hall, 1966). This may be due to their smaller
physical size and their resulting inability to defend territory against the
larger males. It may also be related to the lower aggressiveness levels of most
female mammals. Territorial defense and fighting within the group seems to
be a behavior largely restricted to adult males (Moyer, 1975).

Sex Differences in the Use of Space. There are a number of studies suggesting
that women—like female mamals in general—control less physical territory
than men in our society, and that the personal space of women is smaller and
more frequently violated. Mothers are less likely to have a special room in the
home than fathers, and when they do have a personal area it is more public
and more often violated than the space of the father (Altman and Nelson,
1972). The kitchen is often perceived as the space of the mother, but in most
homes this territory is a public space which can be entered by anyone. The
fact that fathers generally have a chair at the "head" of the dining room table
is another example of their territory in the home. Women, in fact, often have
no private space in the home which is their private territory. Along with the
status implications of these sex differences, this also means that it is harder
for women to do work which requires privacy, since they have no place where
they can work undisturbed.

The pattern of men controlling more territory extends beyond the home
into the business world. Secretarial space, which tends to be public space, is
often women's space, while men usually have more private office space. These
differences may, and often do reflect actual status differences—controlled
studies are needed to test the proposition that even when occupational status
is held constant, women occupy smaller and less desirable space, and are in-
terupted more in their work than men are. This would be consistent with the
general powerlessness of women discussed in Chapter 15.

Several studies show that women also have smaller zones of personal space
than men (Leibman, 1970). When touch is uninvolved and nonreciprocal, it
becomes both a violation of the other person's personal space and an indicator
of higher status for the person who initiates the touch. The higher-status
male is more able to breech the social boundaries of the lower-status female
(Frieze and Ramsey, 1976). Women are more tolerant and accepting of these
personal space violations, especially when the violators are males (Skolnick,
Fraser, and Hadar, 1972).

Body Posture

Another aspect of dominance (or more properly in this case, high status) is
body position and body relaxation. Patterns of how people sit or stand vary

greatly from culture to culture. They are related to the social norms of the culture as well as to clothing styles, architecture, furniture, and the daily tasks people do.

Along with cultural variations, there also appear to be general sex differences in body position. Several positions used cross-culturally appear to be used primarily by women. These include sitting on the floor with one's legs stretched straight ahead or crossed at the knees or ankles, and sitting with the legs folded to one side. Both of these postures serve to keep the legs together and could be correlated with wearing narrow skirts. However, such postures are found even in societies where no clothing is worn. In contrast to these feminine postures, positions where the legs are spread widely apart tend to be associated with men (Birdwhistell, 1964; Hewes, 1957; Frieze and Ramsey, 1976).

Within our society, sex differences in body posture follow similar patterns. Although there is no clear evidence that either men or women sit in more relaxed positions overall, there does appear to be a wider range of possible body positions for males. Women are trained to sit "properly" from young girlhood so that they will sit in "ladylike" ways while men rarely experience the same degree of training (which suggests that male postures are more natural and comfortable). A strong resulting sex difference in body position is that women sit so that their closed legs or hands cover their pubic area even when they wear pants while men typically expose the crotch areas in their pants and not infrequently thrust this area forward. The generality of these sex differences is demonstrated by Figures 1 and 2. These sketches were copied from pictures of men and women in popular magazines, but they have been drawn so as to remove obvious sex cues. These "sexless" men and women in the figures can be readily differentiated from one another solely on the basis of their body positions.

These differences in male and female postures can be interpreted in several ways. Studies with men have demonstrated that men of higher status tend to be more relaxed than those of lower status. Specifically, rigid, straight body and arm and leg positions (which tend to take up minimal space), and learning forward are indices of fearfulness and low status; high-status people, however, tend to lean back and sit in asymmetrical positions which occupy maximal space (Mehrabian, 1971). Women often report that "ladylike" postures are uncomfortable and difficult to stay in. Many women find themselves occasionally sitting in the more comfortable "unladylike " (male) positions and feel they must then modify their postures, especially if men are present. Although not directly testable, it is hypothesized that this monitoring of position and the general lack of comfort of women's body postures are yet another aspect of their lower-status positions. Men are able to sit in their "manlike" positions without a conscious thought and be very comfortable in these positions. The lesser space occupied by women also reinforces their lower status.

Figure 1. Seated posture of women as portrayed in popular magazine.

Figure 2. Seated posture of men as portrayed in popular magazines.

These sex differences in openness of body posture may also be related to sexual attitudes and beliefs (see Chapter 11). Men are seen as more sexually interested and aggressive and are thus encouraged to be more overtly sexual in their nonverbal behaviors. "Good" women, traditionally, have been seen as asexual and are expected to refrain from behavior which might sexually excite men. Sexually provocative postures for women (as shown in magazines like *Playboy*) resemble the open positions more generally associated with men. This may mean that women who do decide to display high-status, relaxed, open postures will be perceived as sexually receptive, if not aggressive.

Physical Size

Another sex difference in dominance expressions is the greater height and weight of men as compared to women. More dominant animals are bigger and stronger, since maintenance of their dominance is dependent upon these characteristics. Physical size may well be a nonverbal dominance message for humans as well. Our language supports this idea. We speak of "looking up to" someone as a way of saying we respect that person. We "look down on" people of inferior status. Also, words like "big," "strong," and "tall" tend to have positive connotations while "little," "weak," and "short" have negative ones.

Although there is presently no specific data on the effects of being tall or short for females, it is clear that most women "look up to" men, a pattern which reinforces higher masculine status. Physical size differences thus create another situation which perpetuates power differences betwen the sexes and necessarily means greater physical coercive power, as well as legitimate power for men (see Chapter 15).

Verbal Space

Verbal space is controlled by men in our society. Research verifies admonitions from books of etiquette that women should be good listeners and encourage men to speak. Men talk more in two-person groups than women, and women in mixed sex groups have trouble getting the group's attention. Women are also interrupted more by men (Bernard, 1972b; Frieze and Ramsey, 1976; Hirschman, 1973). The higher-pitched quality of women's voices may also imply that they are perceived as being more emotional and are taken less seriously in group discussions (Frieze and Ramsey, 1976).

Other Dominance Indicators

All of this suggests a general pattern for men to display dominance and higher status in their nonverbal behavior as compared to women. There may very well be sex differences in other dominance indicators also, but these have not yet been systematically researched. For example, a direct stare is a dominance indicator often used to defend against territorial or other nonverbal violations (Duncan, 1969). Informal evidence suggests that men are more likely to stare at women than women at men. When done by women, staring may be perceived as sexual aggressiveness rather than simple dominance assertion. A student who tried staring at men as part of a class experiment reported that several of her targets thought she was a prostitute. Thus, as with body posture, looking away or downward (submissive response) may be considered appropriate feminine nonverbal behavior but at the same time communicate low status. Violating this norm does not always bring the perception of high status for the "masculine" woman however.

NONVERBAL COMMUNICATION OF EMOTION

Perhaps because of their biological nurturing roles, both human and nonhuman primate females demonstrate nonverbal indicators of liking and warmth more than males. People demonstrate their liking for one another through eye contact and smiling, as well as through their receptiveness to the needs of people they care about. In some ways, however, even these nonverbal behaviors may also be manifestations of lower status. As suggested earlier (see Chapter 15), the apparently greater warmth and expressiveness of women may be due in some cases to the necessities of their submissive roles. Such behavior may reflect attempts of women to gain power in the indirect ways allowed to them.

Eye Contact

Eye contact within the context of verbal conversation is interpreted by others as an indication of attentiveness or liking or a request for feedback (Argyle, 1967; Libby and Yaklevich, 1973). Along with these emotional warmth interpretations of holding eye contact, there may also be a status interpretation, since higher-status individuals display less direct eye contact than lower-status individuals (Exline, 1972).

As might be expected, women display more social eye contact than men do, although both sexes look more at persons of the same sex than at those of the opposite sex in experimental settings (Argyle, 1967; Argyle and Dean, 1965; Exline, 1963; Mehrabian, 1971). Cross-sex looking may be higher when there is a desire to indicate sexual attraction.

These sex differences in eye contact are often seen as indicative of a greater interest for women in the expression of affection and inclusion within a relationship (Russo, 1975). According to one study length of gaze may be a better indicator of intimacy than the amount of eye contact (Argyle, 1967). Taking this into account, women consistently show both greater amount of eye contact and longer length of gaze than men. Again, this may be related to research indicating women's higher affiliative tendencies (Weitz, 1974; Heshka and Nelson, 1972; Russo, 1975). Although data concerning eye contact support the stereotype that women are more emotionally warm and attuned to affiliative factors within a relationship, this responsiveness to the needs and behaviors of others as well as to surrounding events has been suggested in reference to other lower-status groups necessary for survival purposes (Frieze and Ramsey, 1976). Such groups must be aware of the feelings and potential behaviors of higher-status individuals (Goffman, 1967). Act-

ing within the bounds of traditional sex roles, women would thus be attentive to the social information communicated through another's eye behavior.
Research does indeed indicate that women, more than men, show greater
receptivity to the facial affect of others (Buck, et al., 1973).

The lack of social eye contact may also be related to low self-esteem (Frieze
and Ramsey, 1976). Women high in abasement (or low in self-esteem) tend
to look away in social interactions. This corresponds with the general need
many people feel to look away when one feels shamed or embarrassed. Social
experience also demonstrates that it is often a woman who avoids meeting or
holding a man's preexisting stare as they pass on the sidewalk or sit in a bar.
If this nonsocial contact is held, the woman often is the first to look away.
When a woman does engage in prolonged mutual looking, it is a strong cue
that conversation or other interaction will ensue (Cary, 1974).

Smiling

Smiling behavior is similar to social eye contact in its meaning and expression. A smile, however, may indicate happiness, greeting, appeasement, or
approval seeking as well as warmth and liking (Argyle, 1967; Rosenfeld,
1966). Smiling can also represent a buffer against aggressive encounters,
since it can release aggressive tension or soften the impact of hostile words
(Eibl-Eibesfeldt, 1970; Mehrabian, 1972). The meaning of a smile depends
very much upon the context in which it is used since it has so many possible
meanings (Mehrabian, 1971). Women smile more than men, but it is not
entirely clear how this should be interpreted (Mehrabian, 1971). Data
suggests that at least some of the more frequent smiling of women may be attributed to appeasement and approval seeking. Many women report having a
stiff face smiling at a social gathering at which they were not particularly
happy. The ambivalence of smiling for women has been recognized by women's liberation consciousness-raising groups, where a standard discussion
topic is "Do you smile a lot?." The implication of this topic is that smiling
often has negative meanings rather than the positive ones which might be
expected.

Women are seen as deviant when they fail to smile. Thus, a woman's smile
is misleading and probably does not necessarily communicate her true feelings. For example, fathers' smiles at children are frequently accompanied by
positive verbal statements suggesting a generally positive communication.
However, mothers' smiles have little relationship to the verbal messages they
give their children (Bugental, Love, and Gianetto, 1971).

Nonverbal Encoding and Decoding

Women are stereotypically more emotionally expressive than men (Broverman, et al., 1972). Some evidence indicates that nonverbally, women can

express emotions more clearly than men (Buck, et al., 1972). Women are also more able to interpret the nonverbal messages of other people (Argyle, 1967; Buck et al., 1972; Faltico, 1969), although other studies have not replicated this (Buck, Miller, and Caul, 1972). In a study using all male subjects, it was found that individuals who were good at displaying their emotions nonverbally tended to be poor at understanding others nonverbal expressions (Lanzetta and Kleck, 1970). Thus, the data are somewhat ambiguous as to whether men or women are better at interpreting nonverbal cues, but when differences are found it is generally the women who are better at interpreting the nonverbal messages of others. Informal observations support the data that women are more responsive to cues than men in social situations. Women are more receptive to other's facial cues that they wanted to speak (Argyle, 1967). This responsiveness to the cues of others is common for low-status groups as a necessity for their survival, since they must be aware of the feelings of high-status individuals (Gitter, et al., 1972; Goffman, 1967).

NONVERBAL SEX DIFFERENCES: IMPLICATIONS

Research is only beginning to identify the many common sex differences in nonverbal behavior in this society. These continue to suggest that women communicate low status often unconsciously, through their use of "feminine" nonverbal cues. Such behavior, although quite possibly caused originally by their lower status in our society, also serves to perpetuate sex-role stereotypes and lower status for women. Such perpetuation is particularly difficult to confront since so many people are unaware of emitting nonverbal cues or of their interpretation of nonverbal behavior of other people. Additionally, women who are aware of their behavior are placed in the unwanted position of having to choose between "feminine" and assertive behavior. Women are expected to use the various nonverbal behaviors associated with their sex. Failure to perform appropriately is labeled "unladylike" and is reacted to strongly be both men and women (Mehrabian, 1972).

17 Politics and Power

An understanding of the struggles of women to gain political power is important to the study of the psychology of women. The problems women face in the political realm are much the same as the problems they face in trying to find a place for themselves in any other nontraditional area of society. But because politics is such an important and power-laden sphere of life, women's efforts to gain access to political power present these problems writ large.

The efficiency with which a society runs, the goals it pursues, and the values that guide it are largely determined by those who hold powerful positions when important decisions are being made. Since its founding, this nation has denied women, who now comprise a majority of the population, full access to political and economic power. At first this denial was overt: Women were not allowed to vote, were not allowed to pursue certain occupations, and were generally not permitted to serve on juries. Progress has been made since then, but much of it has been slow, and today women are still discriminated against, though now the discrimination is often more subtle (see Chapter 14).

WOMEN AND POLITICS

The Suffrage Movement

Before 1920, women were excluded from any formal participation in American politics. It was not until that year that the Nineteenth Amendment to

Gail Zellman was the primary author of this chapter.

the Constitution was ratified, making it illegal to deny the vote to women. This right was not easily won. In 1848, at a women's rights convention at Seneca Falls, New York, Elizabeth Cady Stanton discussed the need for women's suffrage in America (Bird, 1968). Stanton's ideas were viewed as outrageous by the male establishment as well as by most women. The few who agreed with her formed the National Woman Suffrage Association. This group, headed by Elizabeth Cady Stanton and Susan B. Anthony, began the long battle to win the vote.

Most of the members of NWSA were active in helping with the war effort during the Civil War. This war work increased their resources in a number of ways. Many worked outside their homes for the first time, gaining practical experience and political education. Perhaps more important, the war gave these women an opportunity to earn considerable public recognition and gratitude (O'Neill, 1969). Many suffragists believed that when the war was over, the place of women would be much further advanced than it would have been without the war (Massey, 1966).

In reality, however, women gained little of permanent value from their war work. In particular, women had hoped to gain suffrage along with blacks at the end of the war, but the Fourteenth and Fifteenth Amendments were drafted to extend suffrage only to black males. Women were outraged that

Box 1   Opponents of Suffrage—and Their Reasons

1. Antisuffragist Men and, particularly, Women	Suffrage would defeminize women. It was unnecessary, since women could get what they wanted without the franchise. Women suffrage would not lead to sweeping reforms. Early enfranchisement of women in western territories showed no effect of woman suffrage.
2. Liquor Interests	Leaders of the Women's Christian Temperance Union (WCTU) had espoused woman suffrage to increase the Temperance vote, hence woman suffrage was viewed as likely to lead to prohibition.
3. Big-City Bosses	Bosses feared the volatility and apathy of woman voters. Believed women to be reform-minded and unsusceptible to bribery. Woman suffrage would change the rules of the political game.
4. Southern Males	Southern males had conservative views about women's place. They feared that suffrage would cause women to abandon their husbands and families. Enfranchising women would increase the black vote. Such voters were less controllable than white women.

Box 2   Supporters of Suffrage—and Their Reasons

1. Suffragists	Justice. Women would bring compassion and reform. Women would maintain white and nativist supremacy.
2. Abolitionists	Abolitionists supported universal equality. Since black suffrage had been won, some concern could now be devoted to women.
3. Populists	Support for suffrage would turn women into party loyalists—and such a large number of new supporters would carry the party far.
4. Democrats and Republicans	Depending on the political winds, the parties sought to curry or maintain favor with women.
5. Labor (AFL)	Labor supported women's suffrage when it was tied to equal pay for women. Equal pay would cut down the competitive advantage of cheaper female labor.

the men who had been their abolitionist allies would not support suffrage for women along with blacks.

Women regrouped for a continued and sustained fight over the next fifty years. A major obstacle to winning suffrage, of course, was that women had to be enfranchised by the votes of men. Woman suffrage meant that men had to cede away at least some (and as much as half) of their political control, and groups who profited by the old system, such as the liquor interests and the big-city bosses, had to risk the effects of a doubling of the electorate (Morgan, 1971). Women had to persuade men that neither they nor society would suffer, and perhaps both might benefit, from woman suffrage.

The opponents of suffrage were many, and their reasons were varied and often contradictory (see Box 1). Suffragist arguments evolved and changed over the course of the fight. Some of their arguments are shown in Box 2. The soundest argument, and the first used, was that to deny women the vote in a free country solely because of their sex was undemocratic, unjust, and unconstitutional (O'Neill, 1969). This proposition, though morally and logically sound, failed to adequately arouse the public to action. Hence, suffragists began to attribute functional values to the ballot—they began to promise innumerable benefits and reforms to society if women got the vote.

This linkage between the vote and reform began to dominate suffragist propaganda, and the "justice" argument took a back seat to arguments of expediency and tactics of pragmatism which were often totally devoid of principle (Kraditor, 1968). Instead of arguing that women were entitled to the vote, suffragists said, "you need us to further your aims." In the South, the argument appealed to racist fears: "since there are more white women in the South than blacks of both sexes, woman suffrage will help to maintain white supremacy" (Stimpson, 1972). In the East, however, the same type of argument worked against woman suffrage. Native-born Americans of both sexes were concerned about the enormous influx of immigrants, which reached new heights in the 1880s. Many opposed woman suffrage on the grounds that it would greatly expand the "ignorant vote." A number of prominent suffragists turned away from earlier suffragist principles of universal suffrage to argue for the enfranchisement of women *and* the requirement of a literacy test. In this way could American men save themselves from alien domination (O'Neill, 1969).

Women made little or no progress between 1869 and 1916 in the East; but in the West, women's political rights were expanding along with the frontier. In 1869, the territory of Wyoming granted women full suffrage. Wyoming women did not fight for suffrage—it was a "gift" from men (Cheney, 1973). The reasons were largely pragmatic and political and had little to do with issues of equality. The Democratic-controlled territorial legislature hoped that woman suffrage would stimulate migration of women to female-poor Wyoming. At the same time, many saw woman suffrage as a joke and assumed the Republican governor would veto the bill. But he did not. He felt that if a Republican governor vetoed a Democratic bill granting women suffrage, it would hurt the Republican party severely.

None of the fears most often expressed by opponents of woman suffrage were salient in Wyoming. Women did not campaign for issues relevant to women. Hence fears of female cohesion were minimized, and there were few women to even worry about. The 1870 census reported 1049 women and 6107 men over the age of ten in the territory of Wyoming. This situation led *Harper's Weekly* to declare:

> Wyoming gave women the right to vote in much the same spirit that New York or Pennsylvania might vote to enfranchise angels.

Similar pragmatism and politics led to suffrage in other western territories: in Utah it was hoped that Mormon power against Gentile immigrants would be strengthened by enfranchising women; in Colorado and Idaho the appearance of the Populist Party split Democrats and Republicans. The Populists supported suffrage in part because they hoped (wrongly, it turned out) to attract grateful women to their party (Morgan, 1971; O'Neill, 1969).

As the number of enfranchised women grew, women in other states brought increased pressure on their own state legislators to support state suffrage amendments. They argued that suffrage in the West had brought none of the problems or tragedies that led people to oppose suffrage. Suffrage was fought and won state by state until, in 1916, women had full suffrage in eleven states west of the Mississippi. Carrie Chapman Catt, a leading suffragist, was convinced that now was the time for a federal amendment drive.

Her plan called for the piling up of state victories until their cumulative effect forced the passage of the Nineteenth Amendment. In less than three years the number of presidential electors for whom women could vote jumped from 91 to 339 (NAWSA, 1940). Women used their suffrage to force the passage of the Nineteenth Amendment. In 1920, the Nineteenth Amendment to the U.S. Constitution, which granted full voting rights to women, was ratified after nearly a century of hard work, protest, and personal suffering.

Using Their Power

With the ratification of the Nineteenth Amendment, all women had the right to vote and the potential power that came with the franchise. But women's potential power had to be converted into actual power before women would be a viable political force. For this to happen, women had to be perceived as a unified group by others and especially by themselves; and they, as a group, had to be represented in law-making bodies, government agencies, and political-party structures. But, to achieve representation, the vote had to be used, and few women actually voted. In 1920, the first presidential election in which women had the franchise, only 43 percent of eligible women voted. In the 1924 presidential election, the percentage of eligible women voting had declined to 35 percent. Clearly, women were not going to the polls in large numbers. Over the years, the percentage of eligible women voting has gradually increased. By 1968, the percentage difference between eligible males and females going to the polls had dropped so that more women than men voted for the first time. Since then, the percentage difference has decreased in each presidential election. By 1976 the percentage difference between male and female turnout was less than 1 percentage point, which meant that women cast 53 percent of the ballots in 1976.

To gain power, voting in superior numbers is not enough. The vote has to be used in a way that creates a political power base for the group in question. For this to occur, group members have to be unified on crucial issues, pressure has to be applied to decision-makers at all levels, and group leaders who will articulate and push through group demands must be found and strongly supported. Without such a power base, the franchise remains only a potential resource and not a source of real power (Schattschneider, 1960).

Political Office

Until very recently, women did not perceive themselves as a political force and were not so perceived by others. The most striking demonstration of the lack of real political power among women is found in the huge gulf between their percentage as voters and their tiny representation in elective offices at the national level. In the Ninety-third Congress, there were only 16 women in the House of Representatives and 418 men; in the Senate there were no women at all. The elections of 1974 were described as "a feminist breakthrough" and, indeed, women gained 27 percent more elective offices. However, the Ninety-fourth Congress was comprised of only 18 women—a net gain of 2. In the Ninety-fifth Congress, seventeen women held House seats. The sole woman member of the Senate—Muriel Humphrey—was appointed to finish the term of her late husband. This record of "success" for women politicians on the national level has been as poor in the past as it is in the present. In the half-century since women have had the vote, fewer than 100 women have been members of the House of Representatives and the Senate.

Status of Women Politicians

The political power of a group can also be measured by criteria other than the percentage who hold office at a given level of government. Another important criterion is the power held by group members who do hold office. Power in Congress depends on committee assignments. The ability and opportunity to initiate and amend legislation, call for hearings and budget appropriations is substantially reduced if one is assigned to low-ranked committees. Congressional seniority is closely associated with the most powerful and otherwise desirable committee assignments, though this is changing to some extent. Women tend not to remain long in office. In the Ninety-fifth Congress, only four of the nineteen women House members had served more than two terms. Yet it is widely believed that at least four or five terms are necessary to gain enough power to be an effective legislator (Amundsen, 1971). Thus, it is not surprising that women representatives have, over the years, been assigned to the lesser-status committees (Gehlen, 1969).

The reason for women representatives' brief tenure in Congress stems in large part from the manner in which they are recruited. Nearly half of the women who have served in Congress stepped in to fill a seat vacated by the death of their husbands. They were chosen to capitalize on a sympathy vote or to perpetuate their former husband's policies. They typically lacked any direct political experience or ambition and were motivated by loyalty to their late husbands and their husbands' parties. As soon as an appropriate male successor could be found, most were willing and often glad to step down. In fact, 55 percent of these widows retired upon completion of their husbands' terms (Amundsen, 1971; Bullock and Heys, 1972; Gruberg, 1968).

In the Federal government, power also resides in the executive and judicial branches, especially at the top levels where women are noticeably absent. Since women received the vote, only a few have held cabinet rank, and none have reached the highest levels of the judicial branch (Amundsen, 1971). In the Civil Service system few women are found in policy-making positions. In 1972, less than 2 percent of the employees in each of the top ranks—grades

16 throughout 18—were women (Lepper, 1974). The situation is much the same at the state and local levels of government. Few women have been elected governor of a state since women got the vote in 1920. Of these, only two, Ella Grasso of Connecticut and Dixie Lee Ray of Washington won governorships entirely on their own merits. Several owed their election directly to men:

1. "Ma" Ferguson of Texas (1924–1926, 1932–1936) ran for governor because her husband, a former governor, had been impeached and was therefore not eligible to run again. She offered "two governors for the price of one" (U.S. Civil Service Commission, 1967).
2. Nellie Tayloe Ross ran for the governorship of Wyoming in 1925 to fill the position left vacant by the death of her husband. She did no campaigning at all and presumably was elected on a tide of sympathy and some skill on the part of her campaign manager, a man (Gruberg, 1968).
3. Lurleen Wallace of Alabama ran for the governorship in 1966 because the Alabama Constitution did not permit her husband to seek another consecutive term as governor. It was made clear from the beginning of the campaign that a vote for Lurleen was really a vote for her husband. Her slogan was "Let George do it."

While many politicians are elected to office on the coattails of others, the election of women to fill the seats of their living but ineligible husbands is a unique phenomenon. It involves the filling of the same seat by a person of the same name, who pledges (overtly or not) to be a proxy officeholder. The phenomenon of political sons and nephews following famous fathers and uncles into the political arena is not unusual (and certainly bearing the same name helps the process along, witness the Adams, Goldwaters, Rockefellers, Stevensons, and Tafts). Occasionally a son is elected to the same position held earlier by father or uncle. But never has a son or nephew presented himself as a proxy for his father or uncle. Such an admission of dependence would probably spell the downfall of a male candidate. It is because women are viewed as apolitical and dependent that a proxy status would be believable to the public. A female proxy governor would be less threatening to the male power behind the throne, particularly if she were also his wife. Here, female dependence and lack of ambition and wifely obedience would combine to create the ideal proxy governor.

According to sex-role stereotypes of women as unsophisticated and home oriented, women are not supposed to be prominent in federal or state politics, but are expected to be more involved in local politics. Women are in fact better represented at the local level. For example, in the late sixties, women constituted 9.7 percent of school-board members in the nation. In the big cities, women constituted 23 percent of school boards (Gruberg, 1968). But even here, fewer women were found in the more powerful posts. At the mayoral level, for example, as of April 1976 there were only fourteen women mayors in the 250 largest American cities (U.S. Conference of Mayors, 1976). This was an improvement over 1973, however, when there were only three (World Almanac, 1974). In 1975 women held 4.5 percent of seats in state senates, and 9.3 percent of state house seats. These figures represented an increase of 78 percent above the numbers of women state legislators in 1972 (Center for the American Woman and Politics, 1976).

POLITICAL VIEWS OF WOMEN

Some women have hoped and others have feared that women would be very different from men in ways that had clear political relevance. In general, suffragists portrayed women as pure in spirit, selfless, and dedicated to preserving human life, in contrast to selfish, power-driven, aggressive men. Recent data show that differences between men and women on political issues do exist, though the differences are much smaller than those promised by suffragists. Because of their differing sex roles, and because of the inferior status to which women have been assigned, women's political interests, views, and values are frequently different from men's.

A survey of the public-opinion literature indicates that small but consistent sex differences do exist on a number of important issues. Although these differences rarely exceed 10 percent, they can represent a potentially important factor, since in our two-party system, the outcome of elections is frequently determined by a 1 percent majority difference of the voters (Lansing, 1972).

Aggressive Policies

Some of the most marked sex differences occur on issue positions that deal with the use of military force and situations or policies popularly regarded as risking the danger of American involvement in war. Consistent sex differences also emerge on the issues of capital punishment, gun control, and punishment of criminals.

In 1965, when the Gallup poll asked whether we should have become involved in Southeast Asia, women were much less likely to feel we should have become involved (Gallup, 1965). Other data support the view that women have strong opinions about government war policy. In 1965, women were considerably less likely to favor continuing the Vietnam war (Gallup, 1965). When asked in 1975 if the U.S. should send troops to any of thirteen different nations in the event of attack by communist-backed forces, women were far less supportive than men. The 2:1 approval by men over women was among the sharpest recorded sex difference in the Gallup polls' history (Gallup, 1975). They were also considerably less supportive of a continuation of U.S. bombing of North Vietnam (Gallup, 1967).

Women's attitudes are remarkably consistent across a variety of items dealing with war. They are repeatedly more likely to oppose it. When asked whether the U.S. had made a mistake in entering World War I, the Korean war, and the Vietnam war, women were much less likely than men to disagree but were hardly more likely to agree (Erskine, 1970). This pattern of less disagreement but no more agreement seems to reflect a reluctance on the part of women to directly criticize past government policy, rather than a lack of feelings about the matter.

Women's "don't know" responses have led many to conclude that women are less informed, or even less able, to form political opinions (Greenstein, 1965). A number of studies indicate, however, that giving a "yes" or "agree" or "disagree" response to an interviewer is no assurance that the respondent has a definite opinion on the topic (Converse, 1964). Often, people are responding to the norm which says that citizens ought to be informed about political matters. This norm affects men more profoundly. Hence, ignorant men may say "yes" (or "no") while ignorant women say "no opinion."

Another aggressive policy that has received consistently lower support from women is capital punishment. From 1937 to the present, women have been from 6 to 17 percent less supportive of the death penalty for persons convicted of murder (Erskine, 1970; Gallup, 1976). Women were also less supportive of the death penalty for those convicted of treason, espionage, and sabotage during World War II (Erskine, 1970).

One might hypothesize that less support among women for aggressive solutions stems from less concern about such problems, or less-perceived threat. This is not at all the case. Women tend to be sensitive to violence and feel personally threatened by it. For example, women in 1972 were more likely than men to feel that there had been an increase in crime in their neighborhoods in the past year. This perception of more crime also had more personal implications for women. Fifty-eight percent of women and only 20 percent of men reported that they would be afraid to walk alone in their own neighborhoods at night (Gallup, 1972). By 1975, 68 percent of women and 26 percent of men reported such fears (Gallup, 1975).

While being generally less supportive of aggressive behaviors, women are more supportive of issues that demand or imply prosocial aggression. Women seem to be more concerned than men with moral behavior and the preservation of life. For example, women were more likely than men to feel that parents who abuse their children should be jailed (Cantril, 1951). They were also substantially more supportive of a law that would jail drunken drivers (Gallup, 1968). Women were more supportive of the police in the abstract (Brooks and Friedrich, 1970), and were more favorable than men to a national day to honor police and law enforcement officials (Gallup, 1967). However, in concrete instances, women are more supportive than men only if the police activity in question does not appear to involve direct physical aggression.

Tolerance for Dissent

Women have been less tolerant towards nonconformists. Though the differences here are smaller than those found on issues of war and aggression, differences are quite remarkable in their consistency across nearly all subgroups of women. Thus, even with political interest, education, age, region, and church attendance controlled, women are less tolerant than men (Stouffer, 1955). When asked whether newspapers should be allowed to criticize our form of government in peacetime, women were decidedly less approving (Polls, 1948). In 1948, women were less likely than men to feel that in peacetime members of the Communist party in the United States should be allowed to speak on the radio (Erskine, 1970).

Women are more opposed to protests and demonstrations than men. They were less in favor of peaceful demonstrations against the war in Vietnam and are less likely than men to feel that people have a right to conduct peaceful antiwar demonstrations (Erskine, 1970). They are also less favorable to people being allowed to organize protests against the government; among whites, this difference held at all income levels. However, there is one inconsistency: When asked in 1970 if they thought that everyone should have the right to criticize the government, even if the criticism is damaging to our national interests, slightly more females than males agreed (Erskine, 1970). Recent data indicate *greater* tolerance among women. In a national survey conducted by NBC news in late 1975, respondents were asked whether wiretapping, searching homes without warrants, or opening of mail were justified in the interest of national security. Fifty-seven percent of women and only 45 percent of men reported that none of these actions are justified. This may represent a change in women's attitudes toward dissent which will become more evident in the coming years.

Emotionalism-Nurturance

The greater expression of feelings permitted of women is reflected politically in greater humanitarianism and willingness to sacrifice for others. Women are more supportive of nonmilitary aid to other nations (Hero, 1968). After World War II, women were much more willing than men to go back to rationing so that the U.S. could send food to people in other nations (Polls, 1946).

This greater humanitarianism and concern for human life is usually ignored by political scientists, when they conclude that women are less political than men. Issues that presumably most concern men (waging war and power politics) are considered political, while issues of special concern to women (human needs for clothing and food, adherence to moral principles) are seen as apolitical by political analysts (Borque and Grossholtz, 1974).

Such views contribute to feelings on the part of both men and women that women have no reason to be active in politics.

BARRIERS TO POLITICAL POWER

What has brought about the lack of political power held by women? Two basic beliefs of both men and women in large part explain women's failure to make use of their potential political power. The first belief is that women's interests do not differ from men's interests, even though the data just cited show that this is not always the case. The second is that women—because of temperament and breeding—are not suited to political positions. There are also a number of more direct barriers.

The Power Elite: Men

One reason why women are not in high-level political roles is that individual males have tried to keep them out. Men are frequently hostile to ambitious women, according to a number of women who have succeeded in gaining political positions (Amundsen, 1971). Women often have to run for office without party endorsement (Lamson, 1968). This lack of party support for women was noted by John Bailey, former chairman of the Democratic National Party: "The only time to run a woman is when things look so bad that your only chance is to do something dramatic" (quoted in Lamson, 1968). Pat Schroeder, congresswoman from Colorado, was told by the party not to run in 1972—"it isn't time yet, don't ruffle the waters." When she did win her party's nomination through a primary fight, the party refused to give her the funds usually given to the primary winner (Tolchin and Tolchin, 1971).

Men oppose the entrance of women into politics for many reasons. One reason is self-preservation. If the number of potential candidates were doubled, their own status would be that much less secure. To many, taking women seriously involves high costs and few pay-offs. It is easier to think of women as having no political ambitions of their own and to see their hard work for the party as a labor of love.

Another factor that may limit women's political power is the belief that women by nature, temperament, and training are not suited to politics. The arguments to support this assumption range broadly, but all point to some inconsistency between female sex-role prescriptions and the characteristics of a good citizen, or the great gulf between female sex-role prescriptions and the qualities of a tough politician. The average female is seen by both males and females as passive, illogical, not at all independent, easily influenced, and not knowledgeable about the ways of the world (Broverman, et al., 1972). This is in sharp contrast to the classic democratic ideal which says citizens should be informed, responsible, and independent (Livingston and Thompson, 1966; Sears, 1969). One would guess that the gulf between stereotypes of the average woman and those of a politician would be even greater.

The manner in which political work gets done is also inimical to the female sex role. Politics is conducted outside the boundaries of the home and frequently outside an office as well (Bird, 1968). Politicians must understand and use power and frequently do so in an aggressive way. Both males and females tend to regard the direct exercise of power as masculine (Johnson, 1974). Women are socialized to strive for and achieve their goals through much more indirect means (see Chapter 15).

Others have suggested that women are biologically unsuited to politics. Not surprisingly these voices have come from incumbents of high political offices. In 1970, a high-ranking liberal said that women ought not be in key decision-making positions because they were subject to raging hormonal aberrations during menopause that could affect their ability to make decisions.

Women Themselves

Although the overt discrimination by men against women in politics certainly contributes to the poor representation of women in political positions, women themselves also are an important factor. Until recently, few women have even attempted to run for political office. This may be partially a result of the fact that women have been legally shut out of politics throughout most of our history as a nation and, therefore, politics has become a totally man-made institution, where norms of conduct and issues of importance are decided on the basis of men's concerns. It may also be due to an absence of role models. Young women often do not consider a political career because there are so few women who are visible examples of successful women in politics (Peterson, 1973).

Most occupations are sex-typed, and politics carries a distinctly male label. In general an occupation that has been sex-typed is harder for women to advance in than a new, sex-neutral field, such as computer science (Epstein, 1970). The basis for sex-typing is generally historical and economic: important occupations are male, less important ones female. A typical example involves the primary schoolteacher. Originally, all teachers were male, because women were believed to lack the intellectual stamina needed to be educators of the young. The shortage of men caused by the Civil War and the growing demand for mass education necessitated recruitment of women. Because they would accept lower pay, women were hired more, until teaching was regarded as a suitable female occupation. Stereotypes about women (and teaching) were then reformulated to explain why teaching was woman's work.

Traditionally, women have tended not to enter professions such as law, from which many male politicians are drawn. In 1970–1971, for example, only 7.8 percent of lawyers in the United States were women (Lynn, 1975). This situation is changing, however. The number of women in law schools has more than doubled since 1965. And the number of women running for political office is rapidly increasing. In the 1974 elections, forty-four women survived their primary fights to run for the House, exactly the number that entered primaries in 1970 (*Newsweek*, 1974a).

Early studies found many women did not wish to exercise their new right to vote, because they considered politics to be "unladylike" or "men's business" (Merriam and Gosnell, 1924). Women today vote as much as men, and are only slightly less likely to contribute to campaigns or attend political meetings (Welch, 1977). But when it comes to the most active form of participation, women are much less likely to get involved. Many women also feel that other women should not be in powerful political positions. In a survey of a large metropolitan area 23 percent of the women felt that there should not be more women in public office (Wells and Smeal, 1972). When asked why, over 60 percent gave no other reason than the cultural myth that politics is a man's role and women belong at home. And in another recent survey, 63 percent of both male and female respondents agreed that "most men are better suited emotionally for politics than are most women" (Harris, 1972).

Probably the major causes of the low level of participation of women in politics derive from psychological factors based on socialization into traditional roles. There is some evidence that women are less tolerant of conflict than men. Men and women support the party system in the abstract to about the same degree; but women are considerably more antagonistic to the idea that partisan conflict is beneficial (Dennis, 1966).

Women are also less sophisticated about politics when measured by ability to place the Democratic and Republican parties on a liberal-conservative continuum (Campbell, et al., 1960). Controls for level of education reduce sex differences at the highest levels but do not totally eliminate them even among the college educated. Research suggests that women's lower level of sophistication may be due to the fact that women are less interested in and supportive of the goals of male-dominated politics—military strength and national and personal power (Borque and Grossholtz, 1974). Others imply that it may be women's lower levels of information that prevent them from developing more sophisticated political reasoning (Converse, 1964).

Women are also uncomfortable with the power implicit in most political roles. While little boys learn effectiveness through mastery of the environment, little girls are more likely to learn to get places by eliciting and engaging the help and protection of others (Hoffman, 1972). Raised to be dependent upon adults, the little girl develops few of the skills needed to deal with her environment and less confidence in her ability to acquire such skills. So she continues to be dependent on others to solve her problems and, therefore, needs affective ties. With such strong and deep-seated needs for affiliation, the female is not inclined to do anything that threatens her support, and the biggest threat to such support is her use of whatever power she has to further her own ends. Power is so strongly "male" that women who have come by their power quite legitimately are reluctant to use it directly, for fear they will create conflict, lose support, and be regarded as "castrating."

Women's nonuse of power to get ahead has been labeled the "sleeping beauty syndrome." This is characterized by hard work, loyalty, and non-complaining. Such a strategy is not effective if one's goal is power and influence (Knoblauen, 1974). In politics, such a syndrome, plus a false sense of idealism, holds political women back from demanding a quid pro quo for their votes, money, and services (Tolchin and Tolchin, 1973).

Another reason for women's discomfort with power is that few have had an opportunity to experience it. Women hold few powerful positions outside the home; and at home, in her women's world, the female has not much more power. Children share a strong stereotype that only a male can control potent resources (Bandura, Ross, and Ross, 1963b). This stereotype may arise from the power distribution in most families—unless she works outside the home, the wife has less power in the family than the husband (Blood and Hamblin, 1958). It may also be simply a matter of the greater physical size and muscular strength of males that lead children, regardless of the actual power distribution in the family, to believe Dad has more. Certainly a wife is likely not to directly challenge her husband's authority, though she is ex-pected to and socialized to try to get her own way indirectly. Thus, fear of conflict, dependence, and inexperience in the use of power act as deterrents to political involvement for women.

Self-Hatred among Women

When society views a group as inferior, members of that group who in-ternalize societal beliefs come to hate themselves because they belong to the group. Often a group member will reserve hatred for other members of the group, by placing him or herself outside the boundaries of the group (All-port, 1954). One way to do this is to identify with the dominant group, share their negative attitude toward one's own group, and avoid close rela-tionships with members of one's own group. In the case of women, self-hatred is often expressed when women boast that "all of my close friends are men." In some cases, hatred is limited to certain subgroups. In the case of women, it is not unusual, for example, to discover traditional women find-ing fault with career women. Clearly, self-hatred leads to little group cohe-sion or support for group members.

The internalization of sex-role prescriptions and the self-hatred that this may produce cause women to stay out of political roles themselves and serves to keep other women out as well. Many men believe women do not belong in politics, and a significant number of women agree (Wells and Smeal, 1972). Self-hatred mong women in 1969 was strong enough so that the Gallup poll found that 9 percent more men than women reported that they would vote for a qualified woman for president (Gallup, 1969). By 1971, though, the sex difference had reversed, and 2 percent more women than men reported they would vote for a qualified woman for president. Women are more willing to support other women when their political aspirations are lower. In a survey a year later, 83 percent of men and 84 percent of women said they would vote for a qualified woman who was running for Congress (Gallup, 1970). In another sample, while only 46 percent of the female respondents said they would be as likely to vote for a qualified woman as a qualified man for president, fully 89 percent of the same sample said they would be as likely to vote for a woman as a man for a city council seat (Wells and Smeal, 1972). These findings seem to indicate less self-hatred among women than is typically supposed. However, the fact that support for women decreased as the power of the office increased suggests only that women are sensitive to the sex roles prescribed for them. Women are less biased against other women the more that their behavior conforms to societal norms (Kiesler, 1973).

Lack of Group Identity

As long as many women do not perceive that they have any unique political interests or beliefs that are not being met by male politicians and a male-dominated system they do not feel the necessity for group action. This failure to see themselves as a unique group is the result of both political and psychological factors. Politically, it has been, until recently, difficult for any oppressed minority group to openly work for its own interests in the United States. Additionally, the close proximity of women and men and the numerous statuses men and women share—race, income, class, religion, region—have impaired group consciousness among women. The fact that many of the important issues of the day are not sex-differentiated have led many to feel that political representation of women by women is not important.

Perceiving their interests and beliefs as different from those of men would also require women to act—to take responsibility for their own lives. Responsibility is a frightening prospect for many people, but especially for people who have been trained to see themselves as weak and needing protection. Women have been taught that they can best get things vicariously. Indeed, in a recent survey 41 percent of women and 47 percent of men agreed with the statement:

Women are better off married to public leaders than holding political office themselves; then they get all the pleasure and few of the problems of public life. (Harris, 1972.)

WOMEN CAN BE POLITICAL

In spite of stereotypes and the attainment of few high political offices, women are political and can function effectively at the highest levels of political power. Probably the most telling evidence against the assumption that women are uninterested in or unsuited to politics is the large number of women who do political work. Recent data indicate that women are more likely than men to work for a party or candidate (Welch, 1977). Male candidates know full well that the success of their campaigns depends in large part on a pool of volunteer women who do most of the nitty-gritty work. These women generally do not strive for and rarely are offered leadership positions.

Other evidence suggests that women can do far more than volunteer work. While they have rarely achieved high national office, women have been as likely as men to hold local office (Constantini and Craik, 1972). Many reasons have been offered to explain women's better representation at the local level. Large sums are not required to run a local campaign, and the nonpartisan nature of such campaigns makes them generally less contentious. A number of studies have found that women are more locally oriented in terms of their unsuitability or inability to go higher. Many women, however, feel that they often do not go higher because of barriers created by the men who run the system. The usual ways to get ahead in the party hierarchy do not seem to work for women. Male politicians expect women to work ceaselessly, without receiving any of the rewards (in terms of power, patronage, or support) that would ordinarily be given to men who perform the same services (Tolchin and Tolchin, 1973).

Characteristics of Political Women

The most striking finding of a recent survey of women who held political office at all levels was that these political women were very similar in their family roles to women of voting age in the general population. They were as likely or more likely than other women to be married, and they were no more likely to be divorced, widowed, or single. Nearly all had children. If they worked outside the home, they tended to work in traditionally female occupations. And they were no more likely than women in the general population to report that their parents were very interested in politics.

They did differ in some ways. As is the case for all leaders, they tended to be somewhat older, better educated, and from a higher social class background than the general population of women. But the similarities were most striking. Although office holding is an unconventional behavior for women, their personal lives and roles are traditional (Center for the American Woman and Politics, 1976).

Studies which compare male and female politicians indicate that women differ from men in important ways. In a survey of party leaders in California, differences were found between men and women in family background, personality, and motivations for political involvement (Constantini and Craik, 1972). Women leaders came from higher-class backgrounds than male leaders, though their own current class status was lower than that of their male counterparts. The female leaders came from homes where relatively high socioeconomic status, older American stock, and Protestantism all contributed to a family background in which traditional sex-role typing was less likely. We can assume that these female leaders were less restricted by sex-role training in their seeking of political leadership than other women might be.

Motivation for political involvement varied between men and women. Males were more likely to say they had entered politics to achieve power and influence. In other studies women report that the satisfactions of political work stem from social interaction; men stress the chance to get ahead (Smith and Kornberg, 1970; Merritt, 1977). These findings may reflect both sex-role socialization and past experiences—women office-holders typically have backgrounds in civic and social volunteer work—men are recruited to politics from the professions (Kirkpatrick, 1974; Center for the American Woman and Politics, 1976; Merritt, 1977). There is evidence that successful women politicians are affected and often hindered by sex-role typing. Female political leaders in the Costantini and Craik sample were characterized by self-doubt and ambivalence about their status and were unduly anxious. These factors did not characterize male political leaders, who presumably are free of inconsistency between their sex role and their political activities. Women leaders reported that, as a group, they felt less informed than men on the issues and were more likely to seek out new information. This self-doubt could well inhibit striving and achievement (Constantini and Craik, 1972).

Another study asked successful and unsuccessful *male* candidates to rate and rank the importance of issues, candidate characteristics, and party label in influencing voters' decisions five months after the election in which they had run. Winners were likely to attribute their success to their good, issue-centered campaign, and especially to their positive personal characteristics, and to downgrade the importance of blind party voting. Losers, on the other hand, blamed the electorate rather than themselves for their loss by emphasizing that the voters responded to party labels rather than issues and candidates. In short, winners tended to congratulate the electorate's good judg-

These findings duplicate patterns established in males with high-need achievement—success is attributed to one's ability and effort while failure is attributed to lack of effort (see Chapter 12). Such findings are also compatible with data which indicate that male success on male tasks (and running for political office is certainly male) is attributed to the actor's skill, while female success on the same task is more often attributed to luck (Deaux and Emswiller, 1974). These findings clearly would work in such a way that both winners and losers alike would be likely to campaign again. These general attributional patterns are not as common for women—more often, women attribute success to outside factors and failure to themselves. This tendency would make women candidates—winners and losers alike—less likely to run in another election. Women politicians, already feeling considerable self-doubt and anxiety, would probably have difficulty making the attributions that would be conducive to further achievements or continued attempts to run for political office.

We have already documented the relatively small gains and little power that women leaders have. Even when women do enter politics and attain positions of political power, they are much less oriented towards acquiring or using the power they might have for the taking than their male counterparts. Thus, discrimination in candidate decisions, female sex-role prescriptions, and female "fears" of power all combine to create a dearth of women in positions of potential power, and in the few women who do succeed, few proclivities to turn the potential power implicit in their position into actual power that might benefit women as a group.

Not every woman who enters politics can be assumed to be a supporter of women's issues or other women. This can be explained in part by the self-hatred phenomenon. That is, an oppressed group may be led by people who are not highly identified with the group and who may, to gain points with the dominant group, use their power in ways that are destructive to their own group. While such female "leaders from the periphery" have certainly existed in politics their presence is less likely in the future. Women who feel they owe their election to women are more likely to identify with women. The high visibility of the profession, combined with a growing group consciousness on the part of women is likely to produce more female candidates who feel and are accountable to women and their concerns.

PROSPECTS FOR CHANGE

There are signs of change on a number of points which, if successful, may converge to produce a more equal distribution of political power in our country. Women's level of participation has increased to the point where more women than men are voting. Thus, in terms of power, women have moved a step closer to realizing the potential power that resides in their 53 percent majority.

More women are running for and winning office. There has been an increase in the number of women holding elective office at all levels (*Newsweek*, 1974b; Center for the American Woman and Politics, 1976). Increasingly, younger women are achieving office, which can be seen in a decrease over time in median age at entry into political office (Center for the American Woman and Politics, 1976). Women running on their own are more likely to try to establish a power base for themselves and are far more likely than widows to bid for reelection (Bullock and Hays, 1972). Hence, we can expect to see more women, staying longer, and therefore getting and using more power.

Increased Group Cohesion

Voting in greater numbers than men and having more women in elected offices will not result in political power for women unless this greater participation is combined with some sense of shared group interests and needs. The data indicate that women who perceive discrimination against women are more likely to support other women seeking office (Wells and Smeal, 1972). There is also evidence that a majority of women today perceive discrimination against women in executive jobs and growing numbers of women are sympathetic to women's liberation demands (Gallup, 1970, 1972). However, there is a long way to go before women recognize themselves as a potential political group. For example, only 39 percent of women reported feeling sympathetic towards the efforts of women's liberation groups (Harris, 1972). In a 1975 poll, 46 percent of women favored passage of the Equal Rights Amendment but this was 12 percent less than the level of support from men. Support from working women was much higher than from housewives (NBC News, 1975).

Training in Politics

In 1971, the National Women's Political Caucus was organized in an effort to get women out of volunteer positions and into office-seeking and office-holding roles. The caucus's avowed aim is to increase the participation and influence of women in politics.

The National Women's Political Caucus is trying to achieve its aims by instructing and supporting potential women candidates and policy-makers. Workshops have been offered across the country in campaign techniques and political roles and rules. A workshop in New York City was offered to women who wanted to move out of the "go-fer" role in campaign organizations (go for coffee, go for stamps) and into important policy-making positions (Gerston, 1974). The organizers felt that such a course was unnecessary for men but necessary for women, since male volunteers are automatically given top jobs, while women, regardless of their skills, tend to be shunted off to the typing pool.

WOMEN'S POLITICAL CONCERNS

One way in which women might increase their political participation as a group is if they could unite around common issues. Although not presently regarded as political issues, there are a number of issues which do involve a majority of women and therefore could form a common core for gaining more political cohesion among women.

Child Care

Whether or not we believe the arrangement to be in the best interests of all involved, women are generally held to be primarily responsible for the care of children. In order for a woman with children to be able to work, she must make adequate child-care arrangements herself and must be prepared to miss work or leave early if her personal arrangements break down. The failure to make child care a societal concern means that it remains the individual responsibility of millions of mothers. It places a heavy burden on those who work and may limit the opportunity to work for many others. For example, one out of five unemployed residents of poverty areas reported in a Labor Department survey being unable to look for work because of inability to arrange child care (Keyserling, 1967). Studies by the Bureau of Labor Statistics indicate that labor-force participation among married women is higher among the group with "built-in" child-care facilities, that is, female relatives over eighteen in the family (Waldman and Gover, 1971). Leaving child care in the private sector also means that many children have inadequate or no care in their mother's absence.

Welfare and Social Security

Over three-quarters of welfare recipients in major cities are women. They receive welfare payments largely through the Aid to Dependent Children Programs. Because of a greater life expectancy among women, most Social Security recipients are lone (usually widowed) women. In 1973, the average monthly benefit received by women sixty-five years and over was $145.87 (Statistical Abstract, 1974). Housewives are often unprotected in their later years, or in their own right. A woman who has not worked outside the home is not entitled to her own pension—she must share her husband's. And women who are divorced after less than twenty years of marriage may lose any rights to the former husband's retirement benefits (Seifer, 1973). Hence, benefit levels for welfare and Social Security, and eligibility requirements for such benefits, are a special concern for women.

Employment Benefits

Women constitute the vast majority of part-time and temporary workers. When these workers are denied fringe benefits and vacation leave, these denials fall mainly on women (Bird, 1968). Because women workers are the most marginal group in the labor force, they are expecially susceptible to unfair labor practices. Women have a higher unemployment rate, are paid less for comparable work, and are less likely to be promoted (Rossi, 1970). Even if one were to assume that nonworking women do not share these concerns, the sheer number of working women—31.1 million as of 1970 (Amundsen, 1971)— would be quite enough to have a tremendous impact on legislation—provided that women recognized that they as a group shared these problems.

Protection from Rape

Rape laws in nearly all states discriminate against women. Before and during a trial, the woman often suffers continued questioning and humiliation. The victim is often treated as a criminal: her morals are carefully examined, while the background of the male, including prior arrests on rape charges, is frequently inadmissible as evidence (Le Grand, 1973). This and numerous other inequities result in a conviction rate for rape estimated to be less than 5 percent (National Advisory Committee on Criminal Justice Standards and Goals, 1976). In many states, women are not allowed to protect themselves from rape—the carrying of concealed weapons is illegal.

Equal Rights Amendment

The ERA was written just after the ratification of the Nineteenth Amendment to extend equal rights to women in other domains. It will do so by rendering unconstitutional all laws that make a distinction on the basis of sex. Most of the barriers to women's participation in politics, unlike other areas, are not legal but psychological. Hence, the ERA, if ratified, will have little direct impact on the domain of politics (See Chapter 14).

However, passage of the ERA will contribute to a climate of opinion which enforces new roles for women. For example, it will be illegal to have higher entrance requirements for women for acceptance into special high schools or colleges. Such rules have in the past kept the sex ratio balanced and kept many women out of the best public high schools and graduate training programs.

WOMEN'S ROLE IN POLITICS

Women have been kept out of politics in the same ways that they have been kept out of most other endeavors our society considers important and potentially powerful—but probably more so. After all, politics is directly concerned with power, so that men's desires to keep their power and women's training to believe that power is not within their prescribed sex role are particularly strong barriers to their participation.

It does matter that women are largely unrepresented. Women cannot assume that males who share racial, religious, regional, and partisan status with them will adequately represent their unique interests and concerns. Women should also not assume that their lack of representation indicates that they are unsuited to politics. Here, as in other fields, social expectations have operated so that few women have ever tried to run for major offices.

Change is possible and it is happening. The National Women's Conference held in Houston in November 1977 was an important manifestation of women's growing political consciousness and commitment. The convention, funded by an act of Congress, was attended by 1,442 delegates and thousands of observers. Delegates approved a National Plan of Action which called for passage of ERA, federal and state funds for abortions for poor women, and elimination of housing, employment, and credit discrimination against lesbians, among other things. Recommendations for legislation based on the plan were presented to President Carter and both houses of Congress. Alliances and networks were formed in Houston for future battles. Women learned that concerted action can bring attention and perhaps change. Additionally, many more women are running for and winning offices, though representation at the national level is still slight. What is necessary to gain power for women is an awareness of themselves as group members. Although women now constitute a majority of the electorate, until they use their votes in a group-conscious way, they will not gain power and consequent representation of their concerns and needs. More women need to run for office, and groups like the National Women's Political Caucus are helping to make this possible. Additionally, women, even those in positions of potential power, must be encouraged and trained to use this potential power to further the goals of women.

Part V

Women's Lives Today

18 Making Life Decisions

During the first half of this century, young people entered into their adult roles with less confusion than many have today. Society presented clear guidelines about the appropriate role choices for men and women, and most followed these directives. Everyone was expected to marry and have children. A woman was to make a "good" marriage and subsequently to devote her energies to her children, husband, and home responsibilities. The husband was to support the family and be a father to his children. People could decide who they wanted to marry and had some control over how many children they wanted but, for most men and women, the general life style designated by society as most desirable was accepted without much question.

Generally, people have basic needs for expressing intimacy, nurturance, and competence (McClelland, 1975). The traditional roles outlined for women and men allowed people to fulfill these needs in a particular way. Many were content to do this. Some, however, found that these traditional roles did not fulfill their individual needs. A man might resent his economic responsibilities and see his work as a burden rather than a source of need fulfillment. Similarly, a woman might feel that her wife and mother roles provided her neither a sense of accomplishment nor recognition.

Those who chose to deviate from the traditional roles usually could expect pity or disapproval. Women who remained single or did not have children were viewed as unfulfilled, unhappy, and unfeminine. The assumption was

Irene Frieze and Esther Sales were the primary authors of this chapter.

that these women were unable to find a man or could not bear children. Similar negative opinions were directed toward the married woman who desired to work. She was criticized for harm done to her children by depriving them of a needed mother figure in the home. Additionally, her working implied to others that her husband was unable to support her. Consequently, because a husband often experienced social embarrassment if his wife worked, he would often oppose her efforts to gain employment. Men who did not marry or failed to support their families were similarly disapproved of. Thus, many of the efforts by individuals to restructure their lives in more satisfying ways were defeated or made more difficult by these social pressures. Today, people have more opportunity to structure their adult lives in more personally meaningful ways. Their basic needs can find expression in a greater variety of roles.

This expansion of role possibilities cannot be viewed as an unequivocal gain. With greater freedom of choice comes the burden of choosing from a variety of life-styles that both offer rewards and incur costs. It has become much harder for young adults to make role decisions now that more alternatives are socially acceptable. Instead of being provided with an unquestioned prescription for a happy life, each young adult must take more personal responsibility for choosing life roles that satisfy his or her needs.

This chapter explores the major choices that a woman must confront during her adult years. Basically, these choices involve the traditional set of central adult roles—marriage, parenthood, and work. However, while past generations of women knew that marriage and motherhood were the central sources of their adult satisfactions, contemporary women are more aware of the limitations of these traditional choices. They also realize that other potentially satisfying options exist. Although most women still choose these traditional roles, they are likely to structure these roles in less traditional ways, and are more likely to add work roles to their adult lives.

EXPANDED ROLE OPTIONS

Before we examine the current options in women's lives, we should have some understanding of the social factors that influenced the present choices in women's lives. One critical factor in this trend has been the development of a new attitude about children. The growing concern with ecology and overpopulation over the last two decades, combined with increased recognition of the economic and emotional costs of child-raising, has led many people to question the traditional assumption that children are necessary products of any marriage. Large families today, rather than being held in esteem, are looked down upon by many. Even the assumption that all women should be mothers is being questioned as a result of these changing values. Women today are able to choose not to have children without being perceived as unnatural or sick, and because of improved contraceptive techniques, they are able to implement this choice. Currently, more couples are deciding together not to have children, and these decisions are met with acceptance if not support from others.

Couples who become parents find that the pattern of parenthood has also undergone a change. In the past women spent most of their adult years caring for their children. Today, with women living longer and having smaller families, a major portion of their lives remains after the children are grown. For the traditional woman, this "empty nest" period can be highly traumatic, since it means she must live for many years without a societally defined role (Bart, 1971). However, many women cope with this situation by attempting to find meaningful new roles outside the home. As greater numbers of these women enter the labor force, the idea of married women working becomes increasingly acceptable in this society. Younger women who observe this trend realize that if they are to obtain an involving job they need training and job experience. These women often desire to establish themselves in their jobs before their children are grown. Thus, more and more traditionally married women are, at increasingly younger ages, entering the labor force—the traditional pattern of working only in the home is becoming less prevalent.

Another major change in attitudes has been the increasing rejection of inequalities based on discriminative social practices. Racial barriers were the first to be acknowledged, but this growing awareness of discrimination has been extended to other groups that have been unfairly denied access to equal opportunities. The emergence of the women's movement during the 1960s was both a response to this new social force and an impetus to further change. Its emphasis on personal fulfillment for women provides support to women who wish to seek personal growth through working, remaining single, getting divorced, or refusing to have children. Leaders in the movement often serve as role models who are admired and respected for their beliefs and life choices. Consciousness-raising groups provide social support for women seeking changes in their own lives. Along with helping to change general societal attitudes, the women's movement has also aided in making theoretical alternatives into realistic possibilities. Many legal changes have occurred as a result of its efforts. These new laws have opened job opportunities to women and reduced discriminative practices in financial and domestic arenas. Although the women's movement has been criticized by some for being too radical in the solutions it proposes, it has clearly shown women that they have concrete alternatives to traditional roles. By contrast, some of the smaller changes in roles appear to be more acceptable than they might have been a few years ago. Women are now accepted as workers in a growing number of fields. And although many people still believe that women are biologically suited only for certain types of jobs, increasing numbers of people are reluctant to overtly discriminate against women because of these beliefs.

Another factor in our changing attitudes toward nontraditional life-styles has been a new social emphasis on personal growth (Maslow, 1968; Schutz, 1967; Perls, 1969). There is a general trend toward greater tolerance of nontraditional life-styles. Also, greater public exposure to a diversity of socially deviant alternatives—such as unmarried couples cohabiting or bearing children, equalitarian marriages, and homosexuality—has expanded the awareness of many people, forcing them to examine traditional assumptions about their own expectations for sexual, marital, and child-rearing behavior.

Not only have these more radical alternatives increased in acceptability in recent years, but marriage has lost its idyllic image. Rising divorce rates and increased openness about the problems of marriage have dramatized its risks; some writers are even questioning whether marriage will remain the normative institution for adult relationships in our society (Scanzoni, 1972, Bernard, 1972a). Marriage has traditionally been better for men than for women. Because of this, new role patterns are necessary for the future survival of marriage (Bernard, 1972a).

These social changes have all led to the need for more individualized life planning. To help identify the issues that a woman is likely to confront in choosing her adult roles, we will look at the central role choices involved in fulfilling intimacy, nurturance, and competency needs. After exploring how these needs are fulfilled through love, parenthood, and work options individually, we will consider the issues involved in making decisions about life roles.

LOVE AND INTIMACY

The need for intimacy and love is a major preoccupation of young adulthood for most people (Erikson, 1964). The result of this quest has a major impact upon the remainder of one's life. In the past the search for a love partner was conducted within a rigid framework of social rules, with marriage as the only embodiment of its successful culmination. Women were expected to remain virgins until marriage. They anticipated forming a single central love relationship that would occupy their entire adult life and would define their major role activities as wife and mother. Today the belief in marriage as ensuring happiness ever after as a wife and mother is being questioned. There are many more choices for a young woman to make in her search for intimacy.

The contemporary woman has two central decisions to make in fulfilling her intimacy needs. She has to decide whether or not she wishes to marry, and, if she desires to marry, when this should occur. The recent shift toward later marriages has signified that women may be less subjected to societal pressures to marry in their early twenties, and may use this time to accumulate work and love experiences that will clarify their long-range goals.

Multiple or single relationships, living with or living independent from a partner, sex partners of the same or opposite sex are current alternatives that may be considered as potentially viable ways of satisfying one's intimacy needs. Although some of these options evoke stronger social disapproval than others, none receive the amount of censure or ostracism found in former years. As a consequence, women may be more responsive to their own needs and values and less dictated by external pressures. They may also explore more of the range of options before settling on one that fits best with their lives.

Sexual Behavior

Although many traditional sexual attitudes are still prevalent today, society has become increasingly permissive about the sexual behavior of women (see Chapter 11). In the past, women had little opportunity to explore their sexual natures since this aspect of their identities was shrouded in myth and embarrassment. Clitoral stimulation, self-stimulation, and lesbianism as alternative means of sexual fulfillment are being discussed and explored as women seek to discover their sexual potential. These options, previously viewed as highly inappropriate behaviors denoting sexual inadequacies or problems, now have advocates who publicly expose their advantages over heterosexual intercourse as routes to feminine sexual pleasure (Gagnon and Simon, 1973). While most women still view sexual intercourse as their major source of sexual gratification, many now believe in their right to achieve sexual satisfaction and in their responsibility to actively facilitate this goal through their own behavior. Women are being told that it is permissible and desirable to initiate sex, communicate sexual preferences, and explore new love-making techniques that may enrich their experience. There are still strong moral value guidelines for acceptable sexual behavior, but the range of options has increased and the severity of punishment for experimentation has decreased.

This increased permissiveness in social attitudes, along with advances in contraceptive techniques, has meant that women have more decisions to make about how they wish to behave sexually. Whereas, in the recent past, such evaluative terms as "bad girl," "promiscuous," "tease," "tramp," and "amoral" were used to describe female sexual behavior considered socially unacceptable, such terms are becoming less common as moral standards become increasingly diverse. Consequently, more and more women are engaging in premarital and extramarital sexual intercourse, and a variety of other sexual behaviors.

While many women still continue to reserve sex exclusively for their husbands or fiances, more women are involved in defining their personal standards of sexual behavior morality. Such standards frequently relate to the quality of their total relationship with men, with sexual intimacy contingent on a degree of satisfying overall intimacy. Although these personal guidelines to sexual behavior are often difficult to establish, and can change as a person confronts new life experiences, they may have the virtue of better coordination with a person's overall needs and circumstances. Rather than relying on a socially defined standard for sexual behavior, women are increasingly seeking to understand their own sexual needs and to attain satisfaction of these needs.

The Decision to Marry

Although there is greater opportunity today for women to find satisfying relationships outside of marriage, most women still choose to marry in young adulthood. Marriage commits a couple to an alliance that is respected by society as both central and legitimate. The primacy of the marriage role provides a structure that facilitates the present and future commitment of each partner to the other.

Commitment to a joint future provides a stable context for long-range planning and activities. The couple can share their successes and support each other in their failures. Many people find this interdependence more satisfying than independent living, which requires that a person make choices and experience their consequences without the shared concern of a spouse.

Marriage during one's twenties has some additional advantages for women that should be considered. If a woman intends to have children, she should realize that ease of childbirth decreases during her thirties, with increasing incidence of birth defects. Many women weigh this factor in their planning, along with their desire for a period of time after marriage that is child-free.

The woman who postpones marriage should also consider that she may be reducing her chances of ever marrying. As a woman gets older, the shrinking pool of unmarried men may make it harder for her to find an appropriate mate. In addition, our societal definitions of attractiveness may make her less physically appealing to men after she enters her thirties.

The nonmarried woman may also want to consider the long-range consequences of remaining single. With advancing age she may find herself increasingly cut off from social activities that are oriented around couples or family. If her intimacy needs are to be fulfilled, she may be involved in a series of love relationships with men that can be emotionally taxing and decreasingly rewarding. She may also turn to women to satisfy both friendship and love needs. However, she may have periods when she has no central relationships to satisfy her intimacy needs. She cannot count on the presence of a someone to support her as she confronts the difficulties that continued living inevitably brings. Although the evidence suggests that unmarried women show better psychological and physical health than unmarried men, there have been few studies that examine the consequences of nonmarriage over the life cycle. Currently, few members of our society remain unmarried through all their adult years.

Marriage has other tangible benefits to offer. Sharing a single household is less expensive and less demanding for each partner, since neither assumes the total burden for economic and maintenance activities. Although the division of labor may take a number of forms, it usually ensures that each partner does less work, and has more time and money, than would be possible independently.

What factors contribute to marital discontent for women in traditional marriages? Current literature cites the tedium of household tasks, the absence of achievement rewards, the monotony of everyday life within the husband-wife relationship over time as the most common sources of discontent for the homemaker (Friedan, 1963; Bernard, 1972a). These images of marriage have so dominated recent literature and films that it is difficult to find positive models of a successful traditional marriage.

Modern marriages are more likely to show a diversity of patterns as couples attempt to find a structure responsive to their personal needs. At present, between 40 and 50 percent of married women with children are now working, and the percentage is steadily increasing. This alternative offers many of the advantages of traditional marriage, with the additional benefits of added income and greater stimulation for the wife. On the other hand, this alternative usually results in a greatly increased workload for the wife, since she must now do two jobs instead of one. Also, if the wife wishes to pursue a career instead of a job, she may have difficulties in her career advancement because she usually feels she must put her family first in her priorities (Epstein, 1970; Poloma, 1972).

Another alternative, still relatively infrequent but growing in popularity, is marriage without children. This choice allows the couple more opportunity to nourish their relationship and to attain career goals. They also have more money to spend, since both partners usually work and there are no child-related expenses. An increasing number of couples are delaying their decision to conceive their first child, and some of these couples may eventually choose to remain childless. Currently, childless (or child-free) couples are far more common and encounter less social disapproval than in previous years.

Finally, many couples with and without children are attempting to establish more equalitarian marriages. In the traditional marriage, most decision making and authority lies in the husband's role (Centers, Raven, and Rodrigues, 1971; Scanzoni, 1972). Also, tasks are divided on the basis of traditional sex roles; men work outside the home while women do all or most of the housework and child care. However, the potential contribution of a woman or a man to the marriage can take many forms (Willis and Frieze, in press). In fact, many of the potential liabilities of marriage disappear when the relationship is rid of its sex-role prescriptiveness and tailored to each person's preferences, needs and circumstances.

An equalitarian relationship necessitates an equal weighting of each person's needs and ideas. This can only occur when each partner believes that the other is contributing equally to the marriage. If a partner feels that the other's contribution is greater or lesser than one's own, a power difference (in reward power) is created that threatens mutual satisfaction. A wife who believes that her husband's contribution is greater than her own will not feel that her needs have equal value in negotiation, and will, with some resentment, subordinate her own desires to those of her spouse. If she feels that she is the prime contributor, she will attempt to exert power that may reduce his satisfaction.

Marriage can be viewed as a complex and continuing process of exchange, and each partner will feel satisfied with the relationship only if their rewards are at least equal to their perceived efforts. In the past, women who were dissatisfied with their marriages often felt they had no desirable alternatives. Today, women enter marriage with more work experience and/or education, and have more confidence in their own capacity for independent functioning. If husbands recognize their wives as having options equal to their own, they may be more responsive to the needs of their wives and enhance women's satisfaction with their marriages. Both sexes also know that society is more tolerant of divorce. These factors may reduce their likelihood of people remaining in unsatisfying marriages, and may account, at least partially, for the increasing divorce rate. Furthermore, each partner's efforts to exercise dominance may be tempered by the reality of the other's ability to leave the relationship. These factors may require increased marital negotiations, but may ensure greater satisfaction for each partner as needs are expressed and efforts are made to meet them.

Radical Alternatives

Some people are experimenting with more radical solutions to the problems of contemporary marriage. These experiments involve either limited expansion of sexual behaviors in a traditional marital dyad or an expansion of the nuclear family. The sexual alternatives of group sex or open marriage permit married partners a greater variety of sexual experience. Group sex is a form of structured sexual freedom in which couples meet in small or large groups to openly exchange their spouses for other sexual partners. The expectation is that there will be no emotional involvement with the new partners and that a different partner will be sought each time. Although some arrangements may or may not be satisfying, they do tend to provide a nonthreatening means of exploring various sexual partners. However, this alternative is utilized by only 1 to 2 percent of couples (Hunt, 1974). Open marriage allows both spouses to openly seek friends and sexual partners outside the marriage (O'Neill and O'Neill, 1972). These relationships may be as intimate as either party desires and may, therefore, become a threat to the stability of the marriage. However, they also allow a couple who is willing to risk this possibility an opportunity to experience a variety of meaningful relationships with the added personal growth and individual freedom this brings.

An even more radical transformation of the traditional family structure is found in communal living or group marriage. Both of these alternatives enlarge the nuclear family unit in order to expand the scope for primary relationships and shared tasks. A communal group may be composed of couples and/or single individuals living together in one location as a family. Generally household tasks and child care, as well as the job of economically supporting the group, are distributed among group members. Often these assignments are made along traditional sexual lines, with women doing most of the child care, cleaning, cooking, and laundry, and men working outside the home. However, other groups have purposefully worked to minimize these traditional sex-role divisions (Kanter and Halter, 1973; Tofalo, 1973). Group marriage follows a similar pattern, although the groups are usually smaller. Communes can range from less than ten up to over a thousand people, while group marriages are rarely larger than six people. The group marriage tends to be more intense and more often involves sexual and monetary sharing than found in communes. Both of these life-styles may increase one's possibilities for close and meaningful friendships, but they may also lead to complaints about lack of privacy and resentment over the irresponsibility of some of the members. They tend to be less stable than traditional marriage and often do not provide solutions to women's basic dilemmas about work and family.

PARENTHOOD

While most people still choose to marry, the role of parent has suffered a noticeable decline in popularity. More couples are choosing to remain childless, and the rest are having fewer children than ever before (Chapter 8). It is possible that this trend reflects long-held attitudes toward children that currently are more able to be acted upon as better contraception and abortion have become more available and as childlessness increases in social acceptability. If this is the case, the decreasing birth rate represents a reduction in unwanted births that previously were not avoided because of social or contraceptive factors. Certainly, one seems to hear more expressions of the intention to remain childless, but this change may be occuring solely at the verbal level, as couples feel freer to declare and justify their stance on the grounds of population control, increased marital satisfaction, career facilitation, economic factors, or enhanced freedom.

Today, whether or not to have children is an issue which many couples seriously consider in view of their own needs, circumstances, and life plans. This new deliberation seems reasonable, since the role of parent is the only major adult role that cannot be shed once it has been assumed. Marriage and career decisions can be undone, albeit with difficulty, but the birth of a child creates an irrevocable commitment and responsibility for a major part of one's adult years. No other life decision so strongly commits one's future to a chosen role. Unfortunately, child-bearing must be decided in a fairly narrow time span when the woman is biologically able to have children. In addition, the years between the twenties and forties when this can occur, are also the ages when other roles are still fresh and appealing. Some couples may avoid the complexities of having children because of its short-term inconvenience, only to find that their later lives seem emptier and more routine than the lives of couples with children. Conversely, other couples may fill this time with new life experiences and continue to enjoy their child-free status.

Clearly, children interfere with career advancement for the prime care-giver, usually the mother (Poloma, 1972). Professional women, especially, are likely to cite career interference as a cost of parenthood for themselves (Beckman, 1974). There is also objective evidence that having children decreases a woman's chances of being highly successful in a career (Ginzberg, 1966). Women's increased participation in the labor force means that more couples must deal with the complex issue of how child-raising tasks might be structured to permit continued job involvement for the wife. Although more women with young children currently are remaining in the work force, this joint role involvement is not easily achieved. Although the responsibility for child care in the past has been primarily the woman's, the burden may now be lightened by increased participation by the husband and by external child-care arrangements. In addition these alternatives now have more support within the social sciences; many studies have shown that children of working mothers are not harmed by their mother's absence (e.g., Hoffman and Nye, 1975). Thus, women may feel less guilt than they did in the past if they wish to continue their work but also want the experience of motherhood. In fact, data suggest that children of working mothers have less stereotyped attitudes about women and are more independent (Hoffman and Nye, 1975; Brover-man, et al., 1972).

A final consideration in having children is whether the woman wants to have the children and raise them herself. The rising divorce rate increases the likelihood that married couples will have to consider whether either of them is prepared to assume the child-care responsibilities of a single parent in the event of divorce. Usually, divorce means that the mother will be the single parent (Chapter 8). Also, some women decide to have children without get-ting married. This alternative, although not accepted by many people, has be-come more possible today.

On the positive side, having a child may be viewed as a source of renewal. Marriage and work roles retain their structure over time with relatively minor changes. The birth of a child plunges the parents into a process of growth and change that can be a major source of enrichment. The baby's budding abilities, the child's discovery of the world, and the expansion of the child's sphere to include friends, school, and social groups ensures an ever-changing panorama of experiences. The parents' involvement with their children links them to the future and reawakes childhood memories and feelings from their past. This sense of continuity may become central in middle age when parents die, and children become the only remaining focus for intergenerational caring. Furthermore, children are often a central social contact for many parents during old age.

Along with this sense of renewal and an interest in the growth of the child, women also rated the love relationship between mother and child as a primary benefit of parenthood (Beckman, 1974). Thus, love needs are also met through children as well as one's spouse. Children can also serve achievement needs as one vicariously achieves through the successes of one's children (Beckman, 1974; see Chapter 12).

Since few couples in the past have chosen to remain childless, there are little data on the long-range consequences of this choice today. We do know that childless couples are more satisfied than those with young children during the early years of marriage (Bernard, 1972). However, over their adult lives, women with children report more overall life satisfaction than childless women (Chapter 9).

If one decides to have a child, new issues concerning child-rearing must be resolved. Many women today desire to raise their children in nonsexist ways and to provide opportunities for both boys and girls to explore a variety of alternatives for their lives. However, as discussed in Chapters 7 and 8, this may not be entirely possible. As long as children are exposed primarily to traditional role models in their social environment or on television, they will still tend to define masculinity and femininity in traditional terms.

WORK

An important question for women of all ages is whether they wish to work outside the home, and if they do, in what type of work. A major effect of the women's liberation movement has been to open more jobs to women and thus to greatly increase the range of job options. Although discrimination in hiring, promotions, and salary levels still exist (Chapters 12 and 14), women are now found in nearly every occupation. There are few, if any, jobs in our technological society which women are not physically or psychologically capable of filling (Chapters 4 and 14).

Whatever the field she chooses, a woman can approach her work in various ways. She may work because she needs additional income. As more women get divorced, many are finding that even though they had at one time decided to devote themselves completely to their families, they are now forced to find a job. Other women work to maintain a desired standard of living for the family. For these women work may offer few satisfactions, since the time needed to work and maintain a home may be quite burdensome. Single women may also work out of necessity, but for many of these women work is seen as a temporary activity, something to do until one gets married. In all these cases, the job is seen as secondary to one's major adult roles and goals. Aside from providing needed income it may bring few other satisfactions.

A second reason for working is for personal enrichment. Some women care very much about providing a good home for their children, but find full-time housework boring and unfulfilling. Other women find they need the stimulation of outside work after their children are grown. The completion of their major responsibilities as mothers allows them to seek new roles, perhaps by entering the work world for the first time. A longer life expectancy and smaller family size have had the consequence of greatly lengthening a woman's expected working life, and work-force participation for women aged forty-five to sixty-four tripled between 1900 and 1970 (Chapters 8 and 12). Although they come onto the labor market at an age when employers devalue their contributions, and although as women their job opportunities are more mundane and their salaries are lower than men, they still gravitate to these new work roles. These older women work for many reasons, including: adding to the family income; greater personal autonomy in spending; status inside and outside the family; occupying themselves in an interesting way; meeting people; and having the excitement of being in a contest for advancement (Bergmann and Adelman, 1973). Even though the jobs most of these women have tend to fulfill these desires to a less satisfactory extent than the jobs men have, working does allow them to fulfill these needs better than staying home would.

The wife's decision to work has positive consequences for the marriage and children. Marital satisfaction is much higher for working wives than for nonworking wives during the postparental period (Rose, 1965), and marital conflict is lessened (Dizzard, 1968). Working couples also share decision making, household tasks, leisure-time activities, and experience less decrease in overall marital gratification (Dizzard, 1968; Blood and Wolfe, 1960). In addition, data suggests that a working mother has little if any negative impact upon the children. Rather, the children become more independent and less stereotypic in their views about the nature and abilities of men and women (Hoffman and Nye, 1975).

Women who are working more for personal enrichment, rather than for interest in the job itself, may not be particularly interested in job advancement and may work only when it is convenient within the contect of their family responsibilities (Ginzberg, 1966). Although working outside the home requires more energy and organization for the woman, whe is more likely to accommodate to this willingly since she has freely chosen to work. Such a woman adjusts by doing less entertaining, watching less television, and visiting with neighbors less (Nye and Hoffman, 1963). Furthermore, since her family is first in her priorities, this type of woman experiences little difficulty in her family as a result of her working, but she sacrifices possible satisfactions based on job advancement.

Other women work because they derive more of their primary satisfactions from their work. In such cases, the job might better be labeled a career, regardless of the specific demands of the particular job. A woman interested in her career may be married and have children, but these are of equal or lesser importance to her than her work. She often must work very hard to advance in her field and spend long hours away from her family. Although this pattern potentially provides all the rewards available to the man from his work, it may well be the most difficult choice for the married woman.

For the woman who does pursue a career, there are many role conflicts if she is married or has a family, since her family as well as her work make demands on her time and energy (Chapter 12). Evidence for this is seen in the fact that professional single women tend to be more productive and successful than married professional women (Astin 1970; Rossi, 1967). The opposite is the case for men, probably because the professional man's wife traditionally supports and aids him in his career in a way few men desire or are able to do for their wives.

In addition to questions about who takes primary responsibility for the upkeep of the home and care of the children, there are a number of other types of conflicts which may arise from working. Traditionally, a wife will move with her husband wherever his job takes him, but what about a woman who has a very good job of her own? More and more young couples are deciding to separate and live in different cities under such circumstances, but this option means that intimacy needs are probably not being adequately met if the couple remains married (Gray-Shellberg, et. al., 1972). If there are children, arrangements must be made for someone to care for them when both parents are working. There is also housework to do, in addition to the demands of a full-time job. Studies indicate that working women still end up doing most of the housework (Walker, 1973).

Because of all these difficulties, the emotional support of the husband is enormously important for the working wife. Even in adolescence and young adulthood, women are less afraid of appearing competent if they have a supportive boyfriend (Chapter 12). Although men in general are more traditional in their ideas about sex roles, they have become more sympathetic to women's efforts to change their roles. Consequently, the gap in role expectations between the sexes is narrowing (Pleck, 1976b). Recent studies of men and women show that the same traits tend to be admired for both sexes. These are intelligence (stereotypically a masculine trait), being sensitive to other people (stereotypically a feminine trait), and having a sense of humor. This change in attitude will benefit men also, since it will partially relieve them of the economic burden for their family.

Women must also overcome discriminatory attitudes of employers. If women are expected to be "feminine," it may also be difficult for them to be perceived as competent and assertive (Chapters 14 and 15). Consequently, they may have trouble being hired for responsible positions. Even if they perform well, their work may not be evaluated as highly as similar work by a man, and they may not be promoted as rapidly (Chapter 12). Women must overcome these barriers and learn to be "feminine" in nonsubmissive ways if they hope to be successful in careers. Fortunately, recent data suggest that success-oriented, competent women are not viewed negatively by college students, especially if they express some traditional feminine values. However, these students said that if they were employers they would prefer to hire the women with more masculine values (Shaffer and Wegley, 1974).

As more women choose to work and there are more role models for young women to emulate, we might also expect further changes in women's work orientation. There is already evidence that women are currently entering adulthood with more crystallized work goals, and that these women show personality strengths of competence, independence, and committedness (Gump, 1972; Helson, 1972). As social acceptance of women's work involvement increases, one would anticipate that more women would emerge from adolescence with a firmly rooted sense of self, and with a stronger commitment to work as a source of satisfaction. More and more college women do report that they intend to work all or most of their adult lives (Frieze, Parsons, and Ruble, 1972).

Because of conflicts arising from strong dedication to a career for a married woman, the majority of women, even professional women, currently tend to put family concerns first (Angrist and Almquist, 1975; Poloma, 1972). This means that women generally are not as productive nor as successful as men. Therefore, common stereotypes about women and work are supported. However, within present social barriers, this may be the best possible "blend" for a woman wanting marriage and children. Perhaps with better child-care facilities, or greater acceptance of part-time work, the demands of work and family could better be met.

ISSUES IN ROLE CHOICE

The foregoing discussion has identified the current options available to women in marriage, family, and work areas. As these role sectors become freer from social prescriptions, more women are shaping life plans that reflect their personal preferences and needs. This openness of choice creates new difficulties and responsibilities for women. They may explore a number of different alternatives and role combinations before finding their own best fit of roles. One would expect some confusion and turbulence as women make a variety of tentative role commitments in order to arrive at a satisfying role blend. It is also likely that women will experience more role discontinuity as they adjust their role structure to their changing needs.

If a woman is realistic in her expectations for alternative roles, and honest in the assessment of her personal needs and priorities, the current social permissiveness does offer support for a variety of role choices. Women entering young adulthood today are more aware of having choices to make. This knowledge forces them to examine alternative life-styles, clarify their goals, and orient themselves toward planning for their future. Although many women will continue to follow traditional patterns, they will do so by choice rather than by social imperative. They will also be more aware of the fact that their role choices may need to be restructured as their needs and role demands change over time. These women may more actively engage in long-term life planning rather than seeking ad hoc solutions to their changing lives. Instead of responding haphazardly to situational changes, a woman may anticipate her future needs and prepare for them more realistically.

By setting future goals and actively engaging in their attainment, a woman gains confidence in her ability to manage her life. Furthermore, the diversity of her involvements may cushion her against the loss of any single source of satisfaction. Women who maintain a satisfying role blend should respond less acutely to such common life-cycle events as decreased marital satisfaction, the loss of physical attractiveness, child-launching, menopause, and widowhood. Their embeddedness in other satisfying roles will provide a buffer for these losses.

Thus far, the social trends discussed here have had most influence on the lives of middle-class women. Their educational and economic advantages have given them the luxury of greater role choice. However, the changing attitudes and actions of middle-class women will inevitably exert an effect on everyone's sex-role expectations in the future.

References

ABBOTT, S., and LOVE, B. *Sappho Was a Right-On Woman: A Liberated View of Lesbianism.* New York: Stein and Day, 1972.

ABEL, H., and SAHINKAYA, R. "Emergence of Sex and Race Friendship Preferences." *Child Development,* 1962, *33,* 939–43.

ADAMS, E. B., and SARASON, I. G. "Relation between Anxiety in Children and Their Parents." *Child Development,* 1963, *34,* 237–46.

ADAMS, H. B. "Mental Illness or Interpersonal Behavior?" *American Psychologist,* 1964, *19,* 191–97.

ADLER, A. *Understanding human nature* (W. B. Wolfe, trans.). New York: Greenberg, 1946.

ADORNO, T. W., FRENKEL-BRUNSWIK, E., LEVINSON, D. J., and SANFORD, R. N. *The Authoritarian Personality.* New York: Harper, 1950.

AGASSI, J. B. "The quality of women's working life," in L. E. Davis and A. B. Cherns (eds.), *The Quality of Working Life* (Vol. 1). New York: The Free Press/Macmillan, 1975.

ALBERTI, R. E. and EMMONS, M. L. *Your Perfect Right: A Guide to Assertive Behavior.* San Luis Obispo, Calif.: Impact Press, 1974.

ALLPORT, F. H. *Social Psychology.* Boston: Houghton Mifflin, 1924.

ALLPORT, G. W. *The Nature of Prejudice.* Cambridge, Mass.: Addison-Wesley, 1954.

ALMOND, G. A., and VERDA, S. *The Civic Culture: Political Attitudes and Democracy in Five Nations.* Princeton: Princeton University Press, 1963.

ALMQUIST, E. M., and ANGRIST, S. S. "Role Model Influence on College Women's Career Aspirations." *Merrill-Palmer Quarterly,* 1971, *17*(3), 263–79.

ALPER, T. G. "Achievement Motivation in College Women: A Now-You-See-It-Now-You-Don't Phenomenon." *American Psychologist,* 1974, *29,* 194–203.

ALTMAN, I., and NELSON, P. A. *The Ecology of Home Environments: Final Report* (Project No. 0–0502). U.S. Department of Health, Education, and Welfare, Office of Education, Bureau of Research, January 1972.

ALWOOD, G. "A Developmental Study of Cognitive Balancing in Hypothetical Three-Person Systems." *Child Development,* 1969, *40,* 73–85.

AMUNDSEN, K. *The Silenced Majority: Women and American Democracy.* Englewood Cliffs: Prentice-Hall, 1971.

ANASTASI, A. *Differential Psychology: Individual and Group Differences in Behavior* (3rd ed.). New York: Macmillan, 1958.

ANGRIST, S. S. "Role Constellation as a Variable in Women's Leisure Activities." *Social Forces,* 1967, *45*(3), 423–31.

ANGRIST, S. S., and ALMQUIST, E. *Careers and Contingencies: How College Women Juggle with Gender.* New York: Dunellen, 1975.

ARGYLE, M. *The Psychology of Interpersonal Behavior.* Harmondsworth: Penquin, 1967.

ARGYLE, M., and DEAN, J. "Eye-Contact, Distance and Affiliation." *Sociometry,* 1965, *28*(3), 289–304.

ASTIN, H. S. *The Woman Doctorate in America: Origins, Career, and Family.* New York: Russell Sage Foundation, 1969.

ASTIN, H. S. "Women and Work." Paper presented at the Conference for New Directions for Research on the Psychology of Women, Madison, Wisconsin, 1975.

ATKINSON, J. W. "Motivational Determinants of Risk-Taking Behavior." *Psychological Review,* 1957, *64,* 359–72.

ATKINSON, J. W. *An Introduction to Motivation.* Princeton: Van Nostrand, 1964.

ATKINSON, J. W., and FEATHER, N. T. (eds.). *A Theory of Achievement Motivation.* New York: Wiley, 1966.

AUGER, E. R. "Nonverbal Communication of Normal Individuals and Schizophrenic Patients in the Psychology Interview." Unpublished doctoral dissertation, University of California, Los Angeles, 1969.

BANDURA, A. "Social-Learning Theory of Identificatory Processes," in D. A. Goslin (ed.), *Handbook of Socialization Theory and Research.* Chicago: Rand McNally, 1969.

BANDURA, A., and HUSTON, A. C. "Identification as a Process of Incidental Learning." *Journal of Abnormal and Social Psychology,* 1961, *63*(2), 311–18.

BANDURA, A., ROSS, D., and ROSS, S. A. "Transmission of Aggression Through Imitation of Aggressive Models." *Journal of Abnormal and Social Psychology,* 1961, *63*(3), 575–82.

BANDURA, A., ROSS, D., and ROSS, S. A. "Imitation of Film-Mediated Aggressive Models." *Journal of Abnormal and Social Psychology,* 1963a, *66,* 3–11.

BANDURA, A., ROSS, D., and ROSS, S. A. "Vicarious Reinforcement and Imitative Learning." *Journal of Abnormal and Social Psychology,* 1963b, *67,* 601–7.

BANDURA, A., and WALTERS, R. H. *Social Learning and Personality Development.* New York: Holt, Rinehart and Winston, 1963.

BAR-TAL, D., and FRIEZE, I. H. "Achievement Motivation for Males and Females as a Determinant of Attributions for Success and Failure." *Sex Roles,* 1977, *3*(3), 301–13.

BAR-TAL, D., and SAXE, L. "Physical Attractiveness and Its Relationship to Sex-Role Stereotyping." *Sex Roles,* 1976, *2*(2), 123–33.

BARBACH, L. G. *For Yourself: The Fulfillment of Female Sexuality.* New York: Anchor Books, 1976.

BARDWICK, J. M. *Psychology of Women: A Study of Bio-Cultural Conflicts.* New York: Harper and Row, 1971.

BARKER-BENFIELD, G. J. *The Horrors of the Half-Known Life: Male Attitudes Toward Women and Sexuality in Nineteenth-Century America.* New York: Harper Colophon Books, 1976.

BARR, B. A., GIBBONS, J. L., and MOYER, K. E. "Male-Female Differences and the Influence of Neonatal and Adult Testosterone on Intraspecies Aggression in Rats." *Journal of Comparative and Physiological Psychology,* 1976, 90(12), 1169–83.

BARRY, H., III, BACON, M. K., and CHILD, I. L. "A Cross-Cultural Survey of Some Sex Differences in Socialization." *Journal of Abnormal and Social Psychology,* 1957, 55, 327–32.

BARRY, W. A. "Marriage Research and Conflict: An Integrative Review." *Psychological Bulletin,* 1970, 73, 41–54.

BART, P. B. "Depression in Middle-Aged Women," in V. Gornick and B. K. Moran (eds.), *Woman in Sexist Society: Studies in Power and Powerlessness.* New York: Basic Books, 1971.

BARTNOFF, J. "Title VII and Employment Discrimination in 'Upper Level' Jobs." *Columbia Law Review,* 1973, 73, 1614–40.

BARUCH, G. K. "Maternal Influences upon College Women's Attitudes toward Women and Work." *Developmental Psychology,* 1972, 6, 32–37.

BARUCH, R. "The Achievement Motive in Women: Implications for Career Development." *Journal of Personality and Social Psychology,* 1967, 5(3), 260–67.

BATTLE, E. S. "Motivational Determinants of Academic Task Persistence." *Journal of Personality and Social Psychology,* 1965, 2(2), 209–18.

BAYLEY, N. "Mental Growth During the First Three Years: A Developmental Study of Sixty-one Children by Repeated Tests." *Genetic Psychology Monographs,* 1933, 14, 1–92.

BAYLEY, N. "Comparisons of Mental and Motor Test Scores for Ages 1–15 Months by Sex, Birth Order, Race, Geographical Location, and Education of Parents." *Child Development,* 1965, 36, 379–411.

BECKER, G. "Affiliate Perception and the Arousal of the Participation-Affiliation Motive." *Perceptual and Motor Skills,* 1967, 24, 991–97.

BECKMAN, L. J. "Relative Costs and Benefits of Work and Children to Professional and Non-Professional Women." Paper presented at the meeting of the American Psychological Association, New Orleans, 1974.

BECKWITH, L. "Relationships between Infants' Social Behavior and Their Mothers' Behavior." *Child Development,* 1972, 43(2), 397–411.

BEDELL, J., and SISTRUNK, F. "Power, Opportunity Costs, and Sex in a Mixed-Motive Game." *Journal of Personality and Social Psychology,* 1973, 25(2), 219–26.

BELL, R. Q. "A Reinterpretation of the Direction of Effects in Studies of Socialization." *Psychological Review,* 1968, 75(2), 81–95.

BELL, R. Q., WELLER, G. M., and WALDROP, M. F. "Newborn and Preschooler: Organization of Behavior and Relations between Periods." *Monographs of the Society for Research in Child Development,* 1971, 36(1–2, Serial No. 142).

BELOFF, H. "Two Forms of Social Conformity: Acquiescence and Conventionality." *Journal of Abnormal and Social Psychology,* 1958, *56,* 99–104.

BEM, D. J., and ALLEN, A. "On Predicting Some of the People Some of the Time: The Search for Cross-Situational Consistencies in Behavior." *Psychological Review,* 1974, *81*(6), 506–20.

BEM, S. L. "The Measurement of Psychological Androgyny." *Journal of Consulting and Clinical Psychology,* 1974, *42*(2), 155–62.

BEM, S. L. "Sex Role Adaptability: One Consequence of Psychological Androgyny." *Journal of Personality and Social Psychology.* 1975, *31*(4), 634–43.

BEM, S. L., and BEM, D. J. "Training the Woman to Know Her Place," in D. J. Bem, *Beliefs, Attitudes, and Human Affairs.* Belmont, Calif.: Brooks/Cole, 1970.

BENEDICT, R. "Continuities and Discontinuities in Cultural Conditioning." *Psychiatry,* 1938, *1*(2), 161–67.

BENGIS, I. *Combat in the Erogenous Zone.* New York: Knopf, 1972.

BENNETT, E. M., and COHEN, L. R. "Men and Women: Personality Patterns and Contrasts." *Genetic Psychology Monographs,* 1959, *59,* 101–55.

BENSON, R. C. *Handbook of Obstetrics and Gynecology* (5th ed.). Los Altos, Calif.: Lange Medical Publications, 1974.

BENSTON, M. "The Political Economy of Women's Liberation," in M. H. Garskof (ed.), *Roles Women Play: Readings Toward Women's Liberation.* Belmont, Calif.: Brooks/Cole, 1971.

BERGMANN, B. R., and ADELMAN, I. "The 1973 Report of the President's Council of Economic Advisors: The Economic Role of Women." *The American Economic Review,* 1973, *63*(4), 509–14.

BERMAN, E. F. "Role of Women Sparks Debate by Congresswoman and Doctor." *New York Times,* July 26, 1970.

BERMAN, E. "The Politician Primeval." *Los Angeles Times,* December 6, 1974.

BERMANT, G., and DAVIDSON, J. M. *Biological Bases of Sexual Behavior.* New York: Harper and Row, 1974.

BERNARD, J. "The Paradox of the Happy Marriage," in V. Gornick and B. K. Moran (eds.), *Woman in Sexist Society: Studies in Power and Powerlessness.* New York: Basic Books, 1971.

BERNARD, J. S. *The Future of Marriage.* New York: World, 1972(a).

BERNARD, J. *The Sex Game.* New York: Atheneum, 1972(b).

BERNARD, J. "The Housewife: Between Two Worlds," in P. L. Stewart and M. G. Cantor, *Varieties of Work Experience: The Social Control of Occupational Groups and Roles, a Text with Adapted Original Studies.* Cambridge, Mass.: Schenkman Publishing Co., 1974(a).

BERNARD, J. *Sex Differences: An Overview* (Module 26). New York: MSS Modular Publications, 1974(b).

BERNARD, J. *Women, Wives and Mothers: Values and Options.* Chicago: Aldine, 1975.

BERNARD, J. "Change and Stability in Sex-Role Norms and Behavior," in D. N. Ruble, I. H. Frieze, and J. E. Parsons (eds.), "Sex roles: Persistence and Change." *Journal of Social Issues,* 1976, *32*(3), 207–23.

BERRY, J. W. Temne and Eskimo Perceptual Skills. *International Journal of Psychology,* 1966, *1,* 207–29.

BERRY, J. W. "Ecological and Cultural Factors in Spatial Perceptual Development." *Canadian Journal of Behavioural Science,* 1971, *3*(4), 324–36.

BERSCHEID, E., DION, K., WALSTER, E., and WALSTER, G. W. "Physical Attractiveness and Dating Choice: A Test of the Matching Hypothesis. *Journal of Experimental Social Psychology,* 1971, *7,* 173–189.

BETTELHEIM, B. *Symbolic Wounds; Puberty Rites and the Envious Male.* New York: Collier Books, 1952.

BIDDLE, B. J., and THOMAS, E. J. (eds.). *Role Theory: Concepts and Research.* New York: Wiley, 1966.

BIELIAUSKAS, V. J. "Recent Advances in Psychology of Masculinity and Femininity." *Journal of Psychology,* 1965, *60,* 255–63.

BILLER, H. B. *Father, Child, and Sex Role: Paternal Determinants of Personality Development.* Lexington, Mass.: Heath Lexington Books, 1971.

BINSTOCK, R. H. "Aging and the Future of American Politics." *Annals of the American Academy of Political and Social Science,* 1974, *415,* 199–212.

BIRD, C. *Born Female: The High Cost of Keeping Women Down.* New York: David McKay, 1968.

BIRDWHISTELL, R. L. "The Tertiary Sexual Characteristics." Paper presented at the meeting of the American Association for the Advancement of Science, 1964.

BIRMINGHAM, S. *The Grandees: America's Sephardic Elite.* New York: Harper, and Row, 1971.

BIRNBAUM, J. A. "Life Patterns and Self-Esteem in Gifted Family Oriented and Career Committed Women," in M. T. S. Mednick, S. S. Tangi, and L. W. Hoffman (eds.), *Women and Achievement: Social and Motivational Analyses.* Washington, D.C.: Hemisphere, 1975.

BIRTCHNELL, J., and FLOYD, S. "Attempted Suicide and the Menstrual Cycle—a Negative Conclusion." *Journal of Psychosomatic Research,* 1974, *18,* 361–69.

BLAKE, J. "Coercive Pronatalism and American Population Policy," in K. C. W. Kammeyer (ed.), *Population Studies: Selected Essays and Research* (2nd ed.). Chicago: Rand-McNally, 1975.

BLOCK, J. H. "Another Look at Sex Differentiation in the Socialization Behaviors of Mothers and Fathers," in J. Sherman and F. Denmark (eds.), *Psychology of Women: Future of Research.* New York: Psychological Dimensions, 1977.

BLOOD, R. O., JR., and HAMBLIN, R. L. "The Effect of the Wife's Employment on the Family Power Structure." *Social Forces,* 1958, *36,* 347–52.

BLOOD, R. O., JR., and WOLFE, D. M. *Husbands and Wives: The Dynamics of Married Living.* Glencoe: Free Press, 1960.

BOCK, R. D., and KOLAKOWSKI, D. "Further Evidence of Sex-Linked Major-Gene Influence on Human Spatial Visualizing Ability." *American Journal of Human Genetics,* 1973, *25,* 1–14.

BOGAN, J. E. "The Other Side of the Brain II: An Appositional Mind." *Bulletin of the Los Angeles Neurological Societies,* 1969, *34,* 135–62.

BONCHARD, T. "Sex Differences in Human Opatial Ability: Not an X-Linked Recessive Gene." Unpublished manuscript, 1976.

BORSTELMANN, L. J. "Sex of Experimenter and Sex-Typed Behavior of Young Children." *Child Development,* 1961, *32,* 519–24.

BOURQUE, S. C., and Grossholtz, J. "Politics an Unnatural Practice: Political

Science Looks at Female Participation." *Politics and Society,* 1974, 4(2), 225–66.

BREMER, J. *Asexualization: A Follow-Up Study of 244 Cases.* New York: Macmillan, 1959.

BRIM, O. G., JR. "Family Structure and Sex Role Learning by Children: A Further Analysis of Helen Koch's Data." *Sociometry,* 1958, *21,* 1–16.

BRIM, O. G., JR., and Wheeler, S. *Socialization after Childhood: Two Essays.* New York: Wiley, 1966.

BRINDLEY, C., CLARKE, P., HUTT, C., ROBINSON, I., and WETHLI, E. "Sex Differences in the Activities and Social Interactions of Nursery School Children," in R. P. Michael and J. H. Crook (eds.), *Comparative Ecology and Behaviour of Primates: Proceedings of a Conference Held at the Zoological Society, London, November 1971.* New York: Academic Press, 1973.

BROFENBRENNER, U. "Freudian Theories of Identification and Their Derivatives." *Child Development,* 1960, *31,* 15–40.

BRONSON, F. H., and DESJARDINS, C. "Aggression in Adult Mice: Modification by Neonatal Injections of Gonadal Hormones." *Science,* 1968, *161*(3842), 705–6.

BRONSON, G. W. "Fear of Visual Novelty: Developmental Patterns in Males and Females." *Developmental Psychology,* 1970, *2,* 33–40.

BROOKS, J., and LEWIS, M. "Attachment Behavior in Thirteen-Month-Old, Opposite-Sex Twins." *Child Development,* 1974 45(1), 243–47.

BROOKS, J., RUBLE, D., and CLARKE, A. "College Women's Attitudes and Expectations Concerning Menstrual-Related Changes." *Psychosomatic Medicine,* 1977.

BROOKS, W. D., and FRIEDRICH, G. W. "Police Image: An Exploratory Study." *Journal of Communication,* 1970, *20,* 370–74.

BROVERMAN, I. K., BROVERMAN. D. M., CLARKSON, F. E., ROSENKRANTZ, P. S., and VOGEL, S. R. "Sex Role Stereotypes and Clinical Judgments of Mental Health." *Journal of Consulting and Clinical Psychology,* 1970, *34,* 1–7.

BROVERMAN, I. K., VOGEL, S. R., BROVERMAN, D. M., CLARKSON, F. E., and ROSENKRANTZ, P. S. "Sex-Role Stereotypes: A Current Appraisal." *Journal of Social Issues,* 1972, *28*(2), 59–78.

BROWN, D. G. "Sex-Role Preference in Young Children." *Psychological Monographs,* 1956, *70*(14, Whole No. 421).

BROWN, D. G. "Masculinity-Femininity Development in Children." *Journal of Consulting Psychology,* 1957, *21*(3), 197–202.

BROWN, R. *Social Psychology.* New York: Free Press, 1965.

BROWNMILLER, S. *Against Our Will: Men, Women and Rape.* New York: Simon and Schuster, 1975.

BUCK, R. W., SAVIN, V. J., MILLER, R. E., and CAUL, W. F. "Communication of Affect through Facial Expressions in Humans." *Journal of Personality and Social Psychology,* 1972, *23*(3), 362–71.

BUFFERY, A. W. H., and GRAY, J. A. "Sex Differences in the Development of Spatial and Linguistic Skills," in C. Ounsted and D. C. Taylor (eds.), *Gender Differences: Their Ontogeny and Significance.* Edinburgh and London: Churchill Livingstone, 1972.

BUGENTAL, D. E., LOVE, L. R., and GIANETTO, R. M. "Perfidious Feminine Faces." *Journal of Personality and Social Psychology,* 1971, *17*(3), 314–18.

BULLOCK, C. S., III, and HEYS, P. L. F. "Recruitment of Women for Congress: A Research Note." *Western Political Quarterly,* 1972, *25*(3), 416–23.

BURGESS, E. W., and WALLIN, P. *Engagement and Marriage.* Philadelphia: Lippincott, 1953.

BURR, W. R. "Satisfaction with Various Aspects of Marriage Over the Life Cycle: A Random Middle Class Sample." *Journal of Marriage and the Family,* 1970, *32*(1), 29–37.

BUTLER, R. N. "The Life Review: An Interpretation of Reminiscence in the Aged." *Psychiatry,* 1963, *26*(1), 65–76.

BYRNE, D. "Parental Antecedents of Authoritarianism." *Journal of Personality and Social Psychology,* 1965, *1*(4), 369–73.

CAMPBELL, A. "The American Way of Mating: Marriage Sí, Children Only Maybe." *Psychology Today,* May 1975, pp. 37–41.

CAMPBELL, A., CONVERSE, P. E., MILLER, W. E., and STOKES, D. E. *The American Voter.* New York: Wiley, 1960.

CAMPBELL, D. T. "Social Attitudes and Other Acquired Behavioral Dispositions," in S. Koch (ed.), *Psychology: A Study of a Science* (Vol. 6). New York: McGraw-Hill, 1963.

CAMPBELL, D. T., and STANLEY, J. C. *Experimental and Quasi-Experimental Designs for Research.* Chicago: Rand McNally, 1966.

CANNON, M. S., and REDICK, R. W. *Differential Utilization of Psychiatric Facilities by Men and Women, United States 1970* (Stat. Note 81). Washington, D.C.: U.S. Department of Health, Education, and Welfare, National Institute of Mental Health, 1973.

CANTRIL, H. (ed.). *Public opinion, 1935–1946.* Princeton: Princeton University Press, 1951.

CAREY, G. L. "Sex Differences in Problem-Solving Performance as a Function of Attitude Differences." *Journal of Abnormal and Social Psychology,* 1958, *56,* 256–60.

CAREY, M. S. "Nonverbal Openings to Conversations." Paper presented at the meeting of the Eastern Psychological Association, Philadelphia, 1974.

CARLSON, E. R., and CARLSON, R. "Male and Female Subjects in Personality Research." *Journal of Abnormal and Social Psychology,* 1960, *61,* 482–83.

CARLSON, R. "Stability and Change in the Adolescent's Self-Image." *Child Development,* 1965, *36,* 659–66.

CARLSON, R. "Sex Differences in Ego Functioning: Exploratory Studies of Agency and Communion." *Journal of Consulting and Clinical Psychology,* 1971, *37,* 267–77.

CARLSON, R. "Understanding Women: Implications for Personality Theory and Research." *Journal of Social Issues,* 1972, *28*(2), 17–32.

CARTWRIGHT, D. (ed.). *Studies in Social Power.* Ann Arbor, Mich.: Research Center for Group Dynamics, Institute for Social Research, University of Michigan, 1959.

Center for the American Woman and Politics, Rutgers University. *Women in Public Office.* New York: Bonker, 1976.

CENTERS, R., RAVEN, B. H., and RODRIGUES, A. "Conjugal Power Structure: A Reexamination." *American Sociological Review,* 1971, *36,* 264–78.

CENTRA, JOHN A. *Women, Men and the Doctorate.* Princeton: Educational Testing Service, 1974.

CHAFETZ, J. S. *Masculine/Feminine or Human? An Overview of the Sociology of Sex Roles.* Itasca, Ill.: Peacock publishers, 1974.

CHEIN, I. "Behavior Theory and the Behavior of Attitudes: Some Critical Comments." *Psychological Review,* 1948, *55,* 175–88.

CHERRY, S. H. *The Menopause Myth.* New York: Ballantine Books, 1976.

CHESLER, P. "Women as Psychiatric and Psychotherapeutic Patients." *Journal of Marriage and the Family,* 1971, *33,* 746–59.

CHESLER, P. *Women and Madness.* Garden City: Doubleday, 1972.

CHISHOLM, S. "Racism and Anti-Feminism." *Black Scholar,* 1970, *1*(3–4), 40–45.

CHISHOLM, S. "Sexism and Racism: One Battle to Fight." *Personnel and Guidance Journal,* 1972, *51*(2), 123–25.

CHOWN, S. M. (ed.). *Human Ageing: Selected Readings.* Baltimore: Penguin Books, 1972.

CHRISTIE, R., and JAHODA, M. (eds.). *Studies in the Scope and Method of "The Authoritarian Personality."* Glencoe: Free Press, 1954.

CLARKE-STEWART, K. A. "Interactions between Mothers and Their Young Children: Characteristics and Consequences." *Monographs of the Society for Research in Child Development,* 1973, *38* (6–7, Serial No. 153).

CLAUSEN, J. A. "The Life Course of Individuals," in M. W. Riley, M. Johnson, and A. Foner, *Aging and Society* (Vol. 3). New York: Russell Sage Foundation, 1972.

COATES, B., ANDERSON, E. P., and HARTUP, W. W. "Interrelations in the Attachment Behavior of Human Infants." *Developmental Psychology,* 1972, *6*(2), 218–30.

COATES, S. "Sex Differences in Field Independence among Pre-School Children," in R. C. Friedman, R. M. Richart, and R. L. Vande Wiele (eds.), *Sex Differences in Behavior: A Conference.* New York: Wiley, 1974.

COLLINS, J. K., and THOMAS, N. T. "Developmental Study of Conformity to Unlike-Sex Peer Pressure." *Perceptual and Motor Skills,* 1974, *38*(1), 75–78.

COMSTOCK, J. "Nonverbal communication and the "difficult" patient." Unpublished manuscript, University of California, Los Angeles, 1971.

CONDRY, J., and DYER, S. "Fear of Success: Attribution of Cause to the Victim," in D. N. Ruble, I. H. Frieze, and J. E. Parsons (eds.), "Sex Roles: Persistence and Change." *Journal of Social Issues,* 1976, *32*(3), 63–83.

CONDRY, S., and CONDRY, J. Personal communication. 1976.

CONSTANTINI, E., and CRAIK, K. H. "Women as Politicians: The Social Background, Personality, and Political Careers of Female Party Leaders." *Journal of Social Issues,* 1972, *28*(2), 217–36.

CONSTANTINOPLE, A. "Masculinity-Femininity: An Exception to a Famous Dictum?" *Psychological Bulletin,* 1973, *80*(5), 389–407.

CONVERSE, P. E. "The Nature of Belief Systems in Mass Publics," in D. E. Apter (ed.), *Ideology and Discontent.* Glencoe: Free Press, 1964.

COOK, H., and STINGLE, S. "Cooperative Behavior in Children." *Psychological Bulletin,* 1974, *81*(12), 918–33.

COOKE, W. R. "The Differential Psychology of the American Woman." *American Journal of Obstetrics and Gynecology,* 1945, *49,* 457–72.

COOP, R. H., and SIGEL, I. E. "Cognitive Style: Implications for Learning and In-
    struction." *Psychology in the Schools,* 1971, 8(2), 152–61.
COOPERSMITH, S. *The Antecedents of Self-Esteem.* San Francisco: Freeman, 1967.
COPPEN, A., and KESSEL. N. "Menstruation and Personality." *British Journal of Psy-
    chiatry,* 1963, *109,* 711–21.
CORAH, N. L. "Differentiation in Children and their Parents." *Journal of Personality,*
    1965, *33,* 300–308.
CRANDALL, V. C. "Sex Differences in Expectancy of Intellectual and Academic Rein-
    forcement," in C. P. Smith (ed.), *Achievement-related motives in children.* New
    York: Russell Sage Foundation, 1969.
CRANDALL, V. C., KATKOVSKY, W., and CRANDALL, V. J. "Children's Belief in Their
    Own Control of Reinforcement in Intellectual-Academic Achievement Situa-
    tions." *Child Development,* 1965, *36,* 91–109.
CROKE, J. A. "Sex Differences in Causal Attributions and Expectancies for Success as
    a Function of the Sex-Role Appropriateness of the Task." Unpublished manu-
    script, University of California, Los Angeles, 1973.
CROWLEY, J. E., LEVITIN, T. E., and QUINN, R. P. "Seven Deadly Half-Truths about
    Women." *Psychology Today,* March 1973, pp. 94–96.
CUMMING, E., and HENRY, W. E. *Growing Old: The Process of Disengagement.* New
    York: Basic Books, 1961.
Current Population Reports, Population Characteristics Series P–20, No. 212: "Marital
    Status and Family Status: March 1970." Washington, D.C.: U.S. Government
    Printing Office, 1971.
Current Population Reports, Population Characteristics Series P–20, No. 287: "Marital
    Status and Living Arrangements: March 1975." Washington, D.C.: U.S. Gov-
    ernment Printing Office, 1975(a).
Current Population Reports, Population estimates and projections Series P–25, No.
    545: "Estimates of the Population of the United States and Components of
    Change: 1974 (with Annual Data from 1930)." Washington, D.C.: U.S. Gov-
    ernment Printing Office, 1975(b).
Current Population Reports, Population Characteristics Series P–20, No. 304. Wash-
    ington, D.C.: U.S. Government Printing Office, 1976.
CURTIS, L. A. "Victim Precipitation and Violent Crime." *Social Problems,* 1974,
    21(4), 594–605.
DALTON, K. "Menstruation and Acute Psychiatric Illness." *British Medical Journal,*
    No. 5115, 17 January 1959, 148–49.
DALTON, K. *The Premenstrual Syndrome.* Springfield, Ill.: C. C. Thomas, 1964.
DALTON, K. *The Menstrual Cycle.* New York: Pantheon Books, 1969.
D'ANDRADE, R. G. "Sex Differences and Cultural Institutions," in E. E. Maccoby
    (ed.), *The Development of Sex Differences.* Stanford, Calif.: Stanford University
    Press, 1966.
DARLEY, S. "Big-Time Careers for the Little Woman: A Dual-Role Dilemma," in
    D. N. Ruble, I. H. Frieze, and J. E. Parsons (eds.), "Sex Roles: Persistence and
    Change." *Journal of Social Issues,* 1976, *32*(3), 85–98.
DAVIDSON, M. "Fertility and Childspacing of Women in Marriage Cohorts in the
    United States." Paper presented at the meeting of the Population Association
    of America, Seattle, Washington, April 1975.
DAVIS, K. *Human Society.* New York: Macmillan, 1949.

DAWSON, J. L. M. "Cultural and Physiological Influences upon Spatial-Perceptual Processes in West Africa: Part II." *International Journal of Psychology,* 1967, *2,* 171–85.

DEAUX, K., and EMSWILLER, T. "Explanations of Successful Performance on Sex-Linked Tasks: What's Skill for the Male is Luck for the Female." *Journal of Personality and Social Psychology,* 1974, *29*(1), 80–85.

DEAUX, K., and FARRIS, E. "Attributing Causes for One's Performance: The Effects of Sex, Norms and Outcome." Unpublished manuscript, Purdue University, 1974.

DEAUX, K., and TAYNOR, J. "Evaluation of Male and Female Ability: Bias Works Two Ways." *Psychological Reports,* 1973, *32*(1), 261–62.

DECTER, M. *The New Chastity and Other Arguments Against Women's Liberation.* New York: Coward, McCann, and Geoghegan, 1972.

DeFRIES, J. C., ASHTON, G. C., JOHNSON, R. C., KUSE, A. R., MCCLEARN, G. E., MI, M. P., RASHAD, M. N., VANDENBERG, S. G., and WILSON, J. R. "Parent-Offspring Resemblance for Specific Cognitive Abilities in Two Ethnic Groups." *Nature,* 1976, *261,* 131–33.

DENNIS, J. "Support for the Party System by the Mass Public. *American Political Science Review,* 1966, *60,* 600–615.

DEUTSCH, H. "The Psychology of Women in Relation to the Functions of Reproduction," in J. Chassequet-Smirgel (ed.), *Female Sexuality: New Psychoanalytic Views.* Ann Arbor: University of Michigan Press, 1970.

DEUTSCH, H. *The Psychology of Women* (Vol. 2). New York: Grune and Stratton, 1945.

DEUTSCH, H. "Summary of Symposium on Frigidity," in J. Chasseguet-Smirgel (ed.), *Female Sexuality: New Psychoanalytic Views.* Ann Arbor: University of Michigan Press, 1970.

DEUTSCHER, I. "The Quality of Postparental Life: Definitions of the Situation." *Journal of Marriage and the Family,* 1964, *26*(1), 52–59.

DeVRIES, R. "Constancy of Generic Identity in the Years Three to Six," *Monographs of the Society for Research in Child Development,* 1969, *34*(3, Serial No. 127).

DINITZ, S., DYNES, R. R., and CLARKE, A. C. "Preference for Male or Female Children: Traditional or Affectional?" *Marriage and Family Living,* 1954, *16,* 128–30.

DITTIES, J. E., and KELLEY, H. H. "Effects of Different Conditions of Acceptance upon Conformity to Group Norms. *Journal of Abnormal and Social Psychology,* 1956, *53,* 100–107.

DIZZARD, J. *Social Change in the Family.* Chicago: Community and Family Study Center, University of Chicago, 1968.

DOERING, C. H., BRODIE, H. K. H., KRAEMER, H., BECKER, H., and HAMBURG, O. A. "Plasma Testosterone Levels and Psychologic Measures in Men Over a 2-Month Period," in R. C. Friedman, R. M. Richart and R. L. Vande Wiele (eds.), *Sex Differences in Behavior: A Conference.* New York: Wiley, 1974.

DOERING, C. H., BRODIE, H. K. H., KRAEMER, H. BECKER, MOOS, R. H., BECKER. H. B., and HAMBURG, D. A. "Negative Affect and Plasma Testosterone: A Longitudinal Human Study." *Psychosomatic Medicine,* 1975, *37*(6), 484–91.

DOERING, C. H., KRAEMER, H. C., BRODIE, H. K. H., and HAMBURG, D. A. "A Cycle of Plasma Testosterone in the Human Male." *Journal of Clinical Endocrinology and Metabolism,* 1975, *40*(3), 492–500.

DOHRENWEND, B. S. "Social Status and Stressful Life Events." *Journal of Personality and Social Psychology,* 1973, *28,* 225–35.

DOMHOFF, G. W. *The Higher Circles: The Governing Class in America.* New York: Random House, 1970.

DOOB, L. W. The Behavior of Attitudes. *Psychological Review,* 1947, *54,* 135–56.

DOUVAN, E., and ADELSON, J. *The Adolescent Experience.* New York: Wiley, 1966.

DUNCAN, S., JR. "Nonverbal Communication." *Psychological Bulletin,* 1969, 72(2), 118–37.

DUNN, L. A. "Consideration of Variables in Reward and Coercive Influence Attempts." Unpublished manuscript, Tufts University, 1972.

DUVERGER, M. *The Political Role of Women.* Paris: UNESCO, 1955.

DWECK, C. S. "Sex Differences in the Meaning of Negative Evaluation in Achievement Situations: Determinants and Consequences." Paper presented at the meeting of the Society for Research in Child Development, Denver, April 1975.

DWECK, C. S., and REPPUCCI, N. D. "Learned Helplessness and Reinforcement Responsibility in Children." *Journal of Personality and Social Psychology,* 1973, *25*(1), 109–16.

DWYER, C. A. "Children's Sex-Role Standards and Sex-Role Identification and Their Relationship to Achievement." Unpublished doctoral dissertation, University of California, Berkeley, 1972.

EDWARDS, D. A. "Early Androgen Stimulation and Aggressive Behavior in Male and Female Mice." *Physiology and Behavior,* 1969, *4*(3), 333–38.

EDWARDS, H. T. "Sex Discrimination under Title VII: Some Unresolved Issues." *Labor Law Journal,* 1973, *24,* 411–23.

EHRHARDT, A. A., and BAKER, S. W. "Hormonal Aberrations and Their Implications for the Understanding of Normal Sex Differentiation." Paper presented at the meeting of the Society for Research in Child Development, Philadelphia, 1973.

EHRHARDT, A. A., EPSTEIN, R., and MONEY, J. "Fetal Androgens and Female Gender Identity in the Early-Treated Adrenogenital Syndrome." *Johns Hopkins Medical Journal,* 1968, *122,* 160–67.

EHRHARDT, A. A., GREENBERG, N., and MONEY, J. "Female Gender Identity and Absence of Fetal Gonadal Hormones: Turner's Syndrome." *Johns Hopkins Medical Journal,* 1970, *126,* 237–48.

EIBL-EIBESFELDT, I. *Ethology: The Biology of Behavior* (E. Klinghammer, trans.). New York: Holt, Rinehart and Winston, 1970.

EISENBERG, S. The Sex-Typed Play Behavior of Children in Two Cultural Settings: A Kibbutz Gan and an American Pre-school. Unpublished manuscript, Smith College, 1974.

EKMAN, P. "Cross Cultural Studies of Facial Expression," in P. Ekman (ed.), *Darwin and Facial Expression: A Century of Research in Reviw.* New York: Academic Press, 1973.

ELIG, T. W., and FRIEZE, I. H. "A Multidimensional Scheme for Coding and Interpreting Perceived Causality for Success and Failure Events: The Coding

Scheme of Perceived Causality (CSPC)." JSAS *Catalog of Selected Documents in Psychology,* 1975, *5,* 313 (Ms. No. 1069).

ELLIS, H. *A Study of British Genius.* London: Huret and Blackett, 1904.

ELLIS, H. *The Task of Social Hygiene.* Boston: Houghton Mifflin, 1913.

EMMERICH, W. "Young Children's Discriminations of Parent and Child Roles." *Child Development,* 1959, *30,* 403–19.

EMMERICH, W. "Family Role Concepts of Children Ages Six to Ten." *Child Development,* 1961, *32,* 609–24.

ENGEL, R. and BENSON, R. C. "Estimate of Conceptional Age by Evoked Response Activity." *Biologia Neonatorum,* 1968, *12,* 201–13.

ENTWISLE, D. R., and GREENBERGER, E. "Questions about Social Class, Internality-Externality, and Test Anxiety." *Developmental Psychology,* 1972, *7,* 218.

EPSTEIN, C. F. *Woman's Place: Options and Limits in Professional Careers.* Berkeley: University of California Press, 1970.

EPSTEIN, C. F. "Positive Effects of the Multiple Negative: Explaining the Success of Black Professional Women." *American Journal of Sociology,* 1973, 78(4), 912–35.

ERIKSON, E. H. *Childhood and Society.* New York: Norton, 1950.

ERIKSON, E. H. *Childhood and Society* (2nd ed.). New York: Norton, 1963.

ERIKSON, E. H. "Inner and Outer Space: Reflections on Womanhood," in R. J. Lifton (ed.), *The Woman in America.* Boston: Houghton Mifflin, 1965.

ERIKSON, E. H. *Identity: Youth and Crisis.* New York: Norton, 1968.

ERIKSON, E. H. Womanhood and the Inner Space. In J. Strouse, (ed.), *Women and Analysis: Dialogues on Psychoanalytic Views of Femininity.* New York: Grossman Publishers, 1974.

ERNSTER, V. L. "American Menstrual Expressions." *Sex Roles: A Journal of Research,* 1975, *1,* 3–13.

ERON, L. D., HEUSMANN, L. R., LEFKOWITZ, M. M., and WALDER, L. O. "How Learning Conditions in Early Childhood—Including Mass Media—Relate to Aggression in Late Adolescence." *American Journal of Orthopsychiatry,* 1974, 44(3), 412–23.

ERSKINE, H. "The Polls: Demonstrations and Race Riots." *Public Opinion Quarterly,* 1967, *31,* 665–77.

ERSKINE, H. "The Polls: Recent Opinion on Racial Problems." *Public Opinion Quarterly,* 1968, *32,* 696–703.

ERSKINE, H. "The Polls: Is War a Mistake?" *Public Opinion Quarterly,* 1970, *34,* 134–50.

ERSKINE, H. "The Polls: Women's Role." *Public Opinion Quarterly,* 1971, *35,* 275–90.

ETAUGH, C., COLLINS, G., and GERSON, A. "Reinforcement of Sex-Typed Behaviors of Two-Year-Old Children in a Nursery School Setting." *Developmental Psychology,* 1975, *11*(2), 255.

EXLINE, R. V. "Effects of Need for Affiliation, Sex, and the Sight of Others upon Initial Communications in Problem-Solving Groups." *Journal of Personality,* 1962, *30,* 541–56.

EXLINE, R. V. "Explorations in the Process of Person Perception: Visual Interaction in Relation to Competition, Sex, and Need for Affiliation." *Journal of Personality,* 1963, *31,* 1–20.

EXLINE, R. V. "The Semioptics of Visual Interaction: Is There a Language of the Eyes?" Paper presented at the meeting of the Society for Experimental Social Psychology, Lawrence, Kansas, 1972.

EXLINE, R., GRAY, D., and SCHUETTE, D. "Visual Behavior in a Dyad as Affected by Interview Content and Sex of Respondent." *Journal of Personality and Social Psychology*, 1965, *1*(3), 201–9.

FABRIKANT, B., LANDAU, D., and ROLLENHAGEN, J. "Perceived Female Sex-Role Attributes and Psychotherapists' Sex-Role Expectations for Female Patients." *New Jersey Psychologist*, 1973 (Winter), 13–16.

FAGOT, B. I., and LITTMAN, I. "Stability of Sex Role and Play Interests from Preschool to Elementary School." *Journal of Psychology*, 1975, 89(2), 285–92.

FAGOT, B. I., and PATTERSON, G. R. "An In Vivo Analysis of Reinforcing Contingencies for Sex-Role Behaviors in the Preschool Child." *Developmental Psychology*, 1969, *1*(5), 563–68.

FALTICO, G. J. "The Vocabulary of Nonverbal Communication in the Psychological Interview." Unpublished doctoral dissertation, University of California, Los Angeles, 1969.

FARRIS, E., and DEAUX, K. "The Effects of Sex, Norms, and Outcome on Self-Evaluation of Performance." Paper presented at the meeting of the Midwestern Psychological Association, 1973.

FAULS, L. B., and SMITH, W. D. "Sex-Role Learning of Five-Year-Olds." *Journal of Genetic Psychology*, 1956, 89, 105–17.

FEATHER, N. T. Effects of prior success and failure on expectations of success and subsequent performance." *Journal of Personality and Social Psychology*, 1966, *3*(3), 287–98.

FEATHER, N. T. "Attribution of Responsibility and Valence of Success and Failure in Relation to Initial Confidence and Task Performance." *Journal of Personality and Social Psychology*, 1969, *13*(2), 129–44.

FEIN, G., JOHNSON, N. K., STORK, L., and WASSERMAN, L. "Sex Stereotypes and Preferences in the Toy Choices of 20-Month-Old Boys and Girls." *Developmental Psychology*, 1975, *11*(4), 527–28.

FELDMAN, H. "Changes in Marriage and Parenthood: A Methodological Design," in E. Peck and J. Senderowitz (eds.), *Pronatalism: The Myth of Mom and Apple Pie.* New York: Crowell, 1974.

FELDMAN-SUMMERS, S., and KIESLER, S. B. "Those Who Are Number Two Try Harder: The Effects of Sex on Attributions of Causality." *Journal of Personality and Social Psychology*, 1974, *30*(6), 846–55.

FERRISS, A. L. *Indicators of Trends in the Status of American Women.* New York: Russell Sage Foundation, 1971.

FESHBACH, N. D. "Sex Differences in Children's Modes of Aggressive Responses toward Outsiders." *Merrill-Palmer Quarterly*, 1969, *15*, 249–58.

FESHBACH, N., and SONES, G. "Sex Differences in Adolescent Reactions toward Newcomers." *Developmental Psychology*, 1971, *4*(3), 381–86.

FESTINGER, L., and CARLSMITH, J. M. "Cognitive Consequences of Forced Compliance." *Journal of Abnormal and Social Psychology*, 1959, 58, 203–10.

FESTINGER, L., SCHACHTER, S., and BACK, K. *Social Pressures in Informal Groups: A Study of Human Factors in Housing.* New York: Harper, 1950.

FIELD, W. F. "The Effects on Thematic Apperception of Certain Experimentally

Aroused Needs." in D. C. McClelland, J. W. Atkinson, R. A. Clark, and E. L. Lowell (eds.), *The Achievement Motive*. New York: Appleton-Century-Crofts, 1953.

FIRESTONE, S. *The Dialectic of Sex: The Case for Feminist Revolution*. New York: William Morrow, 1970.

FISHER, J. L., and HARRIS, M. B. "Note Taking and Recall." *Journal of Educational Research*, 1974, 67(7), 291–92.

FITZGERALD, D., and ROBERTS, K. "Semantic Profiles and Psychosexual Interests as Indictors of Identification." *Personnel and Guidance Journal*, 1966, 44(8), 802–6.

FLAVELL, J. H. *Cognitive Development*. Englewood Cliffs: Prentice-Hall, 1977.

FLAVELL, J. H., BOTKIN, P. T., FRY, C. L., JR., WRIGHT, J. W., and JARVIS, P. E. *The development of Role-Taking and Communication Skills in Children*. New York: Wiley, 1968.

FRANCOEUR, R., and FRANCOEUR, A. "Social Sex: The New Single Standard for Men and Women," in M. Tripp (ed.), *Woman in the Year 2000*. New York: Arbor House, 1974.

FRANKENBURG, W. K., and DODDS, J. B. "The Denver Developmental Screening Test." *The Journal of Pediatrics*, 1967, 71, 181–91.

FRENCH, E. G., and LESSER, G. S. "Some Characteristics of the Achievement Motive in Women." *Journal of Abnormal and Social Psychology*, 1964, 68, 119–28.

FRENCH, J. R. P., JR., and RAVEN, B. "The Bases of Social Power," in D. Cartwright (ed.), *Studies in Social Powers*, Ann Arbor, Michigan: Institute for Social Research, 1959.

FRENKEL, E. "Studies in Biographical Psychology." *Character and Personality*, 1936, 5, 1–34.

FREUD, S. "Some Psychical Consequences of the Anatomical Distinction Between the Sexes," in J. Strouse (ed.), *Women and Analysis: Dialogues on Psychoanalytic Views of Femininity*. New York: Grossman, 1974.

FREUD, S. *New Introductory Lectures in Psychoanalysis* (J. Strachey, ed. and trans.). New York: Norton, 1965. (Originally published, 1933.)

FREUD, S. "The Transformations of Puberty," in A. A. Brill (ed. and trans.), *The Basic Writings of Sigmund Freud*. New York: Random House, 1938.

FRIEDAN, B. *The Feminine Mystique*. New York: Norton, 1963; 2nd ed., 1974.

FRIEZE, I. "Studies of Information Processing and the Attributional Process in Achievement-Related Contexts." Unpublished doctoral dissertation, University of California, Los Angeles, 1973.

FRIEZE, I. H. "Changing Self Images and Sex-Role Stereotypes in College Women." Paper presented at the meeting of the American Psychological Association, New Orleans, 1974.

FRIEZE, I. H. "Women's Expectations for and Causal Attributions of Success and Failure," in M. T. S. Mednick, S. S. Tangri, and L. W. Hoffman (eds.), *Women and Achievement: Social and Motivational Analyses*. Washington, D.C.: Hemisphere, 1975.

FRIEZE, I. H. "Causal Attributions and Information Seeking to Explain Success and Failure." *Journal of Research in Personality*, 1976, 10, 293–305.

FRIEZE, I. H. "Social Psychological Theory and Problems of Battered Women." Unpublished manuscript, University of Pittsburgh, 1977.

FRIEZE, I. H., FISHER, J., HANUSA, B., MCHUGH, M., and VALLE, V. A. "Attributions of Success and Failure in Internal and External Barriers to Achievement in Women," in J. Sherman and F. Denmark (eds.), *Psychology of Women: Future Directions of Research.* New York: Psychological Dimensions, 1978.

FRIEZE, I. H., MCHUGH, M., FISHER, J., and VALLE, V. "Attributing the Causes of Success and Failure: Internal and External Barriers to Achievement in Women." Paper presented at the Conference for New Directions for Research on the Psychology of Women, Madison, Wisconsin, 1975.

FRIEZE, I., PARSONS, J., and RUBLE, D. "Some determinants of Career Aspirations in College Women." Paper presented at the Symposium on Sex Roles and Sex Differences, University of California, Los Angeles, 1972.

FRIEZE, I. H., and RAMSEY, S. J. "Nonverbal Maintenance of Traditional Sex Roles," in D. N. Ruble, I. H. Frieze, and J. E. Parsons (eds.), "Sex roles: Persistence and Change." *Journal of Social Issues,* 1976, *32*(3), 133–41.

FROMM, E. "Sex and Character." *Psychiatry,* 1943, 6(1), 21–31.

FRUEH, T., and MCGHEE, P. E. "Traditional Sex Role Development and Amount of Time Spent Watching Television." *Developmental Psychology,* 1975, *11*(1), 109.

GAGNON, J. H., and SIMON, W. *Sexual Conduct: the Social Sources of Human Sexuality.* Chicago: Aldine Publishing Co., 1973.

GALLUP, G. *Gallup Opinion Index* (Report Nos. 1–129). Princeton: Gallup International, 1965–1976.

GANZFRIED, S. *Code of Jewish Law (Kitzur Shulchan Aruch): A Compilation of Jewish Laws and Customs by Rabbi Solomon Ganzfried* (H. E. Goldin, trans.). New York: Star Hebrew Book Co., 1927.

GARAI, J. E. "Sex Differenes in Mental Health." *Genetic Psychology Monographs,* 1970, *81*(2), 123–42.

GARAI, J. E., and SCHEINFELD, S. "Sex Differences in Mental and Behavioral Traits." *Genetic Psychology Monographs,* 1968, 77(2), 169–299.

GARDNER, D. B., and SWIGER, M. K. "Developmental Status of Two Groups of Infants Released for Adoption." *Child Development,* 1958, *29*(4), 521–30.

GEHLEN, F. L. "Women in Congress." *Trans-action,* 1969, 6(11, Whole No. 49), 36–40.

GERGEN, K. J., and MARECEK, J. *The Psychology of Self-Esteem.* Morristown, N.J.: General Learning Press, 1976.

GERSTON, J. "Women Who Want Important Campaign Roles." *New York Times,* May 13, 1974.

GESELL, A., et al. *The First Five Years of Life: A Guide to the Study of the Preschool Child.* New York: Harper and Brothers, 1940.

GERWIRTZ, J. L. "A Factor Analysis of Some Attention-Seeking Behaviors of Young Children." *Child Development,* 1956, *27*, 17–36.

GERWIRTZ, J. L. "Mechanisms of Social Learning: Some Roles of Stimulation and Behavior in Early Human Development," in D. A. Goslin (ed.), *Handbook of Socialization Theory and Research.* Chicago: Rand McNally, 1969.

GIBBONS, J. L. "The Adrenal Cortex and Psychological Distress," in R. P. Michael (ed.), *Endocrinology and Human Behavior.* London: Oxford University Press, 1968.

GIBSON, C. "Changes in Marital Status and Marital Fertility and Their Contribution to the Decline in Period Fertility in the United States: 1961–1973." 1975

Meeting of the Population Association of America (April 17–19), Seattle, reported in *Population Index,* July 1975, *41*(3), 408.

GINZBERG, E. *Life Styles of Educated Women.* New York: Columbia University Press, 1966.

GITTER, A. G., BLACK, H., and MOSTOFSKY, D. Race and Sex in the Communication of Emotion. *Journal of Social Psychology,* 1972, *88,* 273–76.

GLASS, G. S., HENINGER, G. R., LANSKY, M., and TALAN, K. "Psychiatric Emergency Related to the Menstrual Cycle." *American Journal of Psychiatry,* 1971, *128,* 705–11.

GLICK, P. C., and NORTON, A. J. "Perspectives on the Recent Upturn in Divorce and Remarriage." *Demography,* 1973, *10*(3), 301–14.

GLOBIG, L. J., and TOUHEY, J. C. "Sex and Affective Determinants of Lecture Content Retention." *Psychological Reports,* 1971, *29*(2), 538.

GOFFMAN, E. *Interaction Ritual: Essays on Face-to-Face Behavior.* Garden City, NY: Anchor Books, 1967.

GOLDBERG, P. "Are Women Prejudiced against Women?" *Trans-action,* 1968, *5*(5), 28–30.

GOLDBERG, S. *The Inevitability of Patriarchy.* New York: Morrow, 1973.

GOLDBERG, S., and LEWIS, M. "Play Behavior in the Year-Old Infant: Early Sex Differences." *Child Development,* 1969, *40*(1), 21–31.

GOLDMAN, P. S., CRAWFORD, H. T., STOKES, L. P., GALKIN, T. W., and ROSVOLD, H. E. "Sex-Dependent Behavioral Effects of Cerebral Cortical Lesions in the Developing Rhesus Monkey." *Science,* 1974, *186*(4163), 540–42.

GOLDSTEIN, A. G., and CHANCE, J. E. "Effects of Practice on Sex-Related Differences in Performance on Embedded Figures." *Psychonomic Science,* 1965, *3,* 361–62.

GOODENOUGH, E. W. "Interest in Persons as an Aspect of Sex Difference in the Early Years." *Genetic Psychology Monographs,* 1957, *55*(2), 287–323.

GORDON, M., and SHANKWEILER, P. J. "Different Equals Less: Female Sexuality in Recent Marriage Manuals." *Journal of Marriage and the Family,* 1971, *33,* 459–66.

GORDON, R. E., GORDON, K. K., and GUNTHER, M. *The Split-Level Trap.* New York: B. Geis Associates, 1961.

GORE, W. R., and TUDOR, J. F. "Adult Sex Roles and Mental Illness." *American Journal of Sociology,* 1973, *78*(4), 812–35.

GORSKI, R. A. "Influence of Age on the Response to Paranatal Administration of a Low Dose of Androgen." *Endocrinology,* 1968, *82*(5), 1001–4.

GOULD, R. L. "The Phases of Adult Life: A Study in Developmental Psychology." *American Journal of Psychiatry,* 1972, *129*(5), 521–31.

GOULD, R. "Adult Life Stages: Growth toward Self-Tolerance." *Psychology Today,* February 1975, pp. 74–81.

GOY, R. W., BRIDSON, W. E., and YOUNG, W. C. "Period of Maximal Susceptibility of the Prenatal Female Guinea Pig to Masculinizing Actions of Testosterone Propionate." *Journal of Comparative and Physiological Psychology,* 1964, *57*(2), 166–74.

GRAF, R. G., and RIDDELL, J. C. "Sex Differences in Problem-Solving as a Function of Problem Context. *Journal of Educational Research,* 1972, *65*(10), 451–52.

GRANT, E. C. G., and PRYSE-DAVIES, J. "Effect of Oral Contraceptives on Depressive

Mood Changes and on Endometrial Monoamine Oxidase and Phosphates." *British Medical Journal*, 1968, *3*, 777–80.

GRAY, S. W., and KLAUS, R. "The Assessment of Parental Identification." *Genetic Psychology Monographs* 1956, *54*, 87–114.

GRAY-SHELLBERG, L., VILLAREAL, S., and STONE, S. "Resolution of Career Conflicts: The Double Standard in Action." Paper presented at the meeting of the American Psychological Association, Honolulu, 1972.

GREENSTEIN, F. I. *Children and Politics*. New Haven: Yale University Press, 1965.

GREENSTEIN, F. I. *Personality and Politics: Problems of Evidence, Inference, and Conceptualization*. Chicago: Markham, 1969.

GREENWALD, H. *The Call Girl: A Social and Psychoanalytic Study*. New York: Ballantine Books, 1958.

GROSS, E. "Plus Ça Change . . . ? The Sexual Structure of Occupations over Time," in A. Theodore (ed.), *The Professional Woman*. Cambridge, Mass.: Schenkman Publishing Co., 1971.

GROSS, N., MASON, W. S., and MCEACHERN, A. W. *Explorations in Role Analysis: Studies of the School Superintendency Role*. New York: Wiley, 1958.

GRUBERG, M. *Women in American Politics: An Assessment and Sourcebook*. Oshkosh: Academia Press, 1968.

GRUDER, C. L., and COOK, T. D. "Sex, Dependency, and Helping." *Journal of Personality and Social Psychology*, 1971, *19*(3), 290–94.

GUMP, J. P. "Sex-Role Attitudes and Psychological Well-Being." *Journal of Social Issues*, 1972, *28*(2), 79–92.

GUMP, J. P. "Reality and Myth: Employment and Sex Role Ideology in Black Women." Paper presented at the Conference for New Directions for Research on the Psychology of Women, Madison, Wisconsin, 1975.

GURIN, G., VEROFF, J., and FELD, S. *Americans View Their Mental Health*. New York: Basic Books, 1960.

GURIN, P., GURIN, G., LAO, R. C., and BEATTIE, M. "Internal-External Control in the Motivational Dynamics of Negro Youth." *Journal of Social Issues*, 1969, *25*(3), 29–53.

HACKER, H. M. "Women as a Minority Group." *Social Forces*, 1951, *30*, 60–69.

HACKER, H. M. "Women as a Minority Group: Twenty Years Later." Paper presented at the meeting of the American Psychological Association, Honolulu, 1972.

HALL, E. T. *The Silent Language*. Garden City: Doubleday, 1959.

HALL, E. T. *The Hidden Dimension*. Garden City: Doubleday, 1966.

HAMBURG, D. A., and LUNDE, D. T. "Sex Hormones in the Development of Sex Differences in Human Behavior," in E. E. Maccoby (ed), *The Development of Sex Differences*. Stanford: Stanford University Press, 1966.

HAMBURG, D. A., MOOS, R. H., and YALOM, I. D. "Studies of Distress in the Menstrual Cycle and the Postpartum Period," in R. P. Michael (ed.), *Endocrinology and Human Behavior*. London: Oxford University Press, 1968.

HAMILTON, J. A. *Postpartum Psychiatric Problems*. St. Louis: Mosby, 1962.

HANES, L. J. "Sex Differences in Spatial Ability: Possible Environmental, Genetic and Neurological Factors," in M. Kinsbourne (ed.), *Hemispheric Asymmetrics of Function*. Cambridge: Cambridge University Press, 1976.

HARDING, J., PROSHANSKY, H. KUTNER, B., and CHEIN, I. "Prejudice and Ethnic

Relations," in G. Lindzey and E. Aronson (eds.), *Handbook of Social Psychology* (Vol. 5). Reading, Massachusetts: Addison-Wesley, 1969.

HARE, N., and HARE, J. "Black Women 1970." *Trans-action,* 1970, 8(1/2), 65–68.

HARLEY, J. P., KALISH, D. I., and SILVERMAN, A. J. "Eye Movements and Sex Differences in Field Articulation." *Perceptual and Motor Skills,* 1974, 38(2), 615–22.

HARRIS, L., and Associates. *The 1972 Virginia Slims American Women's Opinion Poll.*

HARRIS, S. "Influence of Subject and Experimenter Sex in Psychological Research." *Journal of Consulting and Clinical Psychology,* 1971, 37, 291–94.

HARRIS, S. "The Influence of Patient and Therapist Sex in Psychotherapy." Unpublished paper, Rutgers, The State University, 1974.

HARTLAGE, L. C. "Sex-Linked Inheritance of Spatial Ability." *Perceptual and Motor Skills,* 1970, 31, 610.

HARTLEY, R. E. "Sex-Role Pressures and the Socialization of the Male Child." *Psychological Reports,* 1959, 5, 457–68.

HARTLEY, R. E. "Children's Concepts of Male and Female Roles." *Merrill-Palmer Quarterly,* 1960, 6(2), 83–91.

HARTLEY, R. E. "A Developmental View of Female Sex-Role Definition and Identification." *Merrill-Palmer Quarterly,* 1964, 10(1), 3–16.

HARTLEY, R. E. "Some Implications of Current Changes in Sex Role Patterns," in J. M. Bardwick (ed.), *Readings on the Psychology of Women.* New York: Harper and Row, 1972.

HARTLEY, R. E., and HARDESTY, F. P. "Children's Perceptions of Sex Roles in Childhood." *Journal of Genetic Psychology,* 1964, 105, 43–51.

HARTUP, W. W., MOORE, S. G., and SAGER, G. "Avoidance of Inappropriate Sex-Typing by Young Children." *Journal of Consulting Psychology,* 1963, 27(6), 467–73.

HARTUP, W. W., and ZOOK, E. A. "Sex-Role Preferences in Three- and Four-Year-Old Children." *Journal of Consulting Psychology,* 1960, 24(5), 420–26.

HAWLEY, P. "Perceptions of Male Models of Femininity Related to Career Choice." *Journal of Counseling Psychology,* 1972, 19(4), 308–13.

HEAP, R. B., PERRY, J. S., and CHALLIS, J. R. G. "The Hormonal Maintenance of Pregnancy," in *Handbook of Physiology* (Section 7: Endocrinology, Vol. 2, Pt. 2). Washington, D.C.: American Physiological Society, 1973.

HEATHERS, G. "Emotional Dependence and Independence in a Physical Threat Situation." *Child Development,* 1953, 24, 169–79.

HEIDER, F. *The Psychology of Interpersonal Relations.* New York: Wiley, 1958.

HELPER, M. M. "Learning Theory and the Self Concept." *Journal of Abnormal and Social Psychology,* 1955, 51, 184–94.

HELSON, R. "The Changing Image of the Career Woman." *Journal of Social Issues,* 1972, 28(2), 33–46.

HELSON, R. "Creativity in Women." Paper presented at the Conference for New Directions for Research on the Psychology of Women, Madison, Wisconsin, 1975.

HENLEY, N. M. "The Politics of Touch." Paper presented at the meeting of the American Psychological Association, 1970.

HERO, A. "Public Reactions to Federal Policy: Some Comparative Trends." Unpublished paper, Boston, 1968.

HERSEY, R. B. "Emotional Cycles in Marriage." *Journal of Mental Science,* 1931, *77,* 151–62.

HERZBERG, B., and COPPEN, A. "Changes in Psychological Symptoms in Women Taking Oral Contraceptives." *British Journal of Psychiatry,* 1970, *116,* 161–64.

HESHKA, S., and NELSON, Y. "Interpersonal Speaking Distance as a Function of Age, Sex, and Relationship." *Sociometry,* 1972, *35*(4), 491–98.

HETHERINGTON, E. M. "A Developmental Study of the Effects of Sex of the Dominant Parent on Sex-Role Preference, Identification, and Imitation in Children." *Journal of Personality and Social Psychology,* 1965, *2*(2), 188–94.

HEWES, G. W. "The Anthropology of Posture." *Scientific American,* 1957, *196*(2), 122–32.

HICKS, D. J. "Girls' Attitudes toward Modeled Behaviors and the Content of Imitative Private Play." *Child Development,* 1971, *42,* 139–47.

HIGGINS, E. T. "Social Class Differences in Verbal Communicative Accuracy: A Question of 'Which Question?' " *Psychological Bulletin,* 1976, *83*(4), 695–714.

HILL, K. T., and SARASON, S. B. "The Relation of Test Anxiety and Defensiveness to Test and School Performance over the Elementary-School Years: A Further Longitudinal Study." *Monographs of the Society for Research in Child Development,* 1966, *31*(2, Serial No. 104).

HILTON, T. L., and BERGLUND, G. W. "Sex Differences in Mathematical Achievement—A Longitudinal Study." *Journal of Educational Research,* 1974, *67*(5), 231–37.

HINDLEY, C. B. "Stability and Change in Abilities up to Five Years: Group Trends." *Journal of Child Psychology and Psychiatry,* 1965, *6,* 85–99.

HINDLEY, C. B. "Racial and Sexual Differences in Age of Walking: A Reanalysis of Smith et al. (1930) Data." *Journal of Genetic Psychology,* 1967, *111,* 161–67.

HINDLEY, C. B., FILLIOZAT, A. M., KLACKENBERG, G., NICOLET-MEISTER, D., and SAND, E. A. "Differences in Age of Walking in Five European Longitudinal Samples." *Human Biology,* 1966, *38*(4), 364–79.

HIRSCHMAN, L. "Female-Male Differences in Conversational Interaction." Paper presented at the winter meeting of the Linguistic Society of America, 1973.

HOFFMAN, L. R., and MAIER, N. R. F. "Sex Differences, Sex Composition, and Group Problem Solving." *Journal of Abnormal and Social Psychology,* 1961, *63*(2), 453–56.

HOFFMAN, L. R., and MAIER, N. R. F. "Social Factors Influencing Problem Solving in Women." *Journal of Personality and Social Psychology,* 1966, *4*(4), 382–90.

HOFFMAN, L. W. "Early Childhood Experiences and Women's Achievement Motives." *Journal of Social Issues,* 1972, *28*(2), 129–55.

HOFFMAN, L. W., and NYE, F. I. (eds.). *Working Mothers: An Evaluative Review of the Consequences for Wife, Husband, and Child.* San Francisco: Jossey-Bass, 1974.

HOFFMAN, M. L. "Sex Differences in Empathy and Related Behaviors." *Psychological Bulletin,* 1977, *84,* 712–22.

HOLLANDER, E. P. "Conformity, Status, and Idiosyncrasy Credit." *Psychological Review,* 1958, *65,* 117–127.

HOLMES, D. S. "Male-Female Differences in MMPI Ego Strength: An Artifact." *Journal of Consulting Psychology,* 1967, *31,* 408–10.

HOLTER, H. *Sex Roles and Social Structure.* Oslo, Norway: Universitetsforlaget, 1970.

HOLZMAN, P. S., and GARDNER, R. W. "Leveling-Sharpening and Memory Organization." *Journal of Abnormal and Social Psychology*, 1960, *61*, 176–80.

HORN, H., STATTER, M., and FINKELSTEIN, M. "Estimation of Testosterone in Human Urine." *Steroids*, 1966, *7*, 118–36.

HORNER, M. S. "Toward an Understanding of Achievement-Related Conflicts in Women." *Journal of Social Issues*, 1972, *28*(2), 157–75.

HORNEY, K. "Flight from Womanhood." *International Journal of Psychoanalysis*, 1926, *7*, 324–39.

HORNEY, K. *Feminine Psychology*. New York: Norton, 1967.

HORNEY, K. "The Problem of Feminine Masochism," in J. B. Miller (ed.), *Psychoanalysis and Women*. Baltimore: Penguin Books, 1973.

HOUSE, W. C. "Actual and Perceived Differences in Male and Female Expectancies and Minimal Goal Levels as a Function of Competition." *Journal of Personality*, 1974, *42*, 493–509.

HOVLAND, C. I., JANIS, I. L., and KELLEY, H. H. *Communication and Persuasion*. New Haven: Yale University Press, 1953.

HOWE, L. K. *Pink-Collar Workers*. New York: G. P. Putnam, 1976.

HUNT, M. M. *Sexual Behavior in the 1970s*. Chicago: Playboy Press, 1974.

HUNTER, J. "Images of Woman," in D. N. Ruble, I. H. Frieze, and J. E. Parsons (eds), "Sex Roles: Persistence and Change." *Journal of Social Issues*, 1976, *32*(3), 7–17.

HYDE, J. S., and ROSENBERG, B. G. *Half the Human Experience: The Psychology of Women*. Lexington, Mass.: D. C. Heath, 1976.

IVEY, M. E., and BARDWICK, J. M. "Patterns of Affective Fluctuation in the Menstrual Cycle." *Psychosomatic Medicine*, 1968, *30*(3), 336–45.

JACKAWAY, R. "Sex Differences in Achievement Motivation, Behavior and Attribution about Success and Failure." Unpublished doctoral dissertation, State University of New York, Albany, 1974.

JACKLIN, C. N., MACCOBY, E. E., and DICK, A. E. "Barrier Behavior and Toy Preference: Sex Differences (and Their Absence) in the Year-Old Child." *Child Development*, 1973, *44*, 196–200.

JACOBY, S. "Feminism in the $12,000-a-Year Family: 'What Do I Do for the Next 20 Years?' " *New York Times Magazine*, June 17, 1973.

JAHNKE, J. C., CRANNELL, C. W., and MORRISSETTE, J. O. "Sex Differences and the MAS." *Educational and Psychological Measurement*, 1964, *24*, 309–12.

JENNINGS, M. K., and NIEMI, R. G. "The Transmission of Political Values from Parent to Child." *American Political Science Review*, 1968, *62*, 169–84.

JOHNSON, P. "Social Power and Sex Role Stereotyping." Unpublished doctoral dissertation, University of California, Los Angeles, 1974.

JOHNSON, P. "Women and Power: Toward a Theory of Effectiveness." *Journal of Social Issues*, 1976, *32*, 99–110.

JONG, E. *Fear of Flying*. New York: Holt, Rinehart and Winston, 1973.

JUHASZ, A. MCC. "Changes through History," in A. McC. Juhasz (ed.), *Sexual Development and Behavior: Selected Readings*. Homewood, Ill.: Dorsey Press, 1973.

JUNG, C. "The Stages of Life" (1933) (R. F. C. Hull, trans.), in J. Campbell (ed.), *The Portable Jung*. New York: Viking, 1971.

JUNG, C. G. *Two Essays on Analytical Psychology* (R. F. C. Hull, trans.). New York: Pantheon Books, 1953. (Originally published, 1943.)

JUNG, C. G. *Memories, Dreams, Reflections* (R. and C. Winston, trans.). New York: Pantheon Books, 1961.

KAGAN, J. "Acquisition and Significance of Sex Typing and Sex Role Identity," in M. L. Hoffman and L. W. Hoffman (eds.), *Review of Child Development Research* (Vol. 1). New York: Russell Sage Foundation, 1964(a).

KAGAN, J. "The Child's Sex role Classification of School Objects." *Child Development,* 1964, *35,* 1051–56(b).

KAGAN, J. "Reflection-Impulsivity: The Generality and Dynamics of Conceptual Tempo." *Journal of Abnormal Psychology,* 1966, *71,* 17–24.

KAGAN, J. *Change and Continuity in Infancy.* New York: Wiley, 1971.

KAGAN, J., and KOGAN, N. "Individuality and Cognitive Performance," in P. H. Mussen (ed.), *Carmichael's Manual of Child Psychology* (Vol. 1, 3rd ed.). New York: Wiley, 1970.

KAGAN, J., and MOSS, H. A. *Birth to Maturity, a Study in Psychological Development.* New York: Wiley, 1962.

KAGAN, J., ROSMAN, B. L., DAY, D., ALBERT, J., and PHILLIPS, W. "Information Processing in the Child: Significance of Analytic and Reflective Attitudes." *Psychological Monographs,* 1964, 78(1, Whole No. 578).

KAHN, A., HOTTES, J., and DAVIS, W. L. "Cooperation and Optimal Responding in the Prisoner's Dilemma Game: Effects of Sex and Physical Attractiveness." *Journal of Personality and Social Psychology,* 1971, *17,* 267–79.

KAHN, F. *Man in Structure and Function* (2 vols.; G. Rosen, M.D., ed. and trans.). New York: Knopf, 1943. (Originally published, 1939.)

KAHN, R. L., WOLFE, D. M., QUINN, R. P., and SNOEK, J. D. *Organizational Stress: Studies in Role Conflict and Ambiguity.* New York: Wiley, 1964.

KAHNE, H., with A. I. KOHEN. "Economic Perspectives on the Roles of Women in the American Economy." *Journal of Economic Literature,* 1975, *13*(4), 1249–92.

KALEY, M. M. "Attitudes toward the Dual Role of the Married Professional Woman." *American Psychologist,* 1971, *26,* 301–6.

KALISH, R. A. "The Effects of Death upon the Family," in L. Pearson (ed.), *Death and Dying: Current Issues in the Treatment of the Dying Person.* Cleveland: Case Western Reserve University Press, 1969.

KANTER, R. M., and HALTER, M. "The De-housewifing of Women: Equality between the Sexes in Urban Communes." Paper presented at the meeting of the American Psychological Association, Montreal, 1973.

KATCHER, A. "The Discrimination of Sex Differences by Young Children." *Journal of Genetic Psychology,* 1955, *87,* 131–43.

KATZ, D. "The Functional Approach to the Study of Attitudes." *Public Opinion Quarterly,* 1960, *24,* 163–204.

KATZ, M. "Sex Role Training and Coping Behavior in a Role Conflict Situation: Homemaking-Career Conflicts." Paper presented at the meeting of the American Psychological Association, Chicago, 1975.

KELLAGHAN, T., and MACNAMARA, J. "Family Correlates of Verbal Reasoning Ability." *Developmental Psychology,* 1972, *7,* 49–53.

KENNY, D. A. "The Measurement and Explanation of Population Effects: Sex Differences in Mathematics and Science in a Longitudinal Study." *Dissertation Abstracts International,* 1973, *33,* 4999–B.

KIESLER, S. "Prejudice: Women's Bias toward Other Women." *Intellect,* March 1973, pp. 348–49.

KIMMEL, D. C. *Adulthood and Aging: An Interdisciplinary, Developmental View.* New York: Wiley, 1974.

KIMURA, D. "Functional Asymmetry of the Brain in Dichotic Listening." *Cortex,* 1967, *3*(2), 163–78.

KINGDON, J. W. "Politicians' Beliefs about Voters." *American Political Science Review,* 1967, *61,* 137–45.

KINSEY, A. C., POMEROY, W. B., and MARTIN, C. E. *Sexual Behavior in the Human Male.* Philadelphia: W. B. Saunders Co., 1948.

KINSEY, A. C., POMEROY, W. B., MARTIN, C., and GEBHARD, P. *Sexual Behavior in the Human Female.* Philadelphia: W. B. Saunders Co., 1953.

KIRKPATRICK, J. J. *Political Women.* New York: Basic Books, 1974.

KLEIN, E. B., CICCHETTI, D., and SPOHN, H. "A Test of the Censure-Deficit Model and Its Relation to Premorbidity in the Performance of Schizophrenics." *Journal of Abnormal Psychology,* 1967, *72,* 174–81.

KNOBLAUCH, M. "Women Urged to Abandon Sleeping Beauty Syndrome." *Los Angeles Times,* December 13, 1974.

KNOX, C., and KIMURA, D. "Cerebral Processing of Nonverbal Sounds in Boys and Girls." *Neuropsychologia,* 1970, *8,* 227–37.

KOESKE, R. K., and KOESKE, G. F. "An Attributional Approach to Moods and the Menstrual Cycle." *Journal of Personality and Social Psychology,* 1975, *31*(3), 473–78.

KOHLBERG, L. "The Development of Children's Orientation toward a Moral Order: I. Sequence in the Development of Moral Thought." *Vita Humana,* 1963, *6,* 11–33.

KOHLBERG, L. "A Cognitive-Developmental Analysis of Children's Sex-Role Concepts and Attitudes," in E. E. Maccoby (ed.), *The Development of Sex Differences.* Stanford: Stanford University Press, 1966.

KOHLBERG, L. "Stages and Sequence: The Cognitive-Developmental Approach to Socialization," in D. A. Goslin (ed.), *Handbook of Socialization Theory and Research.* Chicago: Rand McNally, 1969.

KOHLBERG, L., and ZIGLER, E. "The Impact of Cognitive Maturity on the Development of Sex-Role Attitudes in the Years 4 to 8." *Genetic Psychology Monographs,* 1967, *75,* 89–165.

KOMAROVSKY, M. "Cultural Contradictions and Sex Roles." *American Journal of Sociology,* 1946, *52*(3), 184–89.

KOMAROVSKY, M. "Cultural Contradictions and Sex Roles: The Masculine Case." *American Journal of Sociology,* 1973, 78(4), 873–84.

KOPACZ, F. M., II, and SMITH, B. D. "Sex Differences in Skin Conductance Measures as a Function of Shock Threat." *Psychophysiology,* 1971, *8*(3), 293–303.

KRADITOR, A. S. (ed.). *Up from the Pedestal: Selected Writings in the History of American Feminism.* New York: Quadrangle Books, 1968.

KUHLEN, R. G. "Developmental Changes in Motivation During the Adult Years," in J. E. Birren (ed.), *Relations of Development and Aging.* Springfield, Ill.: C. C. Thomas, 1964.

KUHLEN, R. G., and JOHNSON, G. H. "Changes in Goals with Adult Increasing Age." *Journal of Consulting Psychology,* 1952, *16*(1), 1–4.

KUKLA, A. "Attributional Determinants of Achievement-Related Behavior." *Journal of Personality and Social Psychology,* 1972, *21,* 166–74.

LAMBERT, W. E., YACKLEY, A., and HEIN, R. N. "Child Training Values of English Canadian and French Canadian Parents." *Canadian Journal of Behavioral Science,* 1971, *3*(3), 217–36.

LAMPRECHT, F., LITTLE, B., and ZAHN, T. P. "Plasma Dopamine-Beta-Hydroxylase (DBH) Activity During the Menstrual Cycle. *Psychosomatic Medicine,* 1974, *36*(4), 304–10.

LAMSON, P. *Few Are Chosen: American Women in Political Life Today.* Boston: Houghton Mifflin, 1968.

LANCESTER, J. B. "In Praise of the Achieving Female Monkey." *Psychology Today,* September 1973, pp. 30–37; 99.

LANSDELL, H. "The Effect of Neurosurgery on a Test of Proverbs." *American Psychologist,* 1961, *16,* 448.

LANSDELL, H. "A Sex Difference in Effect of Temporal-Lobe Neurosurgery on Design Preference. *Nature,* June 1962, *194,* 852–54.

LANSING, M. "Women: The New Political Class." Unpublished paper, Eastern Michigan University, 1972.

LANSKY, L. M. "The Family Structure Also Affects the Model: Sex-Role Atitudes in Parents of Pre-School Children." *Merrill-Palmer Quarterly,* 1967, *13*(2), 139–50.

LANZETTA, J. T., and KLECK, R. E. "Encoding and Decoding of Nonverbal Affect in Humans. *"Journal of Personality and Social Psychology,* 1970, *16*(1), 12–19.

LAOSA, L. M., SWARTZ, J. D., and HOLTZMAN, W. H. "Human Figure Drawings by Normal Children: A Longitudinal Study of Perceptual-Cognitive and Personality Development." *Developmental Psychology,* 1973, *8,* 350–56.

LAPIERE, R. T. "Attitudes vs. Actions. *Social Forces,* 1934, *13,*230–37.

LASH, J. P. *Eleanor and Franklin.* New York: Norton, 1971.

LAVE, J. R., and ANGRIST, S. S. "Factors Affecting Child Care Expenditures of Working Mothers." Unpublished manuscript, Carnegie-Mellon University, 1974.

LAWS, J. L. "Work Motivation and Work Behavior of Women: New Perspectives." Paper presented at the Conference for New Directions for Research on the Psychology of Women, Madison, Wisconsin, 1975.

LAZOWICK, L. M. "On the Nature of Identification." *Journal of Abnormal and Social Psychology,* 1955, *51,* 175–83.

LEDER, G. C. "Sex Differences in Mathematics Problem Appeal as a Function of Problem Context." *Journal of Educational Research,* 1974, *67*(8), 351–53.

LEDERER, W. *The Fear of Women.* New York: Grune & Stratton, 1968.

LEFKOWITZ, M. M. "Some Relationships between Sex Role Preference of Children and Other Parent and Child Variables." *Psychological Reports,* 1962, *10,* 43–53.

LEGRAND, C. E. "Rape and Rape Laws: Sexism in Society and Law." *California Law Review,* 1973, *61,* 919–41.

LEHNER, G. F. J., and GUNDERSON, E. K. "Height Relationships on the Draw-A-Person Test." *Journal of Personality,* 1953, *21,* 392–99.

LEIBMAN, M. "The Effects of Sex and Race Norms on Personal Space," In H. M. Proshansky, W. H. Ittleson, and L. G. Rivlin (eds.), *Environment and Behavior,* 1970, *2,* 208–46.

LEIBOWITZ, A. "Education and Home Production." *American Economic Review,* 1974, 64(2), 243–50.

LEMASTERS, E.E. "Parenthood as Crisis." *Marriage and Family Living,* 1957, 19, 352–55.

LEON, B. "Sex Prejudice, 1973." Paper presented at the meeting of the Eastern Psychological Association, Philadelphia, 1974.

LEPPER, M. M. "A Study of Career Structures of Federal Executives: A Focus on Women," J. S. Jacquette (ed.), *Women in Politics.* New York: John Wiley, 1974.

LESSER, G. S., KRAWITZ, R. N., and PACKARD, R. "Experimental Arousal of Achievement Motivation in Adolescent Girls." *Journal of Abnormal and Social Psychology,* 1963, 66, 59–66.

LEVENTHAL, D. B., SHEMBERG, K. M., and VAN SCHOELANDT, S. K. "Effects of Sex-Role Adjustment upon the Expression of Aggression." *Journal of Personality and Social Psychology,* 1968, 8(4), 393–96.

LEVI, L. "Sympatho-Adrenomedullary and Related Biochemical Reactions During Experimentally Induced Emotional Stress," in R. P. Michael (ed.), *Endocrinology and Human Behavior.* London: Oxford University Press, 1968.

LEVINE, S. "Sex Differences in the Brain." *Scientific American,* 1966, 214(4), 84–90.

LEVINSON, D. J., DARROW, C. M., KLEIN, E. B., LEVINSON, M. H., and MCKEE, B. "The Psychosocial Development of Men in Early Adulthood and the Mid-Life Transition," in D. F. Ricks, A. Thomas, and M. Roff (eds.), *Life History Research in Psychotherapy* (Vol. 3). Minneapolis: University of Minnesota Press, 1974.

LEVITIN, T., QUINN, R. P., and STAINES, G. L. "Sex Discrimination against the American Working Woman." *American Behavioral Scientist,* 1971, 15(2), 237–54.

LEVY, J. "Possible Basis for the Evolution of Lateral Specialization of the Human Brain." *Nature,* November 1969, 224, 614–15.

LEVY-AGRESTI, J., and SPERRY, R. W. "Differential Perceptual Capacities in Major and Minor Hemispheres." *Proceedings of the National Academy of Sciences of the United States of America,* 1968, 61, 1151.

LEWIN, K. *Resolving Social Conflicts: Selected Papers on Group Dynamics.* New York: Harper and Row, 1948.

LEWIS, M. "Infants' Responses to Facial Stimuli During the First Year of Life." *Developmental Psychology,* 1969, 1(2), 75–86.

LEZINE, I., and BRUNET, O. "Presentation d'une Echelle Française de Tests du Premier Age." *Annales Medico-Psychologiques,* 1950, 108, 479.

LIBBY, W. L., JR., and YAKLEVICH, D. "Personality Determinants of Eye Contact and Direction of Gaze Aversion." *Journal of Personality and Social Psychology,* 1973, 27(2), 197–206.

LIEBERT, R. M., MCCALL, R. B., and HANRATTY, M. A. "Effects of Sex-Typed Information on Children's Toy Preferences." *Journal of Genetic Psychology,* 1971, 119, 133–36.

LINDEMANN, E. "Symptomatology and Management of Acute Grief. *American Journal of Psychiatry,* 1944, 101, 141–48.

LINDER, D. E. *Personal Space* (University Programs Modular Studies). Morristown, N.J.: General Learning Press, 1974.

LINTON, R. *The Study of Man: An Introduction*. New York: Appleton-Century, 1936.

LIPINSKI, B. G. "Sex-role Conflict and Achievement Motivation in College Women. "Unpublished doctoral dissertation, University of Cincinnati, 1965.

LIPMAN-BLUMEN, J. "How Ideology Shapes Women's Lives." *Scientific American*, 1972, *226*(1), 34–42.

LIPMAN-BLUMEN, J., and TICKAMYER, A. R. "Sex Roles in Transition: A Ten-Year Perspective," in A. Inkeles (ed.), *Annual Review of Sociology*. Palo Alto: Annual Reviews, Inc., 1975.

LIVINGSTON, J. C., and THOMPSON, R. G. *The Consent of the Governed* (2nd ed.). New York: Macmillan, 1966.

LOO, C. M. "The Effects of Spatial Density on the Social Behavior of Children." *Journal of Applied Social Psychology*, 1972, *2*, 372–81.

LOPATA, H. Z. *Occupation: Housewife*. New York: Oxford University Press, 1971.

LOPATA, H. Z. *Widowhood in an American City*. Cambridge, Mass.: Schenkman, 1973.

LOWENTHAL, M. F. "Intentionality: Toward a Framework for the Study of Adaptation in Adulthood." *Aging and Human Development*, 1971, *2*, 79–95.

LOWENTHAL, M. F., THURNHER, M., CHIRIBOGA, D., and Associates. *Four Stages of Life: A Comparative Study of Women and Men Facing Transitions*. San Francisco: Jossey-Bass, 1975.

LUBETKIN, B. S., and LUBETKIN, A. I. "Achievement Motivation in a Competitive Situation: The Older Female Graduate Student." *Journal of Clinical Psychology*, 1971, *27*(2), 269–71.

LUBIN, B., GARDENER, S. H., and ROTH, A. "Mood and Somatic Symptoms During Pregnancy." *Psychosomatic Medicine*, 1975, *37*(2), 136–46.

LUCE, G. G. *Biological Rhythms in Psychiatry and Medicine* (Public Health Service Publication No. 2088). Washington, D.C.: U.S. Government Printing Office, 1970.

LYDON, C. "Democrats Hail Charter and Adjourn in Harmony." *New York Times*, December 9, 1974.

LYNN, N. "Women in American Politics: An Overview," In J. Freeman (ed.), *Women: A Feminist Perspective*. Palo Alto,: Mayfield, 1975.

MAAS, H. S., and KUYPERS, J. A. *From Thirty to Seventy: A Forty-Year Longitudinal Study of Changing Life Styles and Personal Development*. San Francisco: Jossey-Bass, 1974.

MACCOBY, E. E. "Sex Differences in Intellectual Functioning," in E. E. Maccoby (ed.), *The Development of Sex Differences*. Stanford: Stanford University Press, 1966.

MACCOBY, E. E. "Differential Socialization of Boys and Girls." Paper presented at the meeting of the American Psychological Association, Hawaii, 1972.

MACCOBY, E. E., and JACKLIN, C. N. "Stress, Activity, and Proximity Seeking: Sex Differences in the Year-Old Child." *Child Development*, 1973, *44*, 34–42.

MACCOBY, E. E., and JACKLIN, C. N. *The Psychology of Sex Differences*. Stanford: Stanford University Press, 1974.

MACCOBY, E. E., and WILSON, W. C. "Identification and Observational Learning from Films." *Journal of Abnormal and Social Psychology*, 1957, *55*, 76–87.

MADDISON, D., and VIOLA, A. "The Health of Widows in the Year Following Bereavement." *Journal of Psychosomatic Research* 1968, *12*(4), 297–306.

MADDOX, G. L. "Fact and Artifact: Evidence Bearing on Disengagement Theory from the Duke Geriatrics Project." *Human Development,* 1965, *8,* 117–30.

MADDOX, G. L. "Persistence of Life Style among the Elderly," in E. Palmore (ed.), *Normal Aging: Reports from the Duke Longitudinal Study, 1955–1969.* Durham: Duke University Press, 1970.

MADDOX, G., and EISDORFER, C. "Some Correlates of Activity and Morale among the Elderly." *Social Forces,* 1962, *40,* 254–60.

MAINARDI, P. "The Politics of Housework," in L. B. Tanner (ed.), *Voices from Women's Liberation.* New York: New American Library, 1971.

MALLICK, S. K., and MCCANDLESS, B. R. "A Study of Catharsis of Aggression." *Journal of Personality and Social Pscyhology,* 1966, *4*(6), 591–96.

"The Mandate of Title VII of the Civil Rights Act of 1964: To Treat Women as Individuals. *Georgetown Law Journal,* 1970, *59,* 221–39.

MANDLER, G., and SARASON, S. B. "A Study of Anxiety and Learning." *Journal of Abnormal and Social Psychology,* 1952, *47*(1), 166–73.

MANES, A. L., and MELNYK, P. "Televised Models of Female Achievement." *Journal of Applied Social Psychology,* 1974, *4*(4), 365–74.

MANN, R. D. "A Review of the Relationships between Personality and Performance in Small Groups." *Psychological Bulletin,* 1959, *56*(4), 241–70.

MARCH, J. G. "Husband-Wife Interaction over Political Issues." *Public Opinion Quarterly,* 1953, *17,* 461–70.

MARKLE, G. E. "Sex Ratio at Birth: Values, Variance, and Some Determinants." *Demography,* 1974, *11,* 131–42.

MARMOR, J. "Changing Patterns of Femininity: Psychoanalytic Implications," in J. B. Miller (ed.), *Psychoanalysis and Women.* Baltimore: Penguin Books, 1973.

MARR, J. "Can Training Change Sex-Role Stereotypes?" *Psychology,* 1974, *11*(2), 10–16.

MASLOW, A. H. *Toward a Psychology of Being* (2nd ed.). Princeton: Van Nostrand, 1968.

MASSEY, M. E. *Bonnet Brigades.* New York: Knopf, 1966.

MASTERS, W. H., and JOHNSON, V. E. *Human Sexual Response.* Boston: Little, Brown, 1966.

MASTERS, W. H., and JOHNSON, V. E. *Human Sexual Inadequacy.* Boston: Little, Brown, 1970.

MAY, R. B., and HUTT, C. "Modality and Sex Differences in Recall and Recognition Memory." *Child Development,* 1974, *45,* 228–31.

MCARTHUR, L. Z., and EISEN, S. V. "Achievements of Male and Female Storybook Characters as Determinants of Achievement Behavior by Boys and Girls." *Journal of Personality and Social Psychology,* 1976, *33*(4), 467–73.

MCCANCE, R. A., LUFF, M. C., and WIDDOWSON, E. E. "Physical and Emotional Periodicity in Women." *Journal of Hygiene,* 1937, *37,* 571–611.

MCCLELLAND, D. C. *Power: The Inner Experience.* New York: Halsted Press, 1976.

MCCLELLAND, D. C., ATKINSON, J. W., CLARK, R. A., and LOWELL, E. L. *The Achievement Motive.* New York: Appleton-Century-Crofts, 1953.

MCEWEN, B. S. "Interactions between Hormones and Nerve Tissue." *Scientific American,* 1976, *235*(1), 48–58.

MCGUIRE, W. J. "The Nature of Attitudes and Attitude Change," in G. Lindzey and

E. Aronson (eds.), *Handbook of Social Psychology* (Vol. 3). Reading, Mass.: Addison-Wesley, 1969.

MCHUGH, M. "Sex Differences in Causal Attributions: A Critical Review." Paper presented at the meeting of the Eastern Psychological Association, New York, 1975.

MCHUGH, M. C., DUQUIN, M. E., and FRIEZE, I. H. "Beliefs about Success and Failure: Attribution and the Female Athlete," in C. A. Oglesby (ed.), *Women and Sport: From Myth to Reality*. Philadelphia: Lea and Febiger, 1977.

MCKEE, J. P., and SHERRIFFS, A. C. "The Differential Evaluation of Males and Females." *Journal of Personality*, 1957, *25*, 356–71.

MCKEE, J. P., and SHERRIFFS, A. C. "Men's and Women's Beliefs, Ideals, and Self-Concepts." *American Journal of Sociology*, 1959, *64*, 356–63.

MCMAHAN, I. D. "Sex Differences in Expectancy of Success as a Function of Task." Paper presented at the meeting of the Eastern Psychological Association, 1972.

MEAD, M. *Sex and Temperament in Three Primitive Societies*. New York: Morrow, 1935.

MEAD, M., and KAPLAN, F. B. (eds.). *American Women: The Report of the President's Commission on the Status of Women and Other Publications of the Commission*. New York: Scribner's, 1965.

MEDDIS, R. "Human Circadian Rhythms and the 48-Hour Day." *Nature*, 1968, *218*, 964–65.

MEDEA, A., and THOMPSON, K. *Against Rape*. New York: Farrar, Straus and Giroux, 1974.

MEHRABIAN, A. "Verbal and Nonverbal Interaction of Strangers in a Waiting Situation." *Journal of Experimental Research in Personality*, 1971, *5*, 127–38.

MEHRABIAN, A. *Nonverbal Communication*. Chicago: Aldine-Atherton, 1972.

MERRIAM, C. E., and GOSNELL, H. F. *Non-Voting, Causes and Methods of Control*. Chicago: University of Chicago Press, 1924.

MERRITT, S. "Winners and Losers: Sex Differences in Municipal Elections." *American Journal of Political Science*, 1977, *21*, 731–43.

MERTON, R. K. *Social Theory and Social Structure* (rev. and enlarged ed.). Glencoe, Ill.: Free Press, 1957.

MEYER, J. W., and SOBIESZEK, B. I. "Effect of a Child's Sex on Adult Interpretations of Its Behavior." *Developmental Psychology*, 1972, *6*, 42–48.

MEYER-BAHLBURG, H. F. L., NAT, R., BOON, D. A., SHARMA, M., and EDWARDS, J. D. "Aggressiveness and Testosterone Measures in Man." *Psychosomatic Medicine*, 1974, *36*(3), 269–74.

MILES, C. C. "Sex in Social Psychology," in C. Murchison (ed.), *A Handbook of Social Psychology*. Worcester: Clark University Press, 1935.

MILLER, J. G. "Information Input Overload and Psychopathology. *American Journal of Psychiatry*, 1960, *116*, 695–704.

MILLETT, K. *Sexual Politics*. Garden City: Doubleday, 1970.

MILTON, G. A. "Sex Differences in Problem Solving as a Function of Role Appropriateness of the Problem Content." *Psychological Reports*, 1959, *5*, 705–8.

MILTON, K. *Women in Policing*. Police Foundation, 1972.

MINCER, J., and POLACHEK, S. "Family Investments in Human Capital: Earnings of Women." *Journal of Political Economy*, 1974, *82*(2, Pt. 2), S76–S108.

MINTON, H. L. "Power as a Personality Construct," in B. A. Maher (ed.), *Progress in*

Experimental Personality Research, Vol. 4. New York: Academic Press, 1967.

MINUCHIN, P. "Sex-Role Concepts and Sex Typing in Childhood as a Function of School and Home Environments." *Child Development,* 1965, *36,* 1033–48.

MISCHEL, W. "The Effect of the Commitment Situation on the Generalization of Expectancies." *Journal of Personality,* 1958, *26,* 508–16.

MISCHEL, W. "A Social-Learning View of Sex Differences in Behavior." In E. E. Maccoby (ed.), *The Development of Sex Differences.* Stanford: Stanford University Press, 1966.

MISCHEL, W. *Personality and Assessment.* New York: Wiley, 1968.

MISCHEL, W. "Continuity and Change in Personality." *American Psychologist,* 1969, *24,* 1012–18.

MISCHEL, W. "Sex-typing and Socialization," in P. H. Mussen (ed.), *Carmichael's Manual of Child Psychology* (Vol. 2, 3rd ed.). New York: Wiley, 1970.

MISCHEL, W. *Introduction to Personality.* New York: Holt, Rinehart and Winston, 1971.

MISCHEL, W. "Continuity and Change in Personality," in H. N. Mischel and W. Mischel (eds.), *Readings in Personality.* New York: Holt, Rinehart and Winston, 1973 (a).

MISCHEL, W. "Toward a Cognitive Social Learning Reconceptualization of Personality. *Psychological Review,* 1973 (b), *80*(4), 252–83.

MISCHEL, W., and GRUSEC, J. "Determinants of the Rehearsal and Transmission of Neutral and Aversive Behaviors." *Journal of Personality and Social Psychology,* 1966, *3*(2), 197–205.

MONEY, J. (ed.). *Sex Research, New Developments.* New York: Holt, Rinehart and Winston, 1965.

MONEY, J., and EHRHARDT, A. A. *Man & Woman, Boy & Girl: The Differentiation and Dimorphism of Gender Identity from Conception to Maturity.* Baltimore: Johns Hopkins University Press, 1972.

MONEY, J., HAMPSON, J. G., and HAMPSON, J. L. "Imprinting and the Establishment of Gender Role." A.M.A. *Archives of Neurology and Psychiatry,* 1957, *77,* 333–36.

MONEY, J., and TUCKER, P. *Sexual Signatures: On Being a Man or a Woman.* Boston: Little, Brown, 1975.

MONTANELLI, D. S., and HILL, K. T. "Children's Achievement Expectations and Performance as a Function of Two Consecutive Reinforcement Experiences, Sex of Subject, and Sex of Experimenter." *Journal of Personality and Social Psychology,* 1969, *13*(2), 115–28.

MONTEMAYOR, R. "Children's Performance in a Game and Their Attraction to It as a Function of Sex-Typed Labels." *Child Development,* 1974, *45,* 152–56.

Monthly Vital Statistics Report, "Advance Report Final Natality Statistics, 1974." February 13, 1976, *24*(11), supp. 2.

MOOS, R. H. "The Development of a Menstrual Distress Questionnaire." *Psychosomatic Medicine,* 1968, *30*(6), 853–67.

MOOS, R. H., KOPELL, B. S., MELGES, F. T., YALOM, I. D., LUNDE, D. T., CLAYTON, R. B., and HAMBURG, D. A. "Fluctuations in Symptoms and Moods During the Menstrual Cycle." *Journal of Psychosomatic Research,* 1969, *13,* 37–44.

MORGAN, D. *Suffragists and Democrats: The Politics of Woman Suffrage in America.* East Lansing: Michigan State University Press, 1972.

MORRIS, L. A. "Attribution Theory and Drug Administration." Unpublished manuscript, 1976.

MOSHER, D. L. "Sex Differences, Sex Experience, Sex Guilt, and Explicitly Sexual Films," in W. C. Wilson and M. Goldstein (eds.), "Pornography: Attitudes, Use and Effects." *Journal of Social Issues,* 1973, *29*(3), 95–112.

MOSS, H. A. "Sex, Age, and State as Determinants of Mother-Infant Interaction. *Merrill-Palmer Quarterly,* 1967, *13,* 19–36.

MOYER, K. E. "Sex Differences in Aggression," in R. C. Friedman, R. M. Richart, and R. L. Vande Wiele (eds.), *Sex Differences in Behavior: A Conference.* New York: Wiley, 1974.

MUSSEN, P. H. "Early Sex-Role Development," in D. A. Goslin (ed.), *Handbook of Socialization Theory and Research.* Chicago: Rand McNally, 1969.

MUSSEN, P., and DISTLER, L. "Masculinity, Identification, and Father-Son Relationships." *Journal of Abnormal and Social Psychology,* 1959, *59,* 350–56.

MUSSEN, P., and RUTHERFORD, E. "Parent-Child Relations and Parental Personality in Relation to Young Children's Sex-Role Preferences." *Child Development, 34,* 589–607.

MYRDAL, G. *An American Dilemma: The Negro Problem and Modern Democracy.* New York: Harper, 1944.

NADELMAN, L. "Sex Identity in American Children: Memory, Knowledge, and Preference Tests." *Developmental Psychology,* 1974, *10*(3), 413–17.

NASH, S. C. "The Relationship among Sex-Role Stereotyping, Sex-Role Preference, and the Sex Difference in Spatial Visualization." *Sex Roles,* 1975, *1*(1), 15–32.

National Advisory Committee on Criminal Justice Standards and Goals. *Criminal Justice Research and Development.* Washington, D.C.: Law Enforcement Assistance Administration, 1976.

National American Woman Suffrage Association. *Victory: How Women Won It: A Centennial Symposium, 1840–1940.* New York: H. W. Wilson, 1940.

National Center for Health Statistics, quoted in the *Pittsburgh Press,* December 31, 1976.

NEBES, R. D. "Handedness and the Perception of Part-Whole Relationship." *Cortex,* 1971 (a), *7,* 350–56.

NEBES, R. D. "Superiority of the Minor Hemisphere in Commissurotomized Man for the Perception of Part-Whole Relations." *Cortex,* 1971 (b), *7,* 333–49.

NEUGARTEN, B. L. (ed.). *Middle Age and Aging: A Reader in Social Psychology.* Chicago: University of Chicago Press, 1968.

NEUGARTEN, B. L., and GARRON, D. C. "Attitudes of Middle-Aged Persons toward Growing Older. *Geriatrics,* 1959, *14*(1), 21–24.

NEUGARTEN, B. L., and KRAINES, R. J. "Menopausal Symptoms in Women of Various Ages. *Psychosomatic Medicine,* 1965, *27,*(3), 266–73.

NEUGARTEN, B. L., MOORE, J. W., LOWE, J. C. "Age Norms, Age Constraints, and Adult Socialization." *American Journal of Sociology,* 1965, *70*(6), 710–17.

NEUGARTEN, B. L., WOOD, V., KRAINES, R. J., and LOOMIS, B. "Women's Attitudes toward the Menopause." *Vita Humana,* 1963, *6,* 140–51.

NEVILL, D. "Experimental Manipulation of Dependency Motivation and Its Effects on Eye Contact and Measures of Field Dependency." *Journal of Personality and Social Psychology,* 1974, *29*(1), 72–79.

N.Y. Narcotic Addiction Control Commission. *Differential Drug Use within the New*

York State Labor Force: An Assessment of Drug Use within the General Population. 1971.

NEWCOMB, T. M., KOENIG, K. E., HACKS, R., and WAURRICH, D. P. *Persistence and Change: Bennington College and Its Students after Twenty-five Years.* New York: Wiley, 1967.

NEWLAND, K. "Many Women Candidates." *New York Times,* May 19, 1974.

NEWLAND, K. *Women in Politics: A Global Review* (Worldwatch Paper 3). Washington, D.C.: World Watch Institute, 1975.

Newsweek. "Womanpower at the Polls." November 18, 1974, p. 39.

Newsweek. July 14, 1976, p. 28.

NICHOLLS, J. G. "Causal Attributions and Other Achievement-Related Cognitions: Effects of Task Outcome, Attainment Value, and Sex." *Journal of Personality and Social Psychology,* 1975, *31*(3), 379–89.

NOWACKI, C. M., and POE, C. A. "The Concept of Mental Health as Related to Sex of Person Perceived." *Journal of Consulting and Clinical Psychology,* 1973, 40(1), 160.

NYE, F. I. "Sociocultural Context," in L. W. Hoffman and F. I. Nye (eds.), *Working Mothers: An Evaluative Review of the Consequences for Wife, Husband, and Child.* San Francisco: Jossey-Bass, 1974.

NYE, F. I., and HOFFMAN, L. W. (eds.). *The Employed Mother in America.* Chicago: Rand McNally, 1963.

OETZEL, R. M. Annotated bibliography, in E. E. Maccoby (ed.), *The Development of Sex Differences.* Stanford: Stanford University Press, 1966.

O'LEARY, V. E. "Some Attitudinal Barriers to Occupational Aspirations in Women." *Psychological Bulletin,* 1974, *81*(11), 809–26.

O'NEILL, N., and O'NEILL, G. *Open Marriage, a New Life Style for Couples.* New York: Evans, 1972.

O'NEILL, W. L. *Everyone Was Brave: The Rise and Fall of Feminism in America.* New York: Quadrangle Books, 1969.

OPPENHEIMER, V. K. *The Female Labor Force in the United States: Demographic and Economic Factors Governing Its Growth and Changing Composition.* Berkeley: Institute of International Studies, University of California, 1970.

OPPENHEIMER, V. K. "Rising Educational Attainment, Declining Fertility and the Inadequacies of the Female Labor Market." *Commission on Population Growth and the American Future, Research Reports* (Vol. 1, 305–28). Washington, D.C.: U.S. Government Printing Office, 1972.

OPPENHEIMER, V. K. "Demographic Influence on Female Employment and the Status of Women." *American Journal of Sociology,* 1973, 78(4), 946–61.

ORDEN, S. R., and BRADBURN, N. M. "Working Wives and Marriage Happiness. *American Journal of Sociology,* 1969, 74(4), 392–407.

PAGE, E. B. "Teacher Comments and Student Performance: A Seventy-four Classroom Experiment in School Motivation." *Journal of Educational Psychology,* 1958, *49,* 173–81.

PAIGE, K. E. "Effects of Oral Contraceptives on Affective Fluctuations Associated with the Menstrual Cycle." *Psychosomatic Medicine,* 1971, *33*(6), 515–37.

PAIGE, K. E. "Women Learn to Sing the Menstrual Blues." *Psychology Today,* September 1973, pp. 41–46.

PALMORE, E. (ed.). *Normal Aging: Reports from the Duke Longitudinal Study, 1955–1969.* Durham: Duke University Press, 1970.

PAPENEK, H. "Men, Women, and Work: Reflections on the Two-Person Career," in J. Huber, (ed.), *Changing Women in a Changing Society.* Chicago: University of Chicago Press, 1973.

PARKES, C. M. *Bereavement: Studies of Grief in Adult Life.* New York: International Universities Press, 1972.

PARKES, C. M., BENJAMIN, B., and FITZGERALD, R. G. "Broken Heart: A Statistical Study of Increased Mortality among Widowers. *British Medical Journal,* 1969, *1,* 740–43.

PARLEE, M. B. "The Premenstrual Syndrome." *Psychological Bulletin,* 1973, 80(6), 454–65.

PARLEE, M. B. "Stereotypic Beliefs about Menstruation: A Methodological Note on the Moos Menstrual Distress Questionnaire and Some New Data." *Psychosomatic Medicine,* 1974, 36(3), 229–40.

PARLEE, M. B. "Psychological Aspects of Menstruation, Childbirth, and Menopause: An Overview with Suggestions for Further Research," in J. Sherman and F. Denmark, eds., *The Psychology of Women: Future Directions of Research.* New York: Psychological Dimensions, 1978.

PARMALEE, A. H., JR., and STERN, E. "Development of States in Infants," in C. D. Clemente, D. P. Purpura, and F. E. Mayer (eds.), *Sleep and the Maturing Nervous System.* New York: Academic Press, 1972.

PARSONS, J. E. "The Development of Achievement Expectancies in Girls and Boys." Paper presented at the meeting of the Eastern Psychological Association, Philadelphia, 1974.

PARSONS, J. E. "The Development of Sex Differences." Unpublished manuscript, Smith College, 1976(a).

PARSONS, J. E. "Sex-Role Choices and Peer Preference in the Middle School Years." Unpublished manuscript, Smith College, 1976(b).

PARSONS, J. E., FRIEZE, I. H., and RUBLE, D. N. Introduction, in D. N. Ruble, I. H. Frieze, and J. E. Parsons (eds.), "Sex Roles: Persistence and Change. *Journal of Social Issues,* 1976, *32*(3), 1–5

PARSONS, J. E., RUBLE, D. N., HODGES, K. L., and SMALL, A. W. "Cognitive-Developmental Factors in Emerging Sex Differences in Achievement-Related Expectancies," in D. N. Ruble, I. H. Frieze, and J. E. Parsons (eds.), Sex roles: Persistence and change. *Journal of Social Issues,* 1976, *32*(3), 47–61.

PARSONS, T. "Full Citizenship for the Negro American? A Sociological Problem." *Daedalus,* 1965, 94(4), 1009–54.

PARSONS, T., and BALES, R. F. *Family, Socialization and Interaction Process.* Glencoe, Ill.: Free Press, 1955.

PEATMAN, J. G., and HIGGONS, R. A. "Development of Sitting, Standing and Walking of Children Reared with Optimal Pediatric Care." *American Journal of Orthopsychiatry,* 1940, *10,* 88–110.

PEDERSEN, D. M., SHINEDLING, M. M., and JOHNSON, D. L. "Effects of Sex of Examiner and Subject on Children's Quantitative Test Performance." *Journal of Personality and Social Psychology,* 1968, *10*(3), 251–54.

PEDERSEN, F. A., and ROBSON, K. S. "Father Participation in Infancy." *American Journal of Orthopsychiatry,* 1969, 39(3), 466–72.

PEPITONE, E. A. "Comparison Behavior in Elementary School Children." *American Educational Research Journal,* 1972, 9, 45–63.

PERLS, F. S. *Gestalt Therapy Verbatim.* Lafayette, Calif.: Real People Press, 1969.

PERRY, D. G., and PERRY, L. C. "Observational Learning in Children: Effects of Sex of Model and Subject's Sex Role Behavior. *Journal of Personality and Social Psychology,* 1975, *31*(6), 1083–88.

PERSKY, H. "Reproductive Hormones, Moods and the Menstrual Cycle," in R. C. Friedman, R. M. Richart and R. L. Vande Wiele (eds.), *Sex Differences in Behavior.* New York: Wiley, 1974.

PERSKY, H., SMITH, K. D., and BASU, G. K. "Relation of Psychologic Measures of Aggression and Hostility to Testosterone Production in Man." *Psychosomatic Medicine,* 1971, *33*(3), 265–77.

PETERSON, I. "Women Get Instructions on Politics." *New York Times,* September 28, 1973.

PETTIGREW, T. F. *A Profile of the Negro American.* Princeton: Van Nostrand, 1964.

PHETERSON, G. I., KIESLER, S. B., and GOLDBERG, P. A. "Evaluation of the Performance of Women as a Function of Their Sex, Achievement, and Personal History. *Journal of Personality and Social Psychology,* 1971, *19*(1), 114–18.

PHILLIPS, L., and RABINOVITCH, M. S. "Social Role and Patterns of Symptomatic Behaviors." *Journal of Abnormal and Social Psychology,* 1958, *57,* 181–86.

PIAGET, J. *The Moral Judgment of the Child* (M. Gabain, trans.). Glencoe, Ill.: Free Press, 1948. (Originally published, 1932.)

PILIAVIN, I. M., RODIN, J., and PILIAVIN, J. A. "Good Samaritanism: An Underground Phenomenon?" *Journal of Personality and Social Psychology,* 1969, *13*(4), 289–99.

PLATH, S. *The Bell Jar.* New York: Harper and Row, 1971.

PLECK, J. H. "The Psychology of Sex Roles: Traditional and New Views," in A. F. Scott (ed.), *Women and Men: Changing Roles, Relationships and Perceptions.* Sanford: Aspen Institute for Humanistic Studies, 1976a.

PLECK, J. H. "The Male Sex Role: Definitions, Problems, and Sources of Change." *Journal of Social Issues,* 1976b, *32,* 155–64.

POLLIS, N. P., and DOYLE, D. C. Sex Role, Status, and Perceived Competence Among First-Graders. *Perceptual and Motor Skills,* 1972, *34,* 235–38.

POLOMA, M. M. "Role Conflict and the Married Professional Woman," in C. Safilios-Rothschild (ed.), *Toward a Sociology of Women.* Lexington, Mass.: Xerox College Publishing, 1972.

POLOMA, M. M., and GARLAND, T. N. "The Married Professional Woman: A Study in the Tolerance of Domestication." *Journal of Marriage and the Family,* 1971, *33,* 531–40.

PRIEST, R. F., and HUNSAKER, P. L. "Compensating for a Female Disadvantage in Problem Solving." *Journal of Experimental Research in Personality,* 1969, *4,* 57–64.

PRIMAVERA, L. H., SIMON, W. E., and PRIMAVERA, A. M. "The Relationship between Self-Esteem and Academic Achievement: An Investigation of Sex Differences." *Psychology in the Schools,* 1974, *11*(2), 213–16.

PUBLIC OPINION POLLS. *Public Opinion Quarterly* (Vols. 4–14), 1940–1950.

RABBAN, M. "Sex-Role Identification in Young Children in Two Diverse Social Groups." *Genetic Psychology Monographs,* 1950, *42*(1), 81–158.

RADLOFF, L. "Sex Differences in Depression: The Effects of Occupation and Marital Status." *Sex Roles,* 1975, *1*(3), 249–65.

RAMEY, E. "Hormonal Bias Is Her Battle." *Los Angeles Times,* February 21, 1972.

RAPH, J. B., GOLDBERG, M. L., and PASSOW, A. H. *Bright Underachievers; Studies of Scholastic Underachievement Among Intellectually Superior High School Students.* New York: Teachers College Press, 1966.

RAVEN, B. H. "Social Influence and Power," in I. D. Steiner and M. Fishbein (eds.), *Current Studies in Social Psychology.* New York: Holt, Rinehart and Winston, 1965.

RAVEN, B. H., and KRUGLANSKI, A. W. "Conflict and Power," in P. Swingle (ed.), *The Structure of Conflict.* New York: Academic Press, 1970.

REBECCA, M., HEFNER, R., and OLESHANSKY, B. "A Model of Sex-Role Transcendence," in D. N. Ruble, I. H. Frieze, and J. E. Parsons (eds.), "Sex Roles: Persistence and Change." *Journal of Social Issues,* 1976, *32*(3), 197–206.

REICH, W. *Sexual Revolution: Toward a Self-Governing Character Structure* (T. Wolfe, trans., 3rd ed.). New York: Orgone Institute Press, 1945.

REICH, W. *Sex-Pol: Essays 1929–1934* (A. Bostock, T. DuBose, and L. Baxandall, trans.). New York: Random House, 1966.

REICH, W. *The Mass Psychology of Fascism* (V. R. Carfagno, trans.). New York: Farrar, Straus and Giroux, 1970.

REID, I., and COHEN, L. "Achievement Orientation, Intellectual Achievement Responsibility and Choice between Degree and Certificate Courses in Colleges of Education." *British Journal of Education,* 1973, *43,* 63–66.

REISS, P. J. "Bereavement and the American Family," in A. H. Kutscher (ed.), *Death and Bereavement.* Springfield, Ill.: C. C. Thomas, 1969.

RENNE, K. S. "Correlates of Dissatisfaction in Marriage." *Journal of Marriage and the Family,* 1970, *32*(1), 54–67.

The Report of the Commission on Obscenity and Pornography. New York: Bantam Books, 1970.

REYNOLDS, E. "Variations of Mood and Recall in the Menstrual Cycle." *Journal of Psychosomatic Research,* 1969, *13,* 163–66.

RICH, A. *Of Woman Born: Motherhood as Experience and Institution.* New York: Norton, 1976.

RICHTER, C. P. "Periodic Phenomena in Man and Animals: Their Relation to Neuroendocrine Mechanisms (a Monthly or Near Monthly Cycle)," in R. P. Michael (ed.), *Endocrinology and Human Behavior.* London: Oxford University Press, 1968.

RICKS, D. F., THOMAS, A., and ROFF, M. (eds.). *Life History Research in Psychopathology* (Vol. 3). Minneapolis: University of Minnesota Press, 1974.

RILEY, M. W., JOHNSON, M., and FONER, A. *Aging and Society* (Vol. 3). New York: Russell Sage Foundation, 1972.

ROBINSON, J. R., and CONVERSE, P. E. *Summary of the U.S. Time Use Survey,* May 30, 1966.

ROBY, P. "Structural and Internalized Barriers to Women in Higher Education," in J. Freeman (ed.), *Women: A Feminist Perspective.* Palo Alto: Mayfield, 1975.

ROCHE, A. F. "Sex-Associated Differences in Skeletal Maturity." *Acta Anatomica,* 1968, *71,* 321–40.

ROHNER, R. P. "Sex Differences in Aggression: Phylogenetic and Enculturation Perspectives." *Ethos,* 1976, *4,* 57–72.

ROIPHE, A. "Confessions of a Female Chauvinist Sow." *New York,* October 30, 1972, pp. 52–53, 55.

ROLLIN, B. "Motherhood: Who Needs It?" *Look,* September 22, 1970, pp. 15–17.

ROLLINS, B. C., and CANNON, K. L. "Marital Satisfaction over the Family Life Cycle: A Reevaluation." *Journal of Marriage and the Family,* 1974, *36*(2), 271–83.

ROLLINS, B. C., and FELDMAN, H. "Marital Satisfaction over the Family Life Cycle." *Journal of Marriage and the Family,* 1970, *32*(1), 20–28.

ROSALDO, M. Z. "Women, Culture and Society: A Theoretical Overview," in M. Z. Rosaldo and L. Lamphere (eds.), *Women, Culture, and Society.* Stanford: Stanford University Press, 1974.

ROSE, A. M. "Factors Associated with the Life Satisfaction of Middle-Class, Middle-Aged Persons," in C. B. Vedder (ed.), *Problems of the Middle-Aged.* Springfield, Ill.: C. C. Thomas, 1965.

ROSE, R. M. "The Psychological Effects of Androgens and Estrogens: A Review," in R. I. Shader (ed.), *Psychiatric Complications of Medical Drugs.* New York: Raven Press, 1972.

ROSE, R. M., BERNSTEIN, I. S., and GORDON, T. P. "Consequences of Social Conflict on Plasma Testosterone Levels in Rhesus Monkeys." *Psychosomatic Medicine,* 1975, *37*(1), 50–61.

ROSE, R. M., HOLADAY, J. W., and BERNSTEIN, I. S. "Plasma Testosterone, Dominance Rank and Aggressive Behavior in Male Rhesus Monkeys." *Nature,* 1971, *231,* 366–68.

ROSEN, B., and JERDEE, T. H. "Effects of Applicant's Sex and Difficulty of Job on Evaluations of Candidates for Managerial Positions." *Journal of Applied Psychology,* 1974(a), *59*(4), 511–12.

ROSEN, B., and JERDEE, T. H. "Influence of Sex Role Stereotypes on Personnel Decisions." *Journal of Applied Psychology,* 1974(b), *59*(1), 9–14.

ROSEN, D. H. *Lesbianism: A Study of Female Homosexuality.* Springfield, Ill.: C. C. Thomas, 1974.

ROSENBLITH, J. F. "Imitative Color Choices in Kindergarten Children." *Child Development,* 1961, *32,* 211–23.

ROSENFELD, H. M. "Instumental Affiliative Functions of Facial and Gestural Expressions." *Journal of Personality and Social Psychology,* 1966, *4*(1), 65–72.

ROSENKRANTZ, P., VOGEL, S., BEE, H., BROVERMAN, I., and BROVERMAN, D. M. "Sex-Role Stereotypes and Self-Concepts in College Students." *Journal of Consulting and Clinical Psychology,* 1968, *32,* 287–95.

ROSENTHAL, R. *Experimenter Effects in Behavioral Research.* New York: Appleton-Century-Crofts, 1966.

ROSENTHAL, R., and JACOBSON, L. F. "Teacher Expectations of the Disadvantaged." *Scientific American,* 1968, *218*(4), 19–23.

ROSS, D. M., and ROSS, S. A. Resistance by Preschool Boys to Sex-Inappropriate Behavior. *Journal of Educational Psychology,* 1972, *63*(4), 342–46.

ROSSI, A. S. "Barriers to the Career Choice of Engineering, Medicine, or Science among American Women," in J. A. Mattfeld and C. G. Van Aken (eds.), *Women and the Scientific Professions: The M.I.T. Symposium on American Women in Science and Engineering.* Cambridge: Massachusetts Institute of Technology Press, 1965.

ROSSI, A. S. "The Roots of Ambivalence in American Women." Paper presented at the Continuing Education Conference, Oakland University, Michigan, May 1967.

ROSSI, A. S. "Job Discrimination and What Women Can Do about It." *Atlantic Monthly,* March 1970, pp. 99–102.

ROSZAK, T. "The Hard and the Soft: The Force of Feminism in Modern Times," in B. Roszak and T. Roszak (eds.), *Masculine/Feminine: Readings in Sexual Mythology and the Liberation of Women.* New York: Harper and Row, 1969.

ROTHBART, M. K., and MACCOBY, E. E. "Parents' Differential Reactions to Sons and Daughters." *Journal of Personality and Social Psychology,* 1966, 4(3), 237–43.

ROTKIN, K. "The Phallacy of Our Sexual Norm." *Loaded,* February 1973, Santa Cruz, Calif.

ROTTER, J. B. *Social Learning and Clinical Psychology.* New York: Prentice-Hall, 1954.

ROTTER, J. B. "Generalized Expectancies for Internal Versus External Control of Reinforcement." *Psychological Monographs,* 1966, 80(1, Whole No. 609).

RUBIN, Z. *Liking and Loving.* New York: Holt, Rinehart and Winston, 1973.

RUBLE, D. N. "Visual Orientation and Self-Perceptions of Children in an External-Cue-Relevant or Cue-Irrelevant Task Situation." *Child Development,* 1975, 46(3), 669–76.

RUBLE, D. N. "Premenstrual Symptoms: A Reinterpretation." *Science,* 1977.

RUBLE, D. N., CROKE, J. A., FRIEZE, I., and PARSONS, J. E. "A Field Study of Sex-Role Attitude Change in College Women." *Journal of Applied Social Psychology,* 1975, 5(2), 110–17.

RUBLE, D. N., FELDMAN, N. S., and BOGGIANO, A. K. "Social Comparison Between Young Children in Achievement Situations." *Developmental Psychology,* 1976, 12(3), 192–97.

RUBLE, D. N., and HIGGINS, E. T. "Effects of Group Sex Composition on Self-Presentation and Sex-Typing," in D. N. Ruble, I. H. Frieze, and J. E. Parsons (eds.), "Sex Roles: Persistence and Change." *Journal of Social Issues,* 1976, 32(3), 125–32.

RUBLE, D. N., and NAKAMURA, C. Y. "Task Orientation Versus Social Orientation in Young Children and Their Attention to Relevant Social Cues," *Child Development,* 1972, 43, 471–80.

RUDEL, R. G., DENCKLA, M. B., and SPALTAR, E. "The Functional Asymmetry of Braille Letter Learning in Normal Sighted Children." *Neurology,* 1974, 24, 733–38.

RUSSO, N. F. "Eye Contact, Interpersonal Distance, and the Equilibrium Theory." *Journal of Personality and Social Psychology,* 1975, 31(3), 497–502.

SAGHIR, M. T., and ROBINS, E. *Male and Female Homosexuality; A Comprehensive Investigation,* Baltimore: Williams and Wilkins, 1973.

SANCHEZ-HIDALGO, E. "El Sentimiento de Inferioridad en la Mujer Puertorriqueña." [The Feeling of Inferiority in the Puerto Rican Female.] *Rev. Asoc. Maestros, P. R.,* 1952, 11(6), 170–71; 193. Cited in J. A. Sherman, *On the Psychology of Women: A Survey of Empirical Studies.* Springfield, Ill.: C. C. Thomas, 1971.

SANDERS, M. K. *The Lady and the Vote.* Boston: Houghton Mifflin, 1956.

SARASON, I. G, and MINARD, J. "Interrelationships among Subject, Experimenter, and Situational Variables." *Journal of Abnormal and Social Psychology,* 1963, 67(1), 87–91.

SARBIN, T. R, and ALLEN, V. L. "Role Theory," in G. Lindzey and E. Aronson (eds.), *Handbook of Social Psychology* (Vol. 1). Reading, Mass.: Addison-Wesley, 1968.

SCANZONI, J. H. *Sexual Bargaining: Power Politics in the American Marriage.* Englewood Cliffs: Prentice-Hall, 1972.

SCHAEFER, L. C. *Women and Sex: Sexual Experiences and Reactions of a Group of Thirty Women as Told to a Female Psychotherapist.* New York: Pantheon, 1973.

SCHATTSCHNEIDER, E. E. *The Semisovereign People: A Realist's View of Democracy in America.* New York: Holt, Rinehart and Winston, 1960.

SCHELL, R. E., and SILBER, J. W. "Sex-Role Discrimination among Young Children." *Perceptual and Motor Skills,* 1968, *27,* 379–89.

SCHLOSSBERG, N. K., and PIETROFESA, J. J. "Perspectives on Counseling Bias: Implications for Counselor Education." *The Counseling Psychologist,* 1973, *4*(1), 44–54.

SCHMIDT, G., and SIGUSCH, V. "Women's Sexual Arousal," in J. Zubin and J. Money (eds.), *Contemporary Sexual Behavior: Critical Issues in the 1970s.* Baltimore: Johns Hopkins University Press, 1973.

SCHONBERGER, R. J. "Inflexible Working Conditions Keep Women Unliberated." *Personnel Journal,* 1971, *50,* 834–37.

SCHULTZ, D. P. "The Human Subject in Psychological Research." *Psychological Bulletin,* 1969, *72,* 214–28.

SCHUTZ, W. C. *Joy: Expanding Human Awareness.* New York: Grove Press, 1967.

SCHWARTZ, N. "Women and the Amendment." *Commonweal,* June 15, 1973, pp. 328–31.

SCHWARTZ, P. "The Social Psychology of Female Sexuality." Paper presented at the Conference for New Directions for Research on the Psychology of Women, Madison, Wisconsin, 1975.

SCOTT, R. B., FERGUSON, A. D., JENKINS, M. E., and CUTTER, F. F. "Growth and Development of Negro Infants: V. Neuromuscular Patterns of Behavior During the First Year of Life." *Pediatrics,* 1955, *16,* 24–30.

SEAMAN, B. *Free and Female: The Sex Life of the Contemporary Woman.* New York: Coward, McCann and Geoheqan. 1972.

SEARS, D. O. "Political Behavior," in G. Lindzey and E. Aronson (eds.), *Handbook of Social Psychology* (Vol. 5). Reading, Mass.: Addison-Wesley, 1969.

SEARS, D. O. "Political Socialization," in F. I. Greenstein and N. W. Polsby (eds.), *Handbook of Political Science* (Vol. 2). Reading, Mass.: Addison-Wesley, 1975.

SEARS, D, O., and FREEDMAN, J. L. "Selective Exposure to Information: A Critical Review." *Public Opinion Quarterly,* 1967, *31,* 194–213.

SEARS, D. O., and WHITNEY, R. E. "Political Persuasion," in I. S. Pool, F. W. Frey, W. Schramm, N. Maccoby, and E. B. Parker (eds.), *Handbook of Communications.* Chicago: Rand McNally, 1973.

SEARS, R. R. "Relation of Early Socialization Experiences to Aggression in Middle Childhood." *Journal of Abnormal and Social Psychology,* 1961, *63,* 466–92.

SEARS, R. R. "Relation of Early Socialization Experiences to Self-Concepts and Gender Role in Middle Childhood." *Child Development,* 1970, *41*(2), 267–90.

SEARS, R. R., MACCOBY, E. E., and LEVIN, H. *Patterns of Child Rearing.* Evanston: Row, Peterson, 1957.

SEARS, R. R., RAU, L., and ALPERT, R. *Identification and Child Rearing.* Stanford: Stanford University Press, 1965.

SEGAL, S. J. "The Physiology of Human Reproduction." *Scientific American,* 1974, *231*(3), 52–62.

SEGAL, S. J., and ATKINSON, L. E. "Biological Effects of Oral Contraceptive Steroids," in *Handbook of Physiology* (Section 7: Endocrinology, Vol. 2, Pt. 2). Washington, D.C.: American Physiological Society, 1973.

SEIFER, N. *Absent from the Majority: Working Class Women in America.* New York: National Project on Ethnic America of the American Jewish Committee, 1973.

SEWARD, G. H. "The Female Sex Rhythm," *Psychological Bulletin,* 1934, *31,* 153–92.

SEXTON, P. C. "Workers (Female) Arise! On Founding the Coalition of Labor Union Women." *Dissent,* 1974, *21,* 380–95.

SHAFFER, D. R., and WEGLEY, C. "Success Orientation and Sex-Role Congruence as Determinants of the Attractiveness of Competent Women." *Journal of Personality,* 1974, *42*(4), 586–600.

SHAW, M. C., and MCCUEN, J. T. "The Onset of Academic Underachievement in Bright Children." *Journal of Educational Psychology,* 1960, *51*(3), 103–8.

SHELTON, P. B. "Achievement Motivation in Professional Women." Unpublished doctoral dissertation, University of California, Berkeley, 1967.

SHEPARD, W. O., and HESS, D. T. "Attitudes in Four Age Groups Toward Sex Role Division in Adult Occupations and Activities." *Journal of Vocational Behavior,* 1975, *6*(1), 27–39.

SHERFEY, M. J. *The Nature and Evolution of Female Sexuality.* New York: Random House, 1972.

SHERMAN, J. A. "Problem of Sex Differences in Space Perception and Aspects of Intellectual Functioning." *Psychological Review,* 1967, *74*(4), 290–99.

SHERMAN, J. A. *On the Psychology of Women: A Survey of Empirical Studies.* Springfield, Ill.: C. C. Thomas, 1971.

SHERMAN, J. A. "Field Articulation, Sex, Spatial Visualization, Dependency, Practice, Laterality of the Brain and Birth Order." *Perceptual and Motor Skills,* 1974, *38*(3, Pt. 2), 1223–35.

SHERMAN, J. A. "Effects of Biological Factors on Sex-Related Differences in Mathematics Achievement." Report prepared for NIE: Women and Mathematics Section, 1977. (Available from author at 3917 Plymouth Circle, Madison, Wisconsin 53705.)

SHNEIDMAN, E. S., and FARBEROW, N. L. "Statistical Comparisons between Attempted and Committed Suicides," in N. L. Farberow and E. S. Shneidman (eds.), *The Cry for Help.* New York: McGraw-Hill, 1961.

SHOCK, N. W. (ed.). *Aging—Some Social and Biological Aspects: Symposia Presented at the Chicago Meeting, December 29–30, 1959.* Washington, D.C.: American Association for the Advancement of Science, 1960.

SILBERGELD, S., BRAST, N., and NOBLE, E. P. "The Menstrual Cycle: A Double-Blind Study of Symptoms, Mood and Behavior, and Biochemical Variables Using Enovid and Placebo." *Psychosomatic Medicine,* 1971, *33*(5), 411–28.

SILVERMAN, A. J., ADEVAI, G., and MCGOUGH, W. E. "Some Relationships between Handedness and Perception." *Journal of Psychosomatic Research,* 1966, *10*(2), 151–58.

SILVERMAN, C. *The Epidemiology of Depression.* Baltimore: Johns Hopkins Press, 1968.

SIMON, J. G., and FEATHER, N. T. "Causal Attributions for Success and Failure at University Examinations." *Journal of Educational Psychology,* 1973, *64,* 46–56.

SIMPSON, G. E., and YINGER, J. M. *Racial and Cultural Minorities: An Analysis of Prejudice and Discrimination* (3rd ed.). New York: Harper, 1965.

SINGER, J. E., WESTPHAL, M., and NISWANDER, K. R. "Sex Differences in the Incidence of Neonatal Abnormalities and Abnormal Performance in Early Childhood." *Child Development,* 1968, *39,* 103–12.

SISTRUNK, F., and MCDAVID, J. W. "Sex Variable in Conforming Behavior." *Journal of Personality and Social Psychology,* 1971, *17*(2), 200–207.

SKLAR, J., and BERKOV, B. "The American Birth Rate: Evidences of a Coming Rise." *Science,* 1975, *189*(4204), 693–700.

SKOLNICK, P., FRASER, L., and HADAR, I. "Do You Speak to Strangers: Studies on Invasions of Personal Space." Paper presented at the meeting of the Western Psychological Association, Portland, 1972.

SMALL, A., NAKAMURA, C. Y., and RUBLE, D. N. "Sex Differences in Children's Outer Directedness and Self-Perceptions in a Problem Solving Situation." Unpublished manuscript, University of California, Los Angeles, 1973.

SMITH, C. "The Development of Sex Role Concepts and Attitudes in Father-Absent Boys." Unpublished master's thesis, University of Chicago, 1966.

SMITH, C. P. (ed.). *Achievement-Related Motives in Children.* New York: Russell Sage Foundation, 1969.

SMITH, J., and KORNBERG, A. "Self-Concepts of American and Canadian Party Officials: Their Development and Consequences." *Social Forces,* 1970, *49,* 210–26.

SOBOL, M. G. "Commitment to Work," in L. W. Hoffman and F. I. Nye (eds.), *Working Mothers: An Evaluative Review of the Consequences for Wife, Husband, and Child.* San Francisco: Jossey-Bass, 1974.

SOMMER, B. "The Effect of Menstruation on Cognitive and Perceptual-Motor Behavior: A Review." *Psychosomatic Medicine,* 1973, *35*(6), 515–34.

SOMMER, R. *Personal Space: The Behavioral Basis of Design.* Englewood Cliffs, N.J.: Prentice-Hall, 1969.

SOUTHAM, A. L., and GONZAGA, F. P. "Systemic Changes During the Menstrual Cycle." *American Journal of Obstetrics and Gynecology,* 1965, *91,* 142–65.

SPENCE, J. T., HELMREICH, R., and STAPP, J. "Ratings of Self and Peers on Sex Role Attributes and Their Relation to Self-Esteem and Conceptions of Masculinity and Femininity." *Journal of Personality and Social Psychology,* 1975, *32*(1), 29–39.

SPERRY, R. W., and LEVY, J. Mental Capacities of the Disconnected Minor Hemisphere Following Commissurotomy. Paper presented at the Symposium on Asymmetrical Function of the Human Brain at the meeting of the American Psychological Association, Miami, 1970.

SPIEGLER, M. D., and LIEBERT, R. M. "Some Correlates of Self-Reported Fear." *Psychological Reports,* 1970, *26,* 691–95.

STAFFORD, R. E. "Sex Differences in Spatial Visualization as Evidence of Sex-Linked Inheritance." *Perceptual and Motor Skills,* 1961, *13,* 428.

STEIN, A. H. "The Effects of Sex-Role Standards for Achievement and Sex-Role Performance on Three Determinants of Achievement Motivation." *Developmental Psychology*, 1971, *4*(2), 219–31.

STEIN, A. H., and BAILEY, M. M. The Socialization of Achievement Orientation in Females. *Psychological Bulletin*, 1973, *80*(5), 345–66.

STEIN, A. H., and SMITHELLS, J. "Age and Sex Differences in Children's Sex-Role Standards about Achievement." *Developmental Psychology*, 1969, *1*(3), 252–59.

STEIN, L. I. "Male and Female: The Doctor-Nurse Game," in J. P. Spradley and D. W. McCurdy (eds.), *Conformity and Conflict: Readings in Cultural Anthropology*, Boston: Little, Brown, 1971b.

STEPHENS, W. N. "A Cross-Cultural Study of Menstrual Taboos." *Genetic Psychology Monographs*, 1961, *64*, 385–416.

STERN, D. N., and BENDER, E. P. "An Ethological Study of Children Approaching a Strange Adult: Sex Differences," in R. C. Friedman, R. M. Richart, and R. L. Vande Wiele (eds.), *Sex Differences in Behavior: A Conference*. New York: Wiley, 1974.

STEVENSON, M. "Women's Wages and Job Segregation." *Politics and Society*, 1973, *4*(1), 83–96.

STEWART, A. J. "Self-Definition and Social Definition in Women." *Journal of Personality*, 1974, *42*, 238–59.

STIMPSON, C. "Thy Neighbor's Wife, Thy Neighbor's Servants: Women's Liberation and Black Civil Rights." In V. Gornick and B. K. Moran (eds.), *Woman in Sexist Society: Studies in Power and Powerlessness*. New York: Basic Books, 1971.

STOGDILL, R. M. *Individual Behavior and Group Achievement*. New York: Oxford University Press, 1959.

STOLLER, R. J. "The Sense of Femaleness." *Psychoanalytic Quarterly*, 1968, *37*, 42–55.

STOUFFER, S. A. *Communism, Conformity, and Civil Liberties: A Cross-Section of the Nation Speaks Its Mind*. Garden City: Doubleday, 1955.

STRATTON, L. O., TEKIPPE, D. J., and FLICK, G. L. "Personal Space and Self-Concept." *Sociometry*, 1973, *36*(3), 424–29.

STROEBE, W., INSKO, C. A., THOMPSON, V. D., and LAYTON, B. D. "Effects of Physical Attractiveness, Attitude Similarity, and Sex on Various Aspects of Interpersonal Attraction." *Journal of Personality and Social Psychology*, 1971, *18*, 79–91.

SZASZ, T. S. "The Myth of Mental Illness." *American Psychologist*, 1960, *15*, 113–18.

TAGIURI, R. "Person Perception," in G. Lindzey and E. Aronson (eds.), *The Handbook of Social Psychology* (Vol. 3). Reading, Mass.: Addison-Wesley, 1969.

TAJFEL, H. "Cognitive Aspects of Prejudice." *Journal of Social Issues*, 1969, *25*(4), 79–97.

TANGRI, S. S. "Determinants of Occupational Role Innovation among College Women." *Journal of Social Issues*, 1972, *28*(2), 177–99.

TAYLOR, S. E. "Some Cognitive Bases of Stereotyping." Unpublished manuscript, Harvard University, 1973.

TEDESCHI, J. T., SCHLENKER, B. R., and LINDSKOLD, S. "The Exercise of Power and Influence: The Source of Influence," in J. T. Tedeschi (ed.), *The Social Influence Processes*. Chicago: Aldine-Atherton, 1972.

THOMAS, A. H., and STEWART, N. R. "Counselor Response to Female Clients with

Deviate and Conforming Career Goals." *Journal of Counseling Psychology,* 1971, *18,* 352–57.

THOMPSON, C. *Psychoanalysis: Evolution and Development.* New York: Hermitage House, 1950.

THOMPSON, C. M. *Interpersonal Psychoanalysis: The Selected Papers of Clara M. Thompson.* New York: Basic Books, 1964.

THOMPSON, S. "Development of Sex-Role Concepts." Unpublished doctoral dissertation. University of California, Los Angeles, 1973.

THOMPSON, S. K., and BENTLER, P. M. "The Priority of Cues in Sex Discrimination by Children and Adults." *Developmental Psychology,* 1971, *5*(2), 181–85.

TIGER, L. *Men in Groups.* New York: Random House, 1969.

TOFALO, R. J. "Self-Image and Dogmatism: Personality Variables within Two Urban Lifestyles—Communal and Noncommunal." Unpublished masters thesis. Howard University, 1973.

TOLOR, A., and TOLOR, B. "Children's Figure Drawings and Changing Attitudes toward Sex Roles." *Psychological Reports,* 1974, *34*(2), 343–49.

TOMASSON, R. F. "Why Has American Fertility Been So High?" in B. Farber (ed.), *Kinship and Family Organization.* New York: Wiley, 1966.

TOMLINSON, J. R. "Situational and Personality Correlates of Predictive Accuracy." *Journal of Consulting Psychology,* 1967, *31,* 19–22.

TOUHEY, J. C. "Effects of Additional Women Professionals on Ratings of Occupational Prestige and Desirability." *Journal of Personality and Social Psychology,* 1974, *29*(1), 86–89.

TRACHTENBERG, J. *Jewish Magic and Superstition.* New York: Behrman's Jewish Book House, 1939; Cleveland: World, 1961.

TREIMAN, D. J., and TERRELL, K. "Sex and the Process of Status Attainment: A Comparison of Working Women and Men." *American Sociological Review,* 1975, *40,* 174–200.

TRESEMER, D. "Fear of Success: Popular But Unproven." *Psychology Today,* March 1974, pp. 82–85.

TRIANDIS, H. C., and DAVIS, E. E. "Race and Belief as Determinants of Behavioral Intentions. "*Journal of Personality and Social Psychology,* 1965, *2*(5), 715–25.

TYLER, B. B. "Expectancy for Eventual Success as a Factor in Problem Solving Behavior." *Journal of Educational Psychology,* 1958, *49,* 166–72.

TYLER, L. E. *The Psychology of Human Differences.* New York: Appleton-Century, 1947.

TYLER, L. E. *The Psychology of Human Differences* (3rd ed.). New York: Appleton-Century-Crofts, 1965.

ULLIAN, D. Z. "The Development of Conceptions of Masculinity and Femininity," in B. Lloyd and J. Archer (eds.), *Exploring Sex Differences.* London: Academic Press, 1976.

U.S. CIVIL SERVICE COMMISSION, STATISTICS SECTION. *Study of Employment of Women in the Federal Government, 1967.* Washington, D.C.: U.S. Government Printing Office, 1968.

U.S. DEPARTMENT OF HEALTH, EDUCATION, and WELFARE. *Vital Statistics of the United States, 1967* (Vol. 1). Washington, D.C.: U.S. Government Printing Office, 1970.

U.S. DEPARTMENT OF LABOR, WAGE and LABOR STANDARDS ADMINISTRATION,

WOMEN'S BUREAU. Facts about Women's Absenteeism and Labor Turnover. Washington, D.C.: U.S. Government Printing Office, 1969(a).

U.S. DEPARTMENT OF LABOR, WAGE AND LABOR STANDARDS ADMINISTRATION, WOMEN'S BUREAU. *1969 Handbook on Women Workers* (Women's Bureau Bulletin 294). Washington, D.C.: U.S. Government Printing Office, 1969(b).

U.S. DEPARTMENT OF LABOR, MANPOWER ADMINISTRATION. *Years for Decision: A Longitudinal Study of the Educational and Labor Market Experience of Young Women* (Manpower Research Monograph 24, Vol. 1). Washington, D.C.: U.S. Government Printing Office, 1971.

U.S. DEPARTMENT OF LABOR AND DEPARTMENT OF HEALTH, EDUCATION, AND WELFARE. *Manpower Report of the President,* transmitted to the Congress, April 1975. Washington, D.C.: U.S. Government Printing Office, 1975.

UNIVERSITY OF CHICAGO REPORTS, *Aging and the Aged,* Vol. 12, No. 2, November 1961.

VAILLANT, G. E., and MCARTHUR, C. C. "Natural History of Male Psychologic Health: I. The Adult Life Cycle from 18–50." *Seminars in Psychiatry,* 1972, 4(4), 415–27.

VALINS, S. "Cognitive Effects of False Heart-Rates Feedback." *Journal of Personality and Social Psychology,* 1966, 4, 400–408.

VALLE, V. A., and FRIEZE, I. H. "Stability of Causal Attributions as a Mediator in Changing Expectations for Success." *Journal of Personality and Social Psychology,* 1976, 33(5), 579–87.

VAN LEEUWAN, K. "Pregnancy Envy in the Male." *International Journal of Psychoanalysis,* 1966, 47, 319–24.

VEEVERS, J. E. "Voluntarily Childless Wives: An Exploratory Study," in E. Peck and J. Senderowitz (eds.), *Pronatalism: The Myth of Mom and Apple Pie.* New York: Crowell, 1974.

VEROFF, J., and FELD, S. *Marriage and Work in America: A Study of Motives and Roles.* New York: Van Nostrand Reinhold, 1970.

WALDMAN, E., and GOVER, K. R. "Children of Women in the Labor Force." *Monthly Labor Review,* 1971, 94(7), 19–25.

WALKER, K. E. "Effect of Family Characteristics on Time Contributed for Household Work by Various Members." Paper presented at the meeting of the American Home Economics Association, Atlantic City, 1973.

WEBSTER, H. *Taboo, a Sociological Study.* Stanford: Stanford University Press, 1942.

WEINER, B. *Theories of Motivation: From Mechanism to Cognition.* Chicago: Markham, 1972.

WEINER, B. "Achievement Motivation as Conceptualized by an Attribution Theorist," in B. Weiner (ed.), *Achievement Motivation and Attribution Theory.* Morristown, N.J.: General Learning Press, 1974.

WEINER, B., FRIEZE, I., KUKLA, A., REED, L., REST, S., and ROSENBAUM, R. M. "Perceiving the Causes of Success and Failure," in E. E. Jones, D. E. Kanouse, H. H. Kelley, R. E. Nisbett, S. Valins, and B. Weiner (eds.), *Attribution: Perceiving the Causes of Behavior.* Morristown, N.J.: General Learning Press, 1972.

WEINER, B., and KUKLA, A. "An Attributional Analysis of Achievement Motivation." *Journal of Personality and Social Psychology,* 1970, 15(1), 1–20.

WEINER, B., and POTEPAN, P. A. "Personality Characteristics and Affective Reactions toward Exams of Superior and Failing College Students." *Journal of Educational Psychology,* 1970, *61*(2), 144–51.

WEINER, E., and BACHTOLD, L. "Personality Characteristics of Women in American Politics." Paper presented at the meeting of the American Political Science Association, Washington, D.C., 1972.

WEISSTEIN, N. "Psychology Constructs the Female, or the Fantasy Life of the Male Psychologist," in M. H. Garskof (ed.), *Roles Women Play: Readings toward Women's Liberation.* Belmont, Calif.: Brooks/Cole, 1971.

WEITZ, S. "Sex Role Attitudes and Nonverbal Communication in Same and Opposite-Sex Interactions." Paper presented at the meeting of the American Psychological Association, New Orleans, 1974.

WELCH, S. "Women as Political Animals? A Test of Some Explanations for Male-Female Political Participation "Differences." *American Journal of Political Science,* 1977, *21, 711*–29.

WELLS, A., and SMEAL, E. "Women's Attitudes toward Women in Politics: A Survey of Urban Registered Voters and Party Committee-Women." Paper presented at the meeting of the American Political Science Association, Washington, D.C., 1972.

WESTOFF, C. F., POTTER, R. G., JR., SAGI, P. C., and MISHER, E. G. *Family Growth in Metropolitan America.* Princeton: Princeton University Press, 1961.

WESTOFF, C. F., and POTVIN, R. H. *College Women and Fertility Values.* Princeton: Princeton University Press, 1967.

WHELAN, E. M. "Attitudes toward Menstruation." *Studies in Family Planning,* 1975, 6(4), 106–8.

WHITE, R. W. *Lives in Progress: A Study of the Natural Growth of Personality* (2nd ed.). New York: Holt, Rinehart and Winston, 1966.

WHITING, B., and EDWARDS, C. P. "A Cross-Cultural Analysis of Sex Differences in the Behavior of Children Aged Three Through Eleven." *Journal of Social Psychology,* 1973, *91, 171*–88.

WHYTE, W. H. *The Organization Man.* New York: Simon and Schuster, 1956.

WILCOXON, L. A., SCHRADER, S. L., and SHERIF, C. W. "Daily Self-Reports on Activities, Life Events, Moods, and Somatic Changes During the Menstrual Cycle." *Psychosomatic Medicine,* 1976, 38(6), 399–417.

WILLIAMS, C. C., WILLIAMS, R. A., GRISWOLD, M. J., and HOLMES, T. H. "Pregnancy and Life Changes." *Journal of Psychosomatic Research,* 1975. *19*(2), 123–29.

WILLIAMS, R. M., JR. *The Reduction of Intergroup Tensions: A Survey of Research on Problems of Ethnic, Racial, and Religious Group Relations.* New York: Social Science Research Council, 1947.

WILLIAMS, T. "Family Resemblance in Abilities: The Wechster Scales." *Behavior Genetics,* 1975, *5,* 405–9.

WILLIS, R. H., and FRIEZE, I. H. "Sex Roles and Social Exchange as Determinants of Attraction and Compatibility in Couples," in K. J. Gergen, M. S. Greenberg, and R. H. Willis (eds), *Social Exchange: Advances in Theory and Research.* New York: Wiley, in press.

WILLS, G. "What? What? Are Young Americans Afraid to Have Kids?" *Esquire,* March 1974, pp. 80–81; 170.

WILSON, G. D. "An Electrodermal Technique for the Study of Phobias." *New Zealand Medical Journal,* 1966, *65,* 696–98.

WILSON, G. D. "Social Desirability and Sex Differences in Expressed Fear." *Behaviour Research and Therapy,* 1967, *5,* 136–37.

WILSON, R. A. *Feminine Forever.* New York: M. Evans/Lippincott, 1966.

WINICK, C., and KINSIE, P. M. *The Lively Commerce: Prostitution in the United States.* New York: Quadrangle Books, 1971.

WINOKUR, G. "Depression in the Menopause." *American Journal of Psychiatry,* 1973, *130*(1), 92–93.

WINSTON, F. "Oral Contraceptives, Pyridoxine, and Depression." *American Journal of Psychiatry,* 1973, *130*(11), 1217–21.

WINTER, D. G. *The Power Motive.* New York: Free Press, 1973.

WITKIN, H. A., DYK, R. B., FATERSON, H. F., GOODENOUGH, D. R., and KARP, S. A. *Psychological Differentiation: Studies of Development.* New York: Wiley, 1962.

WITTIG, M. A. "Sex Differences in Intellectual Functioning: How Much of a Difference Do Genes Make?" *Sex Roles,* 1976, *2,* 63–74.

WOLF, T. M. "Influence of Age and Sex of Model on Sex-Inappropriate Play." *Psychological Reports,* 1975, *36*(1), 99–105.

WOLFE, D. M. "Power and Authority in the Family," in D. Cartwright (ed), *Studies in Social Power.* Ann Arbor: Institute for Social Research, 1959.

Women Mayors in Cities over 30,000 Population. U.S. Conference of Mayors, Washington, D.C., February 1976.

WOOLEY, H. T. "A Review of the Recent Literature on the Psychology of Sex," *Psychological Bulletin,* 1910, *7*(10), 335–42.

YOUNG, W. C., GOY, R. W., and PHOENIX, C. H. "Hormones and Sexual Behavior." *Science,* 1964, *143*(3603), 212–18.

YULISH, S. "The Effectiveness of Storybooks as a Means of Overcoming Sex-Role Stereotyped Behavior Patterns." Unpublished manuscript, Smith College, 1976.

ZAJONC, R. B. "Attitudinal Effects of Mere Exposure." *Journal of Personality and Social Psychology,* 1968, *9*(2), 1–27. (Monograph Supplement, pt. 2.)

ZELDITCH, M. "Family, Marriage, and Kinship," in R. E. L. Faris (ed.), *Handbook of Modern Sociology.* Chicago: Rand McNally, 1964.

ZELLMAN, G. L. "Sex Roles and Political Socialization." Unpublished doctoral dissertation, University of California, Los Angeles, 1973.

ZELLMAN, G. L. "The Role of Structural Factors in Limiting Women's Institutional Participation," in D. N. Ruble, I. H. Frieze, and J. E. Parsons (eds.)," Sex Roles: Persistence and Change." *Journal of Social Issues,* 1976, *32*(3), 33–46.

ZELLMAN, G. L., and CONNOR, C. "Increasing the Credibility of Women." Paper presented at the meeting of the Western Psychological Association, 1973.

ZELLMAN, G. L., and SEARS, D. O. "Childhood Origins of Tolerance for Dissent." *Journal of Social Issues,* 1971, *27*(2), 109–36.

ZUCKERMAN, M., LIPETS, M. S., KOIVUMAKI, J. H., and ROSENTHAL, R. "Encoding and Decoding Nonverbal Cues of Emotion." *Journal of Personality and Social Psychology,* 1975, *32*(6), 1068–76.

Name Index

Subject Index

435